Swinging

Representing Sexuality in the 1960s

Single

Hilary Radner and Moya Luckett, Editors

University of Minnesota Press
Minneapolis
London

Published by the University of Minnesota Press
111 Third Avenue South, Suite 290
Minneapolis, MN 55401-2520
http://www.upress.umn.edu

Printed in the United States of America on acid-free paper

The University of Minnesota is an equal-opportunity educator and employer.

Library of Congress Cataloging-in-Publication Data
Swinging single : representing sexuality in the 1960s / Hilary Radner and Moya Luckett, editors.
    p. cm.
  Includes bibliographical references and index.
  ISBN 0-8166-3351-7 (hardcover). — ISBN 0-8166-3352-5 (pbk.)
    1. Sex in popular culture—United States—History—20th century.
2. Single people—United States—Sexual behavior—History—20th
century.   3. Men in popular culture—United States—History—20th
century.   4. Women in popular culture—United States—History—20th
century.   5. Sexual ethics—United States—History—20th century.
6. Self-realization—Social aspects.   7. Nineteen sixties.
I. Radner, Hilary,   II. Luckett, Moya.
HQ18.U5S95   1999   99-34136
306.7'0973—dc21

11 10 09 08 07 06 05 04 03 02 01 00 99   10 9 8 7 6 5 4 3 2 1

Swinging

Single

Contents

Acknowledgments

This project could not have been completed without the help of many people, first and foremost our colleagues at the University of Notre Dame and the University of Pittsburgh. In particular, we would like to express our gratitude to Don Crafton, chair of the Department of Film, Television, and Theater at the University of Notre Dame, and to the Institute for Scholarship in the Liberal Arts at the University of Notre Dame. Above all, we would like to thank our authors, whose scholarship, intelligence, enthusiasm, discipline, and patience were a source of inspiration to us. We owe a special debt to Janet Staiger, whose advice and counsel guided us through a number of difficult moments. Justin Wyatt was always there for us, generously sharing his time and expertise when our own knowledge fell short. Tom Schatz, with whom many of us have worked as students and as colleagues, was a continual source of encouragement and inspiration, without which this project would have never borne fruit. We owe much more than can be expressed in words to our friends and family who put up with it all during these many months. Finally, we would like to thank the University of Minnesota Press and Doug Armato for transforming a mere manuscript into a book.

Diana Rigg as Emma Peel, circa 1967.

Introduction
Queering the Girl

Hilary Radner

General Concerns

The 1960s conjure up a utopian landscape, a period in which social transformation seemed a cultural reality and a political possibility. Christopher Hitchens, a
child of his times, has written nostalgically about the year 1968 in the popular
magazine *Vanity Fair:* "Man cannot live on Utopias alone. But as Oscar Wilde so
shrewdly remarked, a map of the world that does not include Utopia is not even
worth glancing at. I once had a glimpse of that map in real time."[1] For Hitchens,
as for so many of his generation, the 1960s, 1968 in particular, represent a period
in which the promise of utopia, a social utopia founded upon democracy and
equality, seemed not merely a vision but a tangible social and economic goal.
The young political activists believed that they held the answers to the difficult
questions posed in the 1960s by a series of cultural crises, from the civil rights
movement to the Vietnam War. It was a period of social unrest and social critique but also of optimism and community.

Paradoxically, today the 1960s are also held responsible for contemporary
social ills associated with the dissolution of the "family," from unwed mothers to
low SAT scores. This anticipation of a utopia that seemed near at hand three
decades ago has been lost, replaced by the vision of a culture inevitably and
irrevocably grounded in social anarchy and individual self-indulgence, the illegitimate spawn of a dream gone awry. It is within the context of this widespread
anxiety about culture, the family, and sexual identity that the contributors to this
volume propose to investigate the terms of the new sexualities, new practices,
and new identities that emerged during the 1960s.

This volume elucidates the ways in which it was not the politics of 1960s activism that wrought changes in the contemporary social fabric, changes now associated with the 1960s. Rather, it was popular culture itself, far from resisting change, that posited the personal rather than the political as the new primary arena of experience and citizenship.[2] Fueled by consumer industries' increasing need for new markets, popular culture encouraged the emergence of discourses that formulated an individual whose major preoccupation was the fulfillment of his or her needs and desires as the significant expression of citizenship. This discourse encouraged the individual to realize his or her "self" in the pursuit of pleasure, a pleasure that was first and foremost sexual. Individual fulfillment was the final expression of the citizen's inalienable right to the pursuit of happiness.

Helen Gurley Brown and Betty Friedan, if divided in their sense of how best to achieve this objective, had in common their conviction that each woman has the right to fulfillment defined in her own terms. This sense of the individual as the site of fulfillment became the basis for a discussion of parity between man and woman but also for the assessment of equality across the lines of class, race, and sexual identity. The establishment of the autonomous individual who must perceive her or his pleasure for her- or himself, for whom health can be measured by the body's capacity to experience itself as pleasurable, permeated discourses on child psychology, sexology, marriage, and legal rights. Less obviously, this discourse of autonomy and fulfillment established the terms of a debate about politics, citizenship, and identity that would culminate with the construction of a queer constituency as the authentic political voice of the 1980s and 1990s.

The readings included in this volume focus on the production of new gendered identities dependent upon the articulation of this new cultural arena, a cultural arena that evolved around the assumption of individual fulfillment as the goal of human experience. This cultural arena contests the heterosexual paradigm that is generated by the reproductive model of gender and sexuality. Reproduction then is superseded, supplemented, by the production of other sexualities that cannot be encompassed by this same paradigm in which the self rather than the family becomes the primary unit of social construction. In the words of popular writer Desmond Morris, another child of his times, "It could even be said that we now perform the mating act, not so much to fertilize an egg as to fertilize a relationship."[3] Though it encourages an expanded conceptualization of sexuality, this system in which fulfillment rather than reproduction becomes the goal of sexual activity remains firmly "heterocentric" in its vocabulary.[4] The new sexuality is regulated, in part, by the articulation of a cultural sexual dimorphism, in which masculine and feminine remain distinct categories. The challenge to reproductive sexuality represented by the "Single Girl," for example, is contained by the culturally marked dimorphism of the body that she constructs as "feminine" for herself through consumer culture.

An emerging "third sex" striving for social legitimation served to confirm heterosexuality as the dominant model regulating sexual pleasure by offering a marginalized position that contradicted this model. The binary opposition *heterosexual/homosexual* echoed the opposition *masculine/feminine*, reinforcing existing hierarchies and the centrality of heterosexuality and masculinity as norms by which other positions might be evaluated. The Playboy and the Single Girl were cultural icons who underlined that a new consumer ideology of "singleness" (though perhaps uncomfortably close for some) was not synonymous with gay culture. At the same time, these two figures represented a departure from previous norms defined by kinship and family. To the degree that the focus of the sexual revolution was to emphasize the issue of individual fulfillment as the purpose and goal of sexual activity, the 1960s provided a mise-en-scène that would later enable the enactment of "queer" identities as the focus of political engagement. If the political agenda of the 1960s did not produce the utopia it promised, the sexual revolution resulted in an irrevocable reconfiguration of identity with significant political and economic implications.

This volume addresses the sixties, then, not as a specific period, but in terms of a set of issues that revolve around the constructions of these new identities— in particular, a set of new sexual identities that remain linked to the categories of race, class, and gender. Many of the essays (those by Wyatt and Jordan in particular) focus on topics (the reorganization of the film industry, the emergence of a visible gay community) that have their roots in a transformation of discourse surrounding sexuality that is a product of the 1960s. However, the effects of these transformations and their description moves the analysis inevitably into the 1970s (here the film industry, the gay community). The problem of periodicity is less crucial to this volume than the delineation of certain issues that do not necessarily fit neatly into a specific decade. Rather, these issues reflect a specific sensibility. Similarly, certain issues that we see as typifying the representation of sexuality, and more specifically feminine sexuality, in the 1960s have roots in the late 1950s. Our choice of materials was governed by two concerns:

on the one hand, the desire to demonstrate that the representation of sexuality is best understood as a discourse that is produced through an intersection of social axes (film, television, print, and so on), and, on the other hand, the need to focus on a discrete set of issues. Rather than presenting a cohesive narrative about the 1960s, this volume offers discussion of a set of symptomatic instances that illustrate a specific set of issues. This collection emphasizes the fragmentation of masculine identity; emerging homosexual identities; the intersection of race, ethnicity, and gender; and the transformation of the feminine. The work of Janet Staiger on the avant-garde and Justin Wyatt on popular film gives a social and economic context to the reading of specific texts included in the collection. It is our contention that these new sexualities are best understood as produced through a complex nexus of interdependent cultural, social, and economic developments.

The "sexual revolution" in this context can be seen as a logical extension of social transformations in the twentieth century that posit the individual as the location of identity and fulfillment. In this sense, we can discuss the public discourse surrounding sexuality as part of the formulation of an ethical system (in the terms of Michel Foucault) that defines the relations of the self to the self and that focuses on pleasure as the source of self-fulfillment.[5] Given, however, that this collection does not in fact look at audiences or their behavior, the scope of the contributors' investigations and conclusions is limited. This volume investigates very specifically the representation of sexuality rather than sexual practice itself. Thus, by extension, the authors can comment only on the representation of given ethical systems rather than on, for example, the effects of those systems in practice. In terms of representation one might say, following Foucault, that far from constituting a period of "liberation," the 1960s were characterized by a redefinition and reformulation of sexuality that was largely in the interests of an expanding consumer culture.[6] As Lynn Spigel and Michael Curtin observe:

> The so called "sexual revolution" did not simply amount to a period
> of freedom or enlightenment for all; rather, the sexual revolution was
> a "discourse" through which it became possible to generate a new set
> of statements about what were perceived to be "normal" or "deviant"
> modes of power and pleasure for men and women.[7]

This culture required a mobile workforce with significant discretionary income. The effects of the "sexual revolution" might be termed liberating in the sense that this public discourse produced new norms of behavior. Chastity was no longer the gauge of a woman's value, for example. However, these new norms produced the foundation of new forms of social regulation grounded in "the sexual fix," to borrow from Stephen Heath, in which "sexual fulfillment" legitimated the individual as such.[8] The rights and duties of citizenship came to revolve paradoxically around the pursuit of pleasure, in which sexual pleasure provided the model for all other pleasures. The sexual revolution, unlike the civil rights movement and the antiwar movement, those movements most frequently associated with the 1960s, encouraged the individual to construct him- or herself as individual qua individual. The social became primarily a pretext, the site of opportunities for individual fulfillment.

One might argue that indeed the sexual revolution had important implications for the feminist movement of the 1970s, in spite of the general assessment by most feminists that the sexual revolution just gave men more opportunity to do what they wanted to do all along.[9] The sexual revolution significantly changed women's behavior and affirmed a woman's right (even duty) to take responsibility for her own life and pursuit of happiness.[10] The sexual revolution and its ethos of self-fulfillment clearly encouraged the public acceptance of homosexuality to the degree that its practice was necessary to the individual pursuit of satisfaction. Nonetheless, from an economic and social perspective, one can just as easily argue that the sexual revolution encouraged a public discourse that ignored traditional concepts of public life and that supported gratification at the level of the individual as a political concern. From this perspective, the sexual revolution was hardly a revolution at all; it signified the triumph of bourgeois pragmatism (a Thermadorian reaction) over counterculture idealism, albeit while expanding the category of the bourgeois to include women, gays, lesbians, African Americans, Arabs—the individual in all his or her multicultural variations. Indeed, Sharon Ullman contends that the seeds of current controversies around sexuality are found in late-nineteenth- and early-twentieth-century U.S. culture. At this point we begin to observe a redefinition of sexuality "as a means of self-realization rooted in pleasure and unconnected to reproduction." In a number of different social contexts, a discourse, albeit often contested, emerges that posits sexuality as "central to personal identity and even to a successful life."[11] Paul Robinson argues that "modern" sex can be understood as a reaction against the Victorians. In particular, he claims that "where the Victorians had all but denied woman a sexual existence, the modernists argued her sexual parity with the male, even at the risk of transforming her into an exclusively sexual being."[12] More abstractly, he sees modernist theories as an attempt to reconcile the romantic ideal of transcendent union with the material reality of "human sexual response" defined in empirical terms.[13] Critical in defining this tension was the research of Alfred Kinsey, which substantiated that sexual practice in the mid-twentieth century at least did not conform to either romantic or Victorian ideals among both men and women.[14]

It then should come as no surprise that these new sexualities of the 1960s, which depended as much upon undoing the couple as on constituting it as such, were already manifesting themselves forcefully in popular culture texts of the 1950s. Indeed, Wilhelm Reich's remarkable volume *The Sexual Revolution,* first published in English in 1945, originally appeared in German under the title *Die Sexualität im Kulturkampf* in 1930.[15] In addition to these more notable precursors, Benjamin Spock's cognitively stimulated child,[16] Brigitte Bardot's libidinous sex kitten, and Hugh Hefner's ever-available and ever-eager Playboy prepared the way for the swinging single adult of the 1960s. It is the shifting terrain of these identities, so often dismissed as reactionary, self-indulgent, or self-evident by those concerned with history and politics, that constitutes the topic of this volume.

Unbonding the Bond Girl

> Anyway you mustn't think of being a call girl anymore. You've got a beautiful body. You must keep it for the men you love.
>
> JAMES BOND IN *DR. NO*[17]

In the above injunction, Bond attempts to explain to the naive, impressionable Honey Ryder the proper comportment of the modern young lady. The specifics of this injunction are symptomatic of a shift in the construction of feminine heterosexuality during the late 1950s, a shift the full effects of which are felt in the 1960s. The emphasis here is on *men* (the plural) as opposed to *man* (the singular). This transformation from the singular to the plural implies a fundamental reinterpretation of feminine sexuality. If at the end of the nineteenth century Krafft-Ebing had commented that "the man who avoids women, and the woman who seeks men are sheer anomalies," by the mid-twentieth century attitudes had changed.[18] Typically, in the novel *Marnie* (later a 1964 movie by Alfred Hitchcock, starring Sean Connery, also cinema's first James Bond), the hero explains to his reluctant wife: "Sex is a fundamental instinct that you can't compare to love of music. If it isn't there in some form something is wrong."[19] In Ian Fleming's *Dr. No*, Bond must also reassure Honey that the normal woman likes sex, and that the pleasure that sex affords cannot be reckoned in decimal points. A woman need not look to a man for financial security—perhaps this might even prove to be an unwise investment. The proper exchange between man and woman is one of mutual pleasure.

In fact, at the end of *Dr. No*, Bond makes certain that Honey is well situated before he leaves the islands in pursuit of other women who "love" him. He places her at a school where her many talents, including zoology, will be appropriately developed. Her body and her sexuality are the implicit rather than the explicit measure of her value; most important, it is she herself who reaps the benefits of her well-invested capital.[20] It is perhaps no accident that film's first "Bond girl,"

Doctor No. 1962. Courtesy of Photofest.

Ursula Andress, appears in *Dr. No in* 1961—the first Bond film—as Honey Ryder. The film presents the swinging bachelor and his girls to an eager public as the erotic ideal of the era.

The Bond girl as a cultural icon developed in the popular novel in the 1950s, but came into full bloom only in the 1960s, within the contexts of a renovated publishing industry based on the paperback book and an international post-Hollywood cinema. Her trajectory again suggests the ways in which the "sexual revolution" was hardly a revolution at all. The changes in sexual mores associated with the 1960s were the product of a slow evolution toward an economic and social structure in which the individual rather than the family became the primary locus of identity.

Cultural critics notwithstanding, this transformation was at least as significant to the representation of femininity as it was to the preservation of an existing masculine ideal. Certainly Tony Bennett and Janet Woollacott are correct in claiming, "In, thus, responding to the challenge posed by 'the girl,' putting her back into place beneath him (both literally and metaphorically), Bond functions as an agent of the patriarchal order."[21] Yet these scholars fail to point out that Bond's recognition of feminine pleasure as something that a woman has the right to expect marks a new position in the formulation of feminine identity, even if the woman must achieve it, though not necessarily, missionary style. If it is the patriarchal order that is maintained, it is not tied in the same way to issues of kinship and reproduction. The Playboy circulated outside the norms of family and kinship, his patriarchal identity undermined by his perpetual boyishness, his sense that he had the right to live for himself. Though Bond, as the Playboy surrogate in the world of international intrigue, operates ostensibly in service to his country, he answers to no one. His conscience is his guide. No moral quibbles about the law for him—he is "licensed to kill."

This change at the level of individual identity is tied to changes in marketing in which consumer culture becomes an international rather than a national concern. Michael Denning comments that in the Bond novel,

> consumer capitalism, which relentlessly transcodes politics, religion, and philosophy into sexual terms, fights its ideological battles under the sign of pornography. The battles are not, despite appearances, merely battles between the forces of "liberation" and the forces of "repression." The apparent liberation of sexuality from patriarchal

norms—the so-called "sexual revolution"—is both a genuine change in sexual practices and a reconstitution of sexuality in a fetishized mode that continues to subordinate and oppress women.[22]

That the Bond girl is emblematic of a representational mode that supports the subordination and oppression of women through consumer culture (if not patriarchy) demonstrates how the path of "liberation" was not "free." Rather, redefining feminine identity in particular, sexual identity in general, served the purposes of consumer culture and its industries. These changes are hardly insignificant if regulated by the needs of consumer culture. The Bond girl denotes a change in women's position in which family and kinship no longer necessarily regulated her situation. Economic status, her ability to negotiate consumer culture as both agent and object of exchange, had become the prime determinant of social expectations. The Bond girl has in common with her subsequent popular incarnation the Single Girl that she is a free agent, operating in her own interests.[23] In this sense, feminist commentary notwithstanding, these changes had more fundamental and more immediate implications for femininity than for masculinity.[24]

From Sex Kitten to Single Girl

Feminists in general take a dim view of the sexual revolution. Ellen Willis characterizes the radical feminist position in the following terms:

> The "free love" ideology of male leftists ... was, they argued, nothing but a means of exploiting women sexually while avoiding commitment and responsibility; the "sexual revolution" had not benefited women, but merely robbed us of the right to say no. If some women nonetheless preferred "free love," it was only because marriage under present conditions was also oppressive.[25]

A contemporary feminist talking to the *Guardian* in 1969 had a similar perspective: "The free sexual revolution ... has only served to oppress women and especially radical women. If she doesn't want to sleep with men, a woman is 'hung up.' If she does, she's known as someone's wife or girl friend."[26] The problem posed by this position, as Willis points out, is that this critique leads back to the family as the correct norm. Or it establishes a norm in which all relations with men are considered tainted. In each case, the economic and social reality of women as a demographic category is disregarded in favor of an ideal. In a certain sense, the feminists were always already behind the times. The condemnation of sexuality, the heterosexual world, and bourgeois success expressed by many feminists today evokes the same utopia that Hitchens views with such nostalgia, if no doubt seen from a very different perspective. Was there ever an Edenic moment in which woman acted as one, speaking with a single voice of enlightened self-interest?

The mythic moment of bra burning at the 1968 Miss America pageant ironically echoes advice given by Helen Gurley Brown more than five years earlier, in her best-selling book *Sex and the Single Girl:* the thrifty woman should toss her underwear—or, rather, not buy it in the first place.[27] Certainly, the small-breasted woman could give up her bra as a means of economizing on her wardrobe. In a pinch (so to speak), a Band-Aid could cover an obtrusive nipple more economically than lacy lingerie. Practical, girlish in more than simply her cup size, the Single Girl does not consider the possibility of a world without men; she has more concrete things on her mind, like paying the rent. As Nora Ephron notes, Helen Gurley Brown advocates "that the Single Girl with no other man in her life must somehow make the men that are there serve a purpose."[28] We can only ponder what that purpose might be. Clearly, however, this purpose has as its final goal to uphold the interests of the Single Girl.

I take the Single Girl as emblem of the 1960s because she embodies a new configuration of feminine identity inherent in the public representation of sexuality. Emerging out of the 1950s, rather than simply breaking with her past, the Single Girl presents a utopian fantasy of a woman free from the social and sexual constraints that appeared to limit her mother. Her girlishness also responds to and contains the anxieties that a woman no longer under the yoke of patriarchy (if still subject to the whims of capital) might evoke. She is a girl, in a state of perpetual immaturity. She ultimately cannot challenge an order grounded in the primacy of masculinity. Crucial to the Single Girl's autonomy is her efficacy in the workplace. She is salaried. In her pursuit of pleasure, she may avoid the double bind of the mother/spinster role for which renunciation is the sign of social acceptability; however, she is still subject to the economic imperatives of consumer culture. A working girl, she exacts a paycheck from a boss rather than grocery money from a husband.

During the 1960s, best-selling women writers such as Helen Gurley Brown and later the notorious "J" sought to evolve a technology of feminine sexual practice outside marriage in which nubility (as marriageability) is reproduced through the articulation of the woman as consumer of goods and sexual pleasure. Feminist writer Barbara Ehrenreich points out that from a certain perspective Brown's position in *Sex and the Single Girl* (1962) was more radical than Betty Friedan's in *The Feminine Mystique* (1963), a volume often seen as inaugurating second wave feminism in the United States.[29] Friedan assumed marriage and motherhood, in particular, as the sine qua non of a woman's life; she claimed, however, that a woman could *also* have a career. Brown "announced that marriage was unnecessary and that a new life was already possible, the life of the single, urban working 'girl.'"[30] In many ways the "handbooks" written by Brown (*Sex and the Single Girl*, 1962; *Sex and the Office*, 1964) and "J" (*The Way to Become a Sensuous Woman*, 1969) do not differ substantially from earlier versions such as *Live Alone and Like It* (1936).[31] But as best-sellers, these works represent a democratization of the category of single woman across class lines.

Unlike the author of *Live Alone*, Helen Gurley Brown emphasizes her modest beginnings. Little Helen experienced the failures of patriarchy firsthand. Her mother was widowed when Helen was ten; she supported an invalid sister throughout her life. Without a college education or family connections, she worked her way up from secretary to national figure. In her late thirties, she married David Brown, the prodigiously successful movie producer, a match she frankly saw as beyond her dreams. At the heart of *Sex and the Single Girl* is a chapter titled "Money, Money, Money." Brown advocates the virtues of thrift and self-restraint as integral to the Single Girl's economic success. Though the Single Girl is a consumer, she is a smart consumer. She cannot afford to be otherwise. She must reproduce her body through consumer culture. Her girlish sexuality is her small capital, a capital to which every woman has access and that Brown encourages every woman to exploit.

Finally, *Sex and the Single Girl* is about how a woman might best manage her life given that she and she alone is responsible for her situation. Ironically, Brown is almost never critical of men; rather, she advocates a pragmatic approach in which men constitute neither allies nor enemies, but a series of opportunities and obstacles that a woman encounters in her attempts to achieve economic stability. "Work" is not a "right" for Helen Gurley Brown—it is a necessity. She is quick to realize that marriage is no longer a suitable career for a girl without resources; however, she also underlines the advantages of a life in which a woman enjoys economic autonomy—again making a virtue of necessity.

It would be a mistake, however, to see Helen Gurley Brown or *Sex and the Single Girl* as antimarriage, or to see "singleness" as in and of itself a source of pleasure.[32] Symptomatic of this interpretation are the remarks of media scholar Julie D'Acci: "The bestseller laid out a step-by-step plan for the single woman to forestall marriage, enjoy many sexual partners (including married men), have a job, and spend money on an apartment, furnishings, attractive clothes, and other goods to enhance her appeal."[33] Far from "forestalling marriage," the Single Girl seeks marriage, but realizes that it does not offer her security. The married state, according to Brown, is the ideal position for a woman, but it is not a sinecure. Furthermore, singleness is not necessarily synonymous with spinsterhood. The unmarried woman can lead a fulfilling life, perhaps more fulfilling, if she is careful, than the lives of most of her married counterparts. Finally, all women must face the fact that at some moment, during some period of their lives, they may find themselves unattached. Brown emphasizes this possibility without rancor while simultaneously offering a means of profiting from what might initially seem to be an unprofitable situation. In the opening chapter of *Sex and the Single Girl*, she admonishes her naive audience: "A man can leave a woman at fifty (though it may cost him some dough) as surely as you can leave dishes in the sink. He can leave any time before that too, and so may you leave him when you find your football hero developing into the town drunk."[34] The precarious status of the wife leaves women without a sense of identity. Certainly only a foolish woman would seek economic status and social identity through an institution without stability. Thus Brown proposes, whether married or not, "a single woman is known by what she does rather than by whom she belongs to."[35] The Single Girl's identity, then, is determined in the workplace rather than in the home.

The anxiety generated by the construction of a social hierarchy in which identity is defined in the workplace rather than in the home—in which the salaried individual rather than the family is the fundamental economic unit—has been well documented. Media scholar Lynn Spigel, among others, has mapped out the cultural anxiety surrounding the domestic status of the feminine in her studies on advertising in the late 1940s and early 1950s. She claims that from 1948 to 1955, "women's home magazines ... held to an out dated model of femininity,

The young Brigitte Bardot, sex kitten. Courtesy of Photofest.

ignoring the fact that both working class and middle class women were dividing their time between the family work space and the public work space." In fact, "the fifties witnessed a dramatic rise in the female labor force—and, in particular, the number of married women taking jobs outside the home rose significantly."[36] The Single Girl represents a strand in popular culture that embraces rather than denies work and "singleness" as the emblem of a new sexual order. Helen Gurley Brown's enormously successful transformation of the ailing *Cosmopolitan* in 1965, a magazine that clung to the outmoded domestic ideal described by Spigel, into a publication that spoke to and legitimated the working woman testifies to the importance of these changes.

As if in response to the hyperdomesticity of consumer imagery directed toward women during the 1950s, the Single Girl emerged as the new feminine ideal of consumerism. She represented the supplanting of advertising's domestic ideal by cinema's sex kitten of the 1950s, as embodied in the multiply married Brigitte Bardot.[37] Yet the Single Girl differs from the sex kitten in that she is a working girl, prepared to pay her way if necessary, competent and reliable beneath her girlishness, with her eye on the bottom line. The comparison between the film star Bardot, a daddy's girl all her life, and the feisty, hardworking, waifish Brown illustrates this shift. Unlike Elizabeth Taylor, who has much in common with Bardot, including her "natural endowments," Brown, as the editor of the most influential women's magazine of the second half of the century, is a girl among girls. Her sexuality is subdued and contained by her

Helen Gurley Brown, Single Girl. Courtesy of Helen Gurley Brown.

disciplined consumerism and her pragmatic advice to girls who must depend upon themselves to pay the rent. Symptomatic of the solution was the conflation of the categories of woman/girl into the category of working girl.

The term *girl* maintained or at least represented the woman's status as nubile—marriageable—long past her youth or even her childbearing years. Significantly, Helen Gurley Brown never had children, and as Nora Ephron points out, she was forty-three when she took over *Cosmopolitan* in 1965 and revamped its format from women's service magazine to handbook for the working girl. In so doing, she increased circulation from under 800,000 to more than one million copies a month in five years, from 259 advertising pages a year to 784.[38] Brown's goal was not, however, merely to sell magazines. She told Ephron:

> Self-help ... I wish there were better words, but that is my whole credo. You cannot sit around like a cupcake asking other people to come around and eat you up and discover your sweetness and charms. You've got to make yourself more cupcakable all the time so that you're a better cupcake to be gobbled up.[39]

Perhaps most important is that Brown's agenda transformed the women's magazine. Certainly the success of her new format for *Cosmopolitan*, which became the model for subsequent women's magazines such as *New Woman, Self,* and *Working Woman,* derived from its ability to respond to the new demographics, in which a woman was as likely as not to work outside the home. The terms according to which the women's magazine was reconceived are laid out in *Sex and the Single Girl.*

Importantly, Brown devotes the bulk of the book to the problem of embodiment—that is, the task of the Single Girl is to embody heterosexuality through the disciplined use of makeup, clothing, exercise, and cosmetic surgery, linking femininity, consumer culture, and heterosexuality. The technology of the body that will ultimately produce pleasure as sex is also the process by which the Single Girl will defer marriage by reproducing its possibility. "Sex is a powerful weapon for a single woman in getting what she wants from life, i.e., a husband or steady male companionship. Sex is a more important weapon to her than to a married woman who has other things going for her—like the law!"[40] Thus the technology of sexiness developed by Brown has as its goal, paradoxically, the maintenance of the Single Girl's marriageability. Sexual expertise replaces virginity as the privileged object of exchange outside the law of the family. The seeming contradiction between sex as pleasure and sex as "capital" is never addressed. For the Single Girl, sex as pleasure, her practice, is her capital.

The overdetermination of consumerism and sexual practice works toward the creation of a feminine subject that functions within heterosexuality but nonetheless opens other avenues that lead to other feminine identities outside marriage. Within Brown's discourse, although the woman's pleasure functions as part of her marriageability, it is still marked out as her own. Less obviously, her sexuality is ancillary rather than fundamental to her identity. Helen Gurley Brown is a woman's woman. The goal of her magazine is conversation among women. Ultimately, other women are the Single Girl's most stable resource. Brown explains this explicitly in a later volume:

> A mouseburger's friends are, in some respects, like her lungs or liver—she can't get through life without them. Friends are almost a bigger deal than lover or husband. Those you can get through life without, at least for long periods, but friends—they are a staple of every functional mouseburger.[41]

She adds:

> We've spent pages piloting you through the love affair—which probably won't survive the year—we're only going to spend a paragraph or two on girlfriends who may last your lifetime. Why? Because girlfriends don't need explaining or piloting; they don't bring problems or traumas; they bring solutions and peace.[42]

The term "mouseburger," an epithet coined by her critics, is taken up ironically by Brown. It serves as a metaphor for the disenfranchised state of the Single Girl. Clearly, the mouseburger, in contrast with the "bombshell," is a modest individual, no more than a mouthful, a sorry little "cupcake." The Single Girl is by definition not exceptionally beautiful, rich, or even talented; if she is intelligent, it is the result of hard work and discipline rather than nature or nurture. Brown's message is that every "girl" must make the best of what she has in a world that is neither hostile nor inviting, but rather largely indifferent to her fate. It is this indifference that the Single Girl must combat.

Sex and the Single Girl

Sexuality constitutes a paradox at the center of the Single Girl's ethos. On the one hand, sexuality is part of her capital, her expertise (performance) rather than her chastity enhancing her value; on the other hand, there is no price on pleasure. Her pleasure is valuable only to the extent that it operates as such within a system of mutual exchange. Although the Single Girl does not greet the "call girl" with social disapprobation, as did her predecessors, she eschews this profession in favor of more profitable enterprises, more profitable because ultimately more fulfilling and less precarious.[43] To depend on a man or men, in any way, is an unwise choice on the part of the Single Girl. Equally important, however, is that such dependence renders "unfulfilling" sexual pleasure itself, because "sex" must arise out of mutual erotic need. Prostitution is inequitable in its distribution of pleasure, thus it curtails the Single Girl's freedom of expression in a number of ways: in terms of her personal satisfaction and of her finances. The erotic possibilities of "free" sex constitute a crucial element in the package of rights to which the Single Girl gains access through her willingness to work and her capacity for labor.

These erotic possibilities are further explained, though they differ little in their larger organization, by "J" in *The Way to Become a Sensuous Woman*. "J" encourages women to realize their erotic potential while maintaining standards of a "selfhood" defined by consumer culture. "You must devote a great deal of your time to finding the clothes that flatter you," she advises.[44] In fact, she includes a program designed to teach women, step by step, how to have orgasms. She explains: "There are four keys to sensuality: 1. Heightened sensitivity. 2. Appetite. 3. The desire to give. 4. Sexual skill."[45] The female orgasm itself is legitimated as the means by which a woman may acquire and keep a husband as the guarantor of her heterosexuality. In practice, various forms of masturbation are far more important insofar as these forms of stimulation, and only these forms, serve to guarantee the orgasm.

Well-known feminist writer Barbara Ehrenreich was perhaps the first to recognize the de facto existence of a feminine sexual revolution. Ehrenreich, Hess, and Jacobs stated in 1986:

> Between the mid-sixties and the mid-seventies, the number of women reporting premarital sexual experience went from a daring minority to a respectable majority; and the proportion of married women reporting active sex lives "on the side" is, in some estimates, close to half. The symbolic importance of female chastity is rapidly disappearing.[46]

Crucial to the new feminine sexuality is that it is not based on chastity—on the woman withholding what the man wants. Rather, it is based on "skill" and above all a willingness to engage in sex as a source of mutual pleasure (stressed by both Brown and "J"). This new sexuality is a reconceptualization of the sexual act as an act of exchange. The medium of exchange is the orgasm as the measure of pleasure. For the woman to take on a new function as both agent and object of exchange, it was necessary to define a female orgasm that would be the equivalent of the male orgasm. The clitoral orgasm, rather than vaginal penetration, became the mark of feminine pleasure precisely because it could be measured and recognized as the sign of a woman's pleasure.[47]

Although by 1947 Dr. Helen Wright was already challenging the hegemony of the vaginal orgasm, it was not until the 1960s that Masters and Johnson convinced the U.S. public at large that female pleasure is not dependent on the act of penetration.[48] According to Masters and Johnson, women's sexual disinterest, often termed frigidity, is not the result of nature or nurture, but of male ignorance and ineptitude. Popular writer John Heidenry argues: "The reinvention of the female orgasm, on an almost Copernican scale, had several major ramifications for sex therapy and sexual politics. In the first place, it established the erotic independence of women."[49] Sociologists Patricia Miller and Martha Fowlkes explain that "Masters and Johnson established unequivocally the physiological ability of women to achieve orgasm and dispelled any doubts that females might in any way be possessed of a lesser sexuality than males." According to Miller and Fowlkes, Masters and Johnson's research also indicates that "the female orgasmic response is demonstrably not correlated with—or, more accurately, is negatively correlated with—conventional heterosexual coitus."[50]

The definition of an autonomous female sexuality and an empirically variable method of achieving pleasure independent of coition had a number of consequences:

1. This definition offered the possibility of establishing a system of equivalence among different types of sexual practice in which conventional heterosexual coitus was the definite loser.

2. This formulation challenged the widely held notion that the penis was the privileged instrument of sexual pleasure—if indeed a woman needed a man at all to be sexually satisfied.

3. This definition signaled the creation of a medium of exchange, pleasure

itself, in which pleasure was empirically constituted, and thus measured, as the orgasm.

4. The orgasm permitted "equity" but also firmly established "difference." Feminine sexuality could not be conceived of as "identical" to or in any way dependent on masculine sexuality within this paradigm.

Within a paradigm in which a woman bartered her participation in the sexual act for material goods of one sort or another, her pleasure was irrelevant to the act itself. A different system of exchange was inaugurated in which the woman was the agent rather than the object of exchange, in which she exchanged orgasms as pleasure in a system of equivalence in which her pleasure was measured against his pleasure, or against her pleasure, as the case may be. Thus as Miller and Fowlkes point out, the currency of the orgasm (my term, not theirs) established homosexuality and heterosexuality as equivalent, so that a woman's pleasure did not depend upon "the men in her life." Lesbian sexuality could no longer be described as a weak copy of heterosexuality, and indeed might even be said to offer a greater range of erotic possibilities than heterosexuality. To use Anne McClintock's description, "the autonomy of female clitoral pleasure" challenged "the primacy of the male phallic regime."[51]

This "autonomy" points to another problem: that homosexuality, both male and female, does not in and of itself threaten the existing social hierarchy, which is dependent upon capital and a division between feminine and masculine. Rather, relations of power produce sexual practice as a moment of exchange. The position of the feminine is to be exchanged within patriarchy. Gender itself becomes an irrelevant category. Status and class supersede gender in determining a practice of sexual exchange if the "sex" of the individual is no longer at stake. If pleasure replaces reproduction as the goal of sexuality, then the "sex" of either partner is significant only to the extent that it increases or lessens pleasure given or received.

In a system in which the individual works for him- or herself, Helen Gurley Brown's advice to women working in an office "works" for men or women. She describes a system, an erotics of power, in which sexuality is defined by position within a specific power structure, regardless of who occupies that position. The "Single Girl" is a position that is defined not by gender but by the relation between employer and employee. In this sense, the Single Girl is the prototype of the new model of citizenship within consumer culture, in which the individual is always at risk, never secure, in the struggle to ensure his or her personal fulfill-ment. Inherent in the term *girl* is an attempt to feminize that position—in a sense to naturalize it and to retain the notion of citizenship as inherently mascu-line. Hence gender returns as a socially inscribed category. However, the empha-sis on femininity as a consumer construction also points to the instability of the term.

It is not a coincidence that "sex change" as a medical procedure within the domain of cosmetic surgery developed in the 1950s and received media promi-nence in the 1960s. "Sex changes" are the logical extension of the transforma-tions proposed by surgeons who attempt to make the unpleasing face more beautiful and, in Helen Gurley Brown's terms, more feminine. The "scientific" reorientation of sexuality as an elective process whereby the individual seeks his or her pleasure on a level of parity supported this consumer construction of the self by creating an economy of pleasure that was grounded not in nature but in technique. Thus Heidenry reports that for John Money, who was director of the Johns Hopkins Medical Center when Howard W. Jones performed the first sex-change operation on a man in the United States, "gender-identity was one's pri-vate experience of gender."[52] Similarly, Heidenry claims that "Masters's personal sexual philosophy was that any form of sexual expression between consenting adults in private was acceptable."[53]

The social and scientific recognition of female pleasure within a context in which sexuality was a matter of individual choice opened up erotic practice as an interaction between independent entrepreneurs (or entrepreneuses?) seeking equal returns on their investments. In this sense, Brown's Single Girl represents a certain practice, a construction of "self" that ultimately authorizes gay and les-bian identity. "Queer" identity is the logical result of a self represented through the individual right to pleasure and the consequent right to choose the form (or practice) that this pleasure might take.

Ethics and the Pursuit of Pleasure

A significant development of the 1960s, then, derived from the way in which its discourse was the logical extension of a notion of the pursuit of happiness as both the expression and right of the individual. Similarly, the individual became both the locus and the agent of this happiness. If women were liberated from the necessity of domestic labor, they were also obliged to seek a living under the same terms as the disenfranchised mobile workforce of capital, for whom neither land nor family provided a stable social and economic structure. This new mobile workforce composed of single workers, each worker working for her- or himself, demanded a new ethical system—in the terms of Michel Foucault, a formal discursive system that would define the relationship of the self to the self.[54] This is precisely what *Sex and the Single Girl* attempted to provide for its readers. This ethical system coincided with that offered by "J"; both works, rather than articulating a feminine mandate that history would follow, sought to counsel single working women in their attempts to confront the vagaries of a history that had disenfranchised them. Thus this new ethical system was both a manifestation and a means of reproducing the new feminine self.

According to Michel Foucault, an ethical system can be best understood in terms of four fundamental defining categories: substance, subjectivation, technologies, and telos. In other words, what aspect of the self is regulated? To what "rule" does the subject "subject" itself in order to construct itself as such? What are the means or techniques that the self uses? And finally, what are the legitimating goals of this system? Foucault is largely interested in two systems: the Greek and the Christian. In both cases the substance was the self itself; in other words, the body was a significant site for exercise of ethical practice. Subjectivation was the result of submission to the rules of asceticism—techniques and practices of meditation and control of the body. It was in terms of the telos that these systems most obviously diverged. For the Greeks the goal was self-mastery itself, the construction of the self as a work of art. For the Christians, the goal was salvation, the eradication of the self before God's glory. Though this goal had implications in terms of a practice and an understanding of the first three categories, it was this telos that distinguished Greek ethics from Christian ethics.[55]

Helen Gurley Brown participates in a new ethical system in which the telos is "self-fulfillment." Again, clearly the sexual revolution of the 1960s depended far more on gradual reconfiguration or definition of the self than on any specific scientific development, such as the pill. Indeed, one might say that the pill evolved, and could only have evolved, in response to an ethical system that posited self-fulfillment, including sexual self-fulfillment, as the goal of human existence. As Barbara Ehrenreich and her colleagues remark, the "real function" of the pill was "to legitimize a sexual revolution already in progress: The existence and widespread marketing of a technology for presumably effortless contraception was evidence that millions of women (almost 6 million by 1965) … were 'doing it'—and, apparently with the blessing of the medical profession."[56] The historical context that produced this new subjectivity is extremely complex; we could debate at length whether this new system served to legitimate capitalism's need for a disenfranchised labor force, whether it was the result of or the cause of the disintegration of the family, and so on.

Certainly, this renegotiation of sexual identity manifested itself differently in a number of cultural institutions: the reformulating of film production and exhibition modeled on the success of the pornographic or X-rated film, the development of a countercultural underground cinema, the renovation of *Cosmopolitan* from a general women's service magazine under the direction of Helen Gurley Brown to a narrow-format publication directed toward the new working woman, the development of homosexuality as a political and cultural movement, the construction of youth culture, the centrality of the new sexually liberated woman to certain popular narratives on television, and so on. However, here what I wish to emphasize is the manner in which institutions as disparate as pornography and feminism must be understood, in part, in terms of this new self, which is a sexual self. This self is defined not in terms of gender, but in terms of individual gratification. In this context, the emergence of an autonomous feminine self, one that defines the self primarily in terms of its relationship to itself rather than to others, is a significant sign of the pervasiveness of this new ethical system.

In the case of the Single Girl, it is difficult to read this transformation as utopian. In fact, as a popular icon the Single Girl testifies to the fact that the Enlightenment's promise of universal emancipation can become as easily as not the threat of universal disenfranchisement. Certainly there are significant differences from the ethical model that Foucault characterizes as Christian. Yet if a telos of "self-fulfillment" appears to be in women's interests, the substance, mode of subjectivation, and technologies that define women's practice within consumer culture are less than reassuring. The substance of a woman's practice is her own body, which becomes her primary capital, her resources. She must sell her labor, reinvest her capital, but with little or no hope of ever controlling the means of production, of defining the terms of her indenture. She must subject herself to consumer culture and the codes of femininity as defined by heterosexuality (she must be a "girl," pretty, sexy, perky, and subservient). The techniques available are those offered through consumerism and heterosexuality. Her goal may be self-fulfillment, but this self-fulfillment is confined by the "cupcakeness" of her final incarnations. In considering the predicament of the Single Girl, we are forced to turn to the issues of resistance and agency, issues that have animated feminist debates for the past ten years. In focusing on the terms of representation rather than on practice, the contributors to this volume have in a certain sense removed themselves from the debate. Representation offers sets of possibilities and constraints. It is the theoretical terrain upon which culture inscribes the possibilities of its own existence, a set of relations to "reality" that might be said to define a culture as such. Representation cannot, however, determine the outcome of these relations. Here I would like to argue that in reviewing these historical moments or documents, we may achieve a degree of insight into our own quandaries as "sexually liberated" consumers, our own predicaments as cupcakes and cupcake consumers, and thus reinvent new utopias.

These quandaries might be understood as falling into two sets of dilemmas that arise from our double position as consumers and objects of consumption. The first set of dilemmas is the result of a series of fragmentations, of identity, of sexuality, of race, of masculinity, of nationality. According to the authors of the chapters in Part I of this volume, the resulting crises in representation produce narratives in which the larger institutions of capital and patriarchy are by and large confirmed. Iconography and issues that Janet Staiger sees as supporting experimentation and the interrogation of social norms within the avant-garde community become the basis, Justin Wyatt argues, of a new cinema driven even more directly by the demands of the market than was classical Hollywood cinema. Abdullah AlMaaini's analysis of *Lawrence of Arabia* demonstrates how publicly circulated national histories of the newly liberated, more often than not, ultimately legitimate the centrality of a masculinist European vision. Leerom Medovoi's meticulous rereading of Eldridge Cleaver's *Soul on Ice* suggests how radical politics has served to reinforce racial categories. Mark Jordan's meditation on the ontological problems of gay identity warns us that "gay politics" may become a pretext for the generation of a new set of norms. Jeff Sconce's discussion of Charles Manson as tabloid event points to the ways in which feminism and "free" sex fueled paranoiac fantasies and witch-hunts that confirmed the family as the seat of moral authority. Yet none of these authors would argue that this pessimism should inspire us to return to the more stable values of another era, to dismiss the utopian ideals of the 1960s; rather, the essays as a group testify to necessity and to the difficulties of an ethically engaged cultural politics.

The second set of dilemmas arises out of the specific trajectory of women in consumer culture, who, in achieving economic agency, might appear to have acquired a greater degree of autonomy, to have to a certain extent triumphed over their position as dominated. At the very least, these representations seem to define the terms whereby women might articulate new possibilities for themselves. This review of 1960s femininity takes issue, then, with the traditional feminist perspective on this period, claiming that sexual liberation did indeed offer something to women. The questions that these essays pose but do not resolve revolve around the issue of individual fulfillment: To what extent does the fulfillment of a given woman as individual justify the excesses of consumerism? It is perhaps not an accident that the figures considered in the essays in Part II are white, European, and presented as affluent. The fantasy elements that characterize narratives such as *Barbarella* and *The Avengers* point to the anxieties that underlie this optimism. Nonetheless, the general optimism of these essays, concerned with the development of agency and its relations to a specifically feminine subject, offers a striking contrast to the general pessimism of the essays in Part I. This split is symptomatic of the contradictory heritage of the 1960s, testifying to the complexity and the significance of this period in determining current intellectual debate and to the importance of reconsidering this period.

Re-vision and Identity

The essays that begin this volume take up the problem of identity, in particular sexual identity, within a series of social contexts in which sexuality had become a debated category. Janet Staiger discusses how avant-garde cinema's search for community was tied to the problem of representing sexuality. The political stakes of the avant-garde in this period were explicitly connected to the issues of sexual identity and the aesthetic. Staiger argues that the historical context of this double investigation results in a utopian vision around which a certain alternative community of viewers and artists arises. This vision and community is paradoxically shattered by the film industry itself, which circulates on a mass scale this material that the avant-garde community had initially positioned as resisting dominant culture.

Abdullah AlMaaini examines the other face of moviemaking in the post-Hollywood era: the genre that would later come to be known as the multinational blockbuster production, arguably "Hollywood" in terms of its style and audience, if not its director. The success of *Lawrence of Arabia* (1962) illustrates a trend that began in the later 1950s, in which European films came to compete with Hollywood productions. The inclusion of more explicit representations of sexuality and sexual activity accounted in part for these successes. David Lean's resolve to underline T. E. Lawrence's homosexuality, without making an explicit statement about homosexuality or by extension bisexuality, would have been unthinkable in Hollywood, even after the dissolution of the studio system. At the same time, Lean's desire to mark his own knowledge of Lawrence's sexual practices to the "hip" audience was symptomatic of a general increase in public awareness about "other" sexualities that characterized the 1960s. If the 1950s generated a great deal of work on human sexuality, most notably perhaps that of Alfred Kinsey, the 1960s incorporated this material into a popular vocabulary. This exploration of homosexuality and potentially bisexuality in the film mobilized a vocabulary and iconography described as "Orientalist" by the literary scholar Edward Said. The success of the film both at the box office and at the Academy Awards illustrates how popular cinema borrowed from a nineteenth-century colonialist discourse in order to feed its audience's desire for erotic titillation. The subordination of the pressing political issues of the Arab world to the demands of cinematic drama and spectacle is symptomatic of the inevitable links between the representation of sexuality and the social construction of the categories of race, class, and ethnicity within postcolonial discourse. The inalienable rights of citizenship, which Lawrence paradoxically wishes to "give" the Arab by giving him Damascus, are constructed as dependent upon a journey of personal fulfillment undertaken by the European protagonist, who bravely shoulders "the white man's burden."

If the popularity of *Lawrence of Arabia* depended upon a reinvention of imperialist iconography, the new cinema of the 1960s also drew heavily on the new social mores associated with the sexual revolution. Justin Wyatt discusses how the issues initially raised by the avant-garde in the context of a political and aesthetic interrogation became the basis for a new film industry that is geared toward the autonomous consumer. Wyatt suggests the economic parameters of the intersection between the sexual revolution and the exploitation film. In this context, he examines the strategies utilized by independent distributors to tap into the sexploitation market, the changes in distribution and exhibition practices formed by this market, the "discourse" of sex created in the industry trade papers as the market became identified and expanded greatly, and, finally, the eventual economic impact of the sexploitation film market on the mainstream studios and art film distributors.

Leerom Medovoi and Mark Jordan raise the issues of identity in the context of gender and race: both the African American male and the gay male seek to manifest identity as the visible sign of community. However, these categories are produced in terms that cannot find stable definitions, troubled by the new ethics of the pursuit of individual pleasure. Medovoi explores the uneasy relations in the United States between sexuality and race, highlighting the now equivocal position of the white male. The special intensity of Yippie identification with Black Panther Eldridge Cleaver, Medovoi argues, was also animated by Cleaver's tendency to attribute political importance to the "liberation" of white America's masculine sexuality. Medovoi discusses how in *Soul on Ice* (1968), a collection of essays, some autobiographical and others not, Cleaver articulates the politics of race relations in explicitly sexual terms.

Mark Jordan addresses the problems of visibility in creating gay identity, exploring the difficulties in generating "homosexuality" as a category for citizenship. Jordan claims that if the emblematic beginning of "gay liberation" is now fixed to 1969 and the Stonewall protests, the genealogy of "queer theory" must also be traced back to a tradition of writing exemplified by such figures as Wittman, Altman, and Guy Hocquenghem, among others. These pieces stand at the boundary between strategic popular representation and theoretical justification or historical narrative. Jordan argues from these first writings that in contemporary culture gay identity is defined by the inescapable persistence of tension between "homophilia" or "homosexuality" as categories of political action on the one hand and as sources of representation on the other.

Jeffrey Sconce scrutinizes the terms of masculinity manifested in the Playboy as the representation of an unregulated sexuality. Sconce generates an analysis that elucidates the implicit connections between the narrative generated around Charles Manson to those more commonly associated with Hugh Hefner. Like Hefner, Manson and his cohorts take the ethos of self-fulfillment to its logical limit. The fascination that this story exercises over its public testifies to a social anxiety about the rogue male; it also highlights similar anxieties inspired by a feminine sexuality that is no longer subjected to larger social constraints tied to the nuclear family and that might be harnessed by the unscrupulous *boy* who acts outside the law. The Manson story illuminates a bizarre contradiction between ultraconservative gender roles and unfettered sexual promiscuity, a dynamic that pits a hyberbolic portrait of the patriarchal family against an equally excessive representation of sexual liberation. This analysis isolates the way in which the Manson story exemplifies an unresolved conflict at the heart of contemporary masculinity, a conflict that has come to be discussed as the crisis of masculinity by such scholars as Barbara Ehrenreich and Michael Kimmel.[57]

The New Femininity Unveils Its Mystique

The essays in Part II of this volume center on the problem of femininity within a discursive system in which the individual rather than the family, or the couple, is the primary unit of social construction. Susan McLeland describes the ways in which the figure of Elizabeth Taylor as the "Erotic Vagrant" at the end of the 1950s and the beginning of the 1960s represented certain conflicts over the feminine body: on the one hand, as properly marked within a domestic space, somebody's woman, and, on the other, as the property of the woman herself, which she is free to invest for her own profit. As the last great star in the classical Hollywood tradition, Taylor generates a set of public narratives that document shifts and tensions in the public representation of a feminine ideal. Taylor's specificity as a star lies in the way in which her position as an object of desire (the Hollywood star) serves to authorize her pursuit of sexual pleasure and self-fulfillment while preserving her status as mother and wife.

In contrast, Lisa Parks discusses how Jane Fonda as *Barbarella* (1968) represents a new sexuality, a new body for the woman, that is not aligned with the family as such. Parks argues that the "astronautte," inevitably "astro-naughty," constitutes a discursive embodiment of a number of contradictory strands in popular culture centering on issues of feminine independence and autonomy. By investigating different discourses generated about women in space, taking Vadim's *Barbarella* as her point of departure, Parks explicates the manner in which the "astronaut as woman" constitutes a popular icon that challenges conventional categories of gender difference. The woman in space is a contested figure, Parks claims, because she defies both patriarchal and feminist definitions of "woman."

Moya Luckett describes the ways in which prime-time television promotes the new feminine autonomy while expressing anxieties about the social transformations that are both caused by and the cause of these new femininities. Mid- to late-1960s television capitalized on the new lucrative Single Girl phenomenon. Shows like *Peyton Place* (1964–69), *The Avengers* (1966–69), and *That Girl* (1966–71) presented new feminine fantasies and offered new images of the female body liberated from the constraints of marriage. Rather than positioning women as the (threatening) object of a male gaze or spinning narratives of domestic bliss, these shows presented new visions of female sexuality, with women engaged in public life. In a pointed challenge to the ethics of feminine self-sacrifice, they asserted the physical presence of the woman's body. These shows "liberated" female sexuality, no longer confining it to the private domain of marriage, the boudoir, and the backstreet, in order to highlight the active and sexual female body in public life.

Addressing these same issues of visibility and the female body within disparate landscapes, from the white halls of science to the backstreets of urban erotica, Eithne Johnson highlights the manner in which Masters and Johnson's coloscopic film and the fringe hard-core "beaver loop" unveiled "female sexuality" within the respective discourses of sexology and pornography. The "beaver loop," a low-budget hard-core genre, was a short film that, generally speaking, focused on a woman's sexual performance (as the term *beaver* implies) in which she reveals *all*. The coloscopic film claimed to record the female orgasm within a scientific format, thus revealing *all* in an empirically verifiable form. Both genres worked toward a rewriting of feminine sexuality in which feminine pleasure itself was the central moment in a system of respectively pornographic and scientific representation. It is hardly a coincidence that both pornography and sexology present the terms of feminine sexuality as a site for observation; rather, this coincidence of interests points to the ways in which a reexamination of the feminine and its place characterizes the culture of the 1960s as a whole. Johnson suggests how the repositioning of femininity, though most obviously a concern of a nascent politicized feminism, was hardly its exclusive domain. Femininity, the feminine subject, and her sexuality were interests that cut across class, economic, generic, and disciplinary boundaries.

This rewriting of femininity was not an activity confined to the adult world. Erica Rand discusses how new protolesbian identities manifested themselves in her experiences of teen fiction in the 1960s. In the absence of a visible lesbian community, the protolesbian subject finds moments of identification in the articulation of an autonomous femininity that remains feminine rather than mimicking the masculine. Rusty, the heroine of a teen novel by Viola Rowe, *Freckled and Fourteen* (1965), offers the possibility of singleness as an explicitly feminine position. Though technically heterosexual, Rusty is encouraged to develop as an individual (rather than as a member of a couple, or future couple) whose identity is explicitly feminine. Rusty's independence echoes an ethos of childrearing that hinges upon individual development as well as the self-help discourse (associated with Helen Gurley Brown) that encourages the new Single Girl to find in her "self" a location for identity and self-fulfillment. On a more pessimistic note, Rand also queries whether "cross-readings" ultimately mitigate the heteronormative discourses, inevitably tied to issues of ethnicity, that ultimately characterize these novels.

Concluding Remarks

At a time in which questions about sexuality and identity have been resolved under the rubric of queerness—a category that comprises figures ranging from Mae West as her "self" to Paul Reubens as "Pee-wee Herman"—it seems appropriate to return to the 1960s as that period in which dichotomies of male and female were publicly overturned in the popular arena under the banner of the sexual revolution. The tendency in contemporary analysis is to offer "the queer" as a category that emerges primarily in response to an ethical need rather than a historical situation. This volume reverses that emphasis. These essays have in common that they posit the construction of sexual identity and sexual norms as the product of a complex set of negotiations in which economics, politics, and social mores all play crucial roles. The development of pornography indicates changing social norms of behavior, but also changing senses of an ethical imperative in which ethics is increasingly the domain, if perhaps the sole domain, of the individual in the pursuit of self-fulfillment. Yet the fall of the Hollywood studio system, or perhaps more accurately its transformation, was also crucial to the development of the soft-core pornography industry, the result of a need to define new markets and audiences. It is difficult, then, to separate out the influence of a consumer economy and its emphasis on individual gratification from the seemingly scientific issues raised by the transformation of child-rearing practices, the research of sexologists such as Kinsey and Masters and Johnson, the rise of television, the increase in divorce rates—the list is seemingly endless. The uninhibited child, the sensuous woman, the homophile have in common that they represent configurations of the individual as a perceptual apparatus designed first and foremost to perceive its own pleasure—its "self" as the primary site of its identity and its practice within a social terrain.

If I continue to return to the Single Girl as my point of departure and as a central figure of this new discourse of ethics, it is because she clearly embodies the imperatives of consumer culture and individual fulfillment. The term *girl* suggests that maturation cannot take place within femininity itself; rather, independent of gender, women who do not choose to remain girls must "queer out" —construct identities outside these specific systems of exchange. The men of this era lose or are at least in danger of losing their strategic dominance as masculine. Masculinity does not exempt one from the possible fate of girlishness, of taking the passive position in which to please is the workplace imperative, in which youth, perkiness, and energy are in demand rather than experience, judgment, and consistency. The sexual revolution was not simply about sexual behavior but about the erotics of power. It demarcated a shift in relations of power that continues to inform debates today about power, sexuality, and identity in both the private and public spheres, in particular in terms of a workplace that is increasingly penetrated by the domestic.

The essays in this volume serve to amplify our sense of how the issues of the 1960s remain with us today. In particular, these essays reveal how the terms of the current feminist debate were formulated not only by the groundbreaking work of activists such as Betty Friedan, Gloria Steinem, and Germaine Greer, but also by a generation of women whose initial goal was to pay the rent. The right to her own checkbook became the right to the pursuit of happiness at a fundamental level. The Single Girl was one manifestation of an ethos that emphasized individual rights and individual fulfillment. She was "queer" because her satisfaction was not determined within the family circle. A husband might be desirable, but he was neither necessary nor reliable—a bank account was sine qua non. Still "girlish" and active (somewhere in her seventies, if Nora Ephron is correct) Helen Gurley Brown is as camped out and queer as they come. That Brown continues to talk to an eager audience about woman and her concerns through the vagaries of feminism, postfeminism, and third-wave feminism highlights how popular culture, far from working against "queer" identity, has often worked in its service.[58] The Single Girl was also "queer" because she represented the general disenfranchisement of the worker, whose mobility was not a luxury but a necessity, whose position was always precarious, whose meager earnings were never enough for her to buy into the corporation. To the extent that autonomy also works in favor of capitalism, it is difficult not to interrogate the connection between the development and the authorization of queer identities and the function of a highly mobile workforce with a significant disposable income within a capitalist consumer economy. We have perhaps reached a moment in which we need to consider the category of gender and its transformations as integral to the development of that set of economic and social practices that we group under the rubric of "capital" and consumer culture. The crucial question we face: How can we construct a sense of community within a culture that stresses autonomy as the goal and state of citizenship? What are our alternatives? Certainly, we do not wish to suggest that family be rehabilitated as an authentic location for the production of resistant identities. Rather, these essays direct our attention to the fact that the strategies that position certain sexual and gendered identities as expressions of an "authentic" voice are generated from within the same discourses against which these voices rise up in protest.

Notes

Many people offered me insight and encouragement. I would like to thank Jennifer Moore and Doug Armato for their patience and support, Justin Wyatt for his enthusiasm and understanding, Tom Schatz for his belief in the project, Susan White for giving me a copy of the novel *Marnie*, Janet Staiger for her sense of humor, and of course my coeditor Moya Luckett for her comments on numerous drafts. Above all I would like to thank Kathy Psomiades, whose interest in contemporary feminine culture has been a continual source of inspiration and information.

1. Christopher Hitchens, "The Children of 1968," *Vanity Fair*, June 1998, 103.
2. Though the formula "The personal is political" came to characterize the new feminist values of the 1970s and the 1980s, this position, far from challenging consumer culture, affirmed its continual attempts to collapse the public and the private, to eliminate the public sphere as the forum of a specifically political engagement. This is not to negate the feminists' legitimate contention that private space has a political dimension, but rather to question the direction that this assertion has taken in contemporary everyday life.
3. Desmond Morris, *Intimate Behavior* (New York: Bantam, 1972), 105.

4. In this context, note that Morris, ibid., uses the term *mating* to describe intercourse or, by extension, any other sexual act between one, in his words, "complete and special individual" and another.

5. Much of Michel Foucault's later work, including numerous lectures and interviews, focuses on the issue of ethics; however, this concept, or rather set of concepts, is most concretely and fully documented in the three volumes of *The History of Sexuality* (New York: Vintage, 1990). In this introduction I will refer to brief pieces in *Ethics, Subjectivity, and Truth: The Essential Works of Foucault 1954–1984*, vol. 1, ed. Paul Rabinow, trans. Robert Hurley et al. (New York: New Press, 1997). These last offer a succinct and clear overview of the above-noted concepts written by Foucault himself. For more extensive discussion of these issues, their appearance in Foucault's work, and their significance to feminist scholarship, see Lois McNay, *Feminism and Foucault* (Boston: Northeastern University Press, 1992).

6. See Lynne Segal, *Straight Sex: The Politics of Pleasure* (London: Virago, 1994), 31–69.

7. Lynn Spigel and Michael Curtin, "Introduction," in *The Revolution Wasn't Televised: Sixties Television and Social Conflict*, ed. Lynn Spigel and Michael Curtin (New York: Routledge, 1997), 13.

8. See Stephen Heath, *The Sexual Fix* (New York: Schocken, 1984).

9. See Abe Peck, *Uncovering the Sixties: The Life and Times of the Underground Press* (New York: Citadel, 1991).

10. See Barbara Ehrenreich, Elizabeth Hess, and Gloria Jacobs, *Re-making Love: The Feminization of Sex* (Garden City, N.Y.: Anchor, 1986); Alice Echols, *Daring to Be Bad: Radical Feminism in America 1967–1975* (Minneapolis: University of Minnesota Press, 1989).

11. Sharon Ullman, *Sex Seen: The Emergence of Modern Sexuality in America* (Berkeley: University of California Press, 1997), 3.

12. Paul Robinson, *The Modernization of Sex: Havelock Ellis, Alfred Kinsey, William Masters and Virginia Johnson* (New York: Harper & Row, 1976), 3.

13. Ibid., 191–95.

14. Alfred C. Kinsey, Wardell Baxter Pomeroy, and Clyde E. Martin, *Sexual Behavior in the Human Male* (Philadelphia: W. B. Saunders, 1948); Alfred C. Kinsey, Wardell Baxter Pomeroy, Clyde E. Martin, and P. Gebhard, *Sexual Behavior in the Human Female* (Philadelphia: W. B. Saunders, 1953).

15. Wilhelm Reich, *The Sexual Revolution: Toward a Self-Regulating Character Structure*, trans. Therese Pol (New York: Farrar, Straus & Giroux, 1974).

16. For a discussion of the child in the 1950s, see Henry Jenkins, "The Sensuous Child: Benjamin Spock and the Sexual Revolution," in *The Children's Culture Reader*, ed. Henry Jenkins (New York: New York University Press, 1998).

17. Ian Fleming, *Dr. No* (New York: Charter, 1987), 119. This novel was originally published in 1958.

18. Richard von Krafft-Ebing, *Psychopathia Sexualis with Especial Reference to the Antipathetic Sexual Instinct*, trans. Franklin S. Klaf (New York: Stein & Day, 1965), 8. The Library of Congress lists this volume as published in 1987. Paul Robinson, who describes Krafft-Ebing as "the most influential sexual psychologist of the last quarter of the nineteenth century," notes that it was revised until 1902 (the twelfth edition). *The Modernization of Sex*, 5. An English translation was published in the United States in 1893; however, Library of Congress records indicate that the first "unexpurgated edition . . . in English" was published in 1965.

19. Winston Graham, *Marnie* (New York: Carroll & Graf, 1961), 122.

20. In the novel, the orphaned Honey is already, even without an education, an enterprising businesswoman. She sells exotic shells in order to support herself.

21. Tony Bennett and Jane Woollacott, *Bond and Beyond: The Political Career of a Popular Hero* (New York: Methuen, 1987), 116.

22. Michael Denning, *Cover Stories: Narrative and Ideology in the British Spy Thriller* (London: Routledge, 1987), 113.

23. One popular culture icon did not neatly supplant the other; both continued to function as models of femininity throughout the 1960s, often inhabiting the same star persona, as in the case of Ann-Margret.

24. That "man" has come to see the twentieth century as a closing down of opportunity speaks to the profundity of these transformations within masculinity; however, these effects were slower to manifest themselves. Indeed, we might say that the masculine lament is about loss of privilege rather than loss of opportunity.

25. Ellen Willis, *No More Nice Girls: Countercultural Essays* (Hanover, Conn.: Wesleyan University Press, 1992), 7.

26. Quoted in Peck, *Uncovering the Sixties*, 210–11

27. Abe Peck claims that "burned bras were a mass-media myth, " but that "undergarments were tossed." Ibid., 209.

28. Nora Ephron, *Wallflower at the Orgy* (New York: Bantam, 1970), 18.

29. Helen Gurley Brown, *Sex and the Single Girl* (New York: Random House, 1962); Betty Friedan, *The Feminine Mystique* (New York: Dell, 1963). On the inauguration of second-wave feminism, see Ehrenreich et al., *Re-making Love*, 56.

30. Ehrenreich et al., *Re-making Love*, 56.

31. Helen Gurley Brown, *Sex and the Office* (New York: Random House, 1964); "J," *The Way to Become a Sensuous Woman* (New York: Dell, 1969); Marjorie Hillis, *Live Alone and Like It* (New York: Sun Dial, 1936).

32. In the 1980s, Yves Saint Laurent ran a campaign advertising its scent Rive Gauche with the image of a woman who was "having too much fun to marry"; I would argue that this is a later if logical development of the Single Girl. This image emerged in the late 1970s and the 1980s and is associated with the "New Woman."

33. Julie D'Acci, "Nobody's Woman? Honey West and the New Sexuality" in *The Revolution*

Wasn't Televised: Sixties Television and Social Conflict, ed. Lynn Spigel and Michael Curtin (New York: Routledge, 1997), 76.

34. Brown, *Sex and the Single Girl*, 5.

35. Ibid., 89.

36. Lynn Spigel, "The Domestic Economy of Television Viewing in Postwar America," *Critical Studies in Mass Communication* 6 (1989): 34.

37. For discussion of the cultural significance of Brigitte Bardot, see Cathrine Rihoit, *Brigitte Bardot: Un mythe français* (Paris: Olivier Orban, 1986).

38. Ephron, *Wallflower at the Orgy*, 22, 23, 29.

39. Quoted in ibid., 20.

40. Brown, *Sex and the Single Girl*, 70.

41. Helen Gurley Brown, *Having It All* (New York: Pocket Books, 1982), 303.

42. Ibid., 305.

43. We do, however, witness a change in social attitude toward the prostitute, who becomes a sex worker rather than a "fallen woman." From Helen Gurley Brown's perspective, on the whole, prostitution is simply not a very good job.

44. "J," *The Way to Become*, 56.

45. Ibid., 27, 28.

46. Ehrenreich et al., *Re-making Love*, 2.

47. The debates in contemporary culture about the "G spot" among heterosexuals and lesbians suggest the ways in which such categories are interpretations rather than neutral descriptions.

48. Harriet Gilbert and Christine Roche, *A Woman's History of Sex* (London: Pandora, 1987), x; William Masters and Virginia Johnson, *Human Sexual Response* (Boston: Little, Brown, 1966).

49. John Heidenry, *What Wild Ecstasy: The Rise and Fall of the Sexual Revolution* (New York: Simon & Schuster, 1997), 29.

50. Patricia Miller and Martha Fowlkes, "Social and Behavioral Constructions of Female Sexuality," in *Sex and Scientific Inquiry*, ed. Sandra Harding and Jean F. O'Barr (Chicago: University of Chicago Press, 1987), 151, 152.

51. Anne McClintock, "Gonad the Barbarian and the Venus Flytrap: Portraying the Female and Male Orgasm," in *Sex Exposed: Sexuality and the Pornography Debate*, ed. Lynn Segal and Mary McIntosh (New Brunswick, N.J.: Rutgers University Press, 1992), 119–20.

52. Heidenry, *What Wild Ecstasy*, 99.

53. Ibid., 35.

54. Foucault, *Ethics, Subjectivity, and Truth*, 262

55. Ibid., 223–52.

56. Ehrenreich et al., *Re-making Love*, 41–42.

57. Barbara Ehrenreich, *The Hearts of Men: American Dreams and the Flight from Commitment* (Garden City, N.Y.: Doubleday, 1984); Michael Kimmel, *Manhood in America: A Cultural History* (New York: Free Press, 1996).

58. Helen Gurley Brown did not own *Cosmopolitan*, which remained under the control of the Hearst Corporation. Significantly, though better known than her husband David Brown, she never exerted the same influence within magazine publishing as he did within the world of film production, because she earned only a salary. In this sense, the lesser-known (and younger) Grace Mirabella, who established her own magazine, which she then sold, enjoyed greater autonomy.

Swinging

Part I: Impossible Men

Single

The Connection, 1961. Courtesy of Photofest.

Finding Community in the Early 1960s
Underground Cinema and Sexual Politics
Janet Staiger

In an essay about finding evidence of communities among peoples who believe themselves to be alone,[1] Joan Scott focuses on science fiction writer Samuel Delaney's experience of a St. Mark's bathhouse in 1963: "Watching the scene establishes for Delaney a 'fact that flew in the face' of the prevailing representation of homosexuals in the 1950s as 'isolated perverts,' as subjects 'gone awry.'" Rather, "he emphasizes not the discovery of an identity, but a participation in a movement."[2] It is this same potential of finding others like oneself not only for identity but for community building that I believe the space of the underground cinema of the early 1960s provided. Moreover, the Otherness that seemed so threatening in oneself was, like it was for the St. Mark's bathhouses, a sexual Otherness that did not neatly fit the dominant images of these Others as traditionally conveyed in print, television, and mainstream film. The experience of going to the underground cinema contradicted impressions of isolation as it also elevated images of perverts and subjects gone awry. It vaunted sexual Otherness as an avant-garde aesthetic. It posed sexual Otherness as even a popular culture, as play and laughter, set in a complicated difference against a serious bourgeois art culture. The underground cinema of the early 1960s was a space for validation, empowerment, and often ironic resistance that used sexuality, politics, popular cultural iconography, and humor to establish community among subcultures.

What I wish to emphasize in this essay, then, are three points. One is the clarity with which at least New York intellectuals associated this cinema with the emergence of tacit, if not aggressive, gay sexual liberation activities and with a critique of traditional gendered, heterosexual, same-race/ethnicity sexual norms.[3]

Not merely an identity crisis but a movement was at stake in the American underground cinema explosion of the early to mid-1960s. The second point is that going to these films after midnight was a declaration of where one stood in these debates. The midnight cinema was—like the St. Mark's bathhouse—an expression of community and a site for building a community, which would eventually have its culmination, at least for the mainstream press and for gay men, in the Stonewall events of 1969. Thus I will contribute to refining debates about the history of gay liberation. Third, the ironic appropriations of popular culture were stylistic tactics directed against bourgeois culture but also assertive rhetorical strategies for creating these subcultural community connections. Critical debates about aesthetics and taste are part of this politics of sexual and personal freedom. It is in these years that feminist, civil rights, and gay/lesbian/ transgendered/bisexual movements (hereafter *sexual rights movements*) realize that the personal is political. The significance of my argument in this essay, then, is the suggestion that events do not come from nowhere. While Marxist warnings against teleological historiography need to be respected, simultaneously, it is still the case that prior events prepare the conditions for radical transformations. The subtext for my essay is the emergence, or rather reemergence, of a visible gay culture in New York City in the mid-1960s that parallels its existence in the 1910s and 1920s.[4] I need to stress, however, that the gay culture was not homogeneous. Rather, hierarchies existed within it that required toppling for Stonewall to have the meaning it now has.

Several scholars have studied various parts of these events, noting some of these connections. In particular, David E. James writes: "Contemporary accounts of underground film in the popular press tended, more or less sensationally, to stress the coincidence of formal infractions of orthodox film grammar and parallel moral and social transgressions, interpreting the latter either as evidence of the filmmakers' degeneracy or as their social criticism."[5] I will take up from James's remarks by looking at some of the dialogue among various members of the New York and mass media as they discuss and evaluate the events around the underground cinema of 1959 to about 1966.[6] I will extend his remarks by emphasizing the functions of popular culture and humor in these discussions, although the opposition James finds is not so definitely resistant when camp and sexual desire enter into the complex.

The Scene

What was the contextual scene for the emergence of the underground cinema? New moviegoing behavior, the live theater scene, "beat culture," and politics all influenced the configuration and meaning of the underground cinema.

In terms of mainstream America, moviegoing and movie marketing in the United States were in a transitional stage. While historical epics, male melodramas, and musicals that harbored homosexual themes as subtexts commanded the venues of first-run theaters,[7] by necessity lower-run theaters catered to various subgroups or "niche" markets that opened up taboo areas of content and sometimes violated taste cultures of high art. Art cinemas and 16mm film societies had been flourishing for the full decade of the 1950s and remained committed to a highbrow approach to contemporary themes. But another clientele was being exploited: the teenager.

Thomas Doherty describes the impact of a rather innocent B movie—*Rock around the Clock* (1956). The physical response in the theaters to hearing "our" music included "screaming, foot-stomping, and the occasional scuffle." The in-house fun could spill into the streets, and even staid children of the Midwest were reported to have "snake-danced downtown and broken store windows."[8] The enthusiasm of teens for the less reputable genres of the teen-pix and science fiction and horror films provoked film companies to exploit those passions.

Besides using color and widescreen technologies to draw audiences out of their living rooms and into theaters and drive-ins, film firms also returned to the old ploys of showmen. Gimmicks that relied on being at a theater made a comeback. When coupled with the fantastic genres of the horror film and science fiction, a play-space was created. William Castle's work provides some outstanding examples. In a series of films produced from 1958 through the early 1960s, Castle constructed novel in-house experiences as part of his movies' marketing strategies: a Lloyds of London insurance policy against death from the shock of watching *Macabre* (1958), reinforced by the stationing of ambulances and nurses near the theaters; a skeleton rigged to fly across an auditorium at the climax of *House on Haunted Hill* (1958); an electric current to buzz the bottoms of patrons during *The Tingler* (1959).[9] Moviegoing for youth in the late 1950s could be serious (reserved seats for major openings of Hollywood films), but

often it was fantasy and play in a physically lively environment such as a neighborhood theater that was showing some movie for the teen market or the drive-
in that catered to moving around inside and outside the car. Moreover, in these
places the space was usually away from adults. It was the teens' grounds for
group exchange, just as were certain streets for cruising and drugstore soda
fountains for shakes and fries.

Both the subject matter of these movies and the theater scene become important contexts for the underground cinema. Sexual themes and problems are
commonly explicit in the horror films and other favorite teen-pix of the era. The
most obvious, and probably most influential, horror genre example is *Psycho*
(1960). Norman Bates is not just a serial killer; his behavior is connected to his
mother's sexual choices and his own sexual ambivalences. *Psycho*, of course, does
not support Norman's cross-dressing choice, and it places the blame on mother
—both sexuality and bad mothers being common 1950s discourses. Two aspects
of moviegoing behavior set the stage for the underground cinema, however:
the teenager movie market in terms of the theatrical environment as a place of
isolated community away from adults and the introduction of sexually explicit
themes in fantasy form.[10]

A second salient predecessor for underground movies was the live theater
scene, which also introduced sexual topics and a renewed sense of the physical
environment. As Parker Tyler notes, underground cinema had as one of its
contexts the Happenings of the late 1950s.[11] The cinema had just as immediately
the theatrical context of off-off-Broadway. Historians of American theater date
the beginning of off-off-Broadway "somewhat arbitrarily as September 27,
1960."[12] That was when the revival of Alfred Jarry's *King Ubu* opened at Take 3,
a Greenwich Village coffeehouse. Following this production came many more
café-theater productions.

Off-off-Broadway had multiple connotations for the early 1960s New York
scene. It was promoted as nonprofit (as opposed to the increasing commercialization and capital-intensive Broadway and even off Broadway). It confronted
a tacit boundary between the public and the private by intermingling audience
and performer and by putting theater into the hands of anyone. Although cafés
were initial places for the theater troupes of off-off-Broadway, some of the most
important groups found homes in friendly local churches, such as the Judson
Memorial Baptist-Congregationalist Church on Washington Square and St.

Mark's Church-in-the-Bowerie on the Lower East Side.[13] Off-off-Broadway also produced cutting-edge sexual dramas. Edward Albee's work started within this community, and, as I shall indicate, some of the early underground cinema was exhibited in off-off-Broadway venues.

Albee's work, like that of the underground filmmakers, provoked attacks because of its sexual rights representations. In an early 1960 review of *The Zoo Story*, Robert Brustein of the *New Republic* wrote:

> On the other hand, I am deeply depressed by the uses to which [Albee's] talent has been put. In its implicit assumption that the psychotic, the criminal, and the invert [homosexual] are closer to God than anyone else, "The Zoo Story" embodies the same kind of sexual-religious claptrap we are accustomed to from Allen Ginsberg.... I will not bore you with a discussion of the masochistic-homosexual perfume which hangs so heavily over "The Zoo Story" except to say that Mr. Albee's love-death, like Mr. Ginsberg's poetry, yields more readily to clinical than theological analysis.[14]

Indeed, the "beat" culture (led by Allen Ginsberg) and its currents of homosexuality are a third contextual predecessor for the underground cinema, as David James and Richard Dyer point out.[15] Dyer writes than many of the beat poets (Ginsberg, Robert Duncan, Jack Spicer) were gay, and others (Jack Kerouac and Neal Cassady) thought it "cool." For Dyer, Ginsberg's publication of *Howl* in 1956 associated "beatness" with "homosexuality with revolt against bourgeois convention."[16] James explains the logical dynamic: "Since sex was the sign of social and aesthetic values suppressed in straight society, it could signify deviance and resistance in general, and so social repression of all kinds could be contested via the codes of sexual representation."[17] As early as 1960, one *Village Voice* writer was arguing that an even more radical break was necessary: although "being spokesman for a kind of literary homosexuality" had been valuable, that action was now only a "romanticism."[18] But the *Voice* also continued to describe the doings of the beat culture. In a front-page article in summer 1962, the pilgrimage of beats to Ibiza was detailed, including the fact that "Domino's steam-bath intimacy is probably an important reason for its success."[19]

The beat's appreciation of alternative sexualities was not, however, as liberated as it might seem. The beat's privileged sexuality was of a particular type. As Catharine R. Stimpson argues, "In the late 1940s and 1950s, the Beats prized candor and honesty, energy and rage," not a homosexuality of "concealment and camp, parody and irony." Their homosexual hero was a "rebel who seizes freedom and proclaims the legitimacy of individual desire," who was "'fucked in the ass by saintly motorcyclists' and screamed 'with joy.'"[20] The underground cinema will not take up such a distinction, blurring the various styles and politics of sexual liberation—beat and camp—into one general manifesto of desire.

Indeed, much of this was about politics, a politics of anticonsensus and pro-individual freedoms—my fourth contextual predecessor. Fought out in every arena, one important battle site was civil rights for blacks. Another was the critique of restrictions on subject matter and words on the screen and in the theater. Obscenity laws were under attack as perfect examples of the attempt by Republican conservatives to mold everyone into conformists, thinking the same thing and saying nothing. The early 1960s were the years of the arrests of Lenny Bruce in Greenwich Village and Los Angeles cafés. In the specific area of film, parts of even the mainstream film industry worked to loosen up remnants of the Production Code while more legal forms of restriction were challenged as aftermaths of the Roth case (1957). In 1959, the California State Supreme Court reviewed a case involving Raymond Rohauer's theatrical screening of Kenneth Anger's *Fireworks* (1947) in 1957.[21]

Throughout this scene of context, I have perhaps somewhat reductively, but fairly I believe, characterized a series of oppositions providing at least cultural equivalencies, if not models, for the underground cinema. Alternatives to the dominant of the 1950s are showing up all over the cultural map. (1) Modes of human interaction in a cultural space, (2) modes of producing cultural texts, (3) modes of representation, (4) subject matter, and (5) political agendas are lining up in a series of "either/or"s. Peter Stallybrass and Allon White offer the important observation that hierarchically constructed binary oppositions that are linked with one another are often similarly positioned in terms of evaluation. [22] In one of their examples, the top parts of the human body, like upper parts of geographical maps, are presumed better than the lower halves. Or, if heads are associated with the rational and the good, genitalia are connected to the emotional and the bad.

In the case that I am developing, the following dichotomies are being aligned in a map of oppositions: (1) passive, private involvement with a text; (2) capitalist alienated labor; (3) smooth, seamless modes of mass-produced representation (i.e., dramatic Hollywood movies); (4) repressed (or monogamous, same-race hetero-) sexuality; and (5) conservative consensus politics that restricts individual rights. These are opposed to (1) active, communal participation with a text; (2) cooperative group labor; (3) rough, reflexive modes of popularly produced representations; (4) sexual exploration and confrontation; and (5) libertarian and liberation politics.

In his excellent analysis of the decade of the 1960s, Fredric Jameson places the start of the era in the late 1950s. In a general methodological statement, he argues that periods are theoretically knowable by their "sharing of a common objective situation, to which a whole range of varied responses and creative innovations is then possible, but always within that situation's structural limits."[23] The underground cinema is one such response to the common situation of the conformist 1950s, but one that will be resisted in certain quarters in part because the quintet of oppositions becomes "too much" for certain people. As I shall detail in the cases below, whereas some people could invest in all parts of the map, others could not. Specifically, when rough, reflexive popular culture is replaced by sex play and camp humor, some people draw the line. Of course, for others that last taboo is liberating for its creation of community jokes and pleasure.

The Connection

The appearance of the underground cinema of the early 1960s, like every other cultural phenomenon, is more a transformation of earlier possibilities than some original act of invention. Although I restrict my use of the term *underground cinema* to films that explicitly displayed nondominant sexualities in nonnarrative form and style and were created for the midnight urban movie scene in the early 1960s, underground cinema was part of the larger movement of the New American Cinema, which also met with varied responses to its cultural and political allegiances.

"Created" by manifesto in the summer of 1961 (but also being more a transformation of earlier activities), the New American Cinema was, as Patricia Mellencamp notes, not so much antinarrative as anticommercial and anti-Hollywood.[24] She writes, "The initial impetus was to create alternative narrative features expressive of personal style and link up with the tradition of European art cinema" and its U.S. exhibition circuit.[25] The New American Cinema Group's statement of principles notes the development of a "movement ... reaching significant proportions." It rejects censorship and calls for new forms of financing, labor arrangements, distribution, and exhibition, and for new forms of appreciation for low-budget films from artists. Finally, the group claims that "we are not joining together to make money. We are joining together to make films. ... we have had enough of the Big Lie in life and in the arts.... We don't want false, polished, slick films—we prefer them rough, unpolished, but alive; we don't want rosy films—we want them the color of blood."[26]

This manifesto was fairly successful publicity. By June 1962, Harris Dienstfrey in *Commentary* was able to write a review of "the New American Cinema" that faithfully reproduced its goals, including its common subject-matter concerns about race relations.[27] Among the original filmmaker/signers of the 1961 manifesto were Robert Frank and Alfred Leslie (*Pull My Daisy*, 1959) and Shirley Clarke (*The Connection*, 1961). Named as an ally was John Cassavetes, who had recently completed *Shadows* (1959). What all three of these films (as well as others) had in common were direct public associations with beat culture or off-off-Broadway theater. Thus they had implicit connections to sexual liberation politics. Moreover, Clarke's and Cassavetes's films also directly addressed black civil rights issues.

Pull My Daisy stars beats Ginsberg, Gregory Corso, and Peter Orlovsky and features a witty voice-over narration by Kerouac. Some drugs are shared and jazz is played. Peter (played by Orlovsky) asks a visitor who is proselytizing for an Eastern religion if baseball is holy. Eventually the boys go out together, leaving the wife and child at home.[28] *Shadows* begins with a group listening to rock and roll.[29] Events revolve around a black family in which the older brother, who is a jazz musician, has a couple of white friends, a sister who dates and then has sex with a white man who doesn't realize until later that she is black, and a younger brother. Issues of interracial sex and prejudice are a major part of the film.

The Connection is perhaps a useful example in this group to study further. In the late 1950s, one of the major off-off-Broadway theater groups was the Living Theater, led by Julian Beck and Judith Malina. As Lauren Rabinovitz notes, the Living Theater had a "symbolic allegiance to marginalized and oppressed groups."[30] In 1959, it produced *The Connection*, written by Jack Gelber, about drug addiction. Despite initially bad reviews in the *New Yorker, New York Times,* and *Village Voice,* the play won praise in other quarters. A paid advertisement in the *Village Voice* in August 1959 illustrates the intensity with which supporters viewed *The Connection* as socially significant. After suggesting that critics who disliked the play likely would have also misunderstood James Joyce, D. H. Lawrence, and Henry Miller,[31] the author writes, "This is not one of the regular Broadway, county-fair-type, spun-sugar musicals that both the expense-account trade and the critics find such good 'summer entertainment.' And it is not one of those expanded soap operas (next week East Lynne), alleged 'serious' dramas, in which the hero (emasculated to begin with) is threatened by the tired old buzz-saw dressed and disguised as castration."[32] This assertion of a masculinity to the treatment of the topic of drug addiction is important for understanding the nature of the discursive debates around the film version. The assertion of masculinity also aligns with the general beat attitude against a bourgeoisie that it accused of being soft.

At the same time as the appearance of the play version of *The Connection*, the Living Theater had been showing films as part of a film society run by experimental filmmaker Stan VanDerBeek. Clarke and others shot in 1959 a film version of *The Connection*, which Clarke took to the spring 1961 Cannes Film Festival, accompanied by Ginsberg, Corso, and Orlovsky. The film was a success. Back home, however, *The Connection* had been determined obscene in New York State because it used the word *shit* as a slang term for heroin. During the appeals process, and rejecting the notion the film was obscene, the leadership of an important off-off-Broadway site, the Judson Memorial Church, screened the film without admission charges in October 1962.[33]

New York critics were as unfriendly to the film as they had been to the play. In his weekly column for the *Village Voice*, Jonas Mekas defended the film against criticisms that its content was "'drab,' 'offensive,' 'odd,' 'crude,' 'sick,' 'vulgar,' 'shoddy,' 'sordid,' 'disagreeable,' etc." He countered: "Why don't you admit that you are washed out, that you can't cope with modern cinema?"[34] Mekas's response, of course, had no effect, but over the years the film version of *The Connection* has achieved respect for its tough subject matter and participation in a general opposition to censorship.

Before the film was shown in New York City, the play version altered. It traveled to London in spring 1961, to less than an ecstatic response. And when it was revived in fall 1961 back in New York City, its lead and some textual material had changed, producing a different effect, according to the *Village Voice* reviewer:

"There are many other changes, ... I am not sure they are all for the best. On the other hand, they seem to feed directly into the desires of the audience. Certainly this is not for the best. 'The Connection' is today being played as a comedy, at least as 'camped up' at the late show for the tourist trade on Saturday nights, and as busy as Judith Malina is with newer commitments, I feel that she herself might be well advised to revisit it."[35] If in fall 1961, some late-night versions of *The Connection* had turned to camp, why would that be? The answer has to do, I think, with the overall midnight scene in New York.

Flaming Creatures

As a branch of the New American Cinema, underground cinema was in content sexually explicit and in location "underground"—primarily New York City but also Los Angeles and San Francisco. In the early 1960s, the term *underground* had specific connotations. One *Village Voice* headline on January 25, 1962, declared, "The Bourgeois Mothers' Underground, on the Rise."[36] The story described a group of seventy-five Village housewives who traveled to Washington, D.C., as a public protest about the dangers of nuclear war. Labeled as part of "the peace movement," the group's members had not known each other until they gathered on the train ride.

The repeated phenomenon of individuals taking resistant political action against the norm and then finding others who were like themselves seems an important recurring event in this period. Similar revelations were operating in civil and sexual rights. In these same years, the *Village Voice* published several articles indicating a different stance by some gays toward social and civil repression of homosexuals. In March 1959, Seymour Krim published a "Press of Freedom" column titled "Revolt of the Homosexual."[37] Krim did not take the common 1950s view of homosexuality as an aberration or illness, then even the official view of the Mattachine Society. Instead, he asserted the naturalness and acceptability of homosexuality. Turning to Donald Webster Cory's *The Homosexual in America* to justify his views, Krim claimed:

> We want recognition for our simple human rights, just like Negroes, Jews, and women. . . . Courageous gay people are now beginning to realize that they are human beings who must fight to gain acceptance for what they are—not what others want them to be. . . . In the future you'll see the equally suave acknowledgment of different standards,

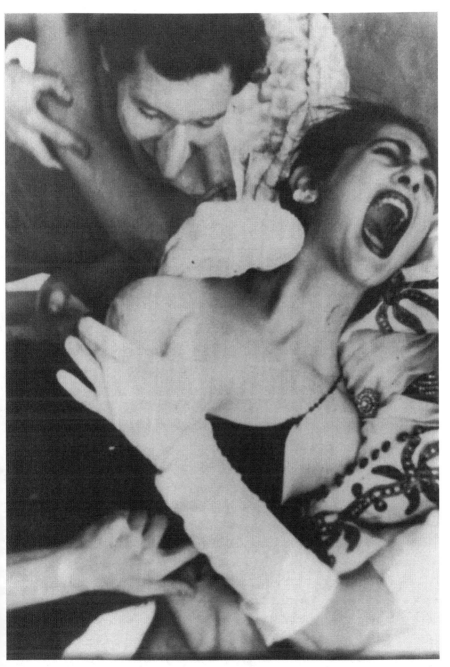

Flaming Creatures, 1963. Courtesy of Photofest.

including the right of the homosexual to fully express himself as a
"healthy" individual in terms of his tradition.... When this movement becomes powerful enough—and gay people refuse either to
hide or flaunt themselves—it will be openly accepted.[38]

Krim was answered the following week in an essay titled "The Gay Underground
—A Reply to Mr. Krim"[39] The author discounted Krim's assertion that a movement was possible, but, again, *underground* refers to the association of minorities not just into resistance against the dominant but also into a common cause
unified by a political agenda for change. In fact, several months later, another
Voice article reported that one gay rights advocate had proposed a third political
party for a homosexual voting bloc.[40] Other articles surveying the sexual politics
for gays continued to appear throughout the period.[41] Thus, for New Yorkers
in the early 1960s, the term *underground* had connotations not of the hidden
but of alternative communities and political activism. Additionally, discourse by
homosexual men about their rights was beginning to take a different rhetorical
tactic than commonly existed in the 1950s.

The movement effect of the underground cinema was partially propelled by
the community associations developed through earlier filmgoing connections.
As scholars have noted, the post–World War II efforts of Maya Deren, Amos
Vogel, and Jonas Mekas to create film distribution organizations, venues, and
journals for filmmakers helped create the sense that numerous individuals were
involved in nontraditional film work. They also created various alliances and
conflicts.[42] Rabinovitz describes several of these; another is mentioned in Calvin
Tomkin's 1973 essay on the scene. Tomkins notes that in 1961 Vogel decided
not to show Stan Brakhage's *Anticipation of the Night* at his Cinema 16 society.
Mekas accepted the piece for his programming, and later with friends began a
competitive film distribution system, Film-Makers' Cooperative, in 1962. For
various reasons, Cinema 16 went out of business in 1963, and Vogel, with Richard Roud, cofounded the New York Film Festival.

Meanwhile, Mekas was championing much more offbeat work in the late-
night shows at various small film theaters. The term *underground* was applied to
movies throughout this period in several ways, but eventually it took on a meaning similar to the wider cultural definition—a liberal or radical agenda with overt
demonstrations of involvement by groups of individuals. In a summer 1960
Film Culture essay, Mekas wrote about the movies he was championing: "The

underground is beginning to boil, to open up, to shoot out."[43] (The masculine eroticism of this image is hard to miss!)

The screenings organized by Mekas and others led to festivals and awards, all of which did not go without their own troubles as the underground cinema began bubbling. Andrew Sarris, asked to judge at the September 1962 Film-Makers' Festival at the Charles Theater, reported his general disgust with the whole lot of films:

> I am aware that Parker Tyler has disassociated himself from the deliberations of a jury which merely wanted to get the hell out of the theatre as quickly as possible. I will go Mr. Tyler one better. I wish to disassociate myself from a primitive movement which fancies itself the moral guardian of cinema. I can take the ineptness, but not the cynical exploitation of the ineptness.[44]

From the context, I am not sure what Sarris means by "cynical exploitation of ineptness," although he does express gratitude "for little favors like clearly focused images, audible sound tracks, an occasional glimpse of a pretty girl, an infrequent glimmer of intelligence, and most rarely of all, a friendly gesture to the audience."[45]

Indeed, the underground cinema of the early 1960s was different from the first wave of the New American Cinema. What Sarris is likely complaining about are films such as *The Flower Thief* (Ron Rice, 1960), *Little Stabs at Happiness* (Ken Jacobs, 1959–63), *Blonde Cobra* (Jacobs, Jack Smith, and Bob Fleischner, 1959–63), and, to come, *Flaming Creatures* (Smith, 1963), *The Queen of Sheba Meets the Atom Man* (Rice, 1963), *Scorpio Rising* (Kenneth Anger, 1963), and *Christmas on Earth* (a.k.a. *Cocks and Cunts;* Barbara Rubin, 1963). All of these are now regarded as the canonical exemplars of the underground cinema.

What is wrong with these films beyond Sarris's general accusation of technical ineptness? I would argue that, along with all of the other stylistic, production, and political connotations, these films' representations of nonheterosexual sex and interracial sex in the context of a playful, humorous, sometimes campy approach to sex rather than a seriousness, an emulation of the high tones of Art, proved hard to take for some people, even devotees of art and experimental cinema. Although Andrew Ross implies that camp became a way for New York intellectuals to deal with popular culture, it is not the case that that was possible for all New Yorkers or that it occurred immediately upon its appearance.[46]

Let me begin with a brief counterexample. In the late 1950s, Brakhage had been exploring the "everyday," including sexuality. *Window Water Baby Moving* —the documentary of the birth of his and his wife's child—showed private body parts. As Tyler would note in 1969, "The emergent message of such films is their novelty in terms of according public exhibition to what has been considered strictly domestic and private."[47] Even earlier, Brakhage had recorded his own masturbation in *Flesh of Morning*.

Tyler connects the sources of Brakhage's work to a longer tradition of high-brow aesthetics, but I wish to stress the effects. Once one creates the binary opposition quintet that I have described above, a series of consequences develops: the verisimilitude of the shooting style of cinema verité is contrasted with the artificiality of Hollywood fiction filmmaking; the obvious explosion of hidden sexual acts is contrasted with the obvious representational repression of those acts; the privileging of the everyday and the popular is contrasted with high culture; the seriousness of Hollywood and even some experimental and art cinema is parodied. These oppositions then become a rallying point for a rebellion from the underground. Recall the metaphors above—the New American Cinema wants a cinema "the color of blood"; Mekas notes that the underground is "beginning to boil, to open up, to shoot out." Brakhage's films are the indication of change, the place for some potential transformations, but Brakhage's alliances with high art, normative sexuality,[48] seriousness, and masculinity provide only a launching pad for the revolution.

The rebellion would come from a new set of filmmakers supported by the underground theatrical scene both as movement and play-space, described so well by J. Hoberman and Jonathan Rosenbaum in *Midnight Movies*. Mekas's share in this venture, despite allegations that his motives were not pure, needs to be recognized as well. These screenings were much like those for the teen-pix of the era but with a Village beat cast: audiences smoked marijuana and very vocally responded to the films. As one critic of *The Flower Thief* acknowledged, "One of the really delightful aspects of the Charles Theatre is that booing, hissing, and applause are all permitted equally, so that one can express one's feelings on the spot." Andy Warhol described these screenings as "a lot like a party."[49]

Beyond the exuberant screening scene, what has not been stressed in the analyses of these films is how linked were nontraditional sexuality, racial civil rights issues, and the fun of popular culture. Each of the canonical films employs variants of these representational materials. *The Flower Thief*'s main character (played by Taylor Mead) wanders through San Francisco accompanied not only by classical music but by progressive jazz and gospel music. Beat poetry provides part of the sound track. Americana in the form of the flag, sparklers, and amusement parks are part of the flower thief's environment. *Little Stabs of Happiness* associates old popular music with scenes of Jack Smith dressed as a clown with balloons and a mirror. In the opening section, Smith performs oral sex on a doll. *Blonde Cobra* is an homage to the 1944 Hollywood film *Cobra Woman*, starring Maria Montez, but Ken Jacobs and Smith's version does not have the reverence and fetishization of Montez that Joseph Cornell brings to Rose Hobart in his *Rose Hobart* (1939).[50] Instead, Smith camps a performance of Montez. Smith's cross-dressing and erotic storytelling follow the nostalgic opening music, "Let's Call the Whole Thing Off."

The notorious *Flaming Creatures* also uses older popular music as background to stylized images of masturbation, cross-dressing, seduction, and rape. Here advertising is employed as commentary in a fabulous second movement that describes the benefits of a new lipstick, which is then liberally applied to lips and penises. Performance is doubly stressed throughout: the characters almost perform performers. Fake noses on "females" gesture toward an obvious ironic use of Freudian symbolism, especially in retrospect after the "women" lift their skirts to reveal their own penises. Hollywood genres are travestied to exaggeration: *Flaming Creatures* references melodrama but also the horror film. As a woman rises out of a coffin, carrying lilies in her hands (a classic image of the femme fatale), the sound track is of the country-and-western "Wasn't It God Who Made Honky Tonk Angels?" Characters appear not only in strange genders but also in odd races. One of the dancers is in blackface. The film closes to an apparent homage to some (to me unknown) classical painting while "Be Bop a Lula, she's my baby" trails away.[51]

Christmas on Earth explores dynamics of couplings in a more serious but equally provocative way. Dated around 1963, the two reels of film are now supposed to be projected one on top of the other (another sexual congress?). Reel A, to be shown at full size, displays close-ups of heterosexuality: penises, anuses, mouths, vaginas. Reel B, to be projected at half of Reel A's size and in the middle of the screen over Reel A, represents 1960s tabooed sex: interracial and homosexual. These images are partially performances. For instance, a white woman appears not only in blackface but in black body (her breasts and stomach remain white, providing a second "face"). At the end of the film, all of the participants wave toward the camera.[52]

Scorpio Rising is another excellent instance of the combination of homosexuality, popular culture, and camp satire, with Anger's appropriation of images of male buddies from Hollywood movies, television, and comic strips. *The Queen of Sheba Meets the Atom Man* pairs a black woman with Taylor Mead, invokes several trashy Hollywood genres, and again uses popular music and jazz.

Although many people appreciated this new cinema, others did not. One recurrent theme is how badly shot by Hollywood standards these films are: out-of-focus and overexposed images, lack of establishing shots, and panning too fast, which prevents the viewer's seeing what is likely (or hopefully) there. These were obviously studied effects by underground filmmakers, and easily justified as that.[53] It is also clear that many people missed or resisted the jokes in the films because other things stood in the way.

An obvious problem was the nontraditional sexuality. It was even nontraditional pornography! Stag movies had been a part of a homosocial scene for males since the 1910s, and exploitation cinema began developing during the late 1950s, but both were still quite nonpublic and unavailable to "innocents" unless they were initiated into them at smokers, lodges, or fraternity parties—in scenes with a strong resemblance to what Warhol and others recall being the case for the underground cinema events.[54] As Thomas Waugh has discovered, some male same-sex scenes exist in traditional pornography, but they are extremely rare.[55] These male same-sex scenes are used as preludes to heterosexual sex and are treated without much emphasis. Beyond these rare images of male same-sex actions, traditional stag films also have some instances of cross-dressing, but mostly as drag performances with the humorous "surprise" of revealing the performer's penis at the end of the act. This humor, and the general treatment of the rare male same-sex scene, might appeal to an individual gay man, but the general structure of heterosexual stag-film pornography works to disavow a homoerotic address to the male spectator.[56]

If this representation of male same-sex sexuality differs from traditional hard-core pornography, it is even nontraditional for the rare examples of early 1960s gay-addressed erotica. Waugh writes that he has found no evidence of any organized gay audience for gay pornography prior to 1960: it was too illegal and taboo.[57] However, gay soft-core erotica was being produced by film companies such as Apollo and Zenith in the 1940s and 1950s. This erotica consists of short narratives justifying nearly complete male nudity (occasionally genitals are displayed). Promises of sexual activities to occur offscreen or after the film's narrative ends may be implicit, but most onscreen same-sex bodily contact is limited to physical sport such as playful wrestling, swimming, or bodybuilding.[58] Thus the rare instances of male same-sex scenes found in heterosexual-addressed stag films are about all the hard-core images of male same-sex sexuality that appear to have existed before 1960.

Thus the underground cinema was multiply confounding in its representation of male same-sex sexuality. It addressed not only heterosexual devotees of avant-garde cinema but gay audiences in a new way. Importantly, it was not using the conventions of a heterosexual stag reel or even standard gay erotica for that audience. Arthur Knight, reviewing *Flaming Creatures* for *Saturday Review* in autumn 1963, objected: "A faggoty stag-reel, it comes as close to hardcore pornography as anything ever presented in a theater.... Everything is shown in sickening detail, defiling at once both sex and cinema."[59] Although it would take almost a year from its initial screening for *Flaming Creatures* to be seized by the police for obscenity, when it and, two weeks later, Jean Genet's *Un Chant d'Amour* were, *Variety* proclaimed in its March 18, 1964, headline: "Cops Raid Homo Films Again."[60] *Variety* described *Flaming Creatures* as "a 58-minute montage of a transvestite orgy." In a formal statement, Mekas argued that the films were art and thus deserved unrestricted availability for viewing. As Tomkins notes, the March 1964 publicity brought the underground out of Greenwich Village: "The public, which had been largely oblivious of the underground's existence, assumed that 'underground' was synonymous with dirty pictures."[61]

Prior to *Flaming Creatures'* obscenity charges, one way to appreciate the underground cinema had been to associate it with art, which was part of the pre-March 1964 public discourse. In his *New York Times* review of *The Flower Thief* in July 1962, Eugene Archer analyzes the film by finding associations with beat culture, but, more significantly, he uncovers highbrow allusions. Among the intertextual references he discovers are *The Seventh Seal*, the "pose of marines planting the flag on Iwo Jima," and "films by Sergei Eisenstein, Charlie Chaplin, Luis Bunuel and Alain Resnais."[62]

Another pre-obscenity-charge response was to treat the films with amused paternalism. A July 1963 *New Yorker* essay considers Mekas, Ken Jacobs, the Film-Makers' Cooperative, and "underground cinema" as diverting New York-iana: "The results range from 'poetic' color and motion studies to blunt documentary denunciations of Society and the Bomb, but most share a total disdain for the traditional manner of storytelling on film, and also for the 'self-consciously art' experimental films of the twenties and thirties."[63] Pete Hamill in the *Saturday Evening Post* in September 1963 also gives an overall positive representation of all of the New American films, and quotes Jacobs as indicating that what he is producing is "art," although Hamill describes *Flaming Creatures* as "a sophomoric exercise in the kind of sex that Henry Miller dealt with 30 years ago" and *Blonde Cobra* as "accompanied by Smith's voice telling fraternity-house stories that presumably are meant to be shocking." Yet the antipathy found in some writers' remarks about these films is not present in Hamill's essay. His conclusion is that by encouraging the filmmakers to be "bad," a new cinema might develop, one that "at least ... won't be Debbie Reynolds or Doris Day, sailing into a saccharine sunset."[64]

After the charges of obscenity, the descriptions shift from art or bemusement to a serious debate, because now the underground cinema represents a political cause, connected to its representations of sex acts and display of parts of the human anatomy. In an editorial, the *Nation* calls for an end to censorship: "Even the banning of hard-core commercial pornography invites trouble." Several weeks later the *Nation* publishes a critical defense of *Flaming Creatures* by Susan Sontag, who ends up calling the film an example of "pop art" in anticipation within this same year of including the film in her essay on camp. Sontag declaims, "Smith's film has the sloppiness, the arbitrariness, the looseness of pop art. It also has pop art's gaiety, its ingenuousness, its exhilarating freedom from moralism."[65] As Ross suggests, Sontag's move to justify this cinema as pop art and camp is a break with "the style and legitimacy of the old liberal intelligentsia, whose puritanism had always set it apart from the frivolous excesses of the ruling class."[66] Sontag will, however, back off of equating camp with homosexuality in her "Notes on 'Camp.'"

The charge of promoting moralism or amoralism through play and sexual diversity is where the film community divides. By mid-1964, two important supporters of experimental and art cinema openly criticized this part of the New American Cinema. In May 1964, Vogel published in the *Village Voice* a statement accusing Mekas and his supporters of inflating the significance of these films and "disregarding even the most advanced and adventurous contemporary artists of the international cinema, such as Antonioni, Resnais, Godard." By promoting only this cinema, Vogel asserted,

> Jonas has become more dogmatic, more extremist, more publicity-conscious. While the flamboyancy and provocative extravagance of the positions taken has [sic] undoubtedly served to make at least one segment of the independent film movement more visible ... it has also been accompanied by an absence of style and seriousness, a lack of concern for film form, rhythm, and theory which leads many people to view the existing works and pretensions with an indulgent, amused air, smiling at the antics of the movement or somewhat repelled by the "camp" atmosphere of its screenings.[67]

Vogel continued by arguing that Mekas was anticipating and perhaps hurting the possibilities of a true revolution in the American cinema: "However justified an objective, the question of timing and tactics is a crucial one." Moreover, *Flaming Creatures*, "despite flashes of brilliance and moments of perverse, tortured beauty, remains a tragically sad film noir, replete with limp genitalia and limp art."[68] Vogel was clearly supporting repeals of obscenity laws and the promotion of expression. What Vogel objected to was the use of what he considered to be a less-than-high art, less-than-serious film, an unmasculine cinema as the test case for obscenity, for fear the masses would not support the cause.

Predictably, letters to the *Village Voice* divided over Vogel's remarks. Two letters supported Vogel, even calling for the *Voice* to drop Mekas's column; a third argued that Vogel was blind to an important evaluative prejudice: "The reason why Genet's film 'Un Chant d'Amour' has been praised by those who cannot stomach 'Flaming Creatures' is not that it is a smoother construction but that it evokes pity: a nice, warm, serious, recognizable emotion. Homosexual love on the screen, yes; a comic conception of human sex, no."[69] "Brooks-Brothers'" gayness, yes; drag queens, no.

Dwight Macdonald was another critic of the proported tone of this cinema. In July 1964, he called *Flaming Creatures* and *Un Chant d'Amour* "two sexually explicit, and perverse, movies."[70] However, his view of the problem is opposite that of Vogel: "Like the Beat littérateurs, the movie-makers of the New American Cinema are moralists rather than artists."[71] Macdonald's widely known attacks against mass culture and in defense of high art and his concern for the social threats of mass culture as standardization inform his opinion. Here Macdonald is responding to many aspects of the underground cinema, but the pop-art features are likely highly influential in his evaluation, as much as the representation of the "perverse."[72]

These debates continued through the summer of 1964, as Macdonald and other leftist colleagues, including Lewis Jacobs, Edouard de Laurot, and Peter Goldfarb, issued a statement:

> The New American Cinema is a movement much vaster in quantity and quality than its restricted and distorted image insistently publicized throughout the world by the New York Village Group of filmmakers (Joanas [sic] Mekas, Adam [sic] Sitney, et al.)
>
>   This misrepresentation is all the more regrettable since the films of the New York Group are on the whole characterized by (a) in their content a solipsistic alienation from reality and society (b) in their form by a lack of originality and professional level (c) in their documentation ... by a specious or superficial realism—justifying these inadequacies with a mystique of spontaneity which in fact hides creative impotence, more often than not.[73]

This split continued through the 1966 New York Film Festival, run by Vogel, Sarris, and others. Sarris justified not showing some of the New American films that were connected to this trend because many people and critics were opposed to it: Warhol was "pointedly excluded from the proceedings so as not to offend the regular reviewers."[74]

Vogel, Macdonald, Lewis Jacobs, and many others were supporters of cinema and radical politics. Yet how cinema might produce radical change was constantly debated among these people. Indications in the rhetoric and discourse of these writers are that part of their difficulties with the underground cinema had to do with its representations—as not serious enough; as pop art and camp; as perverse.[75] Thus to the set of oppositions, play and laughter need to be added in a new category of "attitude," an attitude that was too gay—in the double sense of that term. Some of the antagonisms were probably also personal with Mekas. The debates over *Flaming Creatures* did not end underground cinema; however, the movement took an interesting permutation when the movies of Warhol, excluded from the 1966 New York Film Festival, began to receive national aclaim.

The Chelsea Girls

Andy Warhol's films provide the break from the underground as political movement to aboveground—even general—cinema. It may be a bit too much to
claim that his films permitted the acceptance by a counterculture generation of
soft-core and hard-core pornography. Yet the play with sexual desire explicit in
Blow Job, My Hustler, Chelsea Girls, Lonesome Cowboys, and so many others of
his films took away some of the threat that nontraditional sexuality presented
the middle class. When even *Newsweek* and *Life* could report on this cinema in a
somewhat enthusiastic way, a sexual liberation seemed tolerable, maybe even
fashionable.

Warhol's early involvement with the Mekas underground screenings has
been detailed by Hoberman and Rosenbaum, among others.[76] Warhol liked to
play with his affection for this cinema as he played with his love of dominant
Hollywood and consumer culture. In an interview published in spring 1966 in
Film Culture, David Ehrenstein asked Warhol:

The Chelsea Girls, 1966. Courtesy of Photofest.

DE: Who in the New American Cinema do you admire?

AW: Jaaaacck Smiiiitttth.

DE: You really like Jack Smith?

AW: When I was little, I always ... thought he was my best director. ... I mean, just the only person I would ever try to copy, and just ... so terrific and now since I'm grown up, I just think that he makes the best movies.[77]

By the time Sontag defended *Flaming Creatures*, pop art had become the next New York art fashion, so her stance was a smart tactic for justifying the film. *Film Culture* was also promoting pop art as an iconography worth considering within the New American film scene. In fact, it could even find pop art in the old enemy Hollywood. In *Film Culture*'s summer 1963 issue, Charles Boultenhouse published what I take to be a partially ironic essay, "The Camera as a God," in which he declares that "Hollywood is the Original Pop Art and is GREAT because IT IS WHAT IT IS. Gorgeous flesh and mostly terrible acting! Divine! Campy dialogue and preposterous plots! Divine! Sexy fantasy and unorgasmic tedium! Divine!"[78] Three issues later, Michael McClure did a tribute to Jayne Mansfield in something of the same tone and much like Smith's earlier homage to Maria Montez.[79] Warhol's first films for the underground were *Kiss*, shown weekly as the "serial" at the Grammercy Arts Theater. *Kiss* was three-minute kisses with variant pairings, some heterosexual, others homosexual.[80] The Kuchar brothers rapidly learned the discourse of Hollywood advertising, and their promotions of their forthcoming films are among the most amusing documents of the cinema.[81]

The pop-art and camp inflections of the underground and trends in the New York art scene were—although different—connected, [82] and suspiciously incorporated old Hollywood as part of their subject matter rather than the subject matter many New York intellectuals privileged: the foreign art film and the auteur cinema promoted by Sarris. This makes sense. If foreign art films, auteurs who transcend the mundane of Hollywood, and segments of the New American Cinema are praised for realism and seriousness, then in this binary inversion, grade-B Hollywood could become a "good" object again, albeit inflected by camp humor or exaggerated as commodity by pop art. Aligned with the foreign art film was also high modernism—the American abstract expressionism that Warhol discusses as a "macho" world from which he was excluded as "too swish." [83]

Pop art and camp were contextually associated by opposition to the dominant and so too were pop art and sexual diversity. In fact, in their cases, a dangerous subversion was occurring. In April 1966, Vivian Gornick published in the *Village Voice* an article, "It's a Queer Hand Stoking the Campfire," arguing a homosexual control over pop art. She states: "Popular culture is now in the hands of the homosexuals. It is homosexual taste that determines largely style, story, statement in painting, literature, dance, amusements, and acquisitions for a goodly proportion of the intellectual middle class. It is the homosexual temperament which is guiding the progress of Pop Art."[84] Gornick outlines this influence in a bitter essay, deriving her authority from earlier *Voice* discussions of gay rights and gay sensibilities. Moreover, she declares that camp is not, as Sontag describes it, "tender" but rather a "raging put-on of the middle classes," "a malicious fairy's joke."[85] Thus, whether praised or condemned, the connections of pop art, play, and a camp gay aesthetic were explicitly being made.

Although the exhibition of Warhol's *The Chelsea Girls* into a midtown theater in December 1966 is a good marker of a public acceptance of underground cinema, the way was paved earlier. Two years before, in December 1964, *Newsweek* did a long story on Warhol as pop painter and described his unconventional work in film.[86] Then in January 1965, Shana Alexander described for the mass-circulation *Life* readers what it was like to watch *Flaming Creatures, Scorpio Rising,* and other such films underground. She begins:

> The other night I infiltrated a crowd of 350 cultivated New York sophisticates who were squeezed into a dark cellar staring at a wrinkled bedsheet. The occasion was the world premiere of *Harlot* [Warhol], yet another in the rash of "underground movies" which have become the current passion of New York's avant garde.... if a bunch of intelligent people will spend two solid hours and $2.50 apiece to see a single, grainy, wobbly shot projected onto a bedsheet of a man dressed up as Jean Harlow eating a banana (that's what we saw in the cellar), then the movie business must be in worse shape than anyone has any idea.[87]

Alexander notes the value of Warhol's paintings, retrospectives occurring at the Metropolitan and Carnegie Museums, and Ford Foundation grants to underground filmmakers, although she concludes with some expressions of concern, not about possible effects of pornography, but for "fake artists, phony art, and pompous, pretentious critics."[88] Mekas and his "cinematheque" made the *New York Times Sunday Magazine* later in 1965.[89]

By this time "expanded cinema" was beginning to replace "underground cinema" as the mid-1960s transition to hippie and acid-drug countercultures developed. In late 1965, Mekas did a two-week, mixed-media show; in February 1966, Warhol staged "Andy Warhol, Up-Tight," with the Velvet Underground and with multiple images projected on walls and ceilings. Simultaneously on the West Coast, Ken Kesey, the Merry Pranksters, and the Grateful Dead conducted a series of "acid tests," and Bill Graham staged a large public one at the Fillmore. In April 1966, the famous "Erupting-Exploding-Plastic Inevitable" production with a revolving mirrored ballroom globe and multimedia marked a high point in pop history.

The expanded cinema maintained the tradition of mixed responses. Howard Junker in the *Nation* complained, "How many ill-conceived, half-baked, technically incompetent, faggoty, poetic films can anyone see before announcing: 'I've made that scene. And never mind about the art form of the age.'" Stanley Kauffmann, reviewer for the *New Republic* opined, "Many of [the underground filmmakers] equate radicalism with personal gesture and style—revolt consummated by bizarre hair and dress, unconventional sexual behavior, flirtations with drugs."[90]

It was in September 1966 that *The Chelsea Girls* debuted at Mekas's cinematheque.[91] In a real sense, the praise by *Newsweek* reviewer Jack Kroll marks a mass-media acceptance of these films as potentially art, despite all the other connotations: "It is a fascinating and significant movie event."[92] Warhol's characters are compared with Gelber's, Albee's, and John Updike's—all icons of the epitome of 1960s contemporary aesthetics, and Kroll encourages the distribution of the film to film societies and universities.[93]

Several months later, *Newsweek* published another long essay by Kroll, "Up from Underground," that also brought positive attention to these films as an "'official' avant-garde movement" as in other arts. Kroll declared, "The underground has at last surfaced and is moving into public consciousness with a vengeance."[94] Likewise, *Time* in the same month produced an extended examination of the scene. After describing images from an underground film, the writer indicated that the filmmaker "calls it a work of art. The startling thing is that a great many Americans now agree with him." Pop art, camp art was, finally, Art.[95]

In the history of underground cinema, the commercial success of *The Chelsea Girls* indicates at least a growing toleration of these types of images and attitudes. The success also provided sufficient hopes for packaging underground films and distributing them on a routine basis, first attempted by Mike Getz in late 1966 and then in mid-1967 in London by Raymond Durgnat.[96] The heritage of this distribution of cinema exists most obviously in the late-1960s explosion of feature-length soft-core and hard-core pornography, eventually crossing many prior lines of sexual prohibition, and more generally the sexual revolution opened into mainstream cinema as available for commercialization. Some stylistic tactics of the underground cinema also found their way into mainstream film, particularly the head movies of the late sixties and other "independent" films such as *Easy Rider.*[97]

The critical and commercial success of underground cinema also marked the conclusion of the most lively time for underground cinema as a community film exhibition movement. In 1969, Brakhage filmed *Love Making;* Tyler calmly wrote:

> The second part of the new film, showing two hippie-type males making standardized love (one active, one passive) and featuring unmistakable fellation, does supply some human interest. . . . For the strictly built-in audience at this premiere, the routine homosexual acts passed with no more than a few semisilent gloats, some scattered, suppressed gasps. So far as stirring up articulate moral or emotional reflexes could be observed, they passed like the eight hours Warhol devoted to looking at the Empire State building.[98]

Admittedly, Tyler's fellow viewers were a "built-in" audience, but something significant had happened in the decade between *The Flower Thief* and *Love Making* to allow Tyler to compare an explicit representation of homosexuality with *Empire.*[99]

The emergence of underground cinema is decisively tied to, and I believe participatory in, sexual liberation politics. That is not to suggest that underground cinema was totally liberated itself. As scholars have pointed out, the representation of women fared badly at times. James notes that Carolee Schneemann was moved to create her own representation of lovemaking after being dissatisfied with Brakhage's images, and Mellencamp argues rightly that this avant-garde provides little or no place for the female spectator.[100] Moreover, the degree to which camp reverence for and homages to Hollywood, stars, and popular culture in general is truly resistant and oppositional is worth reflection, as is the commercialization to which this pop/camp culture was employed. This is why I initially labeled this a complex situation.

Yet that the underground cinema was able to so penetrate American culture still deserves notice. Obviously the social conditions of a counterculture and the appropriation of pop culture and comedy made many of the films palatable to people who might otherwise have turned away from them. In fact, the joy and play overrunning the seriousness underpinning the representations likely helped to bind the community and spread it to a larger scene. Although some people may have thought the middle class was unaware of the joke being played on them, I'm not so sure that at least the youth of the middle class were not ready to participate in that joke. In so doing, all those laughing together at the underground scene created a gay community across sexual orientations.

Waugh argues that the gay address of these films was obvious by 1967. Roger McNiven notes that underground movie "camp" was a "pretext for pornography."[101] I believe this study of New York's reception of its underground cinema indicates that the gay address—at least among Villagers—was apparent right away. Moreover, and however, this gay address set up the events at Stonewall in two significant ways. For one thing, these films are not embarrassed by their sexual deviance. They flaunt it and play with it. For another, the sexual deviance was, within its contemporary gay hierarchies, the most underprivileged—it was directed toward fairies and drag queens, not "respectable" middle-class gay men.

Studies of Stonewall seek to explain that 1969 event. In one of the major historical contributions, John D'Emilio suggests that two conditions created the "fairy revolt": a new discourse on gay life away from the 1950s pathological rhetoric and a new militancy.[102] The militancy derived from increasing general resentment of government interference in personal lives, led for homosexuals by individuals such as Franklin Kameny. In 1961, Kameny formed a branch of the Mattachine Society and argued for a civil rights approach (marches, sit-ins) to securing rights for gays and prevention of persecution (such as being fired for supposed security reasons). In New York City in 1962, Randy Wicker founded the Homosexual League of New York, with some good publicity in *Newsweek*, the *New York Times*, and the *Village Voice*. The spring 1965 public attention to abuse of homosexuals in Cuba also set up a valuable contrast for U.S. citizenry.

These actions and related court petitions, as valuable as they were, were conducted by a small number of people in fairly respectable ways. As Elizabeth Lapovsky Kennedy and Madeline D. Davis argue, this homophile movement was still "accommodationist."[103] Kennedy and Davis suggest that the movement needed to incorporate the wide variety of gays and lesbians—men from leather bars, drag queens, butches, and femmes—and to refuse "to deny their difference" in order, finally, to achieve the gay pride symbolized by the events at Stonewall. Most historians of Stonewall stress that it was the transvestites and drag queens who finally fought back, creating the transformation known as the gay liberation movement.

I believe that part of this flaunting of difference derives from the self-identities created in the space of viewing underground cinema in the early 1960s. Several times, screenings flowed into the streets, and confrontations with police or censors at screenings were part of the possible evening events. But most significantly, this underground cinema took up the repressed—even by some homosexuals—images and played with them, had fun, and threw them into the public arena for common consumption. Recognition of this cinema and its makers—from Jack Smith and Andy Warhol to Kenneth Anger—set the stage for validating camp as high style, and gays by association. The underground cinema was not the only early-1960s space for gay play, but it was one that endorsed and even rewarded resistance. It was a scene that "'flew in the face' of the prevailing representation of homosexuals in the 1950s as 'isolated perverts,' as subjects 'gone awry'"—or at least the subjects gone awry were having fun going there! Watching underground movies in New York City in the early 1960s was the beginning of a "participation in a movement"; it was building a community that would later erupt into a revolution.

Notes

This essay is dedicated to Roger McNiven, who introduced me in the mid-1980s to some of these ideas and who died too early of AIDS. I would also like to thank the audience at the 1996 conference of the Society for Cinema Studies, Allan Campbell, and Anne Morey for helpful comments, and David Gerstner for his continuing support and friendship.

1. Cindy Patton discusses the problems with using *community* to describe groups of gays, but chooses to use the term in lieu of a better one. I do as well. See her "Safe Sex and the Pornographic Vernacular," in *How Do I Look? Queer Film and Video*, ed. Bad Object-Choices (Seattle, Wash.: Bay, 1991), 32 n.

2. Samuel Delany in *Motion of Light in Water*, described in Joan Scott, "The Evidence of Experience," *Critical Inquiry* 17 (summer 1991): 773–74.

3. The claims I make in this essay apply only to the reception of this cinema in New York City. I do not assume that people outside of New York were as cognizant as those around the Greenwich Village scene of these connotations. It is the case, however, as Thomas Poe pointed out at the 1996 Society for Cinema Studies conference, that some gay men outside of New York City were aware of these events and took them as signposts for themselves and their future.

4. See the groundbreaking work of George Chauncey, *Gay New York: Gender, Urban Culture, and the Making of the Gay Male World, 1890–1940* (New York: Basic Books, 1994).

5. David E. James, *Allegories of Cinema: American Film in the Sixties* (Princeton, N.J.: Princeton University Press, 1989), 95 n. 7. Also published recently with a similar argument is Juan A. Suárez, *Bike Boys, Drag Queens, and Superstars: Avant-Garde, Mass Culture, and Gay Identities in the 1960s Underground Cinema* (Bloomington: Indiana University Press, 1996).

6. As I indicate below, I use the term *New American Cinema* to describe the widest range of non-Hollywood film practices being produced at this time. I reserve the term *underground cinema* for a specific subset of films that explicitly displayed nondominant sexualities in nonnarrative form and style. To count as underground cinema for the purposes of this essay, a film needs to contain some sexually explicit material and not look like a narrative Hollywood film.

7. The obvious reference is Vito Russo, *The Celluloid Closet: Homosexuality in the Movies* (New York: Harper & Row, 1981), esp. 76–77, 108.

8. Thomas Doherty, *Teenagers and Teenpics: The Juvenilization of American Movies in the 1950s* (Boston: Unwin Hyman, 1988), 82.

9. William Castle, *Step Right Up! . . . I'm Gonna Scare the Pants Off America* (New York: G. P. Putnam's Sons, 1976), 136–59. I am indebted to Alison Macor's research for this information. Castle's activities need to be used to contextualize Alfred Hitchcock's *Psycho* (1960) gimmick of preventing people from entering the theater after the movie started.

10. I shall discuss stag movies and gay erotica of the period below.

11. Parker Tyler, *Underground Film: A Critical History* (New York: Grove, 1969), 11.

12. Nick Orzel and Michael Smith, "Introduction," in *Eight Plays from Off-Off Broadway*, ed. Nick Orzel and Michael Smith (New York: Bobbs-Merrill, 1966), 6.

13. The fact that the troupes' mode of production was often cooperative and communal is important. These were groups of people organizing to produce many plays together, which also marks an alternative politics from commercial theater.

14. Robert Brustein, quoted in Nat Hentoff, "No Paul Whiteman?" *Village Voice*, March 9, 1960, 6.

15. James, *Allegories of Cinema*, 120, 315–16; Richard Dyer, *Now You See It: Studies on Lesbian and Gay Film* (London: Routledge, 1990), 138.

16. Dyer, *Now You See It*, 138.

17. James, *Allegories of Cinema*, 315–16.

18. John Fles, "The End of the Affair, or Beyond the Beat Generation," *Village Voice*, December 15, 1960, 4.

19. Louise Levitas, "Beats Meet at Ibiza," *Village Voice*, June 14, 1962, 1.

20. Catharine R. Stimpson, "The Beat Generation and the Trials of Homosexual Liberation," *Salmagundi* 58–59 (fall 1982–winter 1983), 375, 388 (Stimpson quotes Ginsberg's *Howl*).

21. Russo, *The Celluloid Closet*, 118.

22. Peter Stallybrass and Allon White, *The Politics and Poetics of Transgression* (London: Methuen, 1986), 2–3.

23. Fredric Jameson, "Periodizing the 60s," in *The 60s without Apology*, ed. Sohnya Sayres, Anders Stephanson, Stanley Aronowitz, and Fredric Jameson (Minneapolis: University of Minnesota Press, 1984), 178.

24. New America Cinema Group, "The First Statement of the New American Cinema Group," *Film Culture* 22–23 (summer 1961), reprinted in *The Film Culture Reader*, ed. P. Adams Sitney (New York: Praeger, 1970), 79–83; Patricia Mellencamp, *Indiscretions: Avant-Garde Film, Video, and Feminism* (Bloomington: Indiana University Press, 1990), 1. See also Lauren Rabinovitz, *Points of Resistance: Women, Power and Politics in the New York Avant-Garde Cinema, 1943–1971* (Urbana: University of Illinois Press, 1991), 108–9.

25. Mellencamp, *Indiscretions*, 2.

26. New American Cinema Group, "First Statement," 82–83.

27. Harris Dienstfrey, "The New American Cinema," *Commentary* 33 (June 1962): 495–504.

28. *Pull My Daisy* is not the first film to show beat culture sympathetically. Parker Tyler describes Stan Brakhage's *Desistfilm* (1955) as "the first important beatnik film with the air of a spontaneous Happening. Disarmingly candid in depicting youth in the simple occupation of getting high, being tricksy, and then running harmlessly wild." *Underground Film*, 26. Robert Hatch of the *Nation* liked *Pull My Daisy*, suggesting that the filmmakers "are what we have been needing since Hal Roach left us." Robert Hatch, "Films," *Nation*, June 18, 1960, 540.

29. This is not the first version of the film, but the one Cassavetes reshot and recut. See Jonas Mekas, "Cinema of the New Generation," *Film Culture* 21 (summer 1960): 11.

30. Rabinovitz, *Points of Resistance*, 117.

31. Not coincidentally, these are all writers whose publications earned them obscenity charges.

32. H. B. Lutz, "Some Words on 'The Connection,'" *Village Voice*, August 5, 1959, 9.

33. J. Hoberman and Jonathan Rosenbaum, *Midnight Movies* (New York: Harper & Row, 1983), 40; Rabinovitz, *Points of Resistance*, 118; "'Connection' Film at Judson Church," *Village Voice*, October 18, 1962, 1, 10.

34. Jonas Mekas, column in *Village Voice*, October 11, 1962, reprinted in Jonas Mekas, *Movie Journal: The Rise of a New American Cinema, 1959–1971* (New York: Collier, 1972), 71.

35. J. T., "The Connection Revisited," *Village Voice*, October 26, 1961, 10.

36. "The Bourgeois Mothers' Underground, on the Rise," *Village Voice*, January 25, 1962, 3.

37. Seymour Krim, "Revolt of the Homosexual," *Village Voice*, March 18, 1959, 12, 16. See also Dyer, *Now You See It*, 134–38.

38. Krim, "Revolt of the Homosexual," 12, 16. Krim also remarks, "The old categories of a man being Mars and a woman Venus are artificial: only insensitive people or poseurs pretend to a cartoon image of masculinity vs. femininity."

39. Anonymous, "The Gay Underground—A Reply to Mr. Krim," *Village Voice*, March 25, 1959, 4–5.

40. Stephanie Garvis, "Politics: A Third Party for the Third Sex?" *Village Voice*, September 27, 1962, 3. For more context for this proposition, see my conclusion.

41. See, most immediately, Stephanie Garvis, "The Homosexual's Labyrinth of Law and Social Custom," *Village Voice*, October 11, 1962, 7, 20; Soren Agenoux, review of "City of Night," *Village Voice*, August 1, 1963, 5, 15.

42. Rabinovitz, *Points of Resistance*, 80–84; J. R. Goddard, "'I Step on Toes from Time to Time,'" *Village Voice*, December 14, 1961, 1, 18 (on Amos Vogel and Cinema 16); Hoberman and Rosenbaum, *Midnight Movies*, 39; Calvin Tomkins, "All Pockets Open," *New Yorker*, January 6, 1973, 36–37.

43. Jonas Mekas, "Cinema of the New Generation," *Film Culture* 21 (summer 1960): 9. See also Tomkins, "All Pockets Open," 37; Nat Hentoff, "Last Call for Cinema 16," *Village Voice*, February 21, 1963, 4. Stan VanDerBeek used *underground* a year later likewise to describe a filmmaking trend; his discussion concerned many experimental filmmakers who eventually were not categorized in quite this way. Stan VanDerBeek, "The Cinema Delimina: Films from the Underground," *Film Quarterly* 14 (summer 1961): 5–15. See also Hoberman and Rosenbaum, *Midnight Movies*, 40 n.; James, *Allegories of Cinema*, 94–95; Mellencamp, *Indiscretions*, 3–4. James captures the revolutionary connotations of the terms better than VanDerBeek.

44. Andrew Sarris, "Movie Journal: Hello and Goodbye to the New American Cinema," *Village Voice*, September 20, 1962, 13. Sarris continued to voice his displeasure over this cinema, including an oration at the 1966 New York Film Festival; see below.

45. Ibid.

46. Andrew Ross, *No Respect: Intellectuals and Popular Culture* (New York: Routledge, 1989), 135–36.

47. Tyler, *Underground Cinema*, 37. Tyler notes that Deren objected to the films as an invasion: "Woman's privacy had been deliberately, tactlessly invaded."

48. Although masturbation may not have been publicly approved, it was on the way to being considered normal. It was certainly masculine. Brakhage's heterosexuality was also not in doubt.

49. Tomkins, "All Pockets Open," 31–35; Hoberman and Rosenbaum, *Midnight Movies*, 40–43; David McReynolds, "'The Flower Thief'—Invalid or Incompetent" (letter to the editor), *Village Voice*, July 26, 1962, 13; Andy Warhol and Pat Hackett, *POPism: The Warhol Sixties* (New York: Harper & Row, 1980), 49. Tomkins notes, as others have, that Mekas started out his career with a different aesthetic. In 1955, Mekas attacked experimental cinema as permeated by "the conspiracy of homosexuality that is becoming one of the most persistent and shocking characteristics of American Film poetry today." Jonas Mekas, "The Experimental Film in America," *Film Culture* 3 (May–June 1955), reprinted in *The Film Culture Reader*, ed. P. Adams Sitney (New York: Praeger, 1970), 23. See also Rabinovitz, *Points of Resistance*, 84; Dyer, *Now You See It*, 102.

50. By 1960, the Cornell film was a recognized masterpiece in the American avant-garde. Thus *Blonde Cobra* seems a camp version of *Rose Hobart*. This is reinforced by Smith's homage to Maria Montez in *Film Culture*, which might be read as a parody of auteur/high art criticism; for example, "Don't slander her [Montez's] beautiful womanliness that took joy in her own beauty and all beauty—or whatever in her that turned plaster cornball sets to beauty." Jack Smith, "The Perfect Filmic Appositeness of Maria Montez" *Film Culture* 27 (winter 1962–63): 28.

51. Smith apparently created *Flaming Creatures* to be a comedy, an effect that works for me. However, as J. Hoberman reports, "Smith himself felt burned, bitterly complaining that his film, 'designed as a comedy,' was transformed into 'a sex issue of the Cocktail World.'" J. Hoberman, "The Big Heat," *Village Voice*, November 12, 1991, 61. See also Michael Moon, "Flaming Closets," *October* 51 (1989): 19–54.

52. For background on Barbara Rubin, see J. Hoberman, *Vulgar Modernism: Writing on Movies and Other Media* (Philadelphia: Temple University Press, 1991), 141–42.

53. For criticisms of competence, see George Dowden, "'The Flower Thief'—Invalid or Incompetent" (letter to the editor), *Village Voice*, July 26, 1962, 11; Pete Hamill, "Explosion in the Movie Underground," *Saturday Evening Post*, September 28, 1963, 82, 84. For arguments that this is an intentional choice, see Ron Rice, "Foundation for the Invention and Creation of Absurd Movies," *Film Culture* 24 (spring 1962): 19; P. Adams Sitney, "'The Sin of Jesus' & 'The Flower Thief,'" *Film Culture* 25 (summer 1962): 32–33.

54. Linda Williams, *Hard Core: Power, Pleasure, and the "Frenzy of the Visible"* (Berkeley: University of California Press, 1989), 58–152.

55. Thomas Waugh, "Homoerotic Representation in the Stag Film, 1920–40," *Wide Angle* 14, no. 2 (1992): 14–15. Female same-sex scenes are quite common and, like male same-sex scenes, are usually preludes to heterosexual couplings. See Williams, *Hard Core*.

56. Waugh, "Homoerotic Representation," 14–15.

57. Ibid., 6–8.

58. My special thanks to David Gerstner for alerting me to this cinema. I have viewed a compilation of these films under the general title *Gay Erotica from the 1940s and*

1950s: One to Many (Apollo), *The Beach Bar Nightmare* (Apollo), *Auntie's African Paradise* (Zenith), *Cellmates* (Zenith), *The Cyclist* (Apollo), *Cocktails* (unknown), *Ben-Hurry* (Zenith), *The Captive* (Zenith), and *Fanny's Hill* (Pat Rocco for Bizarre).

59. Arthur Knight, quoted in J. Hoberman, "The Big Heat," 61.
60. "Avant-Garde Movie Seized as Obscene," *New York Times,* March 4, 1964; Stephanie Garvis Harrington, "City Sleuths Douse 'Flaming Creatures,'" *Village Voice,* March 12, 1964, 3, 13; "Mekas Gaoled Again, Genet Film Does It," *Village Voice,* March 19, 1964, 13; "Cops Raid Homo Films Again," *Variety,* March 18, 1964, 5. *Variety's* labeling of these films as "homo" was not without cause: Mekas had previously publicly represented the underground cinema as connected to homosexuality. See his *Village Voice* columns reprinted in *Movie Journal:* "Flaming Creatures and the Ecstatic Beauty of the New Cinema," April 18, 1963, 82–83; "On the Baudelairean Cinema," May 2, 1963, 85–86; "On Blonde Cobra and Flaming Creatures," October 24, 1963, 101–3. *Flaming Creatures* premiered on April 29, 1963. Its seizure occurred March 3, 1964, as part of a New York City cleanup for the 1964 World's Fair. See Hoberman, "The Big Heat," 61; and Hoberman and Rosenbaum, *Midnight Movies,* 59–60, for excellent accounts of the film's legal history. See also Dyer, *Now You See It,* 145–49; Tomkins, "All Pockets Open," 38–39; and, of course, Mekas in *Movie Journal.* Tomkins notes that when Mekas brought *Flaming Creatures* to the December 1963 Knokke-le-Zoute International Experimental Film Competition he showed it privately to Jean-Luc Godard, Roman Polanski, and others. Mekas's version is in "Flaming Creatures at Knokke-le Zoute," *Village Voice,* January 16, 1964, reprinted in *Movie Journal,* 111–15.
61. Tomkins, "All Pockets Open," 40. These films were also being seen and seized in Los Angeles. Knight had viewed the film there, and Mike Getz was found guilty on March 13, 1964, of screening "the obscene film" *Scorpio Rising* on March 7 at the Cinema Theater in Hollywood. Hoberman and Rosenbaum, *Midnight Movies,* 59–60. Mekas's versions are in "On Obsenity," *Village Voice,* March 12, 1964; "Underground Manifesto on Censorship," *Village Voice,* March 12, 1964; "Report from Jail," *Village Voice,* March 19, 1964, reprinted in *Movie Journal,* 126–30; "On the Misery of Community Standards," *Village Voice,* June 18, 1964, reprinted in *Movie Journal,* 141–44.
62. Eugene Archer, "The Flower Thief," *New York Times,* July 14, 1962, 11.
63. "Cinema Underground," *New Yorker,* July 13, 1963, 17.
64. Hamill, "Explosion in the Movie Underground," 82, 84.
65. "Flaming Censorship," *Nation,* March 30, 1964, 311; Susan Sontag, "A Feast for Open Eyes," *Nation,* April 13, 1964, 374–76; Susan Sontag, "Notes on 'Camp,'" *Partisan Review,* 1964, reprinted in *Against Interpretation* (New York: Delta, 1978). Hoberman and Rosenbaum state that the editor who assigned Sontag the *Nation* piece was fired for doing so. *Midnight Movies,* 61. It is not clear to me why this would occur, but the decision may have had to do with the subsequent debates over morality. Do note that the *Nation* published filmmaker Ken Kelman's positive views on New American

Cinema within the month: Ken Kelman, "Anticipations of the Light," *Nation*, May 11, 1964, 490–94. An excellent later analysis of *Flaming Creatures* is in Grandin Conover, "'Flaming Creatures': Rhapsodic Asexuality," *Village Voice*, July 28, 1964, 9, 15.

66. Ross, *No Respect*, 147. Sontag was not the first to make the connection between this cinema and pop art; see Mekas, *Movie Journal:* "On Andy Warhol" (December 5, 1963), 109–10; "On Andy Warhol's Sleep" (January 30, 1964), 116.

67. Amos Vogel, "Flaming Creatures Cannot Carry Freedom's Torch," *Village Voice*, May 7, 1964, 9. See Mekas's response: Jonas Mekas, "Movie Journal," *Village Voice*, May 14, 1964, 15.

68. Vogel, "Flaming Creatures," 18.

69. Elizabeth Sutherland, "Flaming Cause," *Village Voice*, May 14, 1964, 4.

70. Dwight Macdonald, *On Movies* (New York: Berkley Medallion, 1969), 341.

71. Ibid., 361.

72. See also Dwight Macdonald, "A Theory of Mass Culture," *Diogenes* 3 (summer 1953): 1–17; Dwight Macdonald, "Objections to the New American Cinema," in *The New American Cinema*, ed. Gregory Battcock (New York: Dutton, 1967), 197–204. On Macdonald and taste, see Ross, *No Respect*, 42–64.

73. "In Camera," *Films and Filming* 11 (November 1964): 37.

74. Andrew Sarris, "The Independent Cinema" (1966), reprinted in *The New American Cinema*, ed. Gregory Battcock (New York: Dutton, 1967), 51. See also Fred Wellington, "Liberalism, Subversion, and Evangelism: Toward the Definition of a Problem," also in *The New American Cinema*, 38–47. Annette Michelson did not take the festival's prevailing position, siding with Sontag; see her festival address, "Film and the Radical Persuasion" (1966), reprinted in *The New American Cinema*, 83–102.

75. It is perhaps difficult to return to this time for film scholars who are now so familiar with representations of sexuality. Consider that the defense for the 1964 Los Angeles obscenity trial concerning Getz's screening of *Scorpio Rising* was pleased with an all-woman jury: "He feared that a male juror with anxieties about his masculinity might respond hysterically to the homoerotic undertones of Anger's film." Fred Haines, "Art in Court: 1. City of Angels vs. Scorpio Rising," *Nation*, September 14, 1964, 123. The women found Getz guilty.

76. On Warhol's involvement, see Stephen Koch, *Stargazer: Andy Warhol's World and His Films* (New York: Praeger, 1973); Dyer, *Now You See It*, 149–62; Calvin Tomkins, *The Scene: Reports on Post-modern Art* (New York: Viking, 1976), 35–53; Hoberman and Rosenbaum, *Midnight Movies*, 58–75; Matthew Tinkcom, "Camp and the Question of Value" (Ph.D. diss., University of Pittsburgh, 1995). Warhol's version is in Warhol and Hackett, *POPism*, 25–35 and throughout.

77. David Ehrenstein, "Interview with Andy Warhol," *Film Culture* 40 (spring 1966): 41. Ellipses in this quote represent Warhol's pauses, not deletions of text.

78. Charles Boultenhouse, "The Camera as a God," *Film Culture* 29 (summer 1963),

reprinted in *The Film Culture Reader*, ed. P. Adams Sitney (New York: Praeger, 1970), 137.

79. Michael McClure, "Defense of Jayne Mansfield," *Film Culture* 32 (spring 1964), reprinted in *The Film Culture Reader*, ed. P. Adams Sitney, (New York: Praeger, 1970), 160–67.

80. Hoberman, *Vulgar Modernism*, 181. And an echo of the famous 1896 film *The Kiss.*

81. Jonas Mekas, "An Interview with Kuchar Brothers"(March 5, 1964), reprinted in *Movie Journal*, 122–26.

82. Ken Jacobs was to later indicate that he and Smith "hated" pop art. Distinguishing between pop art and camp, or, as Jacobs puts it, his and Smith's "'Human Wreckage' aesthetic" is important for a finer discussion of these features. See Jacob's 1971 interview quoted in Carel Rowe, *The Baudelairean Cinema: A Trend within the American Avant-Garde* (Ann Arbor, Mich.: UMI Research Press, 1982), 39. Also see Sasha Torres, "The Caped Crusader of Camp: Pop, Camp, and the Batman Television Series," in *Pop Out: Queer Warhol*, ed. Jennifer Doyle, Jonathan Flatley, and José Esteban Muñoz (Durham, N.C.: Duke University Press, 1996), 238–55. Torres writes that although pop, camp, and gay sensibilities were by 1966 linked, they were not equivalents. She argues that camp was going through a "de-gaying" in the mid 1960s by Sontag and others, a de-gaying that permitted the potentially suspect Batman series to be considered "camp" but not gay.

83. Warhol and Hackett, *POPism*, 12–15. Ironically, American abstract expressionism, while perhaps macho, was not immune to attacks by conservatives. In the early 1950s, some right-wingers accused creators of these paintings of hiding information in them to pass on to U.S. enemies. William Hauptman, "The Suppression of Art in the McCarthy Decade," *Artforum* 12 (October 1973): 48–52.

84. Vivian Gornick, "It's a Queer Hand Stoking the Campfire," *Village Voice*, April 7, 1966, 1, 20.

85. Ibid., 1.

86. "Saint Andrew," *Newsweek*, December 7, 1964, 102–4.

87. Shana Alexander, "Report from Underground," *Life*, January 28, 1965, 23. See Mekas's reaction, "On the Establishment and the Boobs of the Shana Alexanders," *Village Voice*, February 11, 1965, reprinted in *Movie Journal*, 176–78.

88. Alexander, "Report from Underground," 23.

89. Alan Levy, "Voice of the 'Underground Cinema,'" *New York Times Sunday Magazine*, September 19, 1965. See also Eugene Boe, "Lights! Camera! But Where's the Action?" *Status* (March 1966): 71–74; Elenore Lester, "So He Stopped Painting Brillo Boxes and Bought a Movie Camera," *New York Times*, December 11, 1966.

90. Howard Junker, "The Underground Renaissance," *Nation*, December 27, 1965, 539; Stanley Kauffmann, *A World on Film* (New York: Dell, 1966), 424. See also Robert Hatch, "Media-Mix," *Nation*, January 31, 1966, 139.

91. Hoberman and Rosenbaum, *Midnight Movies*, 68–69; Koch, *Stargazer*, 70–71.

92. Jack Kroll, "Underground in Hell," *Newsweek*, November 14, 1966, n.p. This preparation goes through an interest in pornography by mass media in 1965. See "On Perverts and Art," *Village Voice*, April 22, 1965, reprinted in Mekas, *Movie Journal*, 183–84.

93. But see the review by Dan Sullivan, "The Chelsea Girls," *New York Times*, December 2, 1966, 46.

94. Jack Kroll, "Up from Underground," *Newsweek*, February 13, 1967, 117–19.

95. "The New Underground Films," *Time*, February 17, 1967, 94–99. Bosley Crowther continued to disagree; see his review of *My Hustler*, *New York Times*, July 11,1967, 29, in which he points out that the cinematheque had moved to a new theater that used to show burlesque and nudie films. This was fitting for another "homosexual strip-tease." See also Rosalyn Regelson, "Where Are 'The Chelsea Girls' Taking Us?" *New York Times*, September 24, 1967. These reviewers were a bit late in noticing this trend. In 1962, Rudy M. Franchi, discussing X-rated movies, predicted the underground cinema would be "art" and "exhibited widely in art houses, playing with quality foreign and American films." Rudy M. Franchi, "The Coming of Age in the X-Film," *Cavalier*, July 1962, 85.

96. Hoberman and Rosenbaum, *Midnight Movies*, 73; "In Camera," *Films and Filming* 13 (July 1967), 38.

97. The late 1960s also saw the beginning of the development of erotic films for gay audiences, in part because of changing obscenity laws. See Paul Alcuin Siebenand, *The Beginnings of Gay Cinema in Los Angeles: The Industry and the Audience* (Ann Arbor, Mich.: UMI Press, 1980). On connections between these events and the development of hard-core pornographic exhibition—both hetero and homo, see Hoberman and Rosenbaum, *Midnight Movies*, 76; Tomkins, "All Pockets Open," 45.

98. Tyler, *Underground Film*, 224.

99. Critics of Warhol suggest that *Empire* was a camp joke: eight hours of a hard-on.

100. James, *Allegories of Cinema*, 317; Mellencamp, *Indiscretions*, 21 and throughout.

101. Thomas Waugh, "Cockteaser," in *Pop Out: Queer Warhol*, ed. Jennifer Doyle, Jonathan Flatley, and José Esteban Muñoz (Durham, N.C.: Duke University Press, 1996), 59–73; Roger McNiven, Ph.D. comprehensive exam, New York University, April 1987.

102. John D'Emilio, *Sexual Politics, Sexual Communities: The Making of a Homosexual Minority in the United States, 1940–1970* (Chicago: University of Chicago Press, 1983), 129–75. See also Neil Miller, *Out of the Past: Gay and Lesbian History from 1869 to the Present* (New York: Vintage, 1995), 340–54.

103. Elizabeth Lapovsky Kennedy and Madeline D. Davis, *Boots of Leather, Slippers of Gold: The History of a Lesbian Community.* (New York: Routledge, 1993), 372–73.

Filmography

Blonde Cobra. Ken Jacobs, Jack Smith, and Bob Fleischner, 1959–63; Film-Makers' Cooperative. Viewed September 19, 1995.

Christmas on Earth (a.k.a. *Cocks and Cunts*). Barbara Rubin, 1963; Film-Makers' Cooperative. Viewed July 17, 1995.

Flaming Creatures. Jack Smith, 1963; Film-Makers' Cooperative. Viewed July 24, 1995.

The Flower Thief. Ron Rice, 1960; Film-Makers' Cooperative. Viewed July 18, 1995.

Gay Erotica from the 1940s and 1950s. Apollo, Zenith, and Bizarre Productions. Videotape purchased December 1996 from Little Rickie, New York.

Little Stabs at Happiness. Ken Jacobs, 1959–63; Film-Makers' Cooperative. Viewed July 18, 1995.

Pull My Daisy. Robert Frank and Alfred Leslie, 1959; Library of Congress. Viewed July 11, 1995.

The Queen of Sheba Meets the Atom Man. Ron Rice, 1963; Film-Makers' Cooperative. Viewed July 24, 1995.

Scorpio Rising. Kenneth Anger, 1963; Museum of Modern Art. Viewed September 19, 1995.

Shadows. John Cassavetes, 1959; Bravo television transmission.

Lawrence of Arabia, 1962. Courtesy of Photofest.

"You Are an Interesting Man"
Gender, Empire, and Desire in David Lean's *Lawrence of Arabia*
Abdullah Habib AlMaaini

The stately inauguration of Sir David Lean's cinematic saga *Lawrence of Arabia*, on Sunday, December 9, 1962, was no ordinary event.[1] The cinematic occasion had its political signature from the beginning in that it was treated as a grand national event. The film's London premiere, "following the greatest press excitement ever generated in Britain by a motion picture,"[2] was attended by no less than the imperial symbol herself, Queen Elizabeth II. Present also were Prince Philip and more than two thousand other guests.

> A fanfare was sounded by the Royal Horse Guards as the Queen and her party entered the auditorium and the National Anthem was played by the band of the Welsh Guards.... Hundreds tried to buy tickets up to curtain time despite huge "sold out" signs. Thousands more milled around the entrance to the Odeon [Theatre] during the performance waiting to see the Queen and her guests leave long after midnight.[3]

The royal blessing granted to the film was an expression of political nostalgia to empire and its past glories and was entirely compatible with both an official and a popular feeling of reverence toward its legendary subject matter, Colonel T. E. Lawrence, who came to be known as Prince of Mecca, the Uncrowned King of Arabia, Sheikh Dynamite, and Lawrence of Arabia. Indeed, this man's name had become inextricably linked with the British imperial project in the Arab world.[4] It is remarkable, in this context, that the very advent of David Lean in the British film industry in the post–World War II period was already synchronized with a certain national project and political vision. Gerald Pratley points out that Lean "began to think of new techniques, personalities, stories, to contribute to the new spirit of Britain's reviving film creativity, given an added impetus by the war. This national emergency made the British more aware of the need to seek a unity and recognition of themselves as a nation on the influential cinema screen, previously dominated by American movies."[5]

The lavish British production by Horizon Pictures was not meant, in the words of Sam Spiegel, the producer, "to resolve the enigma of Lawrence but [rather] to perpetuate the legend, and to show why it continues to haunt us after all these years."[6] The mirroring of empire as a colonial narrative in the film is explicit enough. For example, the scene of the Arab National Council meeting in Damascus is, as Edward Said puts it, "the film's political pay off," for the scene shows the Arabs to be "semi-barbaric children," from which representation it follows that the film's political message is that "serious rule was never meant for such lesser species, only for the white man."[7] However, what still needs to be systematically explored are the political implications of the way the film depicts, indeed devolves, Lawrence and his geographic and human milieu sexually and erotically—that is, the identity questions of both the self and the Other, and the gaze that captures the transformations of desire. The discursive plotting of the text as a complex play of empire, gender, and desire thus needs to be investigated.

Gender, Erotics, and Politics of the Gaze

Ella Shohat observes that the introduction of the cinema coincided with the peak of European colonialism at the close of the nineteenth century; she notes that the critique of colonialism in film studies and feminist film theory has not articulated an analysis of gender issues in the context of "the contradictions and asymmetries provoked by (post) colonial arrangements of power." She proposes, then, the study of Western cinema "as a product of a gendered Western gaze, an imbrication reflective of the symbiotic relations between patriarchal and colonial articulation of difference." Drawing on Said's notion that the "Orient" is represented as "feminine," Shohat argues that "Europe's 'civilizing mission' in the Third World is projected as interweaving opposed yet linked narratives of Western penetration of inviting virginal landscapes *and* of resisting libidinal nature."[8] In this context, Western cinema, in such examples as *Lawrence of Arabia*, relies on the figure of the "discoverer": "The camera relays the hero's dynamic movement across passive, static space, gradually stripping the land of its 'enigma,' as the spectator wins visual access to Oriental treasures through the eyes of the explorer-protagonist."[9] In fact, the question of the gaze in *Lawrence* is agilely hinted at at the film's outset in an intriguing shot that appears at the end of the scene depicting the motorcycle crash in which Lawrence was killed. The quite lengthy static shot is a close-up of Lawrence's goggles hanging from the twigs of a tree and "gazing" hauntingly, so to speak, at the viewer. The goggles shot, furthermore, is immediately followed by a medium close-up of a bust of Lawrence at the beginning of the memorial service scene. The bust, again, "gazes" at the audience as the camera slowly zooms out, thereby creating the impression of a gradual sweeping and penetrating look.

Within this general theoretical framework, I propose in this essay a reading of *Lawrence of Arabia* as an exemplary film that illustrates the "engendering" of the Western gaze. Specifically, the film demonstrates how such a gaze crosses gender boundaries while maintaining European cultural hegemony. That is, a discussion of Lawrence's ambiguous sexual identity highlights the ideological, homoerotic, and sadomasochistic underpinnings that govern the shifting images of gender. Ultimately, however, the film privileges a masculinist vision of desire. This interplay is a cinematic contribution to the inscription of empire as a textual practice of desire within a largely oedipal configuration.

Laura Mulvey's argument in her celebrated essay "Visual Pleasure and Narrative Cinema" is useful for understanding the role of the gaze and the relationship to the oedipal subject in *Lawrence*.[10] Mulvey argues that the viewer's unconscious is informed by the dominant patriarchal order. The cinematic narrative thus privileges the male audience with an active scopophilic gaze that objectifies the screen females as images to-be-looked-at for erotic impact. Mulvey therefore identifies three types of gaze: the gaze of the male characters in the film at the female characters, the gaze of the male audience, and the gaze of the camera, which constructs the masculinized audience.

Mulvey's insistence on the masculine nature of the gaze has, however, been subsequently disputed. For example, Steve Cohen in his analysis of *Picnic*, a film directed by Joshua Logan (1955), argues that the film "is an especially revealing ... example of Hollywood cinema's investment in the spectacle of the male body. This film is ... organized, in both its cinematic address and its narrative, around questions of looking at the body of its male star."[11] It is, then, in Cohen's sense that I appropriate Mulvey's discussion of the gaze; that is, the object of the gaze is not exclusively the female, but (also) the male body. Erotically charged, the gaze in *Lawrence* celebrates the male body. As in *Picnic*, the "male body" in *Lawrence* "is the film's primary image of sexual difference."¹² *Lawrence* represents the male body as the locus of ambivalent and dialectical identity and desire. The film, for the most part, avoids setting rigid binary oppositions in its representation of gender. But, as is the case with *Picnic*'s protagonist, "it jeopardiz[es]

Peter O'Toole as T. E. Lawrence.

the masculinity of [Lawrence] only to restore it in the end."[13] Fundamentally, therefore, the film, in spite of all its complex and undeniably interesting ambivalence, succumbs eventually to what Shohat has called "a Western gendered gaze." Cohen's analysis of *Picnic* as an extension of Mulvey's argument is useful for understanding *Lawrence*'s appeal to gendered subjects.

Omar Sharif as Sherif Ali.

At the heart of this appeal is the controversial casting of Peter O'Toole in the title role. Leslie Taubman comments: "The handsome six-foot, blond and blue-eyed actor hardly resembles the relatively mousy-looking five-foot-five T. E. Lawrence."[14] O'Toole, however, is not the only "handsome" actor cast in the film. There is also Omar Sharif, who plays Sherif Ali, a "swarthy, handsome newcomer ... [who] had the girls in the audience oohing."[15] This "oohing," which might not be music to Mulvey's ears, is an encouraging sign to Cohen. It is an example of the way in which *Lawrence* constructs its viewership in terms of gender. The male bodies, in other words, are represented as "to-be-looked-at."

This construction of the gaze is encapsulated, for example, in a slow dolly shot in the scene that takes place in Auda Abu Tayi's huge tent toward the end of the first half of the film.[16] The shot surveys the faces of several unveiled (that is, only with head covers) Arab women. The camera's perspective is that of the audience; it gradually reveals that the women are looking at Majid, Lawrence, and Sherif Ali, who appear, throughout the scene, in close-ups, two-shots, and three-shots. The scene clearly exhibits these men as objects of the feminine gaze. Here, as throughout the narrative, Lawrence and Sherif Ali play a central part in the film's construction of the gaze. Another example can be found in the spectacular scene of the onslaught on Akaba. This scene illustrates the film's restless appropriation of the gaze. Included in the scene is a static shot showing the inside of a tent in the Turkish garrison. The foreground shows the framed black-and-white picture of a belly dancer hanging on the tent's pole, while we see, through the tent's entrance, the charging men, and hear the noise of their action that is taking place in the frame's middle ground. As the extraordinary assault continues, and as the garrison succumbs to the attackers, we see, a moment later, a long shot of three Arab women rushing onto a hill overlooking the battlefield to witness the action. The inclusion of the female as a silent, taxidermic image in the first shot and as actual moving bodies in the second provides a marked contrast. In the first shot, the image of the female as an object of desire is stormed with the rest of that which the sweeping military action storms; in the second, it is the actual women as desiring subjects who watch the symbolic destruction of their image as "to-be-looked-at" and, simultaneously, look at the men as they exhibit their military "manliness." This contrast, in my view, implies no contradiction, for it epitomizes the constant shift of the gendered gaze that punctuates the film. The few shots of veiled Arab women that appear in the film show them as natural voyeurs, so to speak: the transparent black cloth of their veils offers them an ideal tool for voyeurism, because they can see through those veils, which, at the same time, preclude the possibility of others identifying them. Another metonymy representing and stressing this natural voyeurism is found in the camel litters in which the Arab women, surrounded by men, are seated during the journey from Wadi Safra to Yanbu. Here again, the women do see without being seen in their Panopticon-like litters.

Yet in a certain sense, like the protagonist of *Picnic*, the historic and cinematic "Lawrences" are "accused" of "unmanliness." The controversy over Lawrence's homosexuality has never ceased. The debate should be understood as an essential ingredient in the manufacturing of the mythic image of the popular and "extraordinary" figure to whose reputation the passage of time only adds enigma and mystery. Hagiographers such as Jeremy Wilson painstakingly dispute the claim of a homosexual Lawrence and categorically deny it in favor of a pure, "manly" image of the celebrated national hero.[17] A critical biographer, Richard Aldington, however, contends that he was a homosexual.[18] Other biographers, such as Philip Knightley and Colin Simpson, provide evidence that Lawrence had a homosexual tendency that expressed itself in sadomasochistic rituals rather than active homosexuality.[19]

What is perhaps more interesting in this context is that David Lean, the film's director, actually believed that Lawrence was indeed a homosexual. One reason for his displeasure with Michael Wilson's screenplay was that he found "many faceted aspects of Lawrence's character not yet in [the] screen play." Lean then went on to give two specific examples: "masochism.... Let us not avoid or censor out the homosexual aspect of Lawrence's relationships.... The incipient homosexuality of Daud and Farraj must be emphasised."[20] Robert Bolt, the screenplay writer, shared, in effect, the same belief: "Whether [Lawrence] was homosexually active I have no idea. That he was more or less homosexual by nature I think almost certain. He, himself, seems to me to make small bones about it."[21] Yet, although it is true that many spectators and critics "got it," it would be difficult to accept that "the homosexual aspect" is made transparently clear in the film. Indeed, many critics fault the film exactly for neglecting that "aspect." Peter Baker, for example, writes that the film "carefully avoids the issue of homosexuality which [Lawrence] at least condoned, almost praised publicly, in his book [*Seven Pillars of Wisdom*]."[22] Similarly, Brian St. Pierre sees that "Lawrence has been watered down by too much of the milk of Robert Bolt's kindness," which, in terms of the film, translates to "not being too specific about many of the questionable points of [Lawrence's] life, particularly the all-important time he was captured by the Turks."[23] In fact, Bolt has described his strategy in writing the screenplay as "getting at least within hailing distance of the factual truth ... [and] within hailing distance of the truth about the man as well."[24] The final product of this strategy is a vague and problematic sexual identity that adds extra flavors to the mystery of, and fascination by, a "Romantic Fascist," as Bolt calls him.[25]

I should stress, however, that my concern with homosexuality here is diegetic, not historic; the reference to homosexuality is necessitated by the fact that the film poses questions of desire, masculinity, and femininity. "Because masculinity is a category of gender," as Mark D. Jordan argues, "the category 'homosexuality' functions at the level of gender rather than of sexuality, even though it pretends to be a category of sexuality."[26] Homosexuality, role, gender, desire, and identity are constructed in the film as performance—more specifically, performance for Western audiences. General Allenby captures this particular aspect of the film's thematics in his first meeting with Lawrence. He comments on Lawrence's Arab headdress (*hatta* and *ʿiqāl*) and garb by asking him, "What do you mean by coming here dressed like that?! Amateur theatricals?!" "Oh, yes! Entirely!" Lawrence meaningfully answers. This theatricality resides at the heart of the mechanisms producing Orientalist representation. Edward Said has insisted all along not merely that Orientalism is "a learned field," from which representations are produced, but also that "the idea of representation is a theatrical one."[27] Although this might sound supererogatory, it acquires new concreteness and relevance when applied to representations that include questions of gender in political and ideological contexts such as the case in *Lawrence*. Indeed, Colonel T. E. Lawrence himself was consciously specific on the political role of theatrical identity. For example, in his "Twenty-Seven Articles," the manual he produced for British political officers on how to handle Arabs, the imperial officer wrote of the "handling" as "an art, not science." He therefore advised his fellow officers that

> If you can wear Arab kit when with the tribes you will acquire their trust and intimacy to a degree impossible in uniform. ... You will be like an actor in a foreign theatre, playing a part day and night for

months, without rest, and for an anxious task. . . . If you wear Arab things at all, go the whole way. Leave your English friends and customs on the coast, and fall back on Arab habit entirely. It is possible, starting this level with them, for the European to beat the Arabs at their own game, for we have stronger motives for our action, and put more heart into it than they.[28]

The film stresses in all possible ways the struggle for identity and the ambivalence it produces throughout Lawrence's existential, political, erotic, and literal journey. It is useful to recall here that T. E. Lawrence experienced, in real life, an apparent conflict of identity that a colleague of his, Harry St. John B. Philby of the Arab Bureau at the British Headquarters in Cairo, has labeled as "that curious mingling of woman's sensibility with the virility of the male."[29] Lawrence's journey in the film thus stands as a metaphor for self-exploration and the quest for identity, a theme all too familiar in colonialist and Orientalist literature and cinema, in which the Other's space is revealed as the zone on which the anxieties and fantasies of the self are projected. In this context the film shows Lawrence to be captured in a constant oedipal phase, never being able to resolve it.[30] Indeed, Lawrence's identity is the subject of the memorial service episode at Saint Paul's that immediately follows Lawrence's death in the motorcycle crash at the beginning of the film. "Who is Lawrence?" is the implicit, unspoken question that introduces the long flashback that constitutes the rest of the film. Frank McConnell points out that the question "is one that not only puzzles the characters surrounding him in the Arab campaign, but centrally puzzles and obsesses Lawrence himself."[31] As the story unfolds, the question "Who is Lawrence?" becomes more pressing and more explicit at various points throughout the film. Prince Feisal, upon Lawrence's arrival to the just air-bombed desert encampment at Wadi Safra, asks him, "Who are you?" Lawrence, who does not answer the question, is seen here through a thick cloud of smoke, which suggests a murky identity. After the successful assault on the Turkish garrison at Akaba, Sherif Ali, being even more convinced of the Englishman's leadership qualities, throws into the calm waves of the Gulf of Akaba a bouquet of red flowers: "Garlands for the conqueror! Tributes for the prince! Flowers for the man!" he says of and to Lawrence. Lawrence, however, responds with a puzzling answer: "I'm none of those things, Ali!" "What then?!" perplexed Sherif Ali asks. "Don't know!" is Lawrence's answer, which he delivers in a broken voice. After crossing

Sinai, and upon arriving at the Suez Canal, a British soldier on a motorcycle shouts twice to Lawrence from the other bank, "Who are you?!"[32] Lawrence responds with only a silent gaze.

Three Pairs of Men

The film, furthermore, posits Lawrence in obligatory relationships with three pairs of men. The function of those pairs is to externalize metaphorically the masculine and the feminine in/for Lawrence, that is, the identities between which he is torn. I should note again, however, that, for the most part, these pairs do not conveniently stand as neat and rigid binary oppositions: the play of the masculine and the feminine and their varieties intersects and intertwines. And again, in spite of presenting problematic variations of identity, the film eventually insists on inscribing Lawrence as a "man" in the patriarchal sense of the word.

The first pair that reflects Lawrence's paradox, and which is introduced at the film's outset, consists of General Murray, the harsh commander at the British General Headquarters in Cairo, and Mr. Dryden, the politician at the Arab Bureau therein. Cynical and tough, tyrannical and lacking in compassion, the general appears in the role of the father, the masculine role. His office is pre-sented as a rich store of phallic objects and masculinist imagery. The mise-en-scène emphasizes vertical arrangements. There is a conspicuous tank shell placed erect on a table, a marble column, a coat rack, and busts of men. There are also two cannon miniatures as well as a wall painting depicting three pieces of artillery aligned vertically. An obvious phallic symbol, artillery is invoked throughout the film as that which the Arabs lack. Prince Feisal insistently and vainly requests the British to supply his army with artillery; his request is ignored. "If you give them artillery, then you give them independence," Dryden advises General Allenby. We also see through the window a tower in the frame's background, which extends the general's masculinist conception of the world that exists beyond his immediate surroundings. It is General Murray, having reluctantly agreed to Dryden's request to dispatch Lawrence to the desert, who quite explicitly ascribes to Lawrence an undefined—probably homosexual, or perhaps even asexual—identity: "You are the kind of *creature* I can't stand"; it is also he who adds, a short while later, "Who knows, [the arduous mission to Arabia] might even make a *man* of him."

Protecting and sympathetic, Dryden, on the other hand, appears as playing the role of the mother, the role of the feminine. He, for example, signals with his hand for Lawrence to restrain himself in the face of the general's anger, just as a mother would do for her child in dealing with a tyrannical father. In contrast with Murray's office, which is harshly lit, Dryden's is suffused with a warm glow that reveals a mise-en-scène that underlines horizontal arrangements. The office is furnished with circular and oval-shaped objects—for example, a round table on which a round bowl is placed. In addition to a statuette of Venus, the office also houses ancient Egyptian antiquities, such as a statue of Bastet, the cat goddess. The inclusion of this particular Egyptian mythological symbol echoes the notion of a feminine Egypt, a notion that is not alien to the Egyptomania that Western cinema typically invokes.[33]

The problem here, however, is that Dryden, as an experienced and shrewd politician, is associated with the possession of knowledge and wisdom, which is usually associated with the father figure, not with "brute nature," which General Murray paradoxically symbolizes. It is Dryden who explains to Lawrence that the goal of his mission is to find out about the long-term objectives of Prince Feisal. He demonstrates a fairly concrete knowledge about the prince and his people: "They are within 300 miles of Medina. They are Hashemite Bedouins. They can cross 60 miles of desert in a day." By creating these kinds of contradictory positions (Dryden is "feminine" but knowledgeable), the film keeps challenging the traditional associations of gender roles, and it is in terms of these contradictions that Lawrence must inscribe his identity and desire.

The first pair, General Murray/Dryden, exists and functions in a city setting (Cairo), the location of the British, and therefore of civilization.[34] In this setting Lawrence, although wearing his military uniform, is shown to be awkward, out of touch with the masculine professional environment in which he works, and which seems alien to him. He is unable to adhere to strict military rules; even when General Murray has to remind him to salute by directly instructing him to do so, he executes the order in a laughably unsoldierly fashion. In other words, he is depicted at this stage of the story as unmanly, feminine, lacking.

General Murray's and Dryden's irreconcilable positions vis-à-vis Lawrence indicate a split in attitudes within the British military and political institutions that compose the colonial disposition. General Murray (the father) represents the values of the Old Guard, the traditional principles of manliness and military rituals. Dryden (the mother), with his openness and understanding, seems to represent a different, more accommodating trend. It is according to these anti-thetical modes of understanding that Lawrence is judged: on the one hand, the general considers him unqualified for the job; on the other, the politician feels he is quite suited to it ("He knows his stuff, sir"). The point here is that General Murray, who, considering his low opinion of Lawrence, would certainly not entrust him, for example, with the command of a group of British soldiers, gives in to Dryden's assessment that Lawrence is, in fact, perfectly qualified for the mission precisely for the very reasons the general judges him "inadequate." Lawrence's "unmanliness," suspected sexual orientation, and erotic tendencies become therefore assets, not liabilities. This twist has ultimately to do with Dryden's implicit thesis that Lawrence will be able to deal with the Arabs because he is of their sort: he is not a clear-cut "man." Dryden's theory, therefore, is not at odds with the traditional image of the Oriental, in Western construction, as the site of sensual and erotic syntheses and amalgams. Lawrence is the "man" for the job not only because "he knows his stuff" but also because he represents the very "stuff" that would make the Arabs relate to and interact with him. Thus sexuality and (homo)eroticism are included in the film's Orientalist discourse, which produces and reproduces the knowledge of the Other.

Fire, Sun, Veils, and Vales

The ambiguous position that Lawrence occupies in terms of the erotic is thus established early in the film. His masochism signals him as superior in his ability to master pain and inferior in his fascination with his own mortification. The first Cairo sequence introduces Lawrence's masochism. He is shown, at the beginning of the episode, igniting a match and, instead of blowing it out, snuff-ing it out with his fingers. The scene suggests that the practice produces pain and pleasure. "The trick ... is in not minding that it hurts," he explains to a puzzled fellow soldier. Actually, O'Toole's expression reveals that "not minding" is an understatement; it is intense, one might almost say "orgasmic." The last shots in the Cairo episode, after the interview with General Murray, are particularly sig-nificant in terms of dialectically shifting Lawrence's feminine identity, or what arguably has hitherto appeared to be a feminine identity. Lawrence ignites a match, but he does not snuff it out with his fingers at this time; rather, he blows it out in the customary way. A magnificent dissolve connects the burning match with the sun rising over the desert. We then see Lawrence in his first desert appearance, accompanied by his Bedouin guide, Tafas, as we listen to Maurice Jarre's enthusiastic and soaring, romantic and militaristic music, which suggests both conquering and romancing. Michael A. Anderegg aptly argues that by cutting from the match to the burning desert, Lean implies that "Lawrence's penetration of Arabia ... functions as a displacement of his masochism, a painful/ pleasurable testing of the self."[35] With this shot of the desert, "a burning, fiery furnace" in the warning words of Dryden, the film enters the realm of Orientalist iconography and imagery—that is, the Orient as "a place of romance, exotic beings, haunting memories and landscapes, remarkable experiences," as Said puts it.[36] And it is in the introduction of the desert that the film illustrates Shohat's argument that "the exotic films allow for subliminally transexual tropes. The phantasm of the Orient gives an outlet for a carnivalesque play with national and ... gender identities."[37]

It has now become accepted knowledge that Western literature and art have established a strong tradition of depicting the Orient as feminine.[38] Myriad paintings, novels, poems, and travel accounts, especially those produced during the colonial era, provide ample evidence to support this claim. Linked to masculine representational perspectives, images of "barren land" and "blazing sands" in Western cinema, Shohat argues, stand for "'hot' passion."[39] And "hot" in every sense the desert in *Lawrence* is. It is therefore not surprising that such critics as John Simon designate the desert in *Lawrence* as "the second hero of the film" (the first being, of course, Peter O'Toole in the title role). Simon describes the desert poetically in explicitly sexualized and femininized imagery: "It is a virgin desert, and it unfolds its loveliness shyly, dune by dune, vale by vale."[40] Note the telling homophonic evocation of *veil* in *vale* and the paronomastic suggestion of *nude* in *dune*. The masculinist sensibility, in other words, appreciates the desert as a seducing veiled virgin. In revealing the desert's valleys, the camera also denudes the veiled virgin. Simon's comment is perhaps partly inspired by the dissolve from the aforementioned shot of the sun rising to a shot of two neatly curved and juxtaposed golden sand dunes. Evoking the image of two gigantic thighs, the sand dunes occupy the frame's foreground, and the static camera gazes at them for a full forty seconds. The visual details and formations of the desert are hardly a happy accident in *Lawrence*. Thus Joel C. Hodson comments that "[Freddie] Young's [the film's cinematographer] camera work, which made the desert 'sumptuous' was unfavorably compared [in the British press] to a contemporary BBC television documentary by Malcolm Brown about Lawrence that captured the bleakness of the desert."[41]

It is in the desert, the sensual domain, which poses a challenge to identity, that Lawrence has his encounter with the second pair: Sherif Ali and Prince Feisal. The former, fierce and tough, corresponds to General Murray; the latter, gentle and good-hearted, to Dryden. At one point, Prince Feisal signals with his hand to keep Lawrence in the tent after the departure of the others in order to check his intentions and motivations. We recall that Dryden made that very gesture commanding Lawrence to restrain himself in his reaction to General Murray's fury. The gesture functions as a clue that identifies the Arab prince as a replacement for the British politician. But with this pair, too, it would be wrong to ascribe a fixed label in terms of gender to either of the two men. Here again, the prince, like Dryden, is associated with knowledge. For example, he educates Lawrence about Arab history by telling him this anecdote: "In the Arab city of Cordoba were two miles of public lighting in the streets, when London was a village." Lawrence's relationship with Sherif Ali is even more complex, and is intimately tied to his relation with two young boys—Farraj and Daud.

Lawrence meets the Arab boys Farraj and Daud also in the desert; they are metaphoric representations of gender located in the Other's space, as opposed to the space of the self as represented by General Murray and Dryden in the British General Headquarters in Cairo. Daud and Farraj become Lawrence's faithful servants ("We can do *everything*") until their tragic deaths, for which Lawrence is largely culpable: he leads the former into quicksand, into which he sinks, and he executes the latter after he is wounded to spare him the torture and humiliation of Turkish captivity. Identifying Daud and Farraj with the feminine and the masculine is much less difficult. Unlike the other two English and Arab pairs, in which gendered identities intersect, the two boys neatly correspond to clear divisions between masculine and feminine roles. In terms of Arabic etymology, the name Farraj is derived from the infinitive *faraja*, which denotes, among other things, a split, a breach, a cleave, making an opening, to comfort, to drive away grief, to relieve, to be cleft, pleasure, repose. Not surprisingly, therefore, another close derivation from the infinitive *faraja* is *farj* (vulva). Farraj *always* wears headdress, which corresponds to the images of the veiled Arab women who appear in the film, unlike Daud, who is always bareheaded. Farraj is shy, tender, fragile, with a soft voice, and *always* walks behind tough Daud, who is always in possession of leadership and initiative. For example, when Lawrence rides to rescue Gasim from the Nefud desert, it is Daud who goes to meet him halfway, whereas anxious and frightened Farraj waits with the waterskin. In fact, Lawrence himself identifies Farraj with traditional "woman's work." He, for instance, instructs Farraj, not Daud, to wash his clothes.[42] And so does Sherif Ali, who, for example, orders Farraj, not Daud, to bring food to Lawrence. These stereotypical representations clearly feed into Western notions of women's status in Arab culture. Consider, for example, the fact that women are virtually absent in the film. This is flagrantly antithetical to the fact that women are very visible participants in almost every single economic, cultural, and social activity in the nomadic society of Arabia. Women, via their practical absence from the film, reinforce the notion of Arabia as the land of, as it were, female males, or male females, among whom Lawrence searches for an erotic mirroring of his identity and desire. In this context, boys replace women as both subjects and objects of desire.

The young pair Daud and Farraj constitute a couple that is clearly marked as masculine and feminine, which unmistakably accentuates Lawrence's split identity. Moreover, what is equally important about them is the fact that they are "parentless," which echoes directly the biographical fact of Lawrence's illegitimacy. Lawrence, however, will be legitimated in "Arabia" by Sherif Ali. The figure of the sherif comes to define Lawrence's position in a number of ways. Significantly, Sherif Ali appears as if he replaces Lawrence's first guide into the desert, whom the sherif kills.

"I'm Different"

Lawrence's first encounter with Sherif Ali takes place when the former, accompanied by his Bedouin guide, Tafas, is still on his way to find Prince Feisal at Wadi Safra. Initially, Tafas and Lawrence develop a mutual sympathy; as the desert journey progresses, they actually grow fond of one another. Lawrence appears to assume a new identity in the new environment, drinking only when the guide drinks, thus disciplining himself like the "Bedou." The new identity for which Lawrence strives, however, does not replace an acquired "natural" identity, but rather serves to fragment further the concept of identity within the film. In the English military setting in Cairo, Lawrence appears as, and is associated with, the feminine. By contrast, his readiness to accept and cope with hardships in the desert Arab setting signifies a movement to the masculine, simply because the ideological and aesthetic mise-en-scène of the desert, the Other's space, is portrayed in the film as feminine.

Answering Tafas's spontaneous and curious questions, Lawrence says that Britain is "a fat country, with fat people." Reacting to Tafas's comment that Lawrence is "not fat," Lawrence explains that he is "different." This "difference" could be understood, on one level, as a reference to the qualities that set Lawrence apart intellectually from his countrymen (and -women). For example, he knows classical Arabic, represented by his ability to recite Koranic verses in Prince Feisal's tent. It is difficult, however, not to understand this comment in terms of sexual difference, undefined as it may be, especially with the explicit reference to body type and quality. "I'm different" also indicates a readiness to experiment with the questions and practices of new identities and desires. Earlier, as I have already pointed out, General Murray, in the British Headquarters in Cairo, had addressed Lawrence as a "creature," and had expressed the hope that the mission to Arabia might make a "man" of him.

Still wearing his military uniform in the morning following the conversation about his "difference," Lawrence ostentatiously tosses his only service pistol down on his leather bag in front of Tafas. Tafas looks at the pistol with covetous glance. Centered on the pistol, a short exchange of gazes between Lawrence and Tafas ensues. Lawrence then insistently offers the pistol to Tafas. The film diligently portrays Lawrence as being knowledgeable about various aspects of the Bedouin culture, so much so that he, for example, even boasts of his detailed knowledge of Tafas's tribal identity, "a Hazemi of the Beni Salem." I want, therefore, to argue here that Lawrence is familiar with the fact that in this country weapons are both scarce and treasured. Thus he knows that the Bedouin guide will certainly be interested in the pistol; that he wants to solicit a desiring gaze, which the camera captures; and that the surrendering of the classic phallic symbol, the pistol, functions as a gesture that points to the assumption of, or the desire to assume, a new identity. Ironically, after the moment of bonding, Tafas is eliminated; his place is taken by the sherif.

When Lawrence and Tafas reach the water well, Sherif Ali appears as a distant black dot in the desert vastness, in one of the film's most celebrated scenes. As the sherif approaches the well, Lawrence asks Tafas, "Who is he?" Frightened, Tafas draws the pistol and aims. He is immediately shot dead by the sherif, and the pistol lands before Lawrence. Interestingly, Lawrence, in his conversation with the sherif, does not claim the pistol, despite the fact that, objectively speaking, the need for a weapon appears to be absolute at that point of the journey. Instead, Lawrence says that the pistol was Tafas's, thereby allowing the sherif simply to pick it up and slip it into his belt without protest on Lawrence's part. The phallic symbol therefore becomes an object of a willed exchange between men to signify the assumption of a temporary and constantly shifting identity and to emphasize the homoerotic bond.

Lawrence's second meeting with Sherif Ali is as significant as the first. The meeting takes place in the evening (the first happened during the day). Lawrence, who is seated in Prince Feisal's tent, studies the sherif, who is standing behind him in his dark Arab dress, with a gaze in which attraction is mixed with resentment. Slipped into the sherif's belt, the pistol is sought out by Lawrence's gaze, represented through the camera.

The pistol remains in the sherif's possession until the eve of the assault on Akaba. When a member of the tribal coalition that composes the Arab army, a Harith, murders a Huewaitat, Lawrence senses the precarious situation. The tribal homicide threatens Arab unity, of which he is portrayed as the champion. Because he has "no tribe"—that is, no allegiance—and therefore "no one is offended," Lawrence declares that he will fulfill the demands of tribal law by executing the murderer on the spot. He walks toward Sherif Ali and takes the pistol that had been his and was Tafas's and is now Ali's from the sherif, and he empties the rounds decisively at the murderer, Gasim, the very man he brought out of the Nefud desert. This is, obviously, a reclaiming of the phallic, but it is only a temporary one. Once the execution is over, Lawrence looks shaky and terrified. He walks rigidly and stares at the weapon with disbelief and disavowal; he then gets rid of it by hurling it away to the ground, at which point his Arab companions rush to claim it in a mad tumble. Lawrence's horrific gaze here replaces desire with self-loathing; it denudes the sadistic in articulating the connection between violence and pleasure (Lawrence later admits to General Allenby that he "enjoyed" the killing) and suggests his dismay at rediscovering a lost, or abandoned, sense of identity. This realization is still tied to the manifestations and workings of Lawrence's relationship with Sherif Ali.

Symbolic Marriage

The most important workings of gender and homoerotic desire that underscore the relationship between Lawrence and Sherif Ali are illustrated during the march to Akaba, as the mutual attraction becomes more pronounced, before the execution of Gasim. At the beginning of the Nefud desert crossing, Lawrence surrenders his military cap (he puts it on again only in some of his subsequent meetings with British officers) and substitutes it with an Arab headdress *(hatta* and *ʿiqāl)*. He therefore appears as half Arab (with the headdress) and half English (with the military uniform). This synthesis of Lawrence's attire suggests the gradual acquiring of a new self-image, a hybrid identity—a hybridity that also indicates the process of acquiring new erotic desires.

Lawrence succeeds in rescuing Gasim from certain death. This ostensibly manly and heroic deed baptizes the homoerotic attraction between Lawrence and Sherif Ali; that is, the truly "manly" deed becomes a prerequisite of homoeroticism. The sherif, as a gesture of appreciation of and admiration for the courageous rescuer, personally offers Lawrence a drink from his own waterskin. In return, Lawrence declines the invitations of the tribal chieftains to give them the honor of his resting on their carpets; instead, he walks to the sherif's. Interestingly, he begins to unbutton his military uniform, the symbol of military masculinism, for the first and last time in the film, before reposing on his stomach. After getting up in the evening, Lawrence and the sherif have an intimate conversation about identity. Sherif Ali learns that Lawrence's father actually did not marry his mother. He therefore suggests that Lawrence is free to choose his own name. In fact, the sherif suggests the name El Aurens (a term of honor coined in accordance with tribal traditions). The sherif's manner in proposing the name indicates determination and implicit demand ("El Aurens is best") rather than willingness to negotiate and compromise. Having little room to do otherwise, Lawrence accepts the new name. What this suggests, as far as naming and its bearing on gender role are concerned, is that the sherif actually possesses the legal power and social status to impose his will on Lawrence as a husband on a wife. In other words, the sherif is "Westernized" in that he becomes a husband who, according to the cultural practice, has to give his wife a name. Having accepted the name, and saddened by the embarrassing recollection of his illegitimacy, Lawrence ends eye contact with the sherif and turns his back to resume

Peter O'Toole as "El Aurens."

sleeping. The sherif then throws Lawrence's military dress, the symbol of "man-liness," into the fire. Taking place at night, the scene suggests that Lawrence is now legitimated through a symbolic marriage and virtual acceptance. Unlike Sir Edward Chapman, who did not marry Lawrence's mother and thus "dishonored" her by Bedouin standards, the sherif does marry Lawrence and gives him a name.

The subsequent daytime scene provides an elaborate commentary on what happened the preceding evening. The sherif, who is always dressed in dark attire, personally puts the final touches on Lawrence's new dress, a white Arab costume (a robe of a sherif of Beni Wajh), which Lawrence describes as "very fine." Shohat seizes this moment in the film to point out that "the widely disseminated popular images in newspapers and newsreels of T. E. Lawrence in flowing Arab costume have partially inspired films such as *The Sheik* and *Son of the Sheik*, whose bisexual appeal can be located in the closet construction of Western man as 'feminine.'" She explains that

> the coded "feminine" look ... is played out within the safe space of
> the Orient, through the "realistic" embodiment of the Other. David
> Lean's Lawrence, despite his classical association with norms of
> heroic manliness, is also portrayed in a homoerotic light. When he is
> accepted by the Arab tribe he is dressed all in white, and at one point
> set on a [camel] moving delicately, virtually captured like a bride.
> Drawing a [dagger] from his sheath, [he] shifts the gendered signifi-
> cation of the phallic symbol by using it as a mirror to look at his
> own newly acquired "feminine" "oriental" image. More generally, the
> relationship between Lawrence and [Sherif Ali] gradually changes
> from initial male rivalry to an implied erotic attraction in which [the
> sherif] is associated with female imagery, best encapsulated in the
> scene where [Sherif Ali] is seen in close-up with wet eyes, identifying
> with the tormented Lawrence.... The interracial homoerotic sub-
> text in *Lawrence of Arabia* forms part of a long tradition of colonial
> narratives.[43]

Shohat's commentary might seem contradictory in, for example, ascribing two gender identities, masculine and feminine, to Sherif Ali. Shohat emphasizes the issue of homoerotic attraction; however, she indicates, by identifying both Lawrence and the sherif with the feminine at different points in the film's narra-tive, that gender is not a stable category. I have suggested earlier that *Lawrence* challenges gender binary opposition in favor of provisional identities and avoids (except for the case of the Arab boys Farraj and Daud) fixed roles, not because it is philosophically against such binaries and thus wants to collapse them, but exactly because it is a colonialist text, the political narrative and imperial nostal-gia of which encompass (indeed, are aimed at) the Other's space—or more spe-cifically, the Orient, the unlimited realm of fantasy, mystery, and Western action, where Lawrence, as Robert D. Kaplan puts it, "acted out his fantasies while gathering valuable intelligence."[44] Conceived as fantastic, the Orient perfectly matches the medium through which it is represented, namely, film as the domain of fantasy. Film as fantasy, where "the staging of desire has multiple entries," encompasses, in the view of Elizabeth Cowie, the shift of "subject-position across the boundary of sexual difference but do[es] so always in terms of sexual difference."[45]

Identification of Lawrence with the feminine and Sherif Ali with the masculine, as in the symbolic marriage scene discussed earlier, takes place close to the end of the first half of the film, prior to the major military events of the story. Identification of the sherif with the feminine in the shot Shohat discusses above takes place close to the end of the film. The point I want to make here is that the film shifts and relocates not only the gender of its leading characters, but also that of the desert, the "second hero" of the film, as John Simon has suggested. The desert first appears as a serene, calm, inspiring, sensuous, "natural" body. Military and political actions, however, follow. As these progress and take hold of the narrative, Lawrence comes to *discover* and *rediscover* himself, exposing in the process his desires in the exotic setting. Simultaneously, the desert gradually loses its innocence and intimacy, and therefore assumes an increasingly bleak and inhospitable countenance: sandstorms, killing quicksands, harsh, rocky landscapes. Thus the desert generally attracts less attention from the camera gaze in the second half of the film; the short, medium, and long shots allocated to it only emphasize its griminess.[46] The desert is portrayed as a mirror reflecting its narrator, Lawrence, who in the course of his journey defines and redefines its identity as he struggles to define and redefine his own. The shot that associates Sherif Ali with femininity, the shot that Shohat discusses in the quotation above, appears in a scene toward the end of the film in which Lawrence and the Arab army under his leadership, and thanks to his instructions ("No prisoners"), massacre a retreating Turkish column in retaliation for the destruction of an Arab village.

The massacre scene, however, includes the second moment in which Lawrence looks at his image in the dagger, which Shohat, curiously, does not mention. This time Lawrence, the dagger, and the desert are all stained with blood. The Lawrence of the second moment is not the playful Lawrence of the first. Between the two moments there have been blood, death, and destruction—

a violent maturation and articulation of identity and desire. Lawrence, we recall, sets off to the desert as a "creature" who might, General Murray hopes, become a "man" in the course of his mission to "Arabia." After the astonishing capture of Akaba, Lawrence travels to the British General Headquarters in Cairo to report the victory to his superiors. At this point in the film, General Allenby wholeheartedly addresses him, "You are an interesting *man.* There is no doubt about it." In other words, the doubts General Murray had expressed about Lawrence's manliness, which sounded legitimate to us then considering his "unmanly" behavior, are proven to be unfounded by his succesor, General Allenby. This shift in attitude takes place simply because Lawrence has successfully accomplished the rite of passage of becoming a *man,* in "Arabia." The blood on his dagger's blade proves it.

The massacre scene is introduced by a slow pan shot that shows the ruins of the Arab village and the bodies of the victims. Among these are Arab women lying dead with their legs exposed, indicating rape. It is here where Lawrence unleashes his masculinist sadism, looking ecstatic as he rides his camel and fires at the wounded Turkish soldiers. Significantly, the massacre occurs after the Derra incident in which Lawrence was violated,[47] and thus it is punctuated by a sense of vengeance. The military violence committed by Lawrence and the Arabs (killing) and the sexual violence committed by the Turks (rape) are conflated to produce a trope of sadism in which the blood of rape is mixed with that of murder. More significant is the fact the scene takes place toward the end of the film and the end of Lawrence's desert experience. As a spatial metaphor for a violent journey of self-discovery, the desert assumes the appropriate topographical austerity. Caked with dust and mud and stained with blood, Lawrence looks at himself in the bloody dagger, thereby possessing the Other's tamed space once and for all in the name of the phallic symbol. The first desert scene, with the guide Tafas, had introduced Lawrence to the desert, a tabula rasa on which Lawrence inscribed the story of his maturation through several stages and actions. The desert appeared as feminine, and thus Lawrence wanted to be a "Bedou." The audience, meanwhile, was offered both a colonial and erotic gaze as it followed the unfolding of the remarkable story of quest and conquest.

The desert mirrored and responded to Lawrence's identity anxieties; actually, it articulated them, reflecting the series of male couples that constitute the narrative. The erotic gaze was generously offered to the armchair explorers—both males and females—as desiring participants in taming the desert. As the Other's space, the desert was presented as a domain of fantasy and magic, and thus a realm for experimenting with modes of desire and identity. Even though the film allowed—indeed, encouraged—Lawrence to "become a woman" at a certain point, it eventually restored his masculinity through a symbolic act of deflo-ration as represented in his gaze at the bloodstained dagger. Therefore the film, notwithstanding its strategic appeal to both ends of the gender spectrum, is chiefly informed by a masculinist vision, a vision that finds its driving force only in the very discourse of the "civilizing mission" that is drenched with the blood of enumerable (Other) men and women.

Notes

I am very grateful to Hilary Radner for her constant encouragement, patient remarks, and profound interest in the topic of this essay. I also thank Janet Swaffar for her useful comments.

1. *Lawrence of Arabia* (1962, 222 minutes at original release), shot on location in the United Kingdom, Jordan, Morocco, and Spain; director, David Lean; producer, Sam Spiegel; production, Horizon Pictures (U.K.), released by Columbia; screenplay, Robert Bolt; cinematography, Fred A. Young; editing, Anne V. Coates; production design, John Box; music, Maurice Jarre. Cast: *T. E. Lawrence*, Peter O'Toole; *Prince Feisal*, Alec Guinness; *Auda Abu Tayi*, Anthony Quinn; *General Allenby*, Jack Hawkins; *Mr. Dryden*, Claude Rains; *Sherif Ali*, Omar Sharif; *Gasim*, I. S. Johar; *Majid*, Gamil Ratib; *Farraj*, Michel Ray; *Daud*, Tohn Dimech; *Tafas*, Zia Mohyeddin.
2. Mandel Herbstman, "Lawrence of Arabia," *Film Daily*, December 17, 1962, 6.
3. Ibid.
4. It is more than pure coincidence that in 1962, the year in which *Lawrence* had its premiere, and in no other place than Jordan, in whose desert most of the film was photographed, the first Arabic book on Lawrence was published. The book, which was eventually translated into English, critically evaluates Lawrence's Arabia experi-ence and deconstructs his myth from an Arab perspective. See Suleiman Mousa, *T. E. Lawrence: An Arab View*, trans. Albert Butros (London: Oxford University Press, 1966).
5. Gerald Pratley, *The Cinema of David Lean* (Cranbury, N.J.: A. S. Barnes, 1974), 25.
6. Sam Spiegel, untitled essay in the *Lawrence of Arabia* special issue of *Journal of the Society of Film and Television Arts* 10 (1962–63): 5.
7. Edward Said, " 'Lawrence' Doesn't Do Arabs Any Favors," *Wall Street Journal*, Febru-ary 21, 1989, 18.

8. Ella Shohat, "Gender and Culture of Empire: Toward a Feminist Ethnography of the Cinema," in *Visions of the East: Orientalism in Film*, ed. Matthew Bernstein and Gaylyn Studlar (New Brunswick, N.J.: Rutgers University Press, 1997), 19, 20.

9. Ibid., 27.

10. Laura Mulvey, "Visual Pleasure and Narrative Cinema," in *Feminism and Film Theory*, ed. Constance Penley (New York: Routledge, 1988), 57–68.

11. Steve Cohen, "Masquerading as the American Male in the Fifties: *Picnic*, William Holden and the Spectacle of Masculinity in Hollywood Film," *Camera Obscura* 25–26 (1991): 44.

12. Ibid., 49.

13. Ibid., 45.

14. Leslie Taubman, "Lawrence of Arabia," in *Magill's Survey of Cinema: English Language Films*, first series, vol. 2, ed. Frank N. Magill (Englewood Cliffs, N.J.: Salem, 1980), 961.

15. Rober Musel, "'Lawrence' A Brilliant Film Epic Sets New Mark in Cinematic Art," *Hollywood Reporter*, December 17, 1962, 3.

16. The Mexican American actor Anthony Quinn portrays "Auda Abu Tayi." The cinematic Auda Abu Tayi supposedly corresponds to an actual historic figure, an Arab tribal leader, whose name was actually Auda Abu Tayeh. The character is misnamed in the film, and the person is misnamed in many Western historic and biographical sources, simply because he is thus named in the "definitive" source on Arabia and its people, T. E. Lawrence's account *Seven Pillars of Wisdom* (London: Jonathan Cape, 1935). *Tayi* and *Tayeh* are, in fact, two different tribal designations. Thus the "Tayification" of Auda Abu Tayeh is an obvious example of generic tribalism, generic historiography, and generic cinematography, typical of the inscription of the Other (literally and figuratively) in Western writing and art.

17. Jeremy Wilson, *The Authorized Biography of Lawrence of Arabia* (New York: Antheneum, 1990).

18. Richard Aldington, *Lawrence of Arabia: A Biographical Enquiry* (London: Collins, 1969).

19. Philip Knightley and Colin Simpson, *The Secret Lives of Lawrence of Arabia* (New York: McGraw-Hill, 1970).

20. David Lean, quoted in Adrian Turner, *The Making of David Lean's Lawrence of Arabia* (London: Dragon's World, 1994), 71, 73. Wilson, who was blacklisted as a result of his refusal to appear before the House Un-American Activities Committee (HUAC), was commissioned to write the screenplay originally. However, due to mutual dissatisfaction with both the director and the producer, he was replaced by Robert Bolt. Following a bitter struggle, Wilson's writing credit for the film was acknowledged by the Writers Guild of America in 1995.

21. Robert Bolt, "Clues to the Legend of Lawrence," *New York Times Magazine*, February 25, 1962, 16.

22. Peter Baker, "Lawrence of Arabia," *Film and Filming,* February 1963, 32.

23. Brian St. Pierre, "Lawrence of Arabia," *Seventh Art* 1, no. 3 (1964): 19.

24. Robert Bolt, quoted in Gary Crowdus, "Lawrence of Arabia: The Cinematic (Re)Writing of History," *Cineaste* 17, no. 2 (1989): 17.

25. Robert Bolt, quoted in Alain Silver and James Ursini, *David Lean and His Films* (Los Angeles: Silman-James, 1992), 154.

26. See Jordan's chapter in this volume, "Making the Homophile Manifest."

27. Edward Said, *Orientalism* (New York: Vintage, 1979), 63.

28. T. E. Lawrence, *The Essential T. E. Lawrence: A Selection of His Finest Writings* (New York: Oxford University Press, 1992), 136, 139–40.

29. Harry St. John B. Philby, quoted in Robert D. Kaplan, *The Arabists: The Romance of an American Elite* (New York: Free Press, 1995), 51. There is a rare photograph of T. E. Lawrence showing him in Arab women's dress included in Lowell Thomas, *With Lawrence in Arabia* (New York: Century, 1924), facing 251. The caption reads: "Lawrence would occasionally disguise himself as a Gipsy woman of Syria."

30. "The Oedipus complex, in Freud's account, can be resolved in a number of ways, and, unresolved, can have a number of grave consequences." Malcolm Bowie, "Bisexuality," in *Feminism and Psychoanalysis: A Critical Dictionary,* ed. Elizabeth Wright (Oxford: Blackwell, 1996), 28.

31. Frank McConnell, *Storytelling and Mythmaking: Images from Film and Literature* (New York: Oxford University Press, 1979), 126.

32. Adrian Turner points out that "Lean himself dubbed the line of the motorcyclist." "It is," he interprets the gesture, "the director puzzling over the nature of his hero and puzzling over himself as well—the man from the drab suburbs of London who has driven his own army across the desert." *The Making of David Lean's Lawrence of Arabia,* 8.

33. For an elaborate discussion on this topic, see Antonia Lant, "The Curse of the Pharaoh, or How Cinema Contracted Egyptomania," in *Visions of the East: Orientalism in Film,* ed. Matthew Bernstein and Gaylyn Studlar (New Brunswick, N.J.: Rutgers University Press, 1997), 69–98.

34. It is typical of Orientalist films to associate "urban civilization" with the colonizers, British in this case, and the natives with "desolate terrains." Ella Shohat points to *Lawrence* as an example of this tendency. See Ella Shohat, *Israeli Cinema: East/West and the Politics of Representation* (Austin: University of Texas Press, 1989), 149.

35. Michael A. Anderegg, *David Lean* (Boston: Twayne, 1984), 111.

36. Said, *Orientalism,* 1.

37. Shohat, "Gender and Culture of Empire," 52.

38. For an elaborate discussion on this topic, see Said, *Orientalism.*

39. Shohat, "Gender and Culture of Empire," 32.

40. John Simon, *Private Screenings* (New York: Berkeley, 1971), 53.

41. Joel C. Hodson, *Lawrence of Arabia and American Culture: The Making of a Transatlantic Legend* (London: Greenwood, 1995), 119.

42. Lawrence states in "Twenty-Seven Articles" that "Arabs ... leave you if required to do unmanly work like cleaning boots or washing." *The Essential T. E. Lawrence*, 141–42.

43. Shohat, "Gender and Culture of Empire," 53.

44. Kaplan, *The Arabists*, 54.

45. Elizabeth Cowie, "Fantasia," in *The Woman in Question*, ed. Parvene Adams and Elizabeth Cowie (Cambridge: MIT Press, 1990), 193–94.

46. I agree here with Christian B. Kennedy's premise, which is that the changes that take place in Lawrence's character coincide with the changes that occur in the desert itself in the two halves of the film. I disagree, however, with most of the rest of his argument. See Christian B. Kennedy, "The Myth of Heroism: Man and Desert in *Lawrence of Arabia*," in *Place, Power, Situation and Spectacle: A Geography of Film*, ed. Stuart C. Aitken and Leo E. Zonn (London: Rowman & Littlefield, 1994), 161–79.

47. The Derra incident is important and relevant in that Lawrence is, implicitly, sexually assaulted. However, a full discussion of this event in the present essay would take me too far afield.

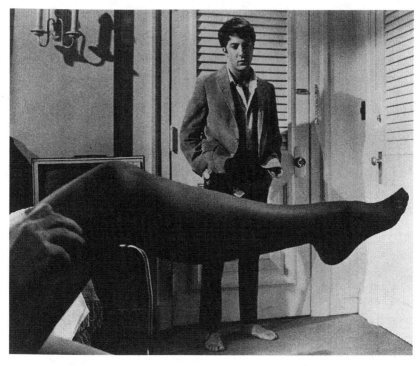

The Graduate, 1967. Courtesy of Photofest.

Selling "Atrocious Sexual Behavior"
Revising Sexualities in the Marketplace for Adult Film of the 1960s
Justin Wyatt

Although the label *independent cinema* usually signifies filmmaking cut off from the commercial advantages and potential of the majors, within film history the independents have been able to specify a market segment several times ahead of the major studios. In this essay, I will concentrate on a particular historical moment in the independent-mainstream relationship, the market for adult film in the late 1960s and early 1970s. In this period, a combination of economic, social, and institutional forces served to configure a separate market for films centered on sexuality; significantly, these films were produced largely outside the world of mainstream cinema. Although popularized as "sexploitation," the films ran the gamut from serious examinations of sexuality and its restrictive conventions (*I am Curious [Yellow]*) to erotica designed to titillate (*Deep Throat, Camille 2000*). The identification and exploitation of this market segment certainly cannot be separated from the turbulent and volatile social context of the period, which helped to make the market segment more legitimate for the "average" moviegoer—suddenly norms of sexuality and sexual expression were being questioned across many media. From an economic standpoint, the range and scope of these films illuminate how a market segment may be identified and exploited apart from the mainstream. Indeed, this commercial lesson proved instrumental for the establishment of several independent companies that are still operating.

The Formation of the Adult Market Segment: Demographics, Sexuality, and the MPAA

Whereas the movement toward the adult film market was driven by a combination of institutional and economic factors, larger sociological and demographic

105

shifts within the film marketplace also aided the constitution of adult films. With the oldest part of the baby boom generation reaching their early twenties by the late 1960s, Hollywood began to recognize the commercial significance of this segment. A market research study conducted by Daniel Yankelovich and Associates in 1968 illustrated that the youth market, aged sixteen to twenty-four, accounted for 48 percent of box-office admissions.[1] As one producer of the era commented on the implications of this statistic, "Each one of the majors should have at least one bright young guy under 30 on its board, just to help in setting up films for today's youth market."[2]

Institutionally, the youth revolution occurred at the same time as the 1969 recession in the film industry. As Tino Balio notes, the majors suffered more than $200 million in losses that year, added to the steadily declining theatrical attendance (weekly attendance was down 17.5 million from the 1946 high of 90 million; revenues had been compensated only slightly by almost tripled admission prices).[3] This recession led Hollywood to believe that the youth picture—low cost, targeting the fifteen to twenty-eight age group specifically—held the key to rejuvenation. In the last few years of the 1960s, *The Graduate*,

Easy Rider, 1969. Courtesy of Photofest.

Goodbye, Columbus, Easy Rider, Alice's Restaurant, and *Midnight Cowboy* all demonstrated, as Abel Green has recounted in *Variety,* "the story of low capital investment versus boffo boxoffice."[4] The youth "revolution" served to feed the increasing freedom in terms of subject matter, further enhancing the marketability of the adult/porno feature.

Within the release schedule circa 1968 for the majors, the youth pictures attained some visibility amid a range of product still targeted at other demographics: thrillers such as *Wait until Dark* and *The Thomas Crown Affair,* science fiction films such as *Planet of the Apes,* mainstream comedies such as *The Odd Couple* and *With Six You Get Eggroll,* musicals (*Star!, Finian's Rainbow, Chitty Chitty Bang Bang*), and war films (*The Green Berets*). Successes of the era suggested to the trade paper *Variety* that the youth demographic was attracted by "a conjunction of original sights and sounds" rather than "straightforward storytelling."[5] The novel sensory experiences were to be augmented by a focus on experiences common to the young, foregrounding rock music, dance, motorcycles, and sex.[6] The tension with which the mainstream industry viewed youth is evident throughout the industry trade papers of the time, with articles stressing that the "older" audiences must not be forgotten by producers, that the youth film audiences are fickle and unpredictable in terms of attendance, and that youth culture is merely a passing phase.[7] In terms of the youth segment, the most visible component, the hippies, were a particular target for the industry, with the trades offering contradictory advice. Whereas one *Variety* piece expounded on the "way-out attire and hippie haircuts" of the European film producers, another from the same year reported on an exhibitor in Toronto who forced an employee to carry a sign in front of the theater proclaiming "No Admittance to Hippies."[8]

Sexuality and the revision of restrictive sexual conventions were often posited within the media as major aspects of the youth counterculture. As Dr. William Masters (coauthor of *Human Sexual Response*) claimed, "The '60s will be called the decade of orgasmic preoccupation."[9] Following Masters's lead, pop sociologist Vance Packard, after demystifying the powers of advertising in *The Hidden Persuaders,* reported on the sexual revolution in his 1968 book, *The Sexual Wilderness.* Packard's major claim centered on the increased sexual experience of unmarried females in North America; he asserted that there had been an increase in sexual intercourse of nearly 60 percent in that group from 1948 to 1968.[10] In reporting Packard's findings, *Time* magazine chose to juxtapose a

Thérèse and Isabelle, 1968. Courtesy of Photofest.

picture of the author with a still from *Blow-Up*, supported by the wording "Aggressive girls in 'Blow Up.' The roles are being reversed." The match illustrates the equation between the arts and freer sexual expression made by the mass media of the era—from Philip Roth's *Portnoy's Complaint* to *Oh, Calcutta* and a large number of independent and imported films (*Coming Apart; Thérèse and Isabelle; I, a Woman; Inga*).

Indeed, the climate for adult filmmaking was also fostered by the abolishment of the Production Code Administration ratings system (established in 1930 and revised in 1966, when many of the taboos in the original code were eliminated).[11] Under fire from the National Catholic Office for Motion Pictures to institute a nationwide ratings system, the Motion Picture Association established the voluntary ratings system (G/M[GP/PG]/R/X) for all films released after November 1, 1968, with the X rating barring those under age sixteen without qualification.[12] Under the MPAA system, nonmember distributors were welcome to self-apply X ratings, but not less restrictive ratings.[13] Even before the new system was instituted, independent distributors lobbied against exhibitors' playing only films with MPAA ratings. Because the majority of independent films were directed at "adult" audiences, the independents felt that their films would have little to gain by having MPAA ratings.[14] Many of these distributors also balked at the cost of submitting their films to the board for ratings that would have no bearing on their potential audience.

In addition to classifying films into one of four ratings categories, the MPAA enacted certain guidelines that aided the board in deciding on ratings. Despite the supposed movement away from moral judgments, the MPAA explicitly listed values and vices that would influence ratings decisions. For instance, "the basic dignity and value of human life shall be respected and upheld," and restraint was requested in the portrayal of, among other things, "evil, sin, crime, wrongdoing," "sex aberrations," "excessive cruelty," and "illicit sex relation-ships."[15] The impacts of these transgressions on ratings were unspecified, leaving wide room for interpretation on the part of the administration. As well as film classification, a system of regulating all advertising and titles for motion pictures was developed. The MPAA warned against "indecent or undue exposure of the human body" in trailers and in print and television advertising and "salacious, obscene, or profane" titles.[16]

At the time of its inception, some producers were optimistic that the MPAA ratings system would actually expand the audience for film, with conservatives admiring the censorship aspects and the self-regulation of the industry and liberals appreciating the anticipated freer themes and content in light of restrictions on admittance to certain films.[17] However, the problems within the structure of the ratings system became evident even before the official starting date of November 1. Perhaps fearing that the age restriction would limit potential audiences, the majors desperately avoided the X rating. Of the initial thirty-nine pictures submitted for ratings, only one (Warner Bros.'s *The Girl on a Motorcycle*) received an X.[18] Following the classification system in Britain, X became associated with a certain breed of "adult" motion pictures, mainly sexually explicit films. In Britain, the X rating gained a reputation as a no-cost marketing tool, advertising to a specific adult demographic; ad lines such as "the sex-x-x-x-iest film ever" were used in British promotional campaigns.

Within six months of the ratings system introduction, several filmmakers and distributors opposed the X rating for their adult-oriented, but not sexually explicit, films: Brian De Palma's antiwar comedy *Greetings* received an X for frontal nudity, as did Lindsay Anderson's *If*. Tiny *Greetings* distributor Sigma III eventually acquiesced to the rating, but Paramount fought the rating of *If* on the basis of strong reviews that had made no mention of the nudity or supposed "exploitation."[19] The rating was upheld, with reediting eventually securing an R rating for the picture. Robert Aldrich's *The Killing of Sister George* also received an X based on the lesbian-centered plot and some relatively mild nudity and largely offscreen simulated sex. Aldrich complained to the trades, fearing that the film would be marginalized based on its rating. As industry analyst Stuart Byron commented at the time, "Despite the MPAA's allegations that the fourply classification system has nothing to do with moral or aesthetic quality, an assumption has grown that films rated X are those which are 'artistically' unworthy of 'higher' tags."[20] Art house exhibitor Walter Reade also complained about the functioning of the X rating a year after the institution of the system, focusing his arguments on the self-application of the X by independents. This process had reinforced the idea that "the code for all practical purposes was basically connected with dirty pictures for a large number of the film-going US public."[21]

The Fox, 1968. Courtesy of Photofest.

The difficulty of judging an X rating was evident only three weeks after the system commenced with the cases of *The Fox*, an adaptation of the D. H. Lawrence novella, and *Birds in Peru*, an erotic drama starring Jean Seberg and directed by Romain Gary. *The Fox*, featuring female masturbation and above-the-waist nudity, received an R, whereas *Birds in Peru*, featuring a sex scene without any nudity whatsoever, received an X rating. As *Variety* commented on the discrepancy, "Many in N.Y. trade simply cannot understand the criteria employed for these two pix."[22] Some considered that the ratings indicated an aesthetic judgment on the part of the MPAA, with *The Fox* garnering a less restrictive rating for its overall "sensitive" treatment of a delicate theme. With the institution of the system, exhibitors' confusions transformed into concerns that would plague the MPAA for the next two decades: a 1969 exhibitor survey on the MPAA concluded that there was a pressing need to distinguish between exploitation X pictures and those with "serious artistic intent," with *Midnight Cowboy* and *Medium Cool* mentioned as examples of the latter category.[23]

The pressure to obtain an R over an X rating by the majors correlates with an increase in the number of R-rated films over the first decade of the ratings system: this shift was most dramatic in the early years, with R ratings accounting for 23 percent in 1968–69, but 37 percent in 1969–70. The figure increased through the early 1970s, reaching a plateau of 48 percent in 1974–75.[24] The increase in the R ratings category is explained by a fall in the number of G/family films. This redistribution aided the separation of the market for X films—in effect, a major studio viewed the X rating as inconsistent with the potential for a mass audience. For the majors, the R rating became the tag that signified adult, yet did not limit attendance, because underage patrons could still attend with parent or adult guardian.

In addition to the growth of R as a ratings category, confusion over the meaning of the X rating within the mainstream film industry furthered that rating's separation from products of the majors. In June 1968, a *Variety* article centered on the widespread bewilderment over the X rating on the part of both exhibitors and distributors. The article reported one claim that any film that was not submitted to the MPAA would automatically receive an X, with no admittance to those under seventeen years old, regardless of the film's content. Another industry spokesman was quoted as saying, "It is not expected that any film submitted for a classification would be placed in the fourth category."[25]

Despite the reluctance of some independents, the MPAA ratings system also acted as an economic benefit, effectively segmenting the marketplace for film— the X rating became synonymous with stronger adult (later pornographic) content. The consequences of the X for the majors were dire: approximately 50 percent of theaters across the country refused to play X films, and as many as thirty large city newspapers, along with many television and radio stations, refused to advertise them.[26] Desperate to maintain their presence in circuit theaters, the studios routinely submitted scripts to the MPAA for readings on the projected ratings for the completed films; for instance, *The French Connection*, the western *Wild Rovers*, and the crime drama *Dealing* were altered at the script level preproduction to avoid an X rating.[27] The fear of the studios to produce X-rated films essentially allowed the independents to exploit this market segment. Within six months of the institution of the MPAA ratings system, companies such as American International, Cinerama, Cinemation, Times Films, and Trans-Lux were self-applying X to their films.[28]

The shift in ratings practice augmented a significant alteration in censorship rule by the U.S. Supreme Court in 1965. In a move that aided the infiltration of adult-themed films, the Court held that the state censorship board had to prove why a certain film under contention could not be shown; the burden was shifted away from the distributor and toward the local board.[29] This change responded to the often lengthy and costly litigation forced upon the independent distributor under the previous system. This litigation acted as a violation of freedom of expression, according to the Court. The move served to highlight the contradictions among definitions of "prurient" and "obscene" material from city to city and from state to state.[30] As these differences were worked through, many adult-oriented films were allowed to play large-scale "art house" releases; censor bans focused on a small number of films, such as Audobon's *Thérèse and Isabelle* and Grove's *I Am Curious (Yellow)*, that already had received great publicity and box office in their runs.[31]

The adult film in this period also was tied strongly to forces within the marketplace for film, particularly to the art film and the underground cinema. Under the rubric of "New American Cinema," underground and avant-garde films developed institutional supports in the early through mid-1960s. Much of the growth in this area was centered in New York: within a five-year period, the Anthology Film Archives devoted to "vanguard, offbeat, underground or poetic experience films" was established (1970), the Filmmakers Cinematheque became a permanent exhibition space for these films (1967), and the Whitney Museum of American Art provided a weekly showcase for independent and experimental films (1970).[32] Most striking from a commercial standpoint, efforts were made to widen the distribution and exhibition possibilities for these films. In 1962, Jonas Mekas guided the development of the Film-Makers' Cooperative, which was devoted to the distribution of avant-garde and experimental works that had little chance of gaining other forms of distribution.[33] Four years later, three of the region's leading directors—Shirley Clarke, Lionel Rogosin, and Mekas—founded the Filmmaker's Distribution Center. Their efforts were devoted to securing a greater number of conventional theatrical bookings for independent film. At the time, only ten to fifteen theaters across the country booked experimental films, and the center's initial ambition was to increase that number to more than a hundred.[34] The center's mission was to aid independent production through this greater visibility. Part of this objective is evidenced in the preferential terms given to filmmakers in their deals with the center: the basic contract stipulated that gross profits would be split fifty-fifty between filmmaker and distributor, with the center absorbing all promotional, advertising, and handling costs.[35] The unprecedented commercial success of Andy Warhol's *The Chelsea Girls* further enhanced the position of the underground cinema "aboveground." Warhol's 3½ hour epic, utilizing two simultaneous 16mm projectors, each projecting different images, moved from the Cinematheque to a regular theatrical run, averaging between ten and fifteen thousand dollars per week.[36] Warhol chose to remain with the Film-Makers' Cooperative for distribution, turning down offers from both United Artists and Twentieth Century Fox as possible distributors.

The efforts of the underground were aided by the already ensconced art cinema world of the larger American cities. Bolstered by the influx of foreign films and auteurs such as Truffaut, Bergman, Fellini, and Antonioni, the art house circuit developed first in New York through the efforts of exhibitors (and later distributors) Walter Reade Jr. and Don Rugoff.[37] Although the leading art film exhibitors relied heavily on foreign product for their theaters, upon the establishment of their own distribution agencies—Cinema V for Rugoff, Continental for Reade—both were instrumental in breaking several American independent films in New York and beyond. Cinema V, for instance, distributed Warhol's *Trash* and Robert Downey's *Putney Swope* to strong art house box office.[38]

Following in a long tradition of avant-garde film, many of these films from the underground questioned both conventions of cinematic construction and codes of sexuality. Warhol's Factory "stars," Kenneth Anger's ode to the homoeroticism of the motorcycle gang (*Scorpio Rising*), and Shirley Clarke's frank portrait of a gay male prostitute (*Portrait of Jason*) ventured into territory untouched by the majors. As described in *Time*, consider Robert Downey's *Chafed Elbows:* "the shaggy-surreal saga of a [Greenwich] Village idiot who hopes to get rich quick by persuading female midgets to use contact lenses as contraceptives."[39] Alternately, Andy Warhol's *Blue Movie* was sold as the first theatrical feature actually to depict intercourse, although the ten-minute lovemaking scene between Viva and Louis Waldon was believed by many critics to be simulated. Nevertheless, the depiction of sex, along with sexual "aberrations" such as male homosexuality and lesbianism, provoked national and local publicity, and ultimately battles of censorship.

Characterizing Adult Cinema: The View from the Center

The MPAA ratings system, the growth of the art and underground cinema, X as a marketing tool, and the confusions around censorship all served to nurture the adult film as a marketplace phenomenon. Although exploitation films had mined the adult market for several decades, the 1960s offered a marked difference from previous eras through the degree of assimilation of adult features into the overall marketplace and through the shifting social attitudes that helped to validate adult film as a legitimate form of entertainment.[40] Growing from the tradition of art films stretching the boundaries of free expression (*La Dolce Vita*, *And God Created Woman*, *Room at the Top*), the adult features of the period were supplied by European producers. The influx of product from Sweden and Denmark played with subtitles in art houses, thus giving an aura of sophistication to the films. The economic power of the adult film became stronger and stronger toward the close of the 1960s—from the foreign imports, such as *I Am Curious (Yellow)*, breaking capacity records in 1969 in New York and placing number one on *Variety*'s Top Grossing Films Chart (November 26, 1969) to the sexploitation films, such as *The Stewardesses*, *I, a Woman*, and *Thérèse and Isabelle*. Of course, today the possibility of any soft-core independent film reaching the top of the *Variety* chart is ludicrous, with the contemporary market for this product dominated primarily by video and cable television.

The increased visibility of the adult feature toward the end of the 1960s was accompanied by more freedom in content. In 1968, for example, a case before the Maryland State Censor Board demonstrated that exploitation features had progressed from upper-torso nudity to full frontal nudity in features such as *Walls of Flesh* and *Savage Blonde*. As a trade paper reported on this transformation, "Time was when a nudie made exclusively for the exploitation house had the male retain some dress, usually a pair of shorts, and the female her panties."[41]

The issue was extended even further with the U.S. distribution of the Swedish film *I Am Curious (Yellow)*. Featuring simulated sexual intercourse in medium and long shot, the film offered a rather unsettling mix of political, sexual, and social satire in a story centering on the "radical" lifestyle choices of Lena, a young Swede unbound by sexual and social conventions. Banned outright in Norway, Vilgot Sjoman's film was censored heavily in Britain, France, and Germany.[42] Grove Press picked up the American distribution rights, only to have the film impounded by the U.S. Customs Service. Until a circuit court of appeals ruled that the film could be shown uncut, Grove Press continued to maximize publicity around the film by releasing a paperback copy of the script with more than

I Am Curious (Yellow), 1969.

250 stills for those who preferred looking at the pictures. When the film finally was cleared for release, Grove Press was able to extract strong terms from exhibitors due to the media controversy surrounding the film: the distributor asked for $50,000 in advance and a 90/10 percent split favoring the distributor after recoupment of the advance.[43] The New York opening in March 1969 was phenomenally successful, with an opening week of $91,785 at two small theaters, the Cinema 57 Rendezvous and the Evergreen.[44] Within six months of release, the film grossed $4 million in fewer than twenty-five theaters. *I Am Curious (Yellow)*'s performance illustrates the power of publicity and the ability of one film to exploit the national dialogue over sexual freedom and expression. The film's foreign origin and the treatment of sexuality as a social issue certainly helped qualify it as within the art, not exploitation, category and therefore worthy of consideration. Reporting on the controversy, *Look* European editor Leonard Gross foregrounded the dramatic and moral qualities of *I Am Curious (Yellow)*: "It is a serious film with a noble theme, and, in dramatic terms, it is original. . . . And [director] Sjoman, whom friends describe as both moral and concerned, uses sex artistically to make a political point: lack of commitment in affairs of state is as disastrous as in affairs of heart."[45] Although the box-office performance was impressive, the figure is extraordinary given the dry, didactic nature of the film, distinguished only by the more sexually frank material. As the reviewer for *Time* noted: "If it were not for the sex scenes, *Yellow* would probably never have been imported. It is simply too interminably boring, too determinedly insular and, like the sex scenes themselves, finally and fatally passionless."[46]

In terms of the marketplace, *I Am Curious (Yellow)*, like many of the break-through adult films, developed primarily in urban centers, opening first in New York, followed by Washington, Chicago, and Philadelphia.[47] Despite the lengthy legal battle ending with the U.S. Court of Appeals (second only in authority to the Supreme Court), exhibitors feared local raids by police. Costly litigation against Audobon's *Thérèse and Isabelle*, for instance, dampened exhibitor interest in booking *I Am Curious (Yellow)* in Pittsburgh.[48] To alleviate some of these concerns, Grove Press agreed to cover the legal costs of any theaters charged. Grove's lawyer, Edward De Grazia, also was placed as legal representative for these theaters.[49] The rural resistance against adult film became formalized through organizations such as the North Central Association of Theatre Owners (a regional division of the National Association of Theatre Owners). President

Ray Vonderhaar appealed for relief from screen "oversexiness," warning the majors that they would lose the small-town market through organized boycotts by the "rebellious" public.[50] The threat was supported by vigorous attempts on the part of local law enforcement in small towns and in the South in general to curtail the showing of adult cinema: Grove faced huge legal fees defending the rights of the Kimo South Theatre in Overland Park, Kansas, to show *I Am Curious (Yellow)*, and Grove fought the stringent obscenity laws in Atlanta before even attempting to secure a playdate for the film.[51]

While the adult film was becoming a serious economic consideration in the marketplace, the awareness and visibility of the adult feature within this market was negotiated by the industry trade papers, *Boxoffice, Motion Picture Herald*, and *Weekly Variety*. Especially for exhibitors, distributors, and producers outside the large urban centers, these trades represented, and to some extent still represent, a significant "lifeline" connecting them to the changing marketplace. Mirroring the larger battles played out in the arena of the sexual revolution, the trade papers offered a (sometimes warped) characterization of the adult cinema as an economic force. This social aspect was matched by a contradictory agenda within the trades. Being a bastion for studio moviemaking, the trades frequently deplored the adult film that could not become the major focus for studio production. Nevertheless, the commercial opportunities of the adult film, and its partial integration into more mainstream studio fare, were discussed continually throughout articles in the trades during the late 1960s.

In the period 1969 through 1971, initially the adult feature was viewed in terms of contagion. The front-page headline in *Variety* on May 7, 1969, proclaimed, "Italy's New 'Lust Horizon': 25 Films with Lesbo Angles."[52] Suggesting that the foreign art film was "to blame" for the frank sexual content in contemporary films, the writer stressed the lack of support, financial and artistic, that these pictures received in their home countries. Not surprisingly, less than two months later, the same writer proclaimed "Italy's porno pix crackdown" from government leaders, political parties, and, of course, the Vatican.[53] The Italian scenario was replicated with *Variety*'s continuing reports on the degradation of New York's 42nd Street in the late 1960s. Clearly invoked as a metaphor for the rising wave of sexploitation across large cities in North America, the articles foregrounded, to use the trades' terms, "pornos-winos-homos" and their unrestrained dominance of the formerly grand theater district.[54] Evidencing a simultaneous repulsion for and fascination with the trend, *Variety* writers balanced pleas for greater police crackdowns on "winos" and "homos" with descriptions of how to spot prostitutes and the most popular street corners for both prostitutes and porno theaters.

Although this thread of puritanism runs throughout, the trades were also interested in the commercial exploitation of sex in cinema, such as an article describing a barbershop that ran soft-core porn for its customers.[55] Marketing sexploitation also became a focus for the trades because many of the features could not be sold through images in mainstream publications. Describing the most inflammatory of advertising campaigns, *Variety* reported that the Presidio Theater in San Francisco refused even to print the title of the theatre's midnight show in the local newspapers. Ads were constituted by a strong disclaimer that read, in part, "Our underground show tonight at midnight is not recommended for those offended at the grotesque and atrocious sexual behavior characteristic of a sick segment of our society."[56]

The trades also attempted to demystify the new sexual freedom of the adult film for those unfamiliar with the boundaries of the sexual revolution. Amazingly, *Variety* even attempted to define the "genre" of the porno film, suggesting that every porno film contains "1. simulated heterosexual congress, a minimum of two scenes; 2. one lesbian segment; 3. at least one orgy; 4. a violence scene; 5. fellatio and/or cunnilingus."[57] This checklist was followed the next month by a front-page article heralding, "New Sex Aberration Discovered for Pic." Describing the practice of tokenism, *Variety* defined tokenism as "what occurs when a person gets a sexual fixation on an object associated with the human body and thus differs from fetishism which refers to items that are human-oriented."[58]

Dividing the Market: Adult, Soft, and Hard

By the end of the 1960s, the market for adult film had branched into three distinct areas: adult dramas, which incorporated increasingly explicit sex scenes and subject matter; soft-core pornography, which often utilized X as a ratings attraction; and hard-core pornography, which was limited to large cities and linked to hard-core bookstores and strip clubs. Soft-core was distinguished from hard-core by the degree of "realism": soft involved simulated sex, whereas hard included insertion and orgasm shots. Reflecting the increased competition from mainstream cinema, the Presidential Commission on Obscenity and Pornography estimated that adult film receipts dropped 10 to 20 percent from 1969 to

Goodbye, Columbus, 1969.

1970, due, in large part, "to increased competition from sexually oriented motion pictures playing outside the exploitation market."[59] The majors responded to the more liberal climate by aligning themselves with more explicit subjects often made "palatable" by their association with adjoining art forms. Adaptations of Carson McCullers's *Reflections in a Golden Eye,* Philip Roth's *Goodbye, Columbus* and *Portnoy's Complaint,* and John Updike's *Rabbit, Run,* all classified as "serious" fiction, arrived on screen with the trades describing their appearance as an attempt by the major studios "to broaden sexploitation."[60] Distributors Cinema V and Continental continued to buttress their release schedules with adult-oriented dramas—*W.R.: Mysteries of the Organism, Ulysses, Putney Swope, Trash* —containing explicit material, yet firmly within the realm of the art cinema. The combined distribution and exhibition arms of both companies aided these films, which were alternately too strong, esoteric, and foreign for the majors and too arty and serious for the porn market.

By 1970, porno films also split into soft-core and hard-core markets. The shift was precipitated by the emergence of 16mm automated hard-core theaters showing "real" or unsimulated sexual intercourse. Until the end of the 1960s, 16mm was considered primarily a nontheatrical mode of exhibition. The porn market seized on the cheaper alternative of 16mm for production and exhibition, with shorts progressing from silent female striptease to sexual intercourse.[61] The hard-core market developed initially in New York, San Francisco, and Los Angeles, and, with a typical admission price of five dollars, the market proved even more profitable than the soft-core business. As Addison Verrill proclaimed in *Variety,* "1970 is sure to emerge as the year of the hardcore porno explosion, a time when every screen sex barrier crumbled before the onslaught of technically slick pornography."[62] To differentiate their product even further from the soft-core market, hard-core theaters began to integrate live entertainment, live sex shows, as special attractions.[63] New York's Mini-Cinema instituted the policy in 1970, offering eleven live shows daily between the hard-core shorts. Soon after, the 47th and 49th Street Playhouses, the Doll Theatre, and the Paree Theater began to include live entertainment.[64]

On a smaller scale, yet still incredibly lucrative, hard-core homosexual films also became a market presence in New York and Los Angeles. In New York, the Park-Miller Theater on 43rd Street grossed in excess of thirty-thousand dollars per week in the early 1970s, with minimal advertising and exhibition expenditures. For the five-dollar admission fee, audience members watched a mixed program that included shorts, slides, and a dubbed minifeature, such as *Truckers—Men of the Road.*[65] As with heterosexual hard-core, live entertainment was added at certain venues to bolster grosses; for instance, the Adonis Theater in New York alternated live go-go boys with hard-core shorts, and the Jewel Theater in the East Village programmed gay hard-core shorts in the daytime and added a live performance piece, *Section 8,* about gay activities in the armed forces, as the only nighttime attraction.[66]

In terms of market structure and organization, the separation of the adult market into three regions—adult, soft, and hard—was enhanced by definite institutional differences between the segments. Whereas adult-oriented material was primarily the domain of the studios, soft- and hard-core were marked for independents through several factors: exhibition (with theaters playing X-rated films solely), pricing (with the higher ticket price for porno theaters), and, despite the intentions of the MPAA, the X rating. With the split of the sexploitation market in 1970, the exhibition house, technology, and additional live entertainment effectively divided hard-core from soft-core through institutional and industrial forces, apart from the differences in explicit sexual content. Consequently, the separation of the market into adult, soft, and hard must be understood not just in terms of cinematic sexual freedom, but also as aided by crucial structural factors within the overall marketplace that subdivided the market into three distinct segments.

Soft-core pornographers such as Radley Metzger and Jay Feinberg became united against hard-core through the Adult Film Association of America (AFAA), a group of producers, distributors, and exhibitors of adult films.[67] The association formed in 1969 to unify soft-core interests against conservative forces by enforcing nonadmittance to minors and complying with antiobscenity laws. The AFAA faced a difficult position with the hard-core producers: although most soft-core industry members advocated free expression for adult material, their own market was being consumed by hard-core producers who were purveying not only explicit sex (insertion shots and unsimulated intercourse), but also subjects, such as bestiality, untouched by the soft-core producers. Radley Metzger, of Audubon Films, one of the most financially successful soft-core distributors of the mid-1960s, claimed that the audience for hard-core simply grew from the soft-core market, although he differentiated hard from soft in terms of erotic appeal: "Part of one's filmgoing should certainly include hard-core pornography, when it's done reasonably well. But I think hard-core is designed less to turn you on and more to shock."[68]

The hard-core market did erode the soft-core audience, as evidenced by the demise of several of the largest soft-core distributors by the early 1970s. Jerry Gross's Cinemation Industries illustrates the difficulty experienced by soft-core distributors after the rise of hard-core film. Formed in 1965, Cinemation relied on a mixture of in-house products and negative pickups for its distribution schedule. Touting the youth of president Gross, the company stressed quick production decisions, low budgets, and artistic freedom for its filmmakers; one press release claimed, "Old line executives, sitting in their Ivory Towers, aloof and far removed from their audiences are ill-equipped to make instantaneous decisions."[69] Although Cinemation handled distribution for the art house company Rizzoli (reissues of *Red Desert*, *Juliet of the Spirits*, and *Baby Doll*, among others), the majority of the release schedule comprised soft-core product emphasizing sex and exploitable, sensationalistic subjects: *Fanny Hill* ("new . . . and from Sweden"), *Teenage Mother* (She did her homework in parked cars!), *God's Little Acre* (See how they live! Their kind of kinship means anything goes!), and *Mondo Cane* nos. 1 and 2 (The "with-it" sex highs! Naked witchcraft murders! See priests on fire!). By 1970, with Gross commenting that "the sexploitation film is definitely on the decline," the company shifted toward other forms of marginalized cinema.[70] With this strategy, Cinemation realized its greatest success in 1971 with Melvin Van Peebles's *Sweet Sweetback's Baadasssss Song*, a classic of black cinema.[71] By the mid-1970s, however, Cinemation's release schedule lost focus, ranging from X-rated cartoons (*Fritz the Cat*) to horror (*I Drink Your Blood*), true-life melodramas (*Abduction*, the Patty Hearst story), and a shift to a more heavily art house–type schedule (*Stavisky, Turkish Delight*, and *La Trompe d'Oeil*). In 1975, Cinemation filed for bankruptcy, and a year later its assets were auctioned; Cinemation's rights to several films, such as Dalton Trumbo's 1971 antiwar drama *Johnny Got His Gun*, were sold for an average price of only nine hundred dollars each.[72] By the end of the decade, Gross returned, under the guise of the Jerry Gross Organization, focused on the post-*Halloween* horror craze through films such as *Blood Beach, Zombie*, and *The Boogeyman*.[73]

One of the most significant commercial successes of hard-core, *Deep Throat* (1972), also illustrates the limits of the hard-core market's shifting into a more mainstream commercial context. With a capsule review from *Variety* stating, "Hardcore hetero sex feature with humor a plus. Tops in the current market," the film initially benefited commercially from a rave review in *Screw* magazine.[74] *Deep Throat*'s opening week at the New Mature World Theatre in Manhattan broke box-office records for an adult feature: $30,033 for the single house.[75] Within nine months, the film had grossed $1.2 million at its initial engagement.[76] This success was replicated in many markets across the country; obscenity cases against the film furthered box-office receipts in some areas and scared potential exhibitors in others.

In New York, Mayor John V. Lindsay's antismut campaign took hold, and the film was seized late in its run at the World Theatre. New York Criminal Court Judge Joel Tyler found the exhibitors guilty on charges of promoting obscenity. Tyler's twenty-nine-page decision discusses in detail the graphic depictions in the film, often almost in lurid tones:

> The camera angle, emphasis and closeup zooms were directed toward a maximum exposure of the genitalia during the gymnastics, gyrations, bobbing, trundling, surging, ebb and flowing, eddying, moaning, groaning and sighing, all with ebullience and gusto. There were

so many and varied forms of sexual activity one would tend to lose count of them. However, the news reporters counted seven separate acts of fellatio and four of cunnilingus.[77]

With the print seized from the theatre and the financial records of the exhibitor impounded, the World Theatre changed its marquee to read "Judge Cuts Throat, World Mourns."[78]

Legal injunctions also interrupted, or in some cases eliminated, runs of *Deep Throat* in Baltimore, Beverly Hills, Memphis, Atlanta, San Antonio, St. Paul, Ft. Worth, Boston, and Houston. Defendants claimed protection of the First Amendment right to freedom of expression, whereas prosecutors, following two different interpretations of obscenity, argued either that the film had "no redeeming social value" or that it was obscene under "local community standards." The latter charge proved thorniest for both sides, with much debate over what constituted "the community" for legal purposes. As Justice John Paul Stevens claimed regarding the trial in eastern Kentucky: "What is the purpose of defining the community? Should it be the economic market of a film's distribution area or a frame of reference for the jurors?"[79] In this specific instance, the community might have been formed by eastern Kentucky, the greater Cincinnati area, or some other geographic region made up of the two. The community standard question led to some curious situations in the *Deep Throat* case; for example, at the same time the film was restricted from Manhattan, a jury in the New York suburb of Binghamton found the film not to be obscene.[80] One exhibitor suggested bus trips from the "more conservative" Times Square to Binghamton for frustrated Manhattan moviegoers.

As *Deep Throat* was the first hard-core feature to attract nationwide attention, it also garnered a large share of interest from authorities. Consequently, despite its reputation, *Deep Throat* actually grossed less than Gerard Damiano's follow-up, *The Devil in Miss Jones*. Amazingly, *Miss Jones* ($7.7 million) ranked as the seventh-largest grosser of 1973, sandwiched between the James Bond film *Live and Let Die* and Peter Bogdanovich's *Paper Moon*. In comparison, *Deep Throat* ($4.6 million) was ranked slightly lower, in eleventh position, between *Deliverance* and *Sleuth*. Following the litigation over *Deep Throat*, however, the attraction of hard-core became more limited in the industry. Particularly noteworthy in terms of a deterrent was Judge Tyler's move to fine the defendants twice the actual gross of *Deep Throat* at the World Theatre, a figure slightly greater than $2 million.[81] In terms of prosecution, authorities shifted from theater employees (cashiers, doormen, projectionists, salaried theater managers) to prosecuting the owners of the hard-core theaters. This move was sufficient to convince some to shift their focus from hard-core to soft-core and to limit the encroachment of hard-core material into the suburbs.

The hard-core market was further undermined by the U.S. Supreme Court's June 21, 1973, decision for "local option" of pornography; in effect, the Court relinquished power over deciding on obscene media to the individual states and localities.[82] Free-speech proponents feared that this move would lead to broader censorship, far beyond hard-core, which had already come under fire. As an example, industry analysts pointed to the *Miller v. California* decision in 1973, in which Justice Burger gave the following as an acceptable definition of obscenity for state law: "patently offensive representations or descriptions of sexual acts, normal or perverted, actual or simulated."[83] Because it included the word *simulated*, this definition opened the possibility for prosecution of soft-core material in which sex acts appear without shots of actual penetration and orgasm. The implications for the porno market were far-reaching—suddenly producers and distributors of both hard- and soft-core feared that their market faced erosion through possible prosecution on a market-by-market basis across the country. As producer Max Stein pleaded to a Supreme Court spokesman, "At least at the onset of Prohibition, one knew that in six months you couldn't sell liquor. But with this nobody knows what you will or won't be able to portray on screen. Can I show a bikini? a navel? What words can I use?"[84]

Although litigation dampened interest in hard-core, the presence of more upscale, "quality" fare, such as *Deep Throat*, actually polarized the hard-core market further. Indeed, while *Deep Throat* earned box-office success, smaller hard-core theaters suffered through a lack of product and a suddenly more discerning hard-core audience. As Addison Verrill reported in *Variety*, in an article headlined "N.Y. Porno Finds Own Level: Selective Buffs Seek 'Quality,'" a 1972 product shortage of feature-length hard-core features forced New York theaters to program hard-core shorts, often on a "sub-sub-run basis."[85] The situation resulted from several factors, including exhibitor disdain for patronage ("They'll sit through anything, even if they've seen it before") and distributors' repackaging old films with new titles. Some hard-core distributors were charged with selling films as "a New York first run" to several theaters in Manhattan under different titles. Gay porno theaters replicated the straight market—a product shortage, few high-quality items—with even the most famous gay hard-core theater, the Park-Miller, reduced to playing a double-bill revival (of *The Right Boy for Peter* and *The Case of the Hooded Man*).[86]

As with most potential threats to the mainstream industry, pornography also was assimilated by the majors. Although content was limited to the arena of soft-core, major studios began to integrate increasingly explicit material. Several films were significant in this regard. After its success with *Midnight Cowboy*, United Artists released Bernardo Bertolucci's *Last Tango in Paris*. The film was also rated X, and it generated much press not only because of its rating but because of its concentration on sexuality and the match of subject matter with an icon from the 1950s. The art house/foreign origins were made more accessible given Marlon Brando's status as American star—the mix of the domestic and the imported framed *Last Tango* as a different breed of adult film. United Artists

Midnight Cowboy, 1969.

maximized this in its advertising—most notoriously through a two-page ad in the *New York Times* that reprinted, in full, Pauline Kael's ecstatic review of the film.[87] Kael claimed that the showing of *Last Tango* at the New York Film Festival represented "a landmark in movie history," and the reprinting of her rapturous comments must be viewed as an attempt by United Artists to broaden the dialogue around the film to include artistic triumph, to encourage discussion of the film other than that based solely around its sex scenes. The accumulation of this evidence—that is, the American star, the talented young foreign director (making his first film since *The Conformist*), an uncompromising vision of sexuality, and the critical acclaim—suggested that perhaps an X rating could signify more than explicit sex scenes. Regardless, the film faced obscenity charges in different areas, although critical accolades and studio legal powers mitigated the charges. Court battles ensued in many markets (Radford, Winnipeg, Lubbock, Shreveport, Atlanta, Toledo, Montgomery, Cincinnati), but United Artists attorney Gerald Phillips countered all allegations with positive results: "Everywhere we were threatened, we brought an action and were successful."[88]

Whereas Bertolucci's film retained a vestige of prestige and serious purpose, Just Jaeckin's *Emmanuelle*, released in North America by Columbia Pictures, could only be described as soft-core porn, pure and simple. Indeed, *Emmanuelle*'s entry into the market, sponsored by a large studio, indicated how comfortable the majors had become with soft-core by 1974. The case of *Emmanuelle* illustrates how the majors' involvement with soft-core was mediated by an attempt to differentiate their product from other forms of pornography. Columbia president David Begelman was attracted to *Emmanuelle* by its audience composition in Paris: as he recounted, "The line outside the theater was made up of about 75 to 80% women. We would have had no interest in the film if its appeal was totally to men. Then it could be taken as pornographic."[89] Begelman and former Young & Rubicam president Steve Frankfurt devised an ad campaign for the North American release centered on the catchphrase "X was never like this." In effect, through the line and the film's European origin, Columbia was able to separate the film from other adult product while still reaping all the commercial benefits of the X rating. In addition, the campaign operated through ambiguity: If X was never like this, Columbia merely implied that *Emmanuelle* was different somehow—but how? That was left to the imagination of the individual moviegoer—to some the phrase could have indicated that *Emmanuelle* was even more graphic in its content than previous X pictures; to others the phrase could have implied that *Emmanuelle* was more artistic or sophisticated than other X pictures.

In large markets, the full text of Columbia's ad campaign helped to demonstrate just how committed the company was to this reorientation of the X rating: the complete ad copy began, "X has never been known for its elegance. Or for its beautiful people. Or for its intelligent story line. X has been known for other things. At Columbia Pictures we're proud to bring you a movie that will change the meaning of X. A movie that begins with the sensual and takes it places X has never been before." The ad continued to position the film as erotica and as a lifestyle alternative to hard-core pornography, suggesting that this X caused no guilt and stimulated the mind, "the most sensual part of your body." Matched to the omnipresent ad line and the film's logo of the title leading to an apple with a woman's head, *Emmanuelle*'s slick ad campaign seems most in line with the blockbuster films of the same decade. Suddenly soft-core porn was being sold through a saturation ad campaign and simple, graphically bold designs that established a visual presence for the film on a repeated basis. In terms of the marketplace, this move also polarized the adult market into just two segments: hard-core films and mainstream studio movies integrating soft-core material. The strategy of redefining the X rating was integral to Columbia's and the other majors' attempts to mine the adult audience while simultaneously separating themselves from the hard-core market.

With hard-core diminished by litigation and the fear of litigation and soft-core integrated into the mainstream through the label of erotica rather than porn, the adult feature ceased to be a major presence in theatrical release for the independents. The period from the late 1960s through the mid-1970s therefore occupies a unique position in film history: it is an era in which institutional and economic forces acting within a larger social context configured a market that was not immediately served by the major studios and thus became a focus for independent production. As the market developed, its fragmentation into adult, soft, and hard diminished the impact of independent companies and increased the majors' presence in the adult marketplace. Although the theatrical market for hard-core never reached the same level of visibility, both soft- and hard-core were rejuvenated by another shift in the market that was just becoming apparent by the mid-1970s: home video.

Notes

My thanks to Eric Schaefer, Hilary Radner, and Tom Schatz for comments on an earlier version of this essay.

1. "Pix Must 'Broaden Market,'" *Variety*, March 20, 1968, 1.
2. Quoted in Lee Beaupre, "Pic Biz Booby-Trap: 'Youth,'" *Variety*, July 31, 1968, 62.
3. Tino Balio, *Hollywood in the Age of Television* (Boston: Unwin Hyman, 1990), 259–62; Robert J. Landry, "To Be 'Youthful' Not Enuf," *Variety*, November 19, 1969, 5.
4. Abel Green, "B.O. Dictatorship by Youth," *Variety*, January 7, 1970, 38.
5. Beaupre, "Pic Biz Booby-Trap," 62.
6. The issues addressed by Beaupre, ibid., are also considered by Robert J. Landry, "Generation-Bridging Pics," *Variety*, July 17, 1968, 8.
7. See, for instance, Addison Verrill, "Youth Angles Can Drop Dead," *Variety*, July 21, 1971, 5; Abel Green, "Over-25 Audience Dormant, Not Dead," *Variety*, December 24, 1969, 1.
8. Stuart Byron, "Way-Out Attire and Hippie Haircuts Common with European Film Folk," *Variety*, September 4, 1968, 2; "Hippies Admittable If They Don't Reek," *Variety*, May 1, 1968, 19.
9. William Masters, quoted in "Sex as a Spectator Sport," *Time*, July 11, 1969, 61.
10. Vance Packard, *The Sexual Wilderness: The Contemporary Upheaval in Male-Female Relationships* (New York: David McKay, 1968); "Ah, Wilderness," *Time*, August 16, 1968, 52.
11. Vincent Canby, "Ratings to Bar Some Films to Children," *New York Times*, October 8, 1968, 1.
12. "MPAA Code Wants Catholic Support," *Variety*, August 17, 1966, 3.
13. "X Marks the Spot (Self-Interest)," *Variety*, April 28, 1969, 3.
14. "'Classification' by Indies?" *Variety*, August 31, 1966, 7.
15. "MPAA's New Code & Ratings Rules," *Variety*, October 9, 1968, 4.
16. Ibid.
17. "'Ratings' an All-Things Thing," *Variety*, September 18, 1968, 5.
18. "39 Pix 'Rated,'" *Variety*, October 23, 1968, 1.
19. "Critics Are Useful Sometimes; Paramount Cites Its Reviews on If; Hope to Erase That X," *Variety*, March 26, 1969, 3.
20. Stuart Byron, "Though Unintended, 'X' Still Is Taken as 'Dirty' or 'Shoddy'; This Condition a Poser for Valenti," *Variety*, February 26, 1969, 7.
21. "Reade Sez Self-Applied X Ratings Dangerous; Brands Code a 'Failure,'" *Variety*, November 12, 1969, 6.
22. "MPAA Ratings to Now: G(43), M(29), R(22); Puzzle: X for 'Birds' but R for 'The Fox,'" *Variety*, December 4, 1968, 18.
23. Robert B. Frederick, "'Young NATO' Group Advises MPAA's 'G' Rating Be Purified in Sex, Gab," *Variety*, November 19, 1969, 22.

24. "MPAA Film Ratings: 1968–81," *Variety*, November 11, 1981, 36.

25. "By Default," *Variety*, June 26, 1968, 16.

26. Stephen Farber and Estelle Changas, "Putting the Hex on 'R' and 'X,'" *New York Times*, April 9, 1972, sec. 2, 1.

27. Ibid., sec. 2, 15.

28. "X Marks the Spot," 3.

29. "Burden on the Censor," *Newsweek*, March 29, 1965, 88.

30. For example, in the case of *Viva Maria!* the Supreme Court ruled against the city (Dallas) on the grounds that the classification guidelines were too vague. Canby, "Ratings to Bar Some Films," 14.

31. "Power of Local Condemning," *Variety*, November 20, 1968, 7.

32. Robert J. Landry, "Up the Underground Film," *Variety*, November 18, 1970, 7; Jack Kroll, "Up from Underground," *Newsweek*, February 13, 1967, 117–19.

33. Jeffrey K. Ruoff, "Home Movies of the Avant-Garde: Jonas Mekas and the New York Art World," *Cinema Journal* 30 (spring 1991): 24.

34. Vincent Canby, "Offbeat Movies Get Selling Unit," *New York Times*, March 30, 1966, 36.

35. "'Film Underground' Would Air Wares in 100 Outlets; Only 12 in US Now," *Variety*, April 27, 1966, 17.

36. Rosalyn Regelson, "Where Are 'The Chelsea Girls' Taking Us?" *New York Times*, September 24, 1967, sec. 2, 15.

37. See Douglas Gomery, "Ethnic Theatres and Art Cinema," in *Shared Pleasures: A History of Movie Presentation in the United States* (Madison: University of Wisconsin Press, 1992), 171–96.

38. *Trash* even established a new record for opening-day gross ($3,565) at Cinema II in New York, and *Putney Swope* more than doubled its opening week's gross (from $6,110 to $14,004) in its eighth week in Cleveland (hardly a bastion of independent cinema).

39. "Art of Light & Lunacy: The New Underground Films," *Time*, February 17, 1967, 94.

40. For a history of the exploitation film in the 1930s and the various institutional and industrial factors bolstering these films, consult Eric Schaefer, "Resisting Refinement: the Exploitation Film and Self-Censorship," *Film History* 6 (autumn 1994): 293–313.

41. "From Nearly to Total Nude Pix," *Variety*, October 2, 1968, 1.

42. "'Curious': Sexy-Dull Shocker," *Variety*, March 19, 1969, 7.

43. Kent E. Carroll, "Some Fear to Be 'Curious,'" *Variety*, April 9, 1969, 5.

44. "Sex Dominates B'way First-Runs," *Variety*, March 19, 1969, 9.

45. Leonard Gross, "After Nudity, What, Indeed?" *Look*, April 29, 1969, 80–81.

46. "Dubious Yellow," *Time*, March 14, 1969, 98.

47. Carroll, "Some Fear to Be 'Curious,'" 5.

48. "Pittsburgh's Yellow," *Variety*, April 9, 1969, 5.

49. "Grove's Rosset: All Censors Wrong, Valenti Is Encouraging Vigilantes," *Variety*, September 17, 1969, 25.

50. "Fed Up With Sex Complaint," *Variety*, April 5, 1967, 13.
51. "'Grove Press Running the Show'; Convoluted Legalistics in Kansas," *Variety*, September 3, 1969, 20. Grove's concerns about Atlanta were fueled by the experience Sherpix had in distributing Andy Warhol's *Lonesome Cowboys*, in which the Atlanta print was seized, the manager/projectionist was arrested, and photographs were taken of audience members.
52. Hank Werba, "Italy's New 'Lust Horizon': 25 films with Lesbo Angles," *Variety*, May 7, 1969, 1.
53. Hank Werba, "Italy's Porno Pix Crackdown," *Variety*, June 25, 1969, 7.
54. See, for example, Joe Cohen, "Hookers, Homos, Pornos Unchecked under Civil Rights, in 'Slime Square,'" *Variety*, November 6, 1968, 1; Abel Green, "Porno-Wino-Homo Gulch (42nd Street) May Be Renewed to Match Times Square," *Variety*, August 13, 1969, 1.
55. For instance, see Aubrey Tarbox, "High Brow Novels to Screen: Broaden 'Sexploitation,'" *Variety*, March 12, 1969, 5.
56. "Selling 'Atrocious Sexual Behavior'" *Variety*, April 16, 1969, 22.
57. Kent E. Carroll, "Porno-Hypo Showmanship," *Variety*, August 13, 1969, 7.
58. "New Sex Aberration 'Discovered' for Pic," *Variety*, September 10, 1969, 1.
59. "Porno Study: 600 US Film Sites Comprise Playoff for Sexploitation," *Variety*, October 7, 1970, 7.
60. Aubrey Tarbox, "High Brow Novels to Screen," *Variety*, March 12, 1969, 8.
61. Addison Verrill, "Skinpix Face 'New Dilemma,'" *Variety*, October 21, 1970, 5.
62. Addison Verrill, "Bill Osco, Boy King of L.A. Porno," *Variety*, December 30, 1970, 5.
63. Addison Verrill, "Porno Vaudfilm Strippers," *Variety*, June 23, 1971, 1.
64. Ibid.
65. "N.Y. Gay Film Underground," *Variety*, May 5, 1971, 7.
66. Verrill, "Porno Vaudfilm Strippers," 56.
67. Verrill, "Skinpix Face 'New Dilemma,'" 5.
68. Richard Corliss, "Radley Metzger: Aristocrat of the Erotic," *Film Comment*, January 1973, 27.
69. Cinemation advertisement, "An Open Letter to the Producers of the World," *Variety*, September 12, 1970, 10.
70. "Cinemation to Release 30 to May 1971," *Boxoffice*, September 7, 1970, 4.
71. "Black-Slanted Pic Looms Next at Cinemation," *Variety*, March 27, 1974, 4.
72. "Auction of Cinemation Films; Attorneys First Assert Claims; $900 Average Price per Pic," *Variety*, March 31, 1976, 10.
73. Jim Robbins, "Jerry Gross Org's Blueprint for Tighter Yet Broader Future," *Variety*, January 6, 1982, 4.
74. Review of *Deep Throat*, *Variety*, June 28, 1972, 26.
75. Advertisement for *Deep Throat*, *Variety*, June 28, 1972, 25.

76. Vincent Canby, "What Are We to Make of Deep Throat?" *New York Times*, January 21, 1973, 1, 33.

77. Quoted in "In 'Greatest Money Notice' Ruling, Judge Tyler Cuts 'Deep Throat' Film," *Variety*, March 7, 1973, 6.

78. Addison Verrill, "No-Jury, 10 Day 'Throat' Trial; 'Obscene' Ruling by Judge Tyler Foreshadows Fine of $2,000,000," *Variety*, March 7, 1973, 6.

79. Quoted in "Bork 'Confesses' Error in Kentucky 'Deep Throat' Case," *Variety*, November 3, 1976, 30.

80. Verrill, "No-Jury, 10 Day 'Throat' Trial," 6.

81. Ibid.

82. Addisson Verrill, "Porno Thicket Now Jungle?" *Variety*, June 27, 1973, 5.

83. Quoted in ibid.

84. Quoted in "Hello, Supreme Court? Listen ..." *Variety*, July 4, 1973, 5.

85. Addison Verrill, "N.Y. Porno Finds Own Level: Selective Buffs Seek 'Quality,'" *Variety*, October 18, 1972, 5.

86. "'Quality' Hardcore Is Lacking," *Variety*, July 10, 1974, 22.

87. Advertisement for *Last Tango in Paris*, *New York Times*, December 24, 1972, D5–6.

88. Harlan Jacobson, "Climaxing Many Legal Wins, Tango Returns to Cincy," *Variety*, March 19, 1975, 17.

89. Quoted in "Analyzing Emmanuelle's B.O. Impact on the U.S. Market," *Variety*, May 7, 1975, 56.

Courtesy of Photofest.

A Yippie-Panther Pipe Dream
Rethinking Sex, Race, and the Sexual Revolution
Leerom Medovoi

Talkin' 'bout a Revolution

It is often recognized that during the late 1960s, *revolution* bore both a political and a sexual valence. The term referred not only to New Left ambitions of toppling the state, but also to the countercultural overthrow of traditional sexual mores. Moreover, these two revolutionary aspirations bore some sort of historical relationship to one another that has yet to be adequately explained. We know that political activists talked about "liberating the people," and that in a different but related way, so did hippies and counterculture gurus. One might say, using the terms of Ernesto Laclau and Chantal Mouffe, that the late sixties were marked by the mutual articulation of radical sexual and political discourse, so much so that this "logic of equivalence" briefly achieved between sex and politics remains one of our most compelling historical memories of those years.[1]

Since the late sixties, the project of liberating eros through a sexual revolution has been decisively abandoned in the United States, even among cultural radicals. From the 1970s on, feminists and gay activists have reworked and deepened the politicization of sexuality that began in the late sixties, but have also rejected that earlier moment's grand revolutionary narrative of sex and politics. The continuities and ruptures between this grand sexual political narrative of the late sixties and relatively recent feminist and queer narratives are what interest me here, for several reasons. One rarely considered feature of the revolutionary discourse of the late sixties is the special role that antiracism played in politicizing sexuality. As I will show, the logic of equivalence between sexual and political revolution was established in the late sixties by a thoroughgoing racialization of sexual revolution and a reciprocal sexual radicalization of antiracism. As one might suppose, sex and antiracist politics in the late sixties were brought together through a series of problematic moves. The articulation of sex and politics often treated race as a naturalized category in certain contexts, or as a voluntaristic one in others (more on this paradox later). Moreover, a phallic and heteronormative discourse of libido was the principal means through which sexuality was politicized by male sixties radicals.

Not suprisingly, early gay and feminist activists established their sexual politics on very different theoretical and practical grounds, ones that called into question the blanket "sex-positivity" of the late sixties. This shift was an important one, allowing sexual violence (both rape and gay bashing) to become a key sexual political issue from the seventies onward. In recent years, however, the growing influence of "pro-sex" feminism and "queer" politics has marked a renewed interest in "sex-positive" radicalism. Queer radicals and pro-sex feminists are once again calling for a liberation of desire. Given the patriarchal and heteronormative assumptions of their predecessors, contemporary sex radicals have struggled to disassociate their political project from that of the sixties, so much so that "sexual revolution" has disappeared even as a problematic legacy or reference point for present-day sex theorists.

This evasion is unfortunate for several reasons. If queer theory and pro-sex feminism mark a reinvention of sexual radicalism, it is worth considering how our present-day radical project differs from that of the past, how it has been reworked through the assimilation of the sex-critical insights that intervened in the seventies and eighties. At the same time, it is also worth considering the nature of the continuities between sixties and present-day sex radicalism. What in effect might we salvage from that earlier project and why? This question motivates my interest in the articulation of sex radicalism and antiracism, an aspect of the sixties project that has largely dropped out of contemporary radical theory and practice. Antiracism and sex radicalism, it seems, have largely parted ways since the sixties. To be sure, analogies are often drawn between the political struggles of racial minorities and those of sexual minorities, but these are related on a metaphoric register of similarity rather than through a metonymic relation of contiguity or connection. In this essay I aim to revisit the political project of the late sixties, both to subject it to an ideological critique and to remind us of the links it tried to forge between race and sex, so as to raise the question of whether contemporary radicalism might be able to renew those connections in a different way that might speak to a broad constituency that includes (but is not limited to) women, queers, racial minorities, and youth subcultures.

The project of linking antiracism and sexual radicalism found many local articulations in the late sixties, but in this essay I name it the Yippie-Panther Pipe Dream, after the high-visibility pact between the Black Panther Party and the Yippies, spearheaded by Eldridge Cleaver and Jerry Rubin, respectively. In part, this selection is motivated by the very unlikeliness of the alliance. Cleaver was a promoter of black power and Third World revolutionary unity. Rubin and the other Yippies believed in the transformative power of the counterculture and aimed to forge a revolutionary youth culture based on sex, drugs, and rock and roll. Nevertheless, their projects intersected in important ways. Racial liberation, for Cleaver, included an important sexual component. It is the way that Cleaver approached the sexual aspects of racial positioning under white supremacy, I will argue, that accounts for his fascination with, and affirmation of, the white counterculture and its promise of sexual revolution. For the Yippies, in turn, sexual liberation was a struggle inextricably imbricated in an American racial order that made white supremacy their enemy. The Panthers and the Yippies were ultimately unable to sustain the articulation of their political projects, but for a time at least they were bound together in ways that enabled the coordination of their political work. If their revolutionary rapprochement turned, in Jerry Rubin's own words, into a "pipe dream," it was one with a visionary power that derived from the seeming convergences of late-sixties social turmoil. It also depended, as we shall see, on a heteronormative model of masculinized libido. I want to acknowledge from the outset, therefore, that the affective power behind the Yippie-Panther alliance was at least in part structured by what we might call homopolitical desire (an identification with one another as idealized images for straight masculine political agency). In deconstructing the Panther and Yippie desire for one another, however, I hope to reopen the question of whether and how a reformulated desire to link antiracism and sexual radicalism might serve an emancipatory project at this turn of the century.

Yippie-Panther Pipe Dream

For Eldridge Cleaver, the Yippie-Panther Pipe Dream developed in the years between 1957 and 1966, which he spent in Folsom Prison. First joining the Nation of Islam, then Malcolm X's Organization of Afro-American Unity, Cleaver was

at last released on parole in late 1966. By then, the "sixties" had moved into a turbulent second phase. Beginning with Harlem in 1964 and Watts in 1965, black
inner cities were the scenes of rioting every summer. The southern civil rights
movement led by the Student Nonviolent Coordinating Committee (SNCC),
the Southern Christian Leadership Conference (SCLC), and the Congress of
Racial Equality (CORE) had given way to a black power movement. The Berkeley free speech movement of 1964 had emboldened white student radicals, and
the New Left was growing quickly as it shifted its energies into the burgeoning
struggle against the Vietnam War. And as the "summer of love" commenced in
Haight-Ashbury, the counterculture was expanding rapidly across the country.
Stepping into this strange new landscape, Cleaver moved to Berkeley and joined
the recently founded Black Panther Party of Oakland, where his extensive self-
education and literary talents quickly won him the high-profile party position
of minister of information. When founder Huey Newton went to prison in
October 1967, Cleaver effectively took over the party and built it into the most
controversial revolutionary organization of the decade.

Between about 1965 and 1967, while in Folsom, Cleaver had written a series
of political, cultural, and autobiographical essays that impressed many highly
reputed writers and critics who had read them.[2] With their help, the collection
was published in early 1968 under the title *Soul on Ice*.[3] Almost overnight,
Cleaver's book achieved a reputation as the key intellectual statement of black
power. *Soul on Ice*, appearing at the height of the sixties' political foment, sold
more than a million copies and even became the *New York Times* Book of the
Year.[4] As Rout puts it, "In its day, *Soul on Ice* was considered the '[Little] Red
Book' of the new American Revolution."[5] And Cleaver's numerous public pro-
nouncements as a Panther spokesman, until he fled the country when his parole
was rescinded late in 1968, reinforced his media reputation as an organic intellectual and leader of the youth movement.

I say youth movement rather than simply the black movement because, at the
same time that he became a hero for many young African Americans, Cleaver
also became a hero for many young whites, including nonactivist participants in
the counterculture. In part, this popularity was a straightforward consequence
of the more coalition-minded politics of the Panthers. Unlike more cultural
nationalist figures, such as Stokely Carmichael, H. Rap Brown, and Ron Karenga,
who presided over SNCC, US, and other radical black organizations of the late

sixties, Huey Newton, Bobby Seale, Eldridge Cleaver, and the other Panther leaders promoted a more cross-racial and internationalist revolutionary politics.[6] In
theory if not always in practice, they welcomed alliances with Chicanos, Puerto
Ricans, and even those white children of the "mother country" who wished to
wage a revolutionary struggle in concert with those of colonized Third World
peoples.

Cleaver was at the forefront of promoting such cross-racial alliances with
whites. In his most famous essay to that effect, "The White Race and Its Heroes,"
Cleaver argues that white youth in America had come to abandon their identification with the white father figures of the past and praises them for making what
he perceives as common cause with the global revolt of Third World peoples
against Western imperialism. Rout notes that in an interview published in *Playboy* magazine, Cleaver referred repeatedly to "the 'deep' radicalization of young
whites, his experience with the Peace and Freedom Party having served to reinforce the impression he had had in prison as articulated in 'The White Race and
Its Heroes,' and [he] adds the observation that these new 'John Browns' will form
a 'coalition' with the Panthers, 'the black-national movement.'"[7] These themes
of cross-racial youth solidarity were repeated by Cleaver throughout his career
as a Panther.

The experience that he refers to with the Peace and Freedom Party, however,
reveals a remarkable fact about exactly which whites Cleaver was most interested
in building an alliance with. In 1968, after the newly formed Peace and Freedom
Party had nominated him (over Dick Gregory) as its presidential candidate,
Cleaver outraged those attending the party convention by insisting that they
select as his running mate not one of their own "straight" left-wing politicos, but
Yippie celebrity Jerry Rubin. Cleaver's interest in young white allies consistently
centered not on pure political activists, but rather on politically inclined countercultural types associated with "sex, drugs, and rock and roll." Cleaver, in this
respect, took his affirmation of white youth one step further than any of his
fellow Panthers. In Marty Jezer's words, "Cleaver ... virtually alone among the
Panther leadership, had an interest in hip, white cultural radicalism."[8] For
Cleaver, the white counterculture was perhaps the most important prong in
the revolt of America's young against their racist, paternalistic government.
Already in "The White Race and Its Heroes," Cleaver had stressed that the white
political allies of the black movement represented only the "third stage" in the

developing revolt of white youth. "The fourth [and final] stage, now in its infancy," Cleaver explains,

> is much deeper than single-issue protest. The characteristic of the white rebels which most alarms their elders—the long hair, the new dances, their love for Negro music, their use of marijuana, their mystical attitude toward sex—are all tools of their rebellion. They have turned these tools against the totalitarian fabric of American society—and they mean to change it.[9]

For Cleaver, the Yippies were the vanguard of this development. Yippie, a distinctly late-sixties entity whose founding was announced by Jerry Rubin, Abbie Hoffman, Paul Krassner, Stew Albert, and others early in 1968, was always more of a media fiction than an organization. These were individuals who had tended to work loosely in New Left politics, but as the sixties picked up steam, had grown more and more attracted to the cultural and sexual liberationist promise of the counterculture. Abbie Hoffman, for instance, began his political career doing support work for SNCC in Massachusetts, but after moving to New York City, he joined the hippie scene of the theatrical, anarchistic Diggers in the East Village. Jerry Rubin similarly started out in the 1964 free speech movement in Berkeley, but by 1967 had moved closer to Haight-Ashbury in spirit. By calling themselves Yippies, Hoffman and Rubin hoped to declare themselves the political vanguard of the counterculture, hippies who had a cause. Officially, Marty Jezer explains, they claimed to be "members of YIP, the Youth International Party. The media would take it seriously as an organized political party representing international youth. The kids would get the joke, however, and understand that there was no organization. Yippie meant political action as excitement and fun. Everyone a revolutionary."[10]

Though promulgated as sort of a joke, then, "Yippie" nevertheless had a serious purpose, namely, to use free media publicity as a means of articulating the counterculture with New Left politics, to unite the hippie with the politico into a new revolutionary youth culture. In places like the 1967 march on the Pentagon, in HUAC hearings (where Rubin dressed as an American Revolutionary of 1776), at the New York Stock Exchange (where Hoffman disrupted trade by tossing money down to the market floor), and most infamously outside the 1968 Democratic Party convention in Chicago, the Yippies devoted their energies to staging theatrical media events that would reach American youth and galvanize them as a revolutionary class.[11] To that same end, "Yippie" also yielded what are probably the most famous manifestos of the sixties, Jerry Rubin's *Do It! Scenarios of the Revolution* and Abbie Hoffman's *Revolution for the Hell of It*.[12] Their message was consistent; politics alone would never draw the young together, the Yippies maintained, but sex, pot, and good music—the liberation of desire—by offering a viable revolutionary alternative lifestyle to American puritanism, would.

The Yippies and Eldridge Cleaver, then, both rose to national public prominence at approximately the same moment in 1967 and 1968, and they saw one another as natural allies and kindred spirits. Cleaver, as I mentioned, selected Jerry Rubin as his Peace and Freedom running mate, and also wrote an introduction for Rubin's book, *Do It!* He also attempted to join the Yippies in Chicago, and when this threatened his parole, he sent Bobby Seale in his stead. And in perhaps his most remarkable show of support for the counterculture, Cleaver encouraged the revolutionary wing of SDS, Weather Underground, to bust Timothy Leary out of prison in 1970 and secrete him to his home-in-exile in Algeria. Rubin, in turn, celebrated Cleaver in *Do It!* culminating in a lyrical solidarity chapter titled "We Are All Eldridge Cleaver!" Abbie Hoffman went on a speaking tour with Cleaver. In perhaps the most extreme instance of Yippie identification with Cleaver, John Sinclair founded an organization called the White Panthers.[13] The alliance was made official in 1968 when Cleaver, Rubin, Hoffman, and Stew Albert published a "Yippie Panther Pact: Pipe Dream #2" in the *Berkeley Barb*.[14] Just preceding the pact was an interview with Huey Newton, "Huey on Yippies," in which Newton concurred that the Panthers would support (though not participate in) Yippie street actions because, "in the long run, it's the same revolution." What motivated this curious rapprochement between the Panthers and the Yippies? Why did they believe for a time that their battles were ultimately the same? To answer these questions, we must look carefully at their discursive points of convergence.

Soul on Ice: Between Black Nationalism and Heteronormative Miscegenation

Eldridge Cleaver's *Soul on Ice* is composed of a wide variety of essays, some personal, some philosophical, some historical. Of these, a number of essays near the middle of the book best articulate a proto-Panther Party line on black power; these essays cogently argue that African America is an "internal colony" of the

United States whose history and fate are tied to the larger history of Western imperialism. And given the exuberant political moment in which they were written (the age of Che Guevara, Ho Chi Minh, and Kwame Nkrumah), these essays propose that blacks represent a potential "fifth column" within the United States for the Third World revolt. In "Rallying around the Flag," Cleaver describes the "link between America's undercover support of colonialism abroad and the bondage of the Negro at home,"[15] which leads him in "The Black Man's Stake in Vietnam" to assert the shared interests of black Americans with the independence movements of former colonized peoples around the world, including the Vietcong. Finally, in "Domestic Law and International Order," he analyzes the police and the military as parallel repressive instruments of state power, the first aimed outward toward the globe and the second directed toward the internal colonies of the black ghettos. The open-ended black nationalist politics that emerges out of these essays is consonant with that of the Black Panthers: Third Worldist, anti-imperialist, and leading logically to militant challenges to the occupation by white police forces of black cities such as Oakland.

Even as he advocates the politics of Third World revolutionary nationalism, however, Cleaver sees this politics as inadequate and incomplete. This is most striking in a piece late in the book titled "The Allegory of the Black Eunuchs." In this brief story, the narrator and three of his young revolutionary contemporaries encounter an older black man who they disparagingly call the Infidel or Lazarus, for his failure to have been reborn as a militant rebel. These young radicals, who embody the militant black youth politics expressed in the earlier essays, perceive old Lazarus as an "Uncle Tom," someone they would entirely expect to see "buck dancing or licking the white man's boots."[16] When they confront him for his political cowardice, however, Lazarus confounds them utterly by entering into a deeply discomforting confessional monologue about his personal repugnance for black women, the reciprocal contempt of black women for him, and his craven attraction to white women. To the youngsters' dismay, Lazarus's talk unveils a whole libidinal economy between the races unaccounted for by their tough talk. As Lazarus retorts, "You cats are setting here all puffed up. You think you got a hell of a thing going for yourselves, but you don't really know anything about yourselves, or about your women, or about white people."[17] From the book's overall point of view, Lazarus is absolutely right. The four would-be revolutionaries are in fact the "black eunuchs" of the allegory's title.

Even as militants they risk castration for their inability to confront and thus transcend the sexual matters that Lazarus describes. In many of the essays that precede and follow this one, Cleaver makes it clear that he takes Lazarus's criticism of the "eunuchs" absolutely seriously. Even the title of the book confirms this point. The phrase *soul on ice* changes meanings as one moves through the collection of essays, but one of its most common allusions is to miscegenation as the key to understanding the psychodynamics of American racism. The very first essay in *Soul on Ice* is an autobiographical one in which Cleaver describes his dismaying discovery while in prison that all his life he had been "brainwashed" to find white women more attractive than black women. The essay concludes on a general note, suggesting that "the black man's sick attitude toward the white woman is a revolutionary sickness that keeps him perpetually out of harmony with the system that is oppressing him," and that political change requires this problem to be "brought out into the open, dealt with and resolved."[18]

Where does this "sick attitude" come from, and what is its nature? In many ways, *Soul on Ice* can be read as a sustained investigation into the political roots of this alleged black male desire for white women, culminating in a full theoretical statement that is found in the penultimate essay of the book, "The Primeval Mitosis." Perhaps the best-known essay in *Soul on Ice*, "Mitosis" is an ambitious, deeply idiosyncratic mythonarrative of the psychopolitical relations of race and sex.[19] Cleaver begins the essay by positing in the indeterminate prehistoric past what he calls the originary "primeval mitosis" of the "Unitary [Human] Self" into male and female hemispheres. The subsequent desire of the two hemispheres ever since to reunite in an "Apocalyptic Fusion" represents the natural libidinal source of heterosexuality. A society divided simply and exclusively along this axis of gender, Cleaver suggests, would be a utopian society, because its men and women would each possess what he calls a "Unitary Sexual Image," a coherent masculine or feminine identity constituted on purely heterosexual terms.

The gender asymmetry of Cleaver's heteronormative vision here is entirely on the surface. Cleaver associates masculinity in conventional patriarchal terms with activity and sovereignty, femininity with passivity and submission. It is equally important to note, however, that Cleaver's hypothetical utopia is entirely nonracial, for unlike gender difference, racial difference introduces a snake into the garden. Cleaver assumes a virtually perfect correspondence between class and racial divisions reaching back to the days of slavery, when the division between white and black corresponded to the division between the mental labor of the master and the manual labor of the slave. This master-slave system, Cleaver explains, disrupts the pure gender opposition of utopian human existence:

> The Class Society projects a fragmented sexual image. Each class projects a sexual image coinciding with its class-function in society. And since its class-function will differ from that of other classes, its sexual image will differ also and in the same proportion.... Man as thinker performs an Administrative Function in society. Man as doer performs a Brute Power Function. These two basic functions I symbolize, when they are embodied in living men functioning in society, as the Omnipotent Administrator and the Supermasculine Menial.[20]

In American society, of course, the former position is occupied by the figure of the white man. Although as Omnipotent Administrator he rules the nation, however, the white man pays a price in his "sexual image." As Cleaver explains:

> Weakness, frailty, cowardice, and effeminacy are, among other attributes, associated with the Mind. Strength, brute power, force, virility, and physical beauty are associated with the Body. Thus the upper classes, or Omnipotent Administrators, are perennially associated with physical weakness, decay, underdeveloped bodies, effeminacy, sexual impotence, and frigidity. Virility, strength, and power are associated with the lower classes, the Supermasculine Menials.[21]

By claiming the right to rule through his association with the mind, the white man paradoxically devalues his masculine sexual image in relation to that of the black man, whose resulting signification of the male body includes a claim on the penis and thus masculine sexual virility.

The white woman's sexual image, Cleaver continues, is required to compensate for the white man's effeminacy. As a result, the quadrant of the white woman becomes associated with "ultrafemininity," physical beauty, and weakness. Rounding out Cleaver's foursome is his least-developed figure, namely, the black woman, who labors manually (like the black man) as a domestic for the white woman. For Cleaver, who equates physicality with masculinity, the black woman's status as a manual laborer compromises her femininity, making her an Amazon.

This iconographic narrative of race and gender relations unambiguously assumes heterosexuality as a natural relation of desire. The notion of the "primeval mitosis" is merely a projecting backward for Cleaver of the self-evident libidinal complementarity of man and woman, which derives from a mythic moment in which they were torn asunder. Restoration depends upon the overcoming of unnatural and alienated desires, primarily homosexual, that Cleaver pathologizes as a symptom of the decadent present.

> Each half of the human equation, the male and female hemispheres of the Primeval Sphere, must prepare themselves for the fusion by achieving a Unitary Sexual Image, i.e., a heterosexual identity free from the mutually exclusive, antagonistic, antipodal impediments of homosexuality (the product of the fissure of society into antagonistic classes and a dying culture and civilization alienated from its biology).[22]

Although this narrative quite obviously undergirds Cleaver's polemics against gays—most notoriously in his attack on James Baldwin as a self-hating race traitor—it also shapes his political views on heterosexuality in less self-evident but consequential ways. The effeminacy of the white man in Cleaver's narrative positions the black man as the only genuinely masculine figure under white supremacy. Similarly, the amazonian masculinization of the black woman leaves the white woman as the only truly feminine figure. As a result, Cleaver is left to conclude that the supermasculine black man and the ultrafeminine white woman are "psychic bridegrooms," representing the purest form of heterosexual union.

Although the narrative scenario of "The Primeval Mitosis" thus allows Cleaver to explain the alleged desire of black men for white women, at the level of his black liberationist agenda this miscegenist complementarity poses a deep political dilemma. On the one hand, Cleaver casts the racial oppression of African Americans in terms of the black man's emasculation under white supremacy and presents racial liberation as the reclaiming of black manhood. On the other hand, given how tightly Cleaver binds masculinity to male heterosexual desire for the feminine, that act of reclaiming would seem to correspond to sexual access to white women, and thus to a state of interraciality.

Of course, this is not a satisfactory conclusion for Cleaver. From the first essay of *Soul on Ice* on, Cleaver repeatedly discusses the attraction of black men to white rather than to black women as a sexual sickness, what amounts to a self-loathing racial death wish that needs to be overcome. Cleaver refers to the white woman as an "ogre" who tyrannizes his inner life, thereby threatening black self-assertion. In this vein, *Soul on Ice* moves narratively from illness to health. The introductory essay, "On Becoming," is Cleaver's notorious confession of how his fury with his "sick" attraction led him to seek "revenge" by becoming a bitter rapist of white women:

> Rape was an insurrectionary act. It delighted me that I was defying and trampling upon the white man's law, upon his system of values, and that I was defiling his women—and this point, I believe, was the most satisfying to me because I was very resentful over the historical fact of how the white man had used the black woman. I felt I was getting revenge.[23]

Cleaver is quick to say, however, that he did not feel justified and quickly lost his self-respect in the process. The only answer for black men, it would seem, is to wrest free of racial hatred and find a route back to racial self-respect and love. By the book's final essay, "To All Black Women, from All Black Men," the figure of the black man has cleansed himself of this diseased desire for whiteness and stands ready to reclaim his African bride, who alone can save him by returning his love:

> Let me drink from the river of your love at its source, let the lines of force of your love seize my soul by its core and heal the wound of my Castration, let my convex exile end its haunted Odyssey in your concave essence which receives that it may give. Flower of Africa, it is only through the liberating power of your re-love that my manhood can be redeemed.[24]

Only by romantically reconstituting its heterosexual couple, Cleaver here suggests, can the black race once again reproduce itself and rebuild its nation. The internal African colony in the United States can then begin its quest for self-determination.

Cleaver's master-slave narrative remains the black power movement's most systematic theorization of American race relations, with all of that moment's strengths and weaknesses. On the one hand, it compellingly maps out the cultural logic of white supremacy in the United States, reconstructing the subject positions into which this racial order attempts to interpellate both whites and blacks, men and women. It is particularly effective in specifying the doubled nature of white and black masculinities within this order. White masculinity is represented as simultaneously omnipotent and impotent. Black masculinity, in a similar fashion, is cast as a position of both castration and hypersexualization. These insights derive from Cleaver's attentiveness to the sexual dimension of racial constructions. By and large this doubledness operates through an ideological separation of the realms of politics and sexuality. The former set of positions—white men's omnipotence and black men's castration—is presented as political. The latter set—white men's impotence and black men's hypersexualization—is presented as sexual. According to a white supremacist logic, these sets of positions balance one another out, because white and black men both have their own arenas of virility, and in this way white supremacy is naturalized. Patriarchy, too, is naturalized, because underlying this racial division of labor is a basic association of masculinity with power and agency—political and sexual, respectively.

This, however, brings us to the ideological blind spot of Cleaver's essay as a work of critical theory. Although it persuasively analyzes the interlocking structures of white supremacist and sexual ideology, it does not attain any critical distance from those ideologies. Cleaver does not present these positions as cultural representations, but instead as social truths. These sorts of positions (Omnipotent Administrator, Supermasculine Menial, Ultrafeminine, Amazon), by mobilizing sexual desire, work to interpellate us into white supremacist, patriarchal, and heteronormative relations of race and sexuality. But Cleaver takes these positions not as ideological self-presentations, but as already given truths. White men really are omnipotent but impotent. Black men really are castrated yet hypersexual.

Many black feminist, queer, and revisionist critics have noted in the intervening years since the black power movement the painful trade-off effected by this face-value acceptance of the sexual race narrative. In adopting it as their own, Cleaver and other black power leaders of the sixties granted straight black men a measure of symbolic power as the charismatic figures of phallic masculinity. In simultaneously associating white men with the feminine, as Robyn Wiegman notes, "Black Power rhetoric invert[ed] the representational economy of lynching and castration, articulating the space of the 'real' masculine solely for the black male himself."[25] However, this strategy was costly in different ways for people in various positions. For black women, it meant that the reclaiming of black manhood came before all else in the black liberation struggle, so that black women were placed in the position of proving their political loyalty by assigning priority to the needs of black men. To quote Cleaver's words to all black women again, "It is only through the liberating power of your re-love that my manhood can be redeemed." Black gay men, because they threatened the simple association of black masculinity with hypersexual virility, could be politically stigmatized as decadents, race traitors, or "false" men. One might also contemplate the costs for nonblacks: what it means for white women to be labeled as intrinsically passive and submissive; what it means for white men who do not possess a political position of "omnipotence" to be told that they do; and, finally, how the exhaustive binarism of Cleaver's iconography denies the very existence of racial positions that are neither black nor white: Asian, Latino, or Native American. All these problems arise if Cleaver's "primeval mitosis" narrative is not firmly recognized as white supremacy's representation of the social world rather than the world itself.

Hypermasculinity, moreover, is a potentially costly position for straight black men as well. To begin with, the narrative that enables a self-identification with phallic masculinity is also, as we have seen, premised on the equation of disenfranchisement with emasculation. Within the terms of such a coercive logic, black (and other) men's experiences of powerlessness come to be experienced as a loss of gender identity, which can be deeply painful and destabilizing. Finally, the social context for this subject position remains white supremacy, and as bell hooks has cautioned, "The very images of phallocentric black masculinity that are glorified and celebrated in rap music, videos, and movies are the representations that are evoked when white supremacists seek to gain public acceptance and support for genocidal assault on black men, particularly youth."[26] Hooks does not deny that "contemporary black men have been shaped by these representations," and that the dual positions of castration and supermasculinization might not be deeply embedded in some or even much of black male subjective life. However, she insists that they are only a small part of the story, that they do not "address the complex gender roles that were so familiar to me [growing up with black men]."[27] Kobena Mercer and Isaac Julien have similarly noted that although many black male pop representations, such as those found in some seventies blaxploitation films, operate according to the codes of black machismo, there are others, including the music and self-presentation of many black male performers ranging from Little Richard to Michael Jackson, that disclose "the 'soft side' of black masculinity (and this is the side we like!). As a way forward in black sexual politics, we feel it is important to tap into and recognize these resources of potential change in popular culture, because they reveal that masculinity can be constructed in a diversity of ways."[28] Viewed against the multiple representations that interest Mercer and Julien, it becomes clear that the position of the black man described in Cleaver's "Primeval Mitosis," although influential, even hegemonic, is not the only available one with which black men may identify, and there are powerful political reasons for black men to look elsewhere and try to avoid reproducing the white supremacist trap for black men embodied in the castration/hypersexualization position.

Having already presumed that blacks and whites, men and women, occupy the precise raced and gendered positions dictated in his narrative, however, Cleaver paints himself into a curious political corner. If the model established in "The Primeval Mitosis" is accepted as de facto reality rather than as an ideological apparatus with only a limited power to organize social and cultural reality, then white women become the necessary ultrafeminine counterparts to black men's supermasculinity. As a result, Cleaver's own sexual axioms on what is sexually "natural" end up designating black heterosexuality as less "normal" than miscegenist heterosexuality. Even in Cleaver's concluding homage to the black woman, the voice of the black man hardly speaks of her in the language of erotic desire, but primarily in terms of pride and respect for her as a figure of African maternity, "the sacred womb that cradled primal man, the womb that incubated Ethiopia, and populated Nubia and gave forth Pharaohs unto Egypt, the womb that painted the Congo black and mothered Zulu, the womb of Mero, the womb of the Nile, of the Niger."[29] Though Cleaver means this final essay as an act of reconciliation and healing between black women and black men, who have been separated too long by the divisive power of white supremacy, the tone of the essay is one of respect and filial devotion, not eroticism. Given that Cleaver has disparagingly posited black women throughout *Soul on Ice* as Amazons, black heterosexuality is limited to becoming the sacred realm of racial reproduction; miscegenist heterosexuality remains the carnal realm of sexual desire.[30]

The final essay's lofty tone contrasts interestingly with several personal love letters that also appear in the book, including the book's second, eponymous essay, "Soul on Ice ." The object of Cleaver's affections in these letters is Beverly

Axelrod, the activist/attorney who took up Cleaver's case and won him the parole that gave him his two free years in the political spotlight. Axelrod's racial identity is never broached in the book, a remarkable fact given how centrally *Soul on Ice* concerns itself with the intersection of race and gender in libidinal relations. Axelrod, however, is white, and the evasion of her racial identity is in many ways crucial for an understanding of the sexual politics of Cleaver's book. The essay "Soul on Ice," for instance, comes immediately after the introductory essay, which, as already noted, is principally concerned with the status of the white woman as an "ogre" in the mental life of the black man. How can Cleaver address Axelrod's whiteness alongside his expression of passionate love for her in the wake of the preceding essay? His growing passion for someone who appreciates his personality and charisma and works tirelessly on his behalf to win his freedom from prison would seem entirely understandable. Yet it becomes impossible for Cleaver to admit explicitly that this love letter is in some sense written to the very "ogre" who tyrannized him for so long. The dilemma is itself embodied in the title of the essay, and by extension in the title of the entire book. As I have noted, the phrase "soul on ice " functions in part as a metaphor for "black on white," or miscegenist desire between black men and white women. In this essay, Cleaver seems to use the phrase in a different, more literal way, describing how his soul, in the misery of prison, had been "on ice," frozen in a state of suspended animation, and awaiting the thaw that only romantic passion can bring:

> Yet I may believe that a man whose soul or emotional apparatus had lain dormant in a deadening limbo of desuetude is capable of responding from some great sunken well of his being, as though a potent catalyst had been tossed into a critical mass, when an exciting, lovely, and lovable woman enters the range of his feelings. What a deep, slow, torturous, reluctant, frightened stirring![31]

But given Axelrod's whiteness, Cleaver's literal use of "soul on ice" still evokes miscegenist desire, if only as the passion that will at last free him from the cold. "Soul on ice" thus paradoxically refers to miscegenation as at once racial sickness and heterosexual health. If in the first essay the white woman is an ogre who evokes self-hatred, in the second she is someone whose femininity is revivifying:

> When she first comes to him his heart is empty, a desolate place, a dehydrated oasis, unsolaced, and he's craving womanfood, without

which sustenance the tension of his manhood has unwound and relaxed. He has imperative need of the kindness, sympathy, understanding, and conversation of a woman ... to sniff the primeval fragrance.... Such is the magic of a woman, the female principle of nature which she embodies, and her power to resurrect and revitalize a long-isolated and lonely man.[32]

The cluster of terms Cleaver uses in this love letter, such as "primeval" (foreshadowing his "Primeval Mitosis"), "hunger," or "female principle," in naturalizing the complementary desire of man and woman, reproduces the racial dilemma I noted earlier. The very "normality" Cleaver grants his longing for Beverly Axelrod confirms the inevitable attraction between supermasculine black men and ultrafeminine white women. Cleaver never suggests in this letter that in wanting Axelrod he has succumbed yet again to the "sexual sickness." There is nothing unwholesome or self-hating in his desire for her. On the contrary, Cleaver presents his passion for her as the expression of a healthy appetite for "Apocalyptic Fusion" between Man and Woman. To sum up, there is an insurmountable contradiction between the two versions of miscegenist desire found in the first and second essays of Cleaver's book. In the first it represents a racial sickness; in the second it represents sexual health. Only silence on Beverly Axelrod's whiteness allows *Soul on Ice* to keep its central dilemma at bay.

Pipe-Dream 1:
White Sexual Liberation as Racial Convalescence

At the heart of Cleaver's conflicting account of miscegenist desire lies an ideological contradiction between the nationalism of his racial agenda and the heteronormativity of his sexual agenda. If heterosexuality is primevally "natural," then it is inevitable that black men and white women will and should desire one another, indeed, that their mutual desire should be the purest, strongest, and most natural of sexual desires. If the masculine and feminine that Cleaver sees divided in the "primeval mitosis" must be re-fused, then miscegenation becomes mandatory, and thus, in time, the abolition of racial difference itself; the utopia Cleaver posits, the "Unitary Society," after all, is a raceless human world. On the other hand, if African Americans constitute a colonized nation that aims for self-realization, then the reclaiming of black manhood needs to be consistent with heterosexual loyalty within the nation.[33]

Given the terms Cleaver has set, there is only one possible way for normative heterosexuality to be made compatible with black nationalism: through a dialectical synthesis of master and slave. The white man and woman must be made to identify with their bodies, and the black man and woman must be made to identify with their minds, so as to transcend the binary opposition that uniquely endows black men with supermasculinity and white women with ultrafemininity. Central to Cleaver's discourse of political revolution is this transcendental scenario that can reconcile his racial and sexual politics. And it is a scenario that play out in several significant ways. One important consequence is that Cleaver's views provided a logic by which black men could make a politicized demand on black women to "feminize" themselves in order to ensure that black men would be attracted to them and that the erotic bonds holding the race together could thereby be strengthened. Insofar as Cleaver's views were diffused and shared among men within the black power movement, one could argue that the rise of black feminism in the early 1970s in many ways constituted a response to this sort of patriarchal pressure.[34]

I would like to focus, however, on what this political solution to the sexualization of race implied for Cleaver's relations to whites. Though Cleaver's model locates the black man as a supermasculine menial, it also casts the black man's oppression as a form of psychic emasculation. The black man has been deprived not of his sexual virility, but rather of the mental potency possessed by the white man. As Cleaver explains:

> The chip on the Supermasculine Menial's shoulder is the fact that he has been robbed of his mind. In an uncannily effective manner, the society in which he lives has assumed in its very structure that he, minus a mind, is the embodiment of Brute Power.... The further away from Brute Power his mental productions stand, the more emphatically will they be rejected and scorned by society, and treated as upstart invasions of the realm of the Omnipotent Administrator.... The struggle of his life is for the emancipation of his mind, to receive recognition for the products of his mind, and official recognition of the fact that he has a mind.[35]

The reclaiming of black manhood, therefore, need not be understood as a claiming of the right to desire white women, but rather as a renewal of the ability and right to think, plan, and act. Moreover, if the black man can reclaim his relationship to the mind, in Cleaver's estimation, the black woman, who now perceives him "essentially as only half a man, an incomplete man," will grow attracted to him once again.

This masculine moment in Cleaver's sexual politics, however, also locates the white man in an emasculated position, and in one that is sexual. All mind, the white man is an erotically repressed figure, unable to realize his desire for the femininity of his own woman. If the white man's dissociation with the body manifests itself in effeminacy and impotence, the consequence for the white woman is frigidity, because her man's lack of a masculine sexual image leaves her "cold":

> Her basic fear is frigidity, the state in which her frantic search for Ultrafemininity collides with an icepack death of the soul: where the fire in her body is extinguished by the ice in her mind. The psychic core of her sensuality, the male-seeking pole of her Female Principle, the trigger of the mechanism of her orgasm, moves beyond the reach or range of the effeminate clitoris of her man. Frigid, cold, icy, ice. Arctic. Antarctic. At the end of her flight from her body is a sky-high wall of ice. (If a lesbian is anything she is a frigid woman, a frozen cunt, with a warp and a crack in the wall of her ice.)[36]

Presenting the lesbian as a victim of thwarted heterosexual desire, Cleaver yet again pathologizes the lesbian (as he does gay men) as having lost her natural sex drive. However, it is worth acknowledging that the figure of the lesbian also expresses, in curiously displaced form, the pathos of the author's incarceration. Cleaver, within the logic expressed in his own book title, identifies his own sexual condition with the same frigidity he attributes to the lesbian. Through the terms of his own logic, therefore, the figure of the lesbian becomes Cleaver's imaginary (if unacknowledged) counterpart, freezing with him in his Antarctic exile, cut off from the erotic energy and intimacy for which he longs.

If these two figures (the lesbian and Cleaver himself) become representative of white women and black men cut off from sexuality, the reciprocal heteronormative desire that might be ignited between them is equally problematic as the "ogre" of miscegenation. How then does Cleaver imagine freeing black men from the erotic structure that he feels so tyrannized by? Much of Cleaver's political vision depends upon a restoration of both black and white heterosexuality. Black heterosexuality will be restored when black men, through their politicization, reclaim the right to mental self-determination that will win back black women's respect. The dysfunctionality that Cleaver attributes to white heterosexuality, however, is associated with white men's gender inadequacy. Ironically enough, then, what Cleaver calls "convalescence" for everyone depends in large part upon the white man's remasculinization. If white men can reconnect with their own bodies, and thereby reestablish their physical virility, white women will no longer look to lesbianism, nor to black men, as their "psychic bridegroom."

This scenario I have been describing is no fanciful extrapolation from the ideological categories of *Soul on Ice*'s mythography, but an actual set of politico-sexual strategies that Cleaver both defended and pursued in the late 1960s. Indeed, much of Cleaver's political optimism at that time derived from a conviction that history was fortuitously bearing out just such a transcendental reconciliation between normative heterosexuality and black nationalism. Located between "The Primeval Mitosis," the third-to-last essay in *Soul on Ice*, and the final essay, "From All Black Men, to All Black Women," and functioning as a bridge between them, is "Convalescence," an essay that briefly interprets American social history since the U.S. Supreme Court ruled against racial segregation in schools in *Brown v. Board of Education*. Cleaver, viewing the Court's decision through the lens of his own racial iconography, declares it an attempt to "graft America's head back onto its body, and vice-versa," and he suggests that if he is right, then what has since followed

> should be a record of the convalescence of the nation.... we should be able to see the Omnipotent Administrators and Ultrafeminines grappling with their unfamiliar and alienated Bodies, and the Super-masculine Menials and Amazons attempting to acquire and assert a mind of their own. The record, I think, is clear and unequivocal. The bargain which seems to have been struck is that the whites have had to turn to the blacks for a clue on how to swing with the Body, while the blacks have had to turn to the whites for the secret of the Mind.[37]

Against this ideological backdrop, Cleaver celebrates whites for "rediscovering" their bodies through the rise of rock and roll music and a new sexual ethos, which he perceives as a complement to black claims on the sovereignty of the "mind" through civil rights struggles and uprisings. The counterculture, it turns out, is the primary agent breaking down the racial mind/body split that has stood in the way of black self-determination. In short, for Cleaver it is the "convalescence" of America, which includes first and foremost the spread of countercultural attitudes among whites, and especially white men in need of remasculinization, that will enable "all black men" to speak once again to "all black women."

Pipe Dream 2: Fucking as Freedom Fighting

It is this precise moment in Cleaver's sexual politics—the explicit importance of white (and implicit importance of male) bodily "convalescence"—that made the Yippies such appealing political allies for him. Unlike "straight" New Left groups like SDS or the Mobe, the Yippies made a countercultural and sexual revolution part of their political agenda. Yippie writer and comedian Paul Krassner endorsed the way that "people, particularly young people, are returning to sexuality" and called for a reversal of civilization's monstrous "separation of sexuality from the rest of life."[38] Central to the Yippie project was the reintegration of sexuality and political activity, or, as the popular expression had it, to "live as though 'the Revolution' has already happened." Historian David Farber claims that, of all the figures of the sixties, Yippie fellow traveler John Sinclair wrote

> perhaps the most explicit paean to free love [of anyone] in an "editorial statement" in the Detroit underground paper, the Sun. "Our position," Sinclair intoned, "is that all people must be free to fuck freely, whenever and wherever they want to . . . in bed, on the floor, in the chair, on the streets, in the parks and fields." "Fucking," Sinclair argued, like dope, helps people to "escape the hangups that are drilled into us in this weirdo country."[39]

What was the political program behind this Yippie advocacy of sexual revolution? Abbie Hoffman claims in *Revolution for the Hell of It* that he had "outgrown" the New Left, which had never come to realize the basic political importance of fun:

> I think fun and leisure are great. I don't like the concept of a movement built on sacrifice, dedication, responsibility, anger, frustration, guilt. All those down things. I would say, Look, you want to have more fun, you want to get laid more, you want to turn on with friends, you want an outlet for your creativity, then get out of school, quit your job. Come on out and help build and defend the society you want.[40]

Sexual revolution, then was part of a larger struggle to liberate the pleasure principle in a repressive and militaristic society bent on denying it. Jerry Rubin was even more specific about the political significance of sexual revolution. In his Yippie manifesto *Do It!* he asks rhetorically:

> How can you separate politics from sex? It's all the same thing: Body politic.
>
> POLITICO-SEXUAL REALITY: The naked human body is immoral under Christianity and illegal under Amerikan law. Nudity is called "indecent exposure." Fuck is a dirty word because you have to be naked to do it. Also it's fun. . . .
>
> We're taught that our shit stinks. We're taught to be ashamed of how we came into the world—fucking. We're taught that if we dig balling, we should feel guilty.
>
> We're taught: body pleasure is immoral!
>
> We're really taught to hate ourselves![41]

White "Amerika's" sexual repression, Rubin continues, is the cause of political and military imperialism. Not only did the Yippies therefore resemble Cleaver in causally relating libidinal repression to political oppression, they also routed their racial and Third Worldist politics through a project of sexual remasculin-ization. "Puritanism leads us to Vietnam. Sexual insecurity results in a super-masculinity trip called imperialism. Amerikan foreign policy, especially in Viet-nam, makes no sense except sexually. Amerika has a frustrated penis, trying to drive itself into Vietnam's tiny slit to prove it is The Man."[42] Central to Rubin's position is the implication that the antiwar movement and the civil rights movement attack only the symptoms, not the underlying psychosexual cause of imperialism or racism: "Neither the civil rights movement, the Free Speech Movement or the antiwar movement achieved its stated goals. They led to deeper discoveries—that revolution did not mean the end of the war or the end of racism. Revolution meant the creation of new men and women."[43] This cre-ative process, for Rubin, is the special province of the counterculture. Unlike a social movement, the counterculture gets to the heart of the political matter, because by liberating white sexuality, by freeing pleasure, hippiedom will bring about a total revolution that will end all oppressive social relations.

As is suggested by his reference to imperialism as a "supermasculinity trip," Rubin, remarkably enough, held the prospects for Third World revolution to be dependent not only upon the liberation of white sexuality, but upon the liberation of white male heterosexuality. So, for example, the implicit reference to styles of white masculinity in Rubin's words on the revolutionary impact of long hair: "Long hair is the beginning of our liberation from the sexual oppression that underlies this whole military society. Through long hair we're engaged in a sexual assault that's going to destroy the political-economic structure of American society."[44] The phallic sexual language of Yippie manifestos ("balling") tends to announce both the masculinity of the desiring subject (the baller) and, just as often, the femininity of his object of genital desire. Thus imperialism becomes, for Rubin, the literal displacement of straight white men's frustrated desire to fuck women.

Setting aside any materialist critique of Rubin's libidinalist reductio ad absurdum, Rubin's sexual revolution seems to have lacked any concern with the inhibition of any desires not reducible to Yippie-style "balling," whether ones that might belong to someone else (women, nonwhites, nonstraights) or ones that might be directed differently (gay, nongenital, fetishistic, racial, or even nonsexual). Only phallic male desire, as fulfilled by a counterculture, could count for Rubin as a political blow against racism, imperialism, and the military-industrial complex.

The phallocentric masculinism of Yippie discourse on sexual liberation does not necessarily mean that it did not help create the conditions for the deepening of sexual radicalism. As the Yippies rightly perceived, countercultural styles and sexual practices represented a symbolic (and gradually a material) blow to hegemonic sexual norms in the United States. Their disarticulation of heterosex from the regimes of marriage, coupling, and reproduction in some significant sense made their sexual project nonheteronormative. In celebrating "freaks" against "straights," Yippie sexual discourses and practices in effect popularized a politics of sexual counternormativity that was able to accommodate in subsequent decades a much broader range of sexual "deviations" from the regimes of heteronormativity. Nevertheless, it would be difficult to overestimate the political costs that accompanied the Yippie privileging of straight white male desire. By defining their project in this way, the Yippies played into a powerful misogynist tradition of male sexual revolt in which women who did not "put out" were held accountable as inhibitors (and hence domesticators) of men. This tradition, ironically enough, given Yippie opposition to the Vietnam War, has deep roots in imperial narratives of adventure and "going native." It tended to fetish-ize male orgasm in the spirit of Wilhelm Reich and Norman Mailer, converged (as Barbara Ehrenreich has shown) in such 1950s phenomena as *Playboy* and the beats, and, finally, in the counterculture itself, clearly worked to coerce women into undesired sexual acts and relations.[45] Whether one does or does not want to struggle in some "last instance" for the liberation of as much desire as socially possible, it seems clear that the ideological privileging of straight white male desire effectively reconstituted in new terms the normativity of a phallic mas-culinist sexuality even as it subverted the regimes of marriage and reproduction.

Prevailing views that the style of countercultural masculinity was peaceful, sexually open, and "soft" belie the need for this critique of Yippie sexual politics. Superficially, for instance, Rubin's critique of aggressive masculinity might seem very different from Cleaver's comparatively macho rhetoric of militancy. The Yippies tended to cast the sexual liberation of white men as a release from a supermasculinity trip rather than, in Cleaver's fashion, as a release from effemi-nacy. But on closer inspection, these two polemics diverge only minimally. Rubin implicitly juxtaposes two models of masculinity, one of a man comfort-able with his body who "likes to ball," and the other of a man who fears sex and compensates by attempting to rule and control others. The latter is very much in keeping with Cleaver's powerful yet sexually insecure "Omnipotent Administrator," whereas the former would seem to be more or less what Cleaver hoped white men would become through the process of "convalescence." More-over, the Yippie presentation of sex, drugs, and rock and roll as cultural weapons is itself suggestive of a certain displacement of male violence that was not lost on the Panthers. As Huey Newton explained in "Huey on Yippies," "Fighting back changes the way blacks think of white rebels. Their original bias is to think of long haired people as being effeminate."[46] Despite the apparent divergences in their rhetoric of masculinity, then, the Yippies still enacted for the Panthers the appropriate role of the white man in a drama of "racial convalescence." Likewise, the Yippies enjoyed the Panthers' endorsement as a political justification for more (but necessarily heteronormative) sex in the counterculture.

In so doing, the Yippies celebrated Eldridge Cleaver as the premier black liberationist who perceived the importance of sex, drugs, and rock and roll for revolutionizing race relations. In the section of *Do It!* titled "Yippie-Panther Pipe Dream No. 2," Rubin acclaims the prophetic powers of *Soul on Ice:*

Eldridge's vision was coming true: young whites rejecting white society. "White" was a state of mind. Hippies were seeking a new identity. Young whites were blowing middle-class Amerika out of their minds and bodies with drugs, sex, music, freedom, living on the streets. They were filling the jails. They were not in the revolution merely to "support" blacks, but were dropouts of white society fighting for their own freedom.[47]

As the Yippies rightly recognized, Cleaver, in placing enormous weight on the need for whites to reconnect with their bodies, had turned the countercultural cry for sexual liberation into a racial issue. Cleaver himself had said (according to Rubin), "The cultural revolution in the white community is to the left of the political left in the white community," presumably because the sexual liberation of straight white men was a deep blow against the repressive underpinnings of white supremacy.[48]

The Yippie articulation of sex and race, however, went one step further than that embraced by Cleaver. Central to the Yippies' effort to politicize the counterculture was their striking assumption that hippiedom was in some significant cultural sense no longer even white. This idea is stated unequivocally in the same section of Jerry Rubin's book cited earlier, where he declared that "long hair is the beginning of our liberation from ... sexual oppression." Rubin uses this section of his book, actually titled "Long Hair, Aunt Sadie, Is a Communist Plot," to stage an imaginary dialogue between himself and his aunt, who, though the communist "black sheep" of his family, is nonetheless distressed by her nephew's hippie appearance. Rubin tries to persuade Aunt Sadie that long hair is accomplishing the very political work she has always promoted:

> Aunt Sadie, long hair is a commie plot! Long hair gets people uptight—more uptight than ideology, cause long hair is communication. We are a new minority group, a nationwide community of longhairs, a new identity, new loyalties. We longhairs recognize each other as brothers on the street.
>
> Young Kids identify short hair with authority, discipline, unhappiness, boredom, rigidity, hatred of life—and long hair with letting go, letting your hair down, being free, being open.
>
> Our strategy is to steal the children of the bourgeoisie right away from the parents.[49]

So far, Rubin appears to be playing out Cleaver's scenario almost to a tee. Longhairs are the new, liberated, in-touch-with-their-bodies white children who have shifted their loyalties away from their elders and toward their colored generational peers. But Rubin enters uncharted territory in the next paragraph: "Aunt Sadie, *long hair is our black skin*. Long hair turns white middle-class youth into niggers. Amerika is a different country when you have long hair. We're outcasts. We, the children of the white middle class, feel like Indians, Vietnamese, the outsiders in Amerikan history.[50] Central to the Yippie creed is the belief that to become a hippie is in effect to become racially oppressed. Like a racial minority, the longhairs are physically marked, instantly recognizable, and thus themselves targets of white supremacy. Indeed, the very word *Yippie* contains the idea that the hippie, a peaceful, apolitical figure, is unsustainable because adult whites will eventually crack his head, and thereby politicize him. After his announcement in *Do It!* that "Eldridge's vision was coming true: young whites rejecting white society," Rubin goes on to write:

> They [young whites] were not in the revolution merely to "support" blacks but were dropouts of white society fighting for their own freedom.
> Eldridge wanted an alliance between bad blacks and bad whites. Criminals of all colors unite.
> Brotherhood through common struggle and oppression.
> Equality-under-the-pigs.
> Black-white unity becomes a real thing only when whites are treated like blacks.[51]

Hippies, maintained the Yippies, were coming to share racial oppression. They too would therefore become political victims of "Amerika." When they began to fight the "pigs" on their own behalf, hippies by definition would become Yippies.[52]

This argument of Rubin's was typical of the Yippies. Abbie Hoffman had made much the same argument as early as September 1967, even before the birth of Yippie. According to biographer Marty Jezer, after the police had arrested a black dope smoker in the East Village, Hoffman headed for the local police house and made a symbolic statement of "hippie-black solidarity" by trashing the station. He then followed up this action in print: "'Digger is Niggery,' he wrote in an article for the underground press. 'On the Lower East Side pot is an effective prop, it is the least common denominator. It makes us all outlaws, brothers, nig-gers.'"[53] In his bestselling *Revolution for the Hell of It*, Hoffman titled a middle section "The New Niggers," meaning of course the Yippies. In one chapter, "The White Niggers," Hoffman echoes Rubin, asking: "You want to get a glimpse of what it feels like to be a nigger? Let your hair grow long. Longhairs, that new minority, are getting the crap kicked out of them by cops all over the country, and with the beatings and jailings comes the destruction of flower power."[54] The next chapter, "Runaways: The Slave Revolt," makes even stronger claims on blackness: "Runaways are the backbone of the youth revolution. We are all run-aways, age is irrelevant. A fifteen-year-old kid who takes off from the middle-class American life is an escaped slave crossing the Mason-Dixon line."[55] Today, Hoffman's claim reads like a satire of countercultural fantasies. Given that middle-class white youth who became hippies in the sixties possessed no history of "slavery" or even "niggery," why would one expect their experiences of abuse or victimization to minoritize them? Did a beating lead to politicization and interracial solidarity, as the Yippies assumed? Or did it lead instead, as Rubin or Hoffman might have joked, to a haircut? To be sure, hippies did physically "mark" their bodies as "other," and thereby placed themselves in moments of physical danger. But the newness, voluntarism, and reversibility of such mark-ings all worked to give the hippies' countercultural identification a more super-ficial identitarian meaning, a fact studiously avoided by the Yippies.

Moreover, the largely voluntaristic quality of "hippie" as subcultural affilia-tion raises the question of why the Yippies presumed that long hair and the other accoutrements of the hippie body would acquire a specifically racial (rather than, say, subcultural) meaning. Although the critical literature on race is wracked by numerous disagreements, one way that race has been theoretically differentiated from other representations of human difference is through the consideration of how its codes signify biologistic criteria of human descent. In their influential analysis of the "racial formation," for example, Michael Omi and Howard Winant provisionally define race as a historically evolving semiotic system that "signifies and symbolizes social conflicts and interests by referring to different types of human bodies" through the invocation of "biologically based human characteristics."[56] Though both long hair and black skin constitute signifying markers of the human body, what and how they signify are therefore very differ-ent. Where skin color (or even nappy hair) signifies a narrative of biological origin from a certain human type (thus racial semiosis), long hair signifies instead an agency of self-fashioning on the part of the subject that bears no presumptive relationship to a narrative of origins. The Yippie equation of long hair and black skin worked (to whatever extent it did) by eliding this difference in bodily signification.

It is not difficult to see that this elision served an unspoken ideological purpose of allowing the Yippies to grant a convenient absolution from white guilt to the counterculture (i.e., if you're no longer white, how can you be the perpetrator of white crimes?). Doubtless this discourse helped to deflect questions about complicities and continuities between the counterculture and a mainstream culture of white supremacy. It must also be granted, however, that at least in the late sixties, long hair did signify an individual's position within a brewing social conflict over the conventional codes of white male adulthood. If, as Omi and Winant suggest, race inscribes in biologistic signifiers the history of a social conflict, then one might view the Yippies' racialization of the counterculture as an effort to align a new and still-fluid social conflict (expressed in the stylistic binary of long/short hair) with the institutionalized racial conflict both regulated and obfuscated by the biologistic binary of black/white. In so doing, the Yippies explicitly aimed to disarticulate countercultural bodies from the prevailing codes of whiteness, even while this strategy in no way ever threatened an ontological discourse of whiteness grounded in lineage.[57] Yet it is important to remember that this elision was itself a partial product of their status as wishful revolutionaries. The Yippies (like Cleaver) had convinced themselves that their articulations of race were a prelude to the overthrow of the racial order itself, along with its set of hierarchical racial categories. It made sense to advocate young white people's disaffiliation from whiteness because, if it actually led to the imagined revolution, then whiteness itself (at least in any recognizable, i.e., supremacist, form) would actually cease to exist.[58] This promise of revolution, as we also saw for Cleaver, made possible a series of slippages through which it became much easier to finesse the articulation of antiracism and sexual revolution, largely because it was assumed that History itself would unravel the categories of sex and race at the precise points where they produced ideological dilemmas for the revolutionaries.

For all their contradictions and evasions, the motives behind the Yippie equation of hippie with nigger deserve one further historicizing comment. Although, as I have suggested, deflecting white guilt played a motivating role in claiming a racial status for the counterculture, this intent was more directly acknowledged by the Yippies than one might expect, and in politically interesting ways. If there was one common thread behind the politics of the Yippies, it was an embrace of pleasure and fun as political principles and an absolute rejection of guilt, responsibility, and duty. In their view, white guilt would not work as a means of mobilizing youth behind black liberation, nor would it be politically progressive if it could, because it would partake of the very denial of pleasure—the repressiveness—endemic to "Amerika." The Yippies, in historian David Farber's words, "gambled that youth, interested above all in the pleasures of the body and the delights of forbidden consumption, would fight for their right to pursue such a plain dream."[59] It was in pursuit of pleasure that white youth had turned to the counterculture, and only a defense of their own pleasure would ever lead them on to the revolution. For the counterculture to actively make common cause with the black power movement, then, "hippie" needed to become a subject of repression who required an alliance with blacks. To repeat Jerry Rubin's words, "Black-white unity becomes a real thing only when whites are treated like blacks."[60]

Given that the Yippies desired a political rhetoric of "white niggers," it is worth noting the ways in which Eldridge Cleaver's own desires helped to facilitate such a discourse.[61] Under Cleaver's narrative model of racial hierarchy, repression and oppression are made equivalent. And in this way, "liberation" took on the doubled meaning (political and sexual) that it did. If white Americans oppress black Americans by denying them mental agency, as Cleaver's paradigm suggests, then they do so at the price of their own sexual repression. And if the masters gave up their claims on the mind and "embodied" themselves, becoming supermasculine menials themselves, then did this not make them slaves, equally subject to the repressive powers of the mind?

Cleaver's narrative, as I noted earlier, reproduces hegemonic racial ideology so exactly that it has little capacity to escape it. Cleaver, for instance, cannot introduce the question of white men's sexual access to black women during slavery, so intent is he on preserving his association of the white man with asexuality and impotence. Nevertheless, Cleaver's formulation thus allows countercultural promiscuity to be declared a revolutionary blow against white supremacy. When Jerry Rubin credits Elvis Presley for beginning the Yippie revolution by "turning our uptight young awakening bodies around. Hard animal rock energy beat/ surged hot through us, the driving rhythm arousing repressed passions," he is building upon Cleaver's own assertions in the penultimate chapter of *Soul on Ice* that America's racial "convalescence" is progressing as its young middle-class whites rediscover their bodies while its young blacks rediscover their minds.[62]

Under the domain of such a sexualized political discourse, the Yippies were able to claim that, by "rediscovering their physicality," young white hippies, and particularly the men, were dropping out of the "white race," becoming "white niggers," "new niggers," and even "white panthers." If Cleaver praised "those whites who abandon the white image of America and adopt the black," he never suggested that they were actually becoming black in the process.[63] But Cleaver did suggest that young whites were learning to swing with their bodies like blacks:

> The white youth of today have begun to react to the fact that the "American Way of Life" is a fossil of history. What do they care if their old baldheaded and crew-cut elders don't dig their caveman mops? They couldn't care less about the old, stiffassed honkies who don't like their new dances: Frug, Monkey, Jerk, Swim, Watusi. All they know is that it feels good to swing to way-out body-rhythms instead of dragassing across the dance floor like zombies to the dead beat of mind-smothered Mickey Mouse music.[64]

From Cleaver's mention of white adult resistance to the new bodily pleasures discovered by white youth, it is only the smallest of slippages for the Yippies to have insisted that young white bodies—no longer "stiffassed honkies" like their parents—were becoming black. This racialized discourse of sexual repression and the necessity of liberation is what lay behind Jerry Rubin's claim that "we are all Eldridge Cleaver," for ironically, the image of Eldridge Cleaver as a political prisoner, locked up for his "sexual passion," came to serve a special role in Yippie rhetoric. Of all things, Cleaver became a figure for the repressed white man who had found the courage to throw off his shackles and liberate himself.

After the Sexual Revolution: The Turn in Sexual Politics

What are we to make of this peculiar discursive convergence between "sexual revolution" and antiracist "political revolution" in the late sixties, with its many ideological elisions regarding gender, heterosexuality, and even race itself? Earlier, in discussing "The Primeval Mitosis," I noted that Cleaver had a dualist model of the construction of race: a political positioning and a sexual positioning. One way to understand the work of Cleaver and the Yippies is to consider that they articulated sexual and antiracist politics through an analysis in which erotic repression and social oppression were causally linked. If in slightly different ways, Cleaver and the Yippies both spoke the language of the repressive hypothesis as developed by a then-influential tradition of Freudian leftists.[65] For Cleaver, asserting political mastery over others involves denying one's corporeal and thus libidinal nature. Oppression thus requires repression. For the Yippies, libidinal self-control (or uptightness) is enacted on the body of an "other." The repressed self projects its own inhibited desires onto another subject, and then, by subjugating that "other," demonstrates its mastery over those denied libidinal urges. Repression thus leads to oppression. Despite the opposing causal directions in which their arguments run, Cleaver and the Yippies therefore effectively agreed that liberating white desire would undermine the psychosexual motivation for American militarism at home and abroad. The countercultural valorization of pleasure therefore promised the demise of white supremacy: the sexual revolution would lead inexorably to the revolution.

Presumptions such as these were rampant in the late sixties, and often seemed to be substantiated by the accelerating social changes. As Todd Gitlin suggests:

> Thanks to the sheer number of youth, the torrent of drugs, the sexual revolution, the traumatic war, the general stampede away from authority, and the trend-spotting media, it was easy to assume that all the styles of revolt and disaffection were spilling together tributaries into a common torrent of youth and euphoria, life against death, joy over sacrifice, now over later, remaking the whole bleeding world.[66]

In the maelstrom of the late sixties, it could seem plausible—and not only to Cleaver and the Yippies—that the many social, political, and cultural upheavals were converging upon some total and cataclysmic transformation based on the liberation of desire. On the other hand, when the zenith of revolutionary hope began to pass, so too did the rapprochement between African American politicos and hippies. By the early seventies, the notion that the countercultural mix of sex, drugs, and rock and roll would help make "the revolution" was clearly collapsing. Even Cleaver broke his alliance with the Yippies after feuding with Timothy Leary, his escapee houseguest in Algiers during 1971. In a KPFA broadcast, Cleaver bitterly attacked the counterculture, making clear that what he had to say

> also applies to the Jerry Rubins, Stew Alperts [sic] and the Abbie Hoffmans and the whole silly psychedelic drug culture/quasipolitical movement of which they are part, and of which we have been part in the past, which we allied ourselves with in the past, which we supported in the past because it was our judgment that at that time this was what we had to work with from white America.
>
> But we're through. We're finished with relating to this madness.[67]

The Yippies furiously denounced Cleaver in turn. Without a symbolic alliance with black power, and without the political valence (however tenuous) gained for hippies through the concept of the "white nigger," any broad program for politicizing the counterculture came to an end. The moment when all revolts seemed to converge had passed, and with it, the Yippie-Panther Pipe Dream of articulating a racial and sexual revolution together.

If the discourse of sexual revolution did not translate into racialized revolt against the state, however, it did break important ground for other forms of sexual politics, although these were politics that did not align easily with the African American struggle. The counterculture must be credited with serving as a vital resource for the new social movements that emerged at the end of the sixties, specifically feminism and gay liberation.[68] In the early sixties, a feminism grounded in the arguments of Betty Friedan was already under way, but this was a liberal feminism focused primarily on women's equal access to the public workplace. By contrast, the radical women's movement of the late sixties derived from the counterculture a concern with sexual freedom, although what this meant for women was not obvious. The counterculture's discourse of sexual liberation was similarly instrumental in creating a cultural environment whereby the pre-1960s "homophile movement" could be transformed into one for gay liberation. Yippie, moreover, was an important reference point for the new sexual politics. The early women's movement group WITCH, for example, where Robin Morgan began her political career, was a splinter group of Yippie. And another Yippie, Jim Fouratt, became an important player in the Stonewall riot of 1969.

In contrast to the sixties-style sexual revolutionary politics from which they emerged, however, both feminism and gay liberation waged struggles not so much against an alleged repression of sexual desire as over the distribution of sexual power and privilege between men and women, straights and gays. Their goals were not to liberate any and all expressions of pleasure, nor did they see such "liberations" as necessarily advancing a broad revolutionary cause. Sexual politics instead developed a far more particularistic emphasis on the relationship of different forms of desire to a dominant regime of sexuality. Most obviously, the gay and women's liberation movements critiqued the countercultural sexual revolution as privileging straight masculine desire. At times, this could mean calling attention to what might constitute specifically female or gay pleasure. The feminist critique of the "myth of the vaginal orgasm" and gay explorations of anal eroticism, for example, both represented efforts to displace phallic pleasure in heterosexual intercourse as the telos of sexual liberation.

In other instances, however, the early gay and women's movements called into question the larger premise of "liberationist" discourse. The women's movement, especially, debated whether "freedom from" sex rather than "freedom to" might be more crucial for erotic empowerment. Ellen Willis, for example, recalls consciousness-raising sessions where "most of the women who testified preferred monogamous relationships, and [determined] that pressure for more sexual freedom came mostly from men (at that point heterosexuality was a more or less unchallenged assumption)."[69] Willis notes that "there were a lot of arguments of how to interpret that material," but one conclusion often reached was that these feelings might represent women's "objective interests" given their lives within a masculinist system of sexuality in which more sex might mean more exploitation by men. It could be read, in other words, as a form of women's resistance to what Adrienne Rich has referred to as "compulsory heterosexuality" under patriarchy. This mode of feminist sexual politics is taken to its logical conclusion in the powerful works of Catharine MacKinnon, who argues that sex is to women under patriarchy what labor is to the worker under capitalism: the thing most your own and yet the most taken away from you, the substance of your exploitation. In some versions of this feminist politics, as we know, lesbianism became privileged as the form of sexuality that resisted patriarchy. In other versions that did not acknowledge lesbianism as outside of patriarchal gender norms, sexual freedom for women might well mean freedom from sex altogether, quite literally celibacy.

The gay movement, too, made a shift away from sexual liberationist discourse, though not to the same degree as the women's movement. Early manifestos like Dennis Altman's often began with Freudian notions that the inherent bisexuality of libido needs to be liberated from the homophobic inhibitions installed by heteronormative culture. In short order, however, the movement began emphasizing the political priority of defending gay subcultural enclaves as a means of creating zones of sexual autonomy, in which the structures of desire in the "straight world" would not prevail. Creating as it did physical spaces for the pursuit of gay pleasure in ways that, like the counterculture, might be conceived as a "postrevolutionary" emancipated space, gay activism remained more "liberationist" in its orientation than the dominant strand of seventies feminism, although even this project was deeply eroded by the AIDS crisis. Both forms of activism, over the course of the seventies, came to drop their "liberationist" middle name. Women's liberation became simply the "women's movement," gay liberation the "gay movement." The early tension between an identity-based form of political activism (for women and gays, respectively) and a universalizing politics of radical sexuality (imagining a world of liberated desire) dissipated as the latter agenda faded away.[70]

In certain respects, this new minority discourse approach to sexual politics still bore continuities with the Yippie-Panther alliance that had preceded it. As Kobena Mercer observes in his essay on the political legacy of "1968," the ten-point platform of the Black Panther Party became a model for similar ten-point charters drafted by both the gay and women's movements, whose terms, he suggests, were "based on a metaphorical transfer of the terms for the liberation of one group into the terms for the liberation of others. It was on the basis of such imagined equivalences that the connotative yield of slogans such as Black Power and Black Pride was appropriated to empower movements around gender and sexual politics."[71] Sexuality for the gay and women's movements, then, may have continued to bear racial connotations drawing upon the logic of equivalence first articulated by the Panthers and the Yippies. More cautious than the Yippies, the gay and women's movements never made a literal claim for femininity or gayness as racial categories.[72] The claim always operated as mere analogy or metaphor. Gender and sexual orientation were "like race" in that they each named a binary relation of power that created a category of oppressed people. One rarely considered result of this shift is that, in creating a relationship of "likeness" (or metaphor) rather than one of "connectedness" (or metonymy), both the gay and women's movements ceased to conceive of sexuality and race as mutually constitutive domains. They instead became two systems that coexist and oppress their respective minorities. To be a black woman or gay person of color therefore found a political narrative of oppression by two systems at once, rather than by one complex sex-race system.[73] In this way, two identity politics of sexuality emerged (for women and gays, respectively) in the seventies and eighties whose strengths lay in their willingness to acknowledge and grapple with nonrevolutionary conditions. At the same time, it became more difficult to articulate their political projects with antiracist social movements. Since the early seventies, the relationship of sexual freedom to antiracism has become increasingly difficult to establish.

Second-Wave Sexual Radicalism: The Future of Antiracism for Queer Theory and Pro-sex Feminism

In the past ten years, a reaction has set in against the anti-sex tendencies in 1980s sexual politics, leading to the emergence of a pro-sex feminism and a queer movement that might loosely be described as second-wave sexual radicalism. In many respects, the pivotal text for this turn is Gayle Rubin's 1984 article "Thinking Sex: Notes for a Radical Theory of the Politics of Sexuality." Rejecting the sex-critical perspective adopted in her own influential feminist essay of the seventies, "The Traffic in Women," Rubin's "Thinking Sex" insists that gender is not the necessary locus for a politics of sexuality and directly attacks "anti-porn feminism" for its demonization of sex and sexual representations rather than gender violence per se. Instead, Rubin describes a sexual system with its own structures of power and its own divisions of legitimate and illegitimate subjects and practices. This system, for Rubin, in turn demands "a radical theory of sex [that] must identify, describe, explain, and denounce erotic injustice, and sexual oppression."[74] Among the ways that Rubin maps out such a sexual system is through a pie chart that represents an inner "charmed circle" of "normal, natural, blessed sexuality" and an "outer limits" of "bad, abnormal, unnatural, damned sexuality."[75]

Given the historical sweep of Rubin's essay, one of the most remarkable things about it is that she never once mentions the sixties or the "sexual revolution" as a reference point for her project. Gayle Rubin writes as though Jerry Rubin and all he represents never existed. Yet implicit in her essay, I would argue, is a desire to resuscitate in a new form the latter's sexual radicalism, his assault on the ideo-logical and social policing of "freaks" by "straights," justified by the idea that "body pleasure is immoral."[76] If Jerry Rubin privileged "fucking in the streets" as the only subversive sexuality, Gayle Rubin's passage through feminist and gay politics allows her to break resolutely with the heteronormativity of Jerry Rubin's vision of body pleasure and to take up marginal sexualities (S/M and cross-generational, for instance) as the benchmarks by which one may measure whether the struggle for liberation from sexual oppression and persecution has deepened. Despite this important difference, Gayle Rubin nevertheless shares with Jerry Rubin an expansive vision of sexual politics as "body pleasure" that is not exclusively minoritarian in its project (though both Rubins construct cer-tain subjects as the counternormative challenges to the sexual order—"freaks" for Jerry, "queers" for Gayle).

Gayle Rubin's bypassing of the "sexual revolution" in developing her radical project is not unusual. Despite refurbishing "sexual radicalism" as a program and even at times the concept of "erotic repression," the new radical queer politics' relationship to the sexual politics of the sixties is a topic for avoidance. Queer Nation, for example, the movement that in many ways launched the new wave of sex radicalism, can be seen as having made its impact through an ingenious revamping, in queer terms, of Yippie strategies for political action (including guerrilla theater, public sex acts, and especially the media-savvy manipulation of national icons). Lauren Berlant and Elizabeth Freeman have noted in passing that Queer Nation's "nationalist-style camp counterpolitics" of sexuality has important reference points in the sixties, whether in such self-description as an "army of lovers" or (fascinating in the light of this essay) the creation of an antibashing foot-patrol unit called the "Pink Panthers."[77] Yet one finds little speculation (of any valence) on the substance of this legacy.

Part of this elision, I would suggest, is politically motivated. The masculinism and heterosexism of countercultural sexuality makes the likes of Jerry Rubin unsavory reference points for queer politics. This desire to disaffiliate queer and pro-sex feminist sexual radicalism from the counterculture, I want to suggest, brings out a troubling aspect of radical sexual discourse—then and now. One of Michel Foucault's motives for writing his highly influential *History of Sexuality* was his desire to respond critically to the sexual liberationist rhetoric of the late sixties. This groundbreaking critique of the repressive hypothesis, which has proven so influential in queer and feminist thought, was partly intended by Foucault as a challenge to self-appointed "sex radicals" who espoused discourses of liberation. Those who have defined the "relationship between sex and power in terms of repression," Foucault warns, may well be motivated by what such assertions offer them as "liberated" speakers, individuals who show themselves to be defiant, subversive, and free.[78]

If Foucault challenges the pro-sex activists of the sixties for constructing their political project in a way that presented them as heroes of the future, it might be worth asking the same question of ourselves to the extent that we pursue a project of sex radicalism. In our contemporary discourse of sex radicalism do we risk presenting (and self-presenting) ourselves as people who, in the Yippies' words once again, might be admired for living as though the revolution had already happened? To what extent might Foucault's opening gambit in *The History of Sexuality*, a description of the sixties, apply once again?

> A great sexual sermon—which has had its subtle theologians and its popular voices—[and] has swept through our societies over the last decades; it has chastised the old order, denounced hypocrisy, and praised the rights of the immediate and the real; it has made people dream of a New City. . . . And we might wonder how it is possible that the lyricism and religiosity that long accompanied the revolutionary project have, in Western industrial societies, been largely carried over to sex.[79]

One of Foucault's motivations in reframing the politics of sexuality in terms of the social regulation of populations was to suggest that we are all subject to the exercise of "biopower," so that the celebration of "liberated" individuals, communities, or zones may serve only to blind us to larger sexual dynamics in which these spaces of "liberation" play their own part in larger regulatory processes.

This insight does not mean that sexual radicalism is hopeless or moot, as pessimistic readers of Foucault might conclude. Rather, it means the politics of sexuality needs a broader scope that does not necessarily privilege as its agents those who conceive of their sexuality as "radical" or "subversive." A radical sexual politics need not, and indeed should not, attach the valorized label of "radical" to particular sexual agents, because this risks dismissing others whose sexualities are less extra-ordinary (stigmatization of the nonnormative inverted as glamour) but just as regulated, and in ways that are tremendously disabling to them.

In the case of the Yippies, I have suggested that phallic and masculinist forms of sexuality were embedded in their notions of the counterculture as the site of sexual radicalism. What sorts of unspoken counternormativities might be at work in contemporary sex radicalism? To address this question, I want to observe a different omission in Gayle Rubin's essay—not the absence of the "sexual revolution" this time, but the absence of its complementary terms in this study, race and antiracism. In her detailed list of the "dos and don'ts" of the hegemonic sexual order, at no point does Rubin address or discuss race, even though in many eras that she mentions, some of the most politically charged sexual desires and practices would have been racialized ones. To restate one last time the central question that arises out of this essay's historical exploration of the late sixties, How and why should antiracism be rearticulated to sexual radicalism in the present?

We might develop one answer by denying that, in order to avoid subordinating one's analysis of sexuality to gender, class, race, or even "sexual orientation," one must discuss sexuality as having, in Gayle Rubin's terms, "its own internal politics, inequities, and modes of oppression."[80] In the moment of the late sixties, as we have seen, radical sexual politics was emphatically not separated from racial politics. Even in Gayle Rubin's own list of persecuted sexual minorities, nominally nonsexual social axes such as generation and class (who are prostitutes, anyway?) keep reemerging. Moreover, insofar as sexuality becomes imbricated in other social relations, one might say that its regulatory power can be even greater in relation to populations that may not typically be understood as "sexual minorities." Despite the absence of such a position on Rubin's pie chart, for instance, it is clear that procreative sex by unwed women of color may be one of the most socially stigmatized and politically attacked sexual acts of the present moment. Although in its strict sexual dimension one would expect relatively little stigma (heterosexual, monogamous, procreative), nevertheless one of the most important battles for sexual justice we could conceivably fight today would be alongside low-income women who are denied basic socioeconomic protection as punishment for their sexual practices. Here our sex radicalism would need to sustain an antiracist and feminist sexual politics that aligns itself with the sexual interests of such a constituency. Just as Cleaver's black nationalism once required sexual liberation, and just as the "sexual revolutionaries" were called upon to be antiracist, so a sex-radical campaign today dealing with the public demonization of "unwed mothers" or "welfare moms" might necessitate new and potentially productive movement affiliations across all sorts of activist lines.

One might attempt to build an even stronger relationship between anti-racism and sexual politics, however, by working more carefully through the more supple Foucauldian paradigm (just as the late-sixties politicos worked through the Freudian one). To see what is at stake here requires a brief digression. Foucault writes little in the *The History of Sexuality* on the subject of race. Yet it hardly seems a coincidence that the Victorian era's rapid development of scientific discourses of sexual knowledge proceeded alongside a similarly scientific discourse of racial knowledge. As Robert Young points out in his study of nineteenth-century race theory, sex and race have long been intimately linked fields of knowledge.[81] Given this historic association, the "incitement to discourse" of which Foucault speaks should perhaps be reinterpreted as the process by which white bourgeois sexuality was constituted in relation to racial difference. It is precisely this reworking of Foucault that constitutes the project of Ann Laura Stoler's book *Race and the Education of Desire*. Extrapolating from Foucault's own comments on the "birth of racism," Stoler argues that "an implicit racial grammar underwrote the sexual regimes of bourgeois culture" such that European colonialism and bourgeois sexuality became inextricably linked technologies of "biopower" for the regulation of populations.[82]

If such a Foucauldian approach to race and sex were brought to bear on the articulation of sexual and racial liberationist projects in the late sixties, we might interpret the developments of those years in terms quite different from those passionately insisted upon by the historical actors themselves. Rather than taking them at their word in their claims to unmask and undermine the repressive origins of social oppression, we can interpret the revolutionary politics of 1968 as an effort to mobilize long-standing discourses of what Abdul Jan Mohammed has called "racialized sexuality" to the mutual purposes of the black power movement and the counterculture.[83] Treating sexual repression as a discourse, constituting white bourgeois sexuality in relation to its "racialized sexual" opposite, allows us to consider how the modern era has established politically volatile fields of desire. Racialized sexuality, that is, may potentially be used to order social life not only in bourgeois or white supremacist terms, but also through the inversion of "negritude," along Third Worldist and/or countercultural lines as well.

The actual political results of this countermoblization of racialized sexual discourse, in point of fact, may not have been what either movement had hoped. Barbara Ehrenreich, for instance, argues in *The Hearts of Men* that the counterculture, in delinking heterosexuality and marriage, prepared the way for a new "singles" consumer culture associated with a therapeutic ethos of the self. In Foucault's terms, it enabled a reconstruction of bourgeois sexuality more in line with the mid-twentieth-century intensification of consumer desire. Ehrenreich's pessimistic evaluation of the counterculture's political effects, then, is that it "ended by affirming the middle-class, materialistic culture it had set out to refute."[84] Like Foucault, Ehrenreich says little about race, but one might imagine that the racialized endorsement by the Yippies and Panthers of "sexual revolution," by creating greater flexibility in imaginary racial identifications, might have played a role in the expansion and mainstreaming of a white consumer market for "black" products that coalesced in the 1970s.

Insofar as a Foucauldian approach to race and sexuality does not depend on a discourse of emancipated libido that plays into the hands of consumerism, it might be used to better political effect than was the Freudian model. If the Foucauldian account of biopower described above is plausible, then the discourses of sexuality and raciality are in effect two faces of the technologies for producing and regulating populations. This in turn suggests that a radical sexual politics capable of engaging the politics of biopower will need to articulate and struggle over the regulation of human life in ways that necessarily address race and sex together (and not merely as identities but as ways of sorting and controlling human behavior). In this context, the AIDS crisis may serve as the single most important lesson in the contemporary politics of biopower. It is a truism of the mass media that AIDS "ended" the sexual revolution. But it is also possible to argue that AIDS led to a new sort of (nonliberationist) politics of sexuality with its own vast potential to articulate sex, race, and many other axes of political interest. The alliances mobilized by ACT UP, for instance, as David Halperin notes, linked "gay resistance and sexual politics with social mobilization around issue of race, gender, poverty, incarceration, intravenous drug use, prostitution, sex phobia, media representation, health care reform, immigration law, medical research, and the power and accountability of 'experts.'"[85] In the struggles it waged, ACT UP remained highly aware of the power of social normativity to determine matters of life and death. "Heteronormativity," however, became a far more complex target for ACT UP, given its broader engagement with the politics of biopower, that made sexual politics inseparable from antiracism and struggle against class inequalities.

On the basis of its very difference from the "liberation of eros" promised by the late sixties, a sexual radicalism of the present might yet be possible that challenges the unfreedoms that accompany our sexual regulation as subjects, not only of sexual orientation, but of class, gender, nationality, and perhaps especially race. This would be a sexual radicalism without a "revolutionary sexuality" that privileges certain subjects as always already living emancipated lives. Instead, such a sexual radicalism would take up, as a foundational plank in its project of erotic freedom, antiracism in its broadest possible sense: social justice for all people as subjects of biopower. Long after the troubled Yippie-Panther Pipe Dream has dissipated, the need for such a meaningful and effective radical joining of sexual and racial politicking seems more vital than ever.

Notes

1. Ernesto Laclau and Chantal Mouffe, *Hegemony and Socialist Strategy: Towards a Radical Democratic Politics* (New York: Verso, 1985), 149–59. See their sophisticated account of "articulation" as a means of politicizing new social relations. For Laclau and Mouffe, "articulation" represents the constitution of a symbolic equivalence between two positions within a discursive structure (i.e., from citizen to worker or woman). This "equivalence" not only transforms both those elements, but may potentially extend the political project of democracy to new domains.

2. Kathleen Rout, in the only literary study of Eldridge Cleaver, writes that Beverly Axelrod, his leftist attorney, "both got Cleaver paroled, and put him in touch with white radicals at *Ramparts* [a New Left magazine], who in turn spread his work among the literati who praised it: Norman Mailer, Leslie Fiedler, Norman Podhoretz, Paul Jacobs, and Maxwell Geismar." Kathleen Rout, *Eldridge Cleaver* (Boston: Twayne, 1991), 4.

3. Eldridge Cleaver, *Soul on Ice* (New York: Dell, 1968).

4. Rout, *Eldridge Cleaver*, 62.

5. Ibid., 40.

6. As Clayborne Carson sums up, "The major line of cleavage within the black militant community was between cultural nationalists, who urged blacks to unite around various conceptions of a black cultural ideal, and self-defined political revolutionaries who were more likely than the cultural nationalists to advocate armed struggle to achieve political or economic goals." The latter, typified by the Panthers, were also more likely to use a rhetoric of alliance with white youth. Clayborne Carson, *In*

Struggle: SNCC and the Black Awakening of the 1960s (Cambridge: Harvard University Press, 1981), 286.

7. Rout, *Eldridge Cleaver*, 89.

8. Marty Jezer, *Abbie Hoffman, American Rebel* (New Brunswick, N.J.: Rutgers University Press, 1992), 177, emphasis added. Jezer overstates this case as Huey Newton's prison interviews also evinced a strong interest in the white counterculture. See, for instance, the interview with Newton on the same page of the *Berkeley Barb* as the actual Yippie-Panther Pact: Stewart E. Albert, "Huey on Yippies," *Berkeley Barb*, October 4–10, 1968, 8. Bobby Seale's participation in the Yippie demonstrations at the Democratic Party convention in Chicago also represents counterevidence.

9. Cleaver, *Soul on Ice*, 77.

10. Jezer, *Abbie Hoffman*, 123.

11. See David Farber, *Chicago '68* (Chicago: University of Chicago Press, 1988); and David Armstrong, *A Trumpet to Arms: Alternative Media in America* (Boston: South End, 1991), for detailed discussions of the media political strategies and theories of the Yippies. Armstrong argues that the Yippies ultimately failed to build support for themselves through the media because ultimately they were unable to "control" the meaning of their own representations on television, as they had believed they could. Farber places more emphasis on the inability or unwillingness of the Yippies to do the hard grassroots work of organizing youth one by one (212–25). In taking the mass-media approach, the Yippies were deeply influenced by the theories of Marshall McLuhan, which implied that electronic media would return us to (in Walter Ong's words) a phase of "secondary orality" corresponding to a neotribal society: McLuhan's famous "global village." Seeing youth and youth counterculture as the vanguard of this new tribalism, the Yippies hoped to speed up this process and precipitate a revolution through their political stagework. Andrew Ross, "Candid Cameras," in *No Respect: Intellectuals and Popular Culture* (New York: Routledge, 1989), 102–34, provides a useful critique of McLuhan's mass-media theory, specifically its inability to address global issues of power.

12. Abbie Hoffman, *Revolution for the Hell of It* (New York: Dial, 1968); Jerry Rubin, *Do It! Scenarios of the Revolution* (New York: Simon & Schuster, 1970).

13. For this group's manifesto, see "White Panther Statement," *Berkeley Barb*, November 29–December 5, 1968, 13. Sinclair went on to form the band MC-5, and I believe he gave Iggy Pop his break.

14. Eldridge Cleaver, Jerry Rubin, Abbie Hoffman, and Stew Albert, "Yippie-Panther Pact: Pipe Dream #2," *Berkeley Barb*, October 4–10, 1968, 9.

15. Cleaver, *Soul on Ice*, 111.

16. Ibid., 145.

17. Ibid., 150.

18. Ibid., 28.

19. Although "The Primeval Mitosis" clearly has a substantial intellectual pedigree, relying

on works Cleaver probably read in prison—Plato's *Symposium*, Hegel's "Master-Servant Dialectic," Engels's "The Origin of Private Property," Fanon's *Black Skin, White Masks*, and many others —Cleaver mentions no sources by name.

20. Cleaver, *Soul on Ice*, 165.

21. Ibid., 167.

22. Ibid., 164.

23. Ibid., 26.

24. Ibid., 189.

25. Robyn Wiegman, *American Anatomies: Theorizing Race and Gender* (Durham, N.C.: Duke University Press, 1995), 85.

26. bell hooks, *Black Looks: Race and Representation* (Boston: South End, 1992), 109.

27. Ibid., 88–89.

28. Kobena Mercer and Isaac Julien, "Black Masculinity and the Sexual Politics of Race," in Kobena Mercer, *Welcome to the Jungle: New Positions in Black Cultural Studies* (New York: Routledge, 1994), 141. I have written in passing on the historical deployment of black masculinity in blaxploitation film. See Leerom Medovoi, "Theorizing Historicity, or the Many Meanings of Blacula," *Screen* 39 (spring 1998): 1–21.

29. Cleaver, *Soul on Ice*, 190–91.

30. Despite Cleaver's efforts in "To All Black Women, from All Black Men," many black women activists understandably found *Soul on Ice* deeply offensive. Indeed, according to Clayborne Carson, this may even have been a factor in the Black Panther Party's failure to merge with SNCC, the premier black civil rights organization of the South. Although SNCC leader Stokely Carmichael joined the Panthers for a time, many other SNCC staff members remained skeptical of the party, particularly women, who, as Carson notes, "were disturbed by Cleaver's disparaging remarks about black women in his best-selling book of essays, *Soul On Ice*, published during 1968." Carson, *In Stuggle*, 283.

31. Cleaver, *Soul on Ice*, 34.

32. Ibid., 34–35.

33. This issue was played out quite literally in Cleaver's personal life, beginning with the infatuation with Beverly Axelrod described in *Soul on Ice*. According to Earl Anthony, in the period immediately after Cleaver's parole, many black nationalists in fact "dismissed him out-of-hand because he was in love with a white woman who was said to be a Communist." Earl Anthony, *Spitting in the Wind: The True Story behind the Violent Legacy of the Black Panther Party* (Malibu, Calif.: Roundtable, 1990), 22. By late 1967, Cleaver had become involved with Kathleen Neal, a black woman and a former SNCC activist. They quickly married and worked side by side in the party.

34. Michele Wallace's *Black Macho and the Myth of Superwoman* (New York: Verso, 1990) is certainly the key text for this black feminist response to the gender politics of the black power movement.

35. Cleaver, *Soul on Ice*, 171–72.

36. Ibid., 170.

37. Ibid., 177.

38. Paul Krassner, "An Impolite Interview with Paul Krassner," in *How a Satirical Editor Became a Yippie Conspirator in Ten Easy Years* (New York: Putnam, 1971), 311.

39. David Farber, *The Age of Great Dreams: America in the 1960s* (New York: Hill & Wang, 1994), 182.

40. Hoffman, *Revolution for the Hell of It*, 61.

41. Rubin, *Do It!* 111.

42. Ibid.

43. Ibid., 56.

44. Ibid., 96.

45. See Barbara Ehrenreich, *The Hearts of Men: American Dreams and the Flight from Commitment* (Garden City, N.Y.: Anchor, 1984).

46. Albert, "Huey on Yippies," 8.

47. Rubin, *Do It!* 195.

48. Ibid., 198.

49. Ibid., 93–94.

50. Ibid., 94.

51. Ibid., 195–96.

52. Indeed, many critics of the Yippies argued that this was a politics based on cruel deception. The Yippies, they argued, led hippie lambs to the slaughter, encouraging them, for example, to come to Chicago for a Woodstock-style "Festival of Life" while actually hoping to politicize them via the blows of Mayor Daley's police clubs. Hippies who came to Chicago would learn firsthand that they shared "equality-under-the-pigs" with blacks. Although it is not fair to say that the Yippies were so coldly premeditative (they also felt answerable to those they had brought to Chicago, and clearly tried to avoid overly violent confrontations), this "barrel-of-a-gun" consciousness-raising strategy was clearly one important component of Yippie politics.

53. Jezer, *Abbie Hoffman*, 92.

54. Hoffman, *Revolution for the Hell of It*, 71.

55. Ibid., 74.

56. Michael Omi and Howard Winant, *Racial Formations in the United States from the 1960s to the 1980s* (New York: Routledge, 1986), 55. Even in post-1945 racialist discourses —which have tended to define race as a form of social over biological difference—racial identity continues to be arbitrated by reference to a reproductive logic of biological descent. Popular wisdom may have it that race is actually a social (not a true biological) category, but nevertheless, when push comes to shove, any particular person's race is still taken as the race of his or her ancestry, an infinite regress of "social" signifiers that ends only with some biological origin gesture, as in "their ancestors . . . came from Asia, Africa, or Europe."

57. In other words, even if one grants that the Yippies had some success in using the diggery-niggery equation to align the counterculture with black social struggle, in no way did they ever broach (let alone challenge) the subject of the stylistic/biologistic distinction between the two subject positions.

58. As I noted earlier, Cleaver himself stopped short of this imaginary revolutionary goal of abolishing race altogether, aiming as he did for a national liberation in which African America could become politically self-determining and reproductively independent of the colonizing mother country. Implicitly, then, this question of the racial status of the counterculture lurked as an unspoken ideological conflict between the black power movement and the sexual liberationists.

59. Farber, *Chicago '68*, 224–25.

60. Rubin, *Do It!* 196.

61. The term *white niggers* also has a discernible genealogy. The Yippies drew the concept from Norman Mailer's essay "The White Negro," in *Advertisements for Myself* (New York: Signet, 1960), 298–33, an essay that Cleaver defended vehemently. Mailer's essay makes a case similar to that the Yippies would make ten years later, namely, that white hipsters were adopting a black code of life, including a highly masculinist "liberated sexuality" of the male orgasm. Mailer, not incidentally, was also among the authors who liked Cleaver's essays and helped get them published.

62. Rubin, *Do It!* 18.

63. Cleaver, *Soul on Ice*, 79.

64. Ibid., 83.

65. Relevant texts in this tradition would include Wilhelm Reich's *The Mass Psychology of Fascism* (New York: Farrar, Straus & Giroux, 1970); Herbert Marcuse's *Eros and Civilization: A Philosophical Inquiry into Freud* (Boston: Beacon, 1966); Norman O. Brown's *Life against Death: The Psychoanalytic Meaning of History* (New York: Random House, 1959); and Norman Mailer's afforementioned essay, "The White Negro."

66. Todd Gitlin, *The Sixties: Years of Hope, Days of Rage* (New York: Bantam, 1987), 255.

67. Quoted in Rout, *Eldridge Cleaver*, 148.

68. It should also be noted that countercultural critiques of the wastefulness of consumer culture also fed into a powerful post-1960s ecology movement.

69. Ellen Willis, "Radical Feminism and Feminist Radicalism," in *The 60s without Apology*, ed. Sohnya Sayres, Anders Stephanson, Stanley Aronowitz, and Fredric Jameson (Minneapolis: University of Minnesota Press, 1984), 94.

70. See Alice Echol, *Daring to Be Bad: Radical Feminism in America, 1967–1975* (Minneapolis: University of Minnesota Press, 1989), for a narrative history of the women's movement's transition from what Echols calls "radical feminism" (a transformative, liberationist politics) to "cultural feminism" (an identity-based movement founded on the notion of "women's culture.") For a parallel study of this transition in the gay

movement, see Stephen Epstein, "Gay Politics, Ethnic Identity: The Limits of Social Constructionism," *Socialist Review* 17, (May–August 1987): 9–54.

71. Kobena Mercer, "1968: Periodizing Politics and Identity," in *Welcome to the Jungle: New Positions in Black Cultural Studies* (New York: Routledge, 1994), 303.

72. For an interesting if limited exception to this rule, however, see Dennis Altman's concept of the "faggot as nigger" in his early gay liberationist book *Homosexual: Oppression and Liberation* (New York: Avon, 1973), 152–226.

73. Nobody has felt this failure to keep race and sexuality connected as political issues more acutely than minority women and gays, who are frequently asked to "choose" between their allegiances. Robyn Wiegman refers to this dilemma as the "contemporary condensation of race and gender into 'blacks and women,'" in which each term is conceived as "something which the other cannot possibly be." *American Anatomies*, 8–9. She then goes on to work with sexuality as an arena where one can discover various historically contingent alignments of race and gender.

74. Gayle Rubin, "Thinking Sex: Notes for a Radical Theory of the Politics of Sexuality," in *The Lesbian and Gay Studies Reader*, ed. Henry Abelove, Michele Aina Barale, and David M. Halperin (New York: Routledge, 1993), 9; see also Gayle Rubin, "The Traffic in Women," in *Toward an Anthropology of Women*, ed. Rayna R. Reiter (New York: Monthly Review Press, 1975), 157–210.

75. Rubin, "Thinking Sex," 13.

76. Rubin, *Do It!* 111.

77. See Lauren Berlant and Elizabeth Freeman, "Queer Nationality" in *The Queen of America Goes to Washington City: Essays on Sex and Citizenship* (Durham, N.C.: Duke University Press, 1997), 149, 156.

78. Michel Foucault, *The History of Sexuality*, vol. 1, *An Introduction*, trans. Robert Hurley (New York: Vintage, 1978), 6.

79. Ibid., 7–8.

80. Rubin, "Thinking Sex," 4.

81. See Robert Young, *Colonial Desire: Hybridity in Theory, Culture, and Race* (New York: Routledge, 1995), in which Young investigates the concern of racial pseudoscience with the sexual reproduction of races.

82. Ann Laura Stoler, *Race and the Education of Desire: Foucault's History of Sexuality and Colonial Order of Things* (Durham, N.C.: Duke University Press, 1995), 12.

83. See Abdul Jan Mohammed, "Sexuality on/of the Racial Border: Foucault, Wright, and the Articulation of 'Racialized Sexuality,'" in *Discourses of Sexuality: From Aristotle to AIDS*, ed. Domna C. Stanton (Ann Arbor: University of Michigan Press, 1992).

84. Ehrenreich, *The Hearts of Men*, 114.

85. David Halperin, *Saint Foucault: Towards a Gay Hagiography* (New York: Oxford University Press, 1995), 63.

Pink Narcissus, 1971. Courtesy of Photofest.

Making the Homophile Manifest
Mark D. Jordan

If the Stonewall demonstrations were not quite a matter of smoke and mirrors, they were certainly preoccupied with mirroring. Indeed, we free ourselves from a number of mystifying clichés when we conceive those demonstrations not as the birth of gay liberation, but as one moment in an ongoing quarrel about how to mirror homosexual lives—about how to make homosexuality visible. The quarrel was partly an intergenerational quarrel, but it was also, perhaps principally, a quarrel between high taste and low, between elite codes of ironic figuration and the passionate earnestness of literal display. Stonewall was one victory in a struggle between tastes. In that victory, what was called "good taste" lost. There was a further and more unhappy casualty: the full force of the question of whether "homosexuality" is the kind of thing that can be represented—or should be.

"Stonewall," Smoke, Mirrors

The quarrel about homosexual representations was easier to hear at the time of Stonewall than it is in clichéd retellings. If the emblematic beginning of "gay liberation" is fixed to 1969 and the Stonewall demonstrations, then the genealogy of a contentious "queer theory" must also be traced back to the late 1960s and early 1970s. There is, for example, the militantly utopian rhetoric that can be heard in some early issues of the new magazines: the *Advocate* (Los Angeles), *Body Politic* (Toronto), *Christopher Street* (New York), *Come Out!* (New York), and *Gay Sunshine* (San Francisco). However naive or touching those revolutionary discourses, they are also, and perhaps overly, theoretical. They are also distinctly American. Elsewhere the first works of "gay liberation" have different parentage. In France, for example, both the FHAR's *Rapport contre la normalité* (1971) and Guy Hocquenghem's *Le Désir homosexuel* (1972) descend from sophisticated conversations about Freud that do not appear in the American writings.[1] In what follows, I will be concerned only with American discourses—and, indeed, with American discourses about men. The automatic linkage of gayness and lesbianism, however important politically, is another cliché that needs to be undone.

Most early works of American gay "theory" show obvious dependence on the discourses of existing political movements, whether the struggles against the Vietnam War or the "liberation movements" focusing on race and gender. Here too it is important to be suspicious of clichés. Our academic or journalistic accounts of activist "theory" in the late sixties remain very general, our explanations correspondingly reductive. The burst of writing on behalf of "gay liberation" is typically explained as one consequence of the fracturing of the New Left. When the antiracist and antiwar movements fissioned, their discourses were picked up by gay writers, many of whom had served in those movements. But to emphasize how "gay liberation" theory came from the earlier movements is to conceal what is most interesting about it—the prominence of puzzles over gay identity.

These puzzles did not afflict the discourses of war or race in the same way. Blackness and war were taken as given. If feminist theory of the 1960s asked insistently who woman was, it did not trouble itself much over who was a woman. Gay writers had not only to challenge the prevailing representations of homosexuality and to call for a redefinition of gayness outside straight categories, they had to master the confusion (shared with their oppressors) about the fixity of the thing itself, if it were a thing. The closet was a practicable response to oppression only because homosexuality was something one could conceal—hence, something that seemed much more like an option or opinion than a biological fact. Again, the realm of sexual activity (as opposed to genital anatomy) had long been treated as pliable both to regulation and to taste. The political uses devised for the Stonewall demonstrations, which is what we really mean by saying "Stonewall," were worked out in the muddle of incipient theoretical disputes about identity, hiddenness, pliability, taste. We can see this most clearly by recovering a context for the gay liberationists of the late sixties, the context of their opposition to the already existing "homophile" organizations.

What was at issue between those organizations and the liberationists was precisely what was to count as a truly homosexual identity—which is to say, as appropriate homosexual visibility. How was homosexuality to be acted out, and how indiscreetly?

In taking up this question, I mean to do some mirroring of my own. The debates over homosexual visibility registered in the first writings of gay liberation seem to me to resemble certain puzzles in gay film of the same years—not to say in the first writing about gay film. I am not interested in discovering or projecting causal connections between the two. I am interested in how the efforts of representation in gay film play out so strikingly the murkier debates of the political and theoretical writings. But I should be emphatic here in order to prevent a fundamental misunderstanding. I do not regard film as essentially or principally a social record—any more than I regard political or theoretical writings as social records. My juxtaposition of film and political text is the juxtaposition of two mirrors between which certain figures pass. Both film and text are mirrors. Neither one is to be privileged as more real or more accurate. Indeed, and as I will try to show, it is in the "unreal" and "fictional" mirror of gay film that the figures appear most plainly.

Gay Manifesto

From the hundreds of speeches, resolutions, placards, posters, pamphlets, leaflets, newsletters, from the lists of nonnegotiable demands and the caucus working papers, the protocols for consciousness-raising, and the open letters of denunciation that were multiplied early in the "gay liberation movement," I pluck out Carl Wittman's *Gay Manifesto*. The *Manifesto* may or may not have had lasting influence, may or may not have been typical or representative or important. Many people at the time thought it influential, typical, representative, important, but none of this matters to my selection. I am not writing social history. I expect from Wittman only that he will introduce ways of speaking about homosexuality that enact the quarrel over the visibility of homosexuals. This quarrel itself was and is important. It discloses the extent to which "gay liberation" remains a disagreement among male homosexuals about how to become visible—about what was to be made visible and within which frames. The quarrel shows further something of why the category "homosexual" was and is so elusive—why it works better as a means of political assertion than as a category for theory, that is, for thinking. But I must say one or two more things by way of situating Wittman's *Manifesto*.

Wittman himself first became visible as president of the Swarthmore Political Action Club in the fall of 1963. He passed from organizing integration actions in Chester, Pennsylvania, to the National Committee of Students for a Democratic Society (SDS) and its Economic and Action Research Project.[2] In 1967, Wittman moved to San Francisco, where he continued his antiwar activities. Wittman "came out" as a homosexual in print during 1968. By 1969 he was involved with the West Coast's Committee on Homosexual Freedom.[3] He participated in the group's unsuccessful picketing of States Steamship Line for its dismissal of a gay employee.[4] Wittman wrote his *Gay Manifesto* in May and June 1969—that is, in the weeks just before the Stonewall demonstrations took place on the other coast. The difference between San Francisco and New York is not negligible. The central images of Wittman's text are local images, images of San Francisco rather than of New York. In any case, the *Manifesto* was first published in the 1969 year-end issue of the *San Francisco Free Press*.[5] Its full title was *Refugees from Amerika*—Amerika with a *k*, of course—*Refugees from Amerika: A Gay Manifesto*. The text was widely reprinted in the underground press.[6]

I do not mean to situate the text of the *Manifesto* in a narrative of Wittman's evolution. Wittman's earlier writings, so far as I can locate them, are fairly standard pieces of the self-righteous, numbingly serious "Marxism" common enough in the mid-1960s. There are no mentions in the earlier Wittman of gender issues.[7] Indeed, Wittman seems to talk about every kind of social division except gender—he mentions race, ethnicity, age, occupation, and geography. So I will not try to retrace the discursive stages through which Wittman may have passed on his way to the *Manifesto*. I want to emphasize the newness that the issues of homosexuality have for Wittman, who could speak their newness only with borrowed categories and tropes. Just because Wittman's *Manifesto* is in many ways an uninformed and tentative witness to the quarrels about homosexual visibility, it is a revealing witness.

The doctrine of the *Manifesto* cannot be summarized, in part because it is so self-contradictory. For example, the "gender" of the "object of sexual desire" is both "imposed socially" and beyond the reach of "taboo" or "indoctrination" (1.1).[8] Homosexuality is neither "genetic" nor the result of upbringing. It *is* a transitional stage on the way to bisexuality, which alone is "complete" (1.2).

And so on. These doctrinal contradictions are less interesting than the *Manifesto*'s rhetorical strategy. The rhetorical strategy proceeds from and is bound by assumptions about homosexual visibility.

Note first that the speaker of the *Manifesto* shifts faces, voices. Most often, the voice is a plural, "we homosexuals." The plural voice addresses a plural audience. We homosexuals speaking to ourselves, trying to provide ourselves with "a starting point of discussion" (pref.). Then, abruptly and briefly, the speaker is an "I," the defensive and apologetic voice of a homosexual who is "white, male, middle-class." This single voice is soliciting or anticipating the voice of a "group-consciousness" that does not yet exist. Moreover, this speaker in the *Manifesto* concedes that he stands only within "the gay male viewpoint" (2.1): "It would be arrogant to presume this to be a manifesto for lesbians." "We homosexuals" can be, then, no more than the illusion of male faces still to be united who speak under false generality when they presume to speak for each other collectively or for women. More: a single male speaks so as to hasten the appearance of a group that is itself on the way to extinction by becoming something as yet unrepresentable—the "bisexual," here as fleeting an ideal as Virginia Woolf's glimpsed androgyne.

The shifting of the speaker, the difficulty of fixing the homosexual voice, determines the central image of the *Manifesto*, the image of the ghetto. These are the text's opening words:

> San Francisco is a refugee camp for homosexuals. We have fled here from every part of the nation, and like refugees elsewhere, we came not because it is so great here, but because it was so bad there. . . . And we have formed a ghetto, out of self-protection. It is a ghetto rather than a free territory because it is still theirs. Straight cops patrol us, straight legislators govern us, straight employers keep us in line, straight money exploits us. (pref.)

A "ghetto," a "refugee camp"—these are places in which the invisible mechanisms of tyranny are made to be visible. They are thus also places in which the identity of the tyrannized becomes visible by becoming separate. If homosexuality is not something visible—indeed, if it is not so much a thing as a transitional stage—a ghetto is visible, is constituted precisely by its having boundaries, by its being a place enforced from outside. Wittman shows this when he talks about the ghetto as a zone of economic exploitation, a place that bar owners and corrupt police officers and rapacious landlords want to be very separate indeed (pref. and sec. 6).

Some of Wittman's strongest recommendations have to do with expanding the space of the ghetto, especially beyond the triad of "our meeting places: bars and baths and parks" (4.1). He sees already in the gay ghetto the signs of incipient liberation: "We are full of love for each other and are showing it" (pref.). Wittman wants more spaces, "rural retreats, political action offices, food cooperatives, a free school, unalienating bars and after hours places," all pieces of what should one day become a "free territory" (sec. 6). "Free territory" is not only an assembly of places in which gayness can show itself, it is itself the showing of gayness—its incarnation in an identifiable territory. The troubles of identity try to resolve themselves into untroubled boundaries of places.

Still Wittman cannot hold off what troubles gay visibility even by advocating that gayness become concrete by becoming visible in places. Counternotions of visibility keep appearing in his text. One is the notion of "mimicry" or "role playing," especially, of course, as applied to the "mimicry of straight society," which is at worst a kind of "burlesque" (3.1–2). Successful gay mimicry is invisibility. Gayness becomes visible only when it stops playing the role and makes a ghetto. Or else it becomes visible when it changes roles. Wittman writes: "There is a tendency among 'homophile' groups to deplore gays who play visible roles—the queens and the nellies. As liberated gays we must take a clear stand. . . . Gays who stand out have become our first martyrs" (3.4). Wittman adds, at the very end of the *Manifesto:* "We've been playing an act for a long time, so we're consummate actors. Now we can begin *to be,* and it'll be a good show!" (Conclusion 4). Our being will be a show. Our being is no more than a showing. Gayness becomes visible by appropriating its extreme roles—which is the same as redirecting the habit of performance from mimicry to display. Display of what?

Gayness becomes visible for Wittman most forcefully and most problematically in sex. Wittman writes piously that sex is "both creative expression and communication, good when it is either, and better when it is both" (5.1). "For us, sexual objectification is a focus of our quest for freedom. . . . Learning how to be open and good with each other sexually is part of our liberation" (5.2). Expression, communication, objectification—not just between or among the parties to a sexual act, but publicly, democratically. "We strive for democratic, mutual, reciprocal sex. This does not mean that we are all mirror images of each other in bed" (5.3). Not mirror images, but images still. For Wittman, the image is not the body so much as the act, not the "plastic stereotypes of a good body" (5.4), but the "highly artistic endeavor, the ballet" of sexual action (5.5, 4). Wittman acknowledges that the visibility of the sexual act may indeed offend against certain tastes: "A few liberated women will be appalled or disgusted at the open and prominent place that we put sex in our lives" (*sic*; 5.2,). But he does not seem to doubt that making sex visible, making it "open and prominent," is an essential moment in liberation.[9]

Gayness becomes visible as place, as performed role, as open sexual act. This visibility is resisted by the oppressive forces of straightness. On Wittman's account, visibility is also resisted by what he refers to condescendingly as the "homophile groups," about which Wittman can only counsel toleration: "Reformist or pokey as they sometimes are, [the members of homophile groups] are our brothers. They'll grow as we have grown and grow.... [We should] cooperate where cooperation is possible without essential compromise of our identity" (7.6). *Identity* here must mean not identity as male homosexual, but identity as gay liberationist. What distinguishes the gay liberationist from the homophile, from the older generation's political program, is just the commitment to a certain kind of visibility—a revolutionary visibility, a "democratic, mutual, and reciprocal" visibility. As Wittman tells it, his *Manifesto* makes manifest what the homophiles wanted to keep hidden or to represent in less literal, less public ways.[10]

Screening the Sexes

Parker Tyler's *Screening the Sexes* was published originally in 1972, though it proclaims itself as surveying the scene "circa 1971" (xix), a scant two years after the completion of the *Gay Manifesto*.[11] By then Tyler had been writing on film for about thirty years, including long service at *View Magazine*.[12] He had begun to write earlier as a poet, though his poetry making was not segregated from his love for the movies. Indeed, within Tyler's *Granite Butterfly* (1944) there is encoded his own homoerotic attraction to the silent-screen star Carlyle Blackwell.[13] In the same year, Tyler published the first of his books on film, *The Hollywood Hallucination*. Hallucination, indeed. Andrew Sarris recalls attending one of Tyler's lectures in 1948—and there being summarily crushed.[14] In the years following, Tyler continued to write copiously about films, perhaps most prominently in *Partisan Review*.

Parker Tyler's stated purpose in *Screening the Sexes* can seem much like Wittman's in the *Manifesto*. Tyler writes: "The chief purpose of this book is to expand that limited idea [of sex] (the pleasure of making and rearing children) with an idea of sexual behavior that achieves magnitude through variety of form, hence variety of sensation and emotion" (xx).[15] He says this more enthusiastically with a reference to *Fellini Satyricon:* sex is "a thing naturally, perennially taking offbeat forms—truly *free* forms" (xx). But the freedom of form is precisely not the freedom envisaged by gay liberation, for which Tyler has only disdain. Nor is the visibility he wants for homoeroticism the same as the visibility of love in Wittman's "free territory." Tyler writes:

> The really odd, rather humorous truth of current homosexual affairs is that, while homosexuality duly inherits its puritanic social critics and its dogged medical opponents …, it also has its pop, quasi-political cults as evidenced in the gay-power newspapers (most as pornographically vulgar as they dare to be) and even by street demonstrations. (20)[16]

The vulgarity of newspapers and demonstrations is to be explained as "self-advertising," "group hysteria," and "the modern obsession (still underestimated) for basking at whatever price in publicity's many spotlights" (20). Here is Tyler's essential contrast: the "vogue," "now-now-now," "corny," "grotesque," "low," "out" visibility of gay liberation as against the "high" and "esoteric."[17] This is, again, the contrast between advertisement and art, between the "happy porno violence" of "untrammeled sexual expression" and a taste for the "aesthetic and historical" (49–50).

"So far Tyler's stance can seem uninteresting cinematic snobbery of the Eurocentric species. What begins to make Tyler's stance interesting is his appropriation of the game of camping as a weapon of the esoteric, the aesthetic, the historical. "My longtime position on Hollywood art has been that serious movies may be unwittingly, though not always unrewardingly, pretentious. Their unsophisticated pretensions tell us something, and the game is to guess just what it is" (73). Tyler invokes throughout a set of contrasts between camp and grotesque, between the free/imaginative and the mechanical/literal, between the poetic and the aggressive. The contrasts are applied densely to homosexuality itself. He is most scathing when attacking the "common enough assumption that 'being homosexual' is usually, even basically, a professional act, a nightclub routine, implying ... that homosexuality is a myth invented by heterosexuals to amuse theater audiences" (264). But Tyler does not mean to combat this myth with what he regards as the contrary myth, the contrary charade of "Gay Liberation." The street demonstration of the liberationists is no more than "rudimentary theatricalization of some hypothetic set of performances.... [It] is a lot like the circus parade, whose only purpose is to titillate appetite and to advertise the joys to come at the *real* performance" (321). The demonstration belongs, in other words, to the disvalued sphere of vulgar advertising, aggressive titillation, pornography. The only visibility enacted in the street is the crude manifestation of blunt separation, of standing off from others in order to show them just how outrageous you are.[18] The visibility sought by gay liberation is the visibility of the homosexual exhibitionist who can think of no better way of being seen than by standing in a park and dropping his (doubtless flamboyant) pants.

To this charade of exhibitionism, Tyler opposes what he insistently calls the poetry of imaginative figure. *Imaginative* in this use should call up *image*, because Tyler also means further to contrast the image with the object. The image of flesh is more powerful, more problematically traumatic, than flesh itself (191). "Movie actors appear automatically as sex *images* rather than sex *objects*. Their true realm is the liberal imagination" (348). A similar valuation should be used within the realm of cinematic images. Tyler at one point counts honesty the great virtue, and he elsewhere excoriates film critics for lying about such limited views of homosexuality as the movies do afford.[19] Tyler's honesty is not some species of documentary realism, certainly not newsreel footage of men fucking. He is perfectly clear that pornography is just bad taste: "Beaver films, all-male or all-female, are viewed here as 'bad,' in any department, entirely on grounds of taste" (134). They can be discussed by the critic only under the rubric of freedom of sexual expression—not, that is, cinematically.

Now certain pornographic or quasi-pornographic films are allowed to contain or permit what Tyler calls "poetic eroticism" or simply the "poetic."[20] He speaks about this at greatest length in describing the effects of *Pink Narcissus*, an 8mm blowup released (if that is the word) in 1971. Tyler writes:

> Frontal nudity is glimpsable enough to make the film a true beaver, but more than that, the nudity is sometimes both insinuative and imaginative.... I don't wish to flatter what is mainly only ultrarich faggot fudge, ludicrously embarrassing, but the truth is that the

erotic effects and the camera work occasionally, aided by music,
become the vehicles of genuine plastic imagination and true poetic
mood. (177–78)

I take Tyler to mean that the male nude can be shown in sexual situations imag-
inatively only if insinuatively, that is, as troped by the fantastic or surreal, as
manipulated beyond the literal, as freed from the earnestness of political program or the solicitation of advertising.

Tyler says something like this in discussing nudity itself: "I have always felt,
personally, that the primary sexual characteristics (the organs of reproduction)
were last, not first, in the hierarchy of sex magnetism.... In fact, culturally, the
sex organs are just Stone Age cosmetics" (204). Again, Tyler assumes "that, in the
truly realistic sense, there are as many sexes as there are individuals; that sex,
empirically, is an infinitely variable spectrum; that the seeming neat correspondence between male and female organs is not the end, but the beginning, of sexuality" (343). So too for images of sexed bodies. The literal visibility of an erect
penis is not the end of homoerotic film, only its beginning. The more potent
visibility—I mean the pun—is a visibility achieved through irony, trope, free
camping, imaginative reassembly, that is, through what Tyler means by "poetry."

The danger of literal visibility is not just the danger of bad taste. It is the danger of repeating the morbid inflexibility of sexual categorization that is killing
off heterosexuality. It is the danger, in short, of refusing to recognize, now on the
grounds of good gay politics, that "Eros is a metamorphose god with a million
honest pleasures and a million dishonest ruses" (346). Tyler finds the unstylish-
ness of gay liberation, its vulgar and aggressive self-advertisement, its preference
for the slogan over the aphorism, only another battle in the old war against the
"metamorphose god." Perhaps something more will come after it—a real circus
at the end of the circus parade. For the moment, in 1971, we are better off with
Passolini's *Teorema*, with a "straightforward fable, told realistically but with
much nuance," than with *The Boys in the Band*, that piece of propagandistic
"special pleading"; better off with Mae West than Myra Breckenridge, with the
real "secret" life and violent death of the matinee idol Ramón Novarro than with
the calculated pathos of Harrison and Burton in *Staircase*.[21] We are better off
writing encrypted poems to a silent-screen idol than flaunting our love in some
neighborhood we describe as a ghetto. Image against object. Fable against document. To make the homoerotic visible as gay liberation is, for Tyler, to betray its
freedom, its instability, its danger, most treacherously, from within.

Live Homosexual Acts

In the *New York Times* of February 23, 1969, there appeared a pseudonymous article on behalf of homosexuals, "Why Can't 'We' Live Happily Ever After, Too?"[22] The article surveyed several dozen novels, plays, and films to show that in all of them the homosexual character was presented as doomed to rejection in favor of straight marriage, to chronic depression, to terrible murder, to death by misadventure (recall the fatal falling tree of *The Fox*), and especially to suicide. It was a just complaint, of course.[23] But one correspondent replied to the article's question some issues later by asking, in turn, whether it wasn't obvious that "living happily ever after is a kind of abomination whether for hetero or homo?"

We see again the quarrel over how to control representations of homosexuality in the mass media. We now call this *mainstreaming*, but the quarrel remains the same under the new name. Why can't homosexuals have happy endings? That is, why can't they be represented as deserving members of the bourgeoisie, whether *haute* or *moyenne?* Why can't they too be shown as participants in whatever version of the American Dream is being hawked this season? This line of questioning can become, as in Bruce Bawer, the complaint that homosexuals would have happy endings if only they would learn to behave properly. But the quarrel deserves more consideration than that kind of prescription allows. There are more difficult questions hiding in it. Is homosexuality essentially marginal, essentially the life of a ghetto? If so, does it make any sense to attempt to set up a miniature city inside the ghetto? Why not rather live parasitically, ironically within the mainstream? Why not mock it by camping it? And what kind of "identity" is homosexuality, anyway? Is it necessarily transitional to some other identity? Is it one identity at all?

The questions cannot stop here. Further in, behind these questions about the varieties of homosexual life, there lies what now seems to me the core of the debate in these texts from the late sixties and early seventies. It remains the resistant core in many current debates. To Wittman's conviction that homosexuality should be made manifest, Tyler has replied that it cannot become manifest as political image without betraying itself into false fixity. No representation will be adequate unless it is as equivocal, as "metamorphose" as the thing itself—if it is any kind of thing. This is the issue invoked by saying that what we call "homosexuality" is itself intrinsically a performance. I don't mean this in the sense that

Judith Butler has made famous, the sense now reduced to formula as "All gender is performance."[24] I mean it more narrowly as describing the particular identity conditions for the category "homosexuality." The category is a subjectivity turned inside out—or rather an outside pushed in to make a subject.

For most of the historical European moralities, whether legal, customary, or theological, the prohibition of same-sex relations is officially a prohibition of acts—of certain genital contacts, their adjuncts and preludes. But the prohibition of acts has long been extended into the hypothesis of a subject, an abiding disposition, an identity from which the prohibited acts proceed. The extension from acts to their inner ground is made not by the participants in the acts, but by those who want to prohibit, punish, or cure them. The category "homosexual" is a category projected by self-proclaimed or normatively assumed "heterosexuals." When "homosexual" men are in bed with each other, there are no homosexuals present. There are just men having sex with men. Those men become "homosexuals" when heterosexual society peers in or else feverishly imagines what must be taking place. The participants are then taught to describe themselves as homosexuals and to behave accordingly. They are allotted a certain repertoire of performances by which they must declare their being homosexual for onlookers—including onlooking homosexuals, given that we must learn to make ourselves visible to one another across the public spaces of heterosexual society. Public transactions of homosexuality always presume onlooking heterosexuals.

It should be objected here that similar remarks could be made about any gender role and certainly about the projection of femininity by men. I would agree with the objection, as I would agree with Irigaray's conclusion from it that in patriarchy there is really only one sex. What distinguishes homosexuality as performance from other gender roles is that it was originally presumed to be pure performance, to be something that could be sustained against the force of nature only by ongoing performance. We give sanction to our prescriptions for gender behaviors by insisting on just how natural they are. Boys walk this way, girls that. It is unnatural for a boy to walk like a girl. Someone who persists in behaving unnaturally is judged to do so perversely or pathologically or at least eccentrically—and so is assigned the further performance of perversity or pathology or eccentricity. This further performance is prescribed as the backdrop, as the diorama against which the prohibited acts will take place. If men who sleep with men can sometimes forget themselves in bed, they are supposed to behave as homosexuals at every other moment, in their least gesture, accent, taste, sentiment. They are supposed to perform what they do so stubbornly in private, as they are to try to conceal that acting out by being what is called discreet.

The conviction that homosexuality is inescapably performative appears in both Wittman and Tyler. It does so negatively as burlesque or charade, positively as show or camp. Tyler in particular enriches the conviction by dwelling on the further layers of performance introduced in the cinematic performance of homosexuality—the layers of person, star, role, and so on. Imagine a gay man who, as star, must be normatively straight, and who is asked to play the role of a straight man who pretends to be a gay man in order to avoid the draft or who does bad drag in order to join an all-female band leaving Chicago—delicious complexities. They should not become so delicious that they distract us from asking *why* homosexuality is seen to be always, especially performative.

Here Wittman is unclear because naive, Tyler unclear because overly invested in the pleasure of homosexuality as elite, ironic performance. The pertinent problem with the category of "homosexuality" is not that it traps us into a binary opposition between heterosexual and homosexual, that it holds us up from getting to the paradise of bisexuality. The pertinent problem is that "homosexuality" is a projection by a viewing eye that is normatively heterosexual. Wittman can claim, as he does, to be writing primarily for other homosexuals, but he cannot really do what he says. The invocation of the category "homosexual" says the opposite. To be writing *for homosexuals* is to be writing under the view of heterosexuals. To be urging homosexuals to make themselves manifest is to remind them that they are most on view not for each other, but for the normatively heterosexual audience peering into the ghetto, watching the show.

Tyler does and does not undertake further explorations. He resists at many points the notion that homosexuality is only a kind of charade, only playacting, and so he cannot trace out how far homosexuality is, in its categorical logic, always a performance for heterosexuals. This is unfortunate, because the outward direction of homosexual visibility is nowhere more apparent than in film, where the camera is normatively heterosexual so far as it registers or re-creates publicly available points of view. That is why, I think, Tyler keeps finding that so many homosexual performances on film have the feel of playacting, of charade, of bad camp. Much more than the writing of manifestos, the making of films can acquiesce in the prevailing politics of visibility. It also forces them into their final paradoxes.

Much has been written since the late sixties about the heteronormativity of cameras, including still ones.[25] Many proposals have been made for queering the camera. These claims do not seem to me to take seriously enough the paradoxes embedded in any program of gay visibility. Let me illustrate this from two distinguished examples.

Teresa de Lauretis reads Sheila McLaughlin's *She Must Be Seeing Things* (1987) as refiguring the "standard," heterosexist relation of viewer to film by including centrally within itself constitutive and multiple acts of lesbian viewing.

> The originality of McLaughlin's film ... consists precisely in its foregrounding [of the male gaze], making *it* visible, and at the same time shifting it, moving it aside, as it were, enough to let us see through the gap, the contradiction; enough to create a space for questioning not only what *they* see but also what *we* see in the film; enough to let us see ourselves seeing, and with what eyes.[26]

De Lauretis links the displacements produced by the inclusion of lesbian filmmaking within the film with the structure of fantasy as pictured psychoanalytically.

> It is in that space between the fantasy scenario and the self-critical, ironic lesbian gaze—a space the film constructs evidently and purposefully—that I am addressed as spectator and that a subject-position is figured out and made available in terms of a sexual difference that is not a difference between woman and man, between female and male sexuality, but a difference between heterosexual and lesbian.[27]

De Lauretis suggests in a note that Fassbinder would be a good place to start with similar transformations into a male homosexual viewer, and, indeed, a nuanced reading of Fassbinder's *Querelle* has been used by Steven Shaviro to just that end.[28] On Shaviro's reading, *Querelle* ensnares the male viewer in its endlessly reduplicated, gilt-framed mirrors of pornography, violence, virility, self-immolation. The snare is artfully set within the film itself.

> In his impotent distance from the events of the narrative, the passively voyeuristic Seblon is a stand-in for the audience, the one figure with whom the spectator is forced to "identify." Overwhelmed and incapacitated by the desire for "boys with big cocks," Seblon is nothing but a pure gaze.[29]

Fassbinder "makes the viewer complicit" in the process of the pornographic ide-alization of men's physical violation by other men. Shaviro links this sense of the viewer's violent manipulation by the film with an almost mystical doctrine about the loss of self in anal intercourse. Being on the bottom becomes the way to escape the economy of images, to enter into unfantasmatic "spasms of ecsta-tic self-annihilation."[30] The viewer is invited to go and do likewise as a means of escaping the heterosexist disposition of the camera.

I confess to finding these two claims for the transformation wrought by more recent lesbian and gay films unconvincing. They are unconvincing in part because they commit what used to be disdained as the "intentional fallacy." Whatever the fate of the author under postmodernism, the auteur seems to flourish. De Lauretis's McLaughlin and Shaviro's Fassbinder are very strong pre-postmodern auteurs, working all kinds of effects precisely and unproblem-atically on the viewer. But my lack of conviction comes from something more than worries over the persistence of auteurship. It comes from the nagging suspicion that the elements singled out as innovative in *She Must Be Seeing Things* and *Querelle* are rather familiar from the sixties (to go no further back). Indeed, they all appear in what Parker Tyler calls "ultrarich faggot fudge," I mean, in the "ludicrously embarrassing" *Pink Narcissus*. In it, they come fabu-lously apart.

Pink Narcissus

For many years, *Pink Narcissus* was officially anonymous. Tyler tells us that "according to rumor" the director/producer/author—a real auteur—might be "a VIP" (177). In 1971, at the time of the film's first public screenings, the reviewer for *Variety* reported that it was made over seven years by a young film-maker whose nerve failed when it came time to edit a version for release. Martin Jay Sadoff was hired to do the editing and, with Gary Goch, the scoring.[31] When the film was "rediscovered" at the 1984 New York Gay Film Festival, its principal maker was identified as Jim Bidgood. This information is now regularly repeated in film guides.[32] A variant narrative tells that the film's producers, fed up with long years of production and fearing many more, cut and released the *Pink Nar-cissus* we know rather than wait on the much larger project Bidgood intended.[33] Bidgood refused to let his name be used on the fragment. Bidgood or not, VIP or not, young or old, costume maker or set painter or both, the film's maker has man-aged to stuff *Pink Narcissus* with more images of performance, spectatorship, and camp than might seem possible. Let me cite two sets of images from the abundance.

The first images are of the masculine gaze. There are so many gazes crosscut in so many directions that the viewer simply loses track. I single out what might be called the "matador/tearoom" sequence. The protagonist (played by Bobby Kendall) begins in front of an iconostasis of mirrors. The protagonist is always in front of mirrors—Narcissus, remember. (We should further remember that "narcissism" was popularly understood to be Freud's candidate for the cause of homosexuality.) The film cuts to Narcissus in front of a line of urinals at what is obviously a public men's room. In case there should be any question, there is an extreme close-up of trash stirred over the porcelain by the stream of fresh urine. Back to the mirror: Narcissus now moves forward to caress himself in it, obliterating with his fingers the image of his mouth, his eyes. Reverse angle to become the mirror looking through the fingers to his eyes. There is some languorous finger sucking.

The next cut is to the night landscape in which the film opened and in which it will close. There is a glimpse of Narcissus lying on the grass. Crowd sounds cue a cut to Narcissus dressed as a matador, then as a (Mexican?) peasant boy, seen stereotypically as a crouched supplicant. The peasant boy removes an astonishingly artificial narcissus flower from his sombrero and throws it in wobbling flight across various backdrops, through a vortex, to land before the matador—who stands, of course, in front of arches that trace the outline of the original mirrors. Back to the men's room, where Narcissus is approached by a leatherman, who gropes him (in realistic footage) even as he rides a motorcycle through his cape (in fantasy footage). Each of the sequences contains numerous gazes back and forth between Narcissus and leatherman. What is more interesting, both the "realistic" and the "fantasy" shots are intercut with the uplifted face of the peasant boy and with an (anonymous) POV long shot of the gropings taken through a partly opened door—that is, from the viewpoint of an arresting officer or a hidden third participant or both. So there are at least eight incorporated gazers in this segment, not counting the camera itself: Narcissus caressing the mirror, Narcissus and the leatherman in the men's room, Narcissus as matador, leatherman as motorcyclist, peasant boy, the unspecified voyeur(s), and the mirror itself. Eight gazers for the rubbings and suckings of at most two bodies—the Panopticon, indeed.

The second set of images, which I can describe more briefly, consists of allusions to or quotations from previous Hollywood films, especially films that suggest homoeroticism in one way or another. Now the whole of *Pink Narcissus* is done in a style that can only be described as Kenneth Anger for the lamé-conscious. It is often linked with Anger's *Fireworks* (1947), and there are indeed both visual and thematic connections.[34] But the design—the texture—of the later film is entirely other. So I prefer to think of *Pink Narcissus* as *Puce Moment* (1949) stretched out to a *Puce Half Hour.* Or perhaps we are to think of the camping of Hollywood performed famously in Jack Smith's *Flaming Creatures* (1963), but also in other of his films and in his performance pieces. Or perhaps we are to see that *Pink Narcissus* invokes Hollywood both directly and through the already available camp version. Its pretitle sequence is a prolonged tracking shot through a nightmarish moonlit landscape that resembles nothing so much as Sebastian Venable's garden in *Suddenly, Last Summer* (1959). The "matador" sequence has to be a send-up of the 1941 version of *Blood and Sand,* starring Tyrone Power, whose offscreen life was indeed pink. The motorcycle-straddling leatherman—James Dean, of course, only in this film it is Dean, not the queer Sal Mineo, who ends up "dying" on the pavement. And perhaps *Pink Narcissus* means even to invoke the Maas and Moore production of *Narcissus* (1957), which is also set in a shabby urban "theater" and is also very much concerned with homosexuality and its fantasies. I am willing to argue that most, if not all, of these quotations are meant to be appreciated precisely as quotations. *Pink Narcissus* may be "ludicrously embarrassing," but it is cunningly well-informed about American movies, both above and below ground level.

The soliciting multiplication of gendered gazes, the mimicry of fantasy mechanisms, the parody of Hollywood styles and scenes—these and other features found in *Pink Narcissus* are supposed to mark the undoing of the straight camera in later films. But if there is a film that reinforces the clichés of gay performance for the straight world, a film that relishes being naughtily disobedient to straight rules, a film that keeps looking over its shoulder at straight viewers to gauge their outrage, the film is *Pink Narcissus.* I draw the conclusion that the kinds of mechanisms identified by de Lauretis and Shaviro do not, in fact, bring about the queering of the camera. If they could, some cameras would have been perfectly queer from 1967 on.

There is, I suspect, a more stubborn puzzle here, having to do with the notion of a queer optics. We can catch a glimpse of it by looking at the other half of the genealogy of *Pink Narcissus*—its debt to the conventions of gay pornography. Thomas Waugh has now shown how old those conventions are, in still photography and in film.[35] It is interesting to note how frequently the gaze figures as a theme in what little plot some of the the early films have. Among the "physique" and "naturist" films of the 1950s, for example, any number concern an artist and his models (with variations on the Pygmalion story) or bodybuilders and their mirrors, or swimmers and their voyeurs.[36] A viewer who had been raised up on these films would have greeted *Pink Narcissus* as a slightly more explicit and definitely better designed restaging of earlier clichés. It is important that it be only slightly more explicit, that it stand "at the juncture of the gay underground tradition and the porno industry."[37] What makes *Pink Narcissus* suitable for Parker Tyler's attention is that it is not simply pornography. If it were, his own principles would have required him to keep silent about it. But that ambiguous position is also what allows the film to push so many of the puzzles about queer film to their limits. *Pink Narcissus* is constantly aware of the threatening gaze of the straight world. It constantly flirts at the edge of unmistakable pornography. So too do the first "hard-core" gay films of a few years later. Sometimes visually or in incidental detail (as in *The Boys in the Sand*, 1971), sometimes in dialogue or plot (as in *Adam and Yves*, 1974), the viewer is reminded of the threat posed by straight society. The sexual deeds being performed for the viewer are as homoerotic as one would want. The presumptive audience is, too—and, as it were, by definition. But these "hard-core" films share with the "soft-core" *Pink Narcissus* an inability to shake off the intruding gaze of heterosexuality. They cannot shake it off, I think, because they cannot get out of the category of homosexuality.

I want to go further. I suggest that no mechanisms yet in view can queer the camera. We have not thought far enough into the paradoxes of gay "identity" to understand the ways in which filming gayness is impossible without an endless replication of performance paradoxes. This is especially the case with the pretense of literal or documentary representation, but true as well of "theatrical" films.[38] We would do much better, I think, to follow Monique Wittig in thinking that we don't yet know what a nonheterosexist representation of homosexuality would be. Or, to say this precisely, what it would be to have a nonheterosexist representation of what heterosexuals call homosexuality.[39] What is more, gay theory cannot here follow the lead of feminist/lesbian theory. The conditions for

representing male homosexuality are not the conditions for representing lesbianism. The visibility of gayness is always conditioned by its being a rejection of
the most visible gender of all, straight masculinity.

Losing Sight of Homosexuals

What blocks thinking here is nothing so simple as an "essentialism" of gay or
straight that could be fingered and thrown out. Wittman and Tyler, in their different ways, are both suspicious of "gayness" as essence. Other texts from the late
1960s reject essentialism more emphatically. One such text is Altman's *Homosexual Oppression and Liberation*, the last chapter of which is titled with a question: "The End of the Homosexual?"[40] The rejection of essentialism and a sketch
of what we now call "social constructionism" is found even more clearly in an
essay by Mary McIntosh titled, quite precisely, "The Homosexual Role."[41] For
McIntosh, modern homosexual identity is a historical artifact, neither a nature
nor a pathology of nature. The rejection of essentialism has long been clear in
principle. What is not clear is how far the rejection was thought through. The
rejection always seems to give way before a need to reify, to bring forward concrete categories. The quarrel about how to make male homosexuality manifest
seems to assume an answer to the question, Is male homosexuality the kind of
thing that can be made manifest? I would like to end by insisting that the question deserves long thought.

Conceive what we call "homosexuality" for a moment, not as an identity, but
as a societal status. Conceive it as an analogy to the institution of private property. The analogy should suggest not just that "homosexuality" is an elaborate
and strictly enforced social construction, but that it is best understood in terms
of utility to nonhomosexuals. To be identified as a male homosexual is to take on
a disposability to certain uses by others—say, the uses of ridicule, scapegoating,
fag bashing, rape. Here it is important to recall that the social valuation of male
homosexuality is primarily conditioned not by the contrast with heterosexuality,
but by the contrast with normative masculinity. Young gays are stigmatized not
because they desire penises, but because they are sissies. Sissyness is simultaneously conceived as both innate and corrigible, a contradiction much like the contradictions embedded in the conception of private property. The insult or identification "You're such a sissy" is typically linked to the command, "Stop acting
that way!" This command can seem to mean something like "Stop performing a

disvalued status." What it actually means is, "Stop doing what 'impels' us straight men to treat you as a gender traitor, as something lower even than a woman." In short, "Stop acting in a way that 'forces' me to abuse you."

Conceived in this way, the category "homosexual" contains a threat of social sanction on behalf of majority gender anxieties. How can this kind of category be represented? Only as a relation, potential or actual, to the punishing power, to the severe norm of straight masculinity. The homosexual can be shown only in eternal reaction, fearful or angry, "excessively" promiscuous or dryly celibate, hysterically nelly or drearily butch. More: the homosexual can appear only as the first part of a conditional sentence, the end of which is inevitably a judgment. A homosexual appears on screen and we hold our breath in expectation, just as we do in a horror show. The association may be important. Homosexuality is an essentially gothic identity, an identity that carries with it, that produces, a plot of exposure, retribution, and cleansing. There are no happy endings for homosexuals because homosexuality as a category requires a very different denouement.

Pink Narcissus can serve once again to illustrate the point. The film ends with the destruction of its protagonist. It is night in a spectral forest marked by spiders' webs and the cold moon. Naked, Narcissus exposes himself to a rainstorm. Suddenly he is threatened by what seem to be the forces of brute nature, of the earth and its overly heavy vegetation. He runs, he struggles. In the end, he is swallowed up by vegetative soil. Note two things. First, this is not in fact how the classical myth of Narcissus ends. It is a free invention of the scriptwriter. Second, this ending is invented by a presumptively gay filmmaker for a presumptively gay audience. One might call it internalized homophobia, but it is more helpful to call it the logic of the category "homosexuality." That category is a mirror, not of same-sex desire, but of the dominant models for straight masculinity. The mirror must show the annihilation of the male homosexual in order to ensure the stable differentiation of the male heterosexual.

This is, I keep suggesting, a matter of categorical logic. It points to the central twist in the category "homosexuality." The category is only secondarily about same-sex desire; it is principally about nonmasculinity. Because masculinity is a category of gender rather than of sex, the category "homosexuality" functions at the level of gender rather than of sexuality, even though it pretends to be a category of sexuality. Gender categories are represented as nonsexual behaviors, hence as performances. The performances are supposed to be about sexuality.

They are supposed to result from sexuality, to derive from it as outward manifestations from inner cause. This is a fiction. "Homosexuality" is in fact a category dependent on the anxieties of male gender. It is, in this way, a radical misdescription of same-sex desire—and, even more emphatically, of same-sex love. It is a misdescription by being a misleading overdescription. The description begins to fall apart when it is transferred to the screen.

One way to see this is by contrast with the term *homophile*. Some of its advocates used this term precisely to say that there is more to homosexuality than mere sex. There is the full range of affection, friendship, and passion, and there is an element of necessity. Any man can have sex with other men, but the homophile (on this understanding) was compelled to seek deep emotional attachment only with other men.[42] Now it would certainly seem possible to make a homophile movie by adapting the conventions of the heterosexual love story. In fact, in the years since the 1960s, just this has been done any number of times, including quite recently in *Beautiful Thing* (1996). But the category "homosexual" seems to claim less and to cover more than the category "homophile" understood in that way. It pretends to be essentially about sex between men—not about love or anything complicated like that. But representations of "homosexuality" in film cannot take the form of just sex acts without running afoul of the complex cinematic codes that separate pornography from what is not pornography.

Here the fiction of homosexuality has been supported in curious ways by the general prohibition against pornographic depictions in "mainstream" movies. If homosexuality has to do with men having sex, then it would seem that representations of homosexuality should show men having sex. The representation of same-sex relations should evidently center on the representation of sexual acts. Wittman is surely right about this: the essential enactment of copulation with (a) partner(s) of similarly shaped genitals is just copulation with (a) partner(s) of similarly shaped genitals. Traditionally, that representation has been called pornography and has been differentiated from "legitimate" or "serious" film. So no film about homosexuality can show unequivocally what homosexuality is about.

The enactment of homosexuality must then be transposed into a complex set of manners of many different kinds. Just here the prohibition against pornography joins up with the central confusion in the category "homosexuality." We cannot show sex. We must displace it onto nonsexual manners. These are generally stereotyped gender traits in no way determined by what is supposed to be their origin, a "desire" for same-sex copulation. The paradox in representing the homosexual arises from the disjunction between same-sex copulation and homosexual manners, between the (always absent) pornographic enactment and its (always deceptive) surrogate, which is not so much a surrogate as a counterfeit. But that paradox of representation is built into the category itself. The category is not about what it pretends to be about. Homosexuality tangles itself in invisibility because homosexuality as a category does not represent what it claims to represent. It claims to represent the sexual cause of same-sex copulation. It represents in fact the enforcement of the gender of masculinity.

Both Wittman and Tyler collaborate in different ways with this game of substitution. They must collaborate so long as they employ the category "homosexuality." Wittman collaborates unknowingly, Tyler knowingly. I conclude this because I find in Tyler the winking mention of a strong alternative. "There are," he murmurs in a passage already quoted, "as many sexes as there are individuals." This equation would undo the enforcement of gender expectations, hence the sleight of hand that substitutes homosexuality for same-sex sexuality. Tyler's individual sexes are constituted not by enforced categories of manners, but by the individual's juxtaposition of copulations, by a specific history of couplings. Tyler's title, *Screening the Sexes*, is quite deliberate in its vague plural. By his reckoning, sexual identity would be no more than the vector of a sequence of sexual episodes. It would, in short, be essentially montage. Imagine the cinema of this plurality. No quarrel about happy endings. No need for narrative endings at all. The innumerable sexes would screen themselves, edit themselves, manifest themselves just as sexes, not as the anxious excess of the ruling gender. Who knows? We might then discover what is really meant by the gender of the camera—not to say the gender of an author's voice.

Notes

1. On these documents and their relations, see the original preface by Jeffrey Weeks to Guy Hocquenghem, *Homosexual Desire* (Paris: Editions Universitaires, 1972; rev. ed., Durham, N.C.: Duke University Press, 1993).
2. Kirkpatrick Sale, *SDS* (New York: Random House, 1973), 104–5.
3. Wayne R. Dynes, ed., *Encyclopedia of Homosexuality* (New York: Garland, 1990), 1400. Given its very uneven quality, I have generally used information from this publication only when I had independent confirmation.
4. On the protest action, see Donn Teal, *The Gay Militants* (New York: Stein & Day, 1971; rev. ed., New York: St. Martin's, 1994), 29–32. To judge from the documents Teal reproduces, the principal motive was not, as the *Encyclopedia of Homosexuality* says, to protest the line's participation in shipping war supplies to Vietnam (1400).
5. Teal, *The Gay Militants*, 95, n. 51.
6. It was republished in 1970 in New York, for example, by the Red Butterfly collective, which added its own commentary. Ibid., 86, 95.,Teal himself wrote in 1971 that the *Manifesto* "has become, in effect, the bible of gay liberation." Ibid., 95.
7. See Carl Wittman, "Students and Economic Action," and Carl Wittman and Thomas Hayden, "An Interracial Movement of the Poor," both reprinted in *The New Student Left: An Anthology*, ed. Mitchell Cohen and Dennis Hale (Boston: Beacon, c. 1966), 170–219.
8. I cite the *Manifesto* parenthetically by section and paragraph, following the version in *Out of the Closets: Voices of Gay Liberation,* ed. Karla Jay and Allen Young (New York: Pyramid, 1972; rev. ed., London: GMP, 1992), 330–42.
9. In an amicus curiae brief written originally during November 1984, Alan Bérubé suggests that gay sex goes public because criminal law already treats it as always public—even when "performed" in private. "Because *all* sex acts between men were considered public and illegal," gay men found or established marginally public places in which they could have a furtive privacy, that is, a kind of secrecy. Alan Bérubé, "The History of Gay Bathhouses," reprinted in *Policing Public Sex,* ed. Dangerous Bedfellows (Boston: South End, 1996), 189.
10. What Wittman says about gay spaces echoes in more recent quarrels over gay visibility. See, for example, the defense of a public "sexual culture" in Lauren Berlant and Michael Warner, "Sex in Public," *Critical Inquiry* 24 (1998): 561–63.
11. I cite parenthetically from Parker Tyler, *Screening the Sexes: Homosexuality in the Movies* (New York: Holt, Rinehart & Winston, 1972; rev. ed., New York: Da Capo, 1993). The terminus of 1971 also figures, for example, on 50, 61.
12. The most piquant presentation of biographical information is by Tyler's lover, Charles Boultenhouse, in "Parker Tyler's Own Scandal," *Film Culture* 77 (fall 1992): 10–23.

13. Ibid., 12–14.

14. See Andrew Sarris, "Foreword," in Tyler, *Screening the Sexes*, ix–x.

15. I wonder if these lines are meant to allude to Walter Pater's infamous (and once suppressed) conclusion to *Studies in the History of the Renaissance* (1873). Consider this familiar sentence: "A counted number of pulses only is given to us of a variegated, dramatic life."

16. Compare Tyler's remarks on "moral crusades" (20), "the new homosexual militance" (49), and "militant minorities" (52, 61).

17. See, for example, Tyler's scathing criticisms of $M^*A^*S^*H$ (33, 43) and other deprecatory phrases (188, 194).

18. See, for example, Tyler's image of the stars and planets (233).

19. Tyler remarks on honesty: "This is what I mean by what I oppose to the virtuous: the vicious; that which militates against *honest* truth" (183). On the dishonesty of critics: "Up till very lately, when homosexuality is a high minority fashion, critics have resorted to every possible 'fair' tactic to suppress homosexual angles whenever movies dared be explicit and realistic about them" (138).

20. Recall, for example, the phrases "hauntingly poetic eroticism" (140), "conscious poetic eroticism" (153), "a truly poetic thing" (222), "a poetically exquisite drama" (288).

21. For Tyler's characterization of *Teorema*, see 122; for *Boys*, 49; Mae and Myra, chap. 1, passim, with the conclusion, 15; for the contrast between Novarro and *Staircase*, 148–49.

22. See the introduction by Jonathan Ned Katz to the revised edition of Teal, *The Gay Militants*, xv–xvi.

23. Vito Russo provides a marvelous summary of the deaths of cinematic homosexuals in the "Necrology" appended to *The Celluloid Closet: Homosexuality in the Movies*, 2d ed. (New York: Harper & Row , 1987), 347–49.

24. Butler's own view is more complex than the formula allows. One can see this, for example, in her reply to some questions posed by Eve Kosofsky Sedgwick in "Queer Performativity: Henry James's *The Art of the Novel*," *GLQ: A Journal of Lesbian and Gay Studies* 1 (1993): 1–16. Judith Butler's "Critically Queer" appears in the same issue of *GLQ* (17–32).

25. See, to select but a few examples, Richard Meyer, "Robert Mapplethorpe and the Discipline of Photography," in *The Lesbian and Gay Studies Reader*, ed. Henry Abelove, Michèle Aina Barale, and David M. Halperin (New York: Routledge, 1993), 360–80, esp. 362, with the reference to Martha Rosler; and any number of essays in *In a Different Light: Visual Culture, Sexual Identity, Queer Practice*, ed. Nayland Blake, Lawrence Rinder, and Amy Scholder (San Francisco: City Light, 1995).

26. Teresa de Lauretis, "Film and the Visible," in *How Do I Look? Queer Film and Video*, ed. Bad Object-Choices (Seattle, Wash.: Bay, 1991), 255.

27. Ibid., 251.

28. Ibid., n. 27; Steven Shaviro, *The Cinematic Body* (Minneapolis: University of Minnesota Press, 1993), 159–98.

29. Shaviro, *The Cinematic Body*, 171–72.

30. Ibid., 181, 187.

31. Review of *Pink Narcissus*, *Variety*, May 25, 1971. *Variety*'s subhead on the review reads, "A homosexual masturbation fantasy, very artistically made. And not hardcore." The film was also reviewed by Vincent Canby for the *New York Times*, May 24, 1971, who judged it "sad and very vulnerable and as serious as it is sappy" (44). See also the entry in Raymond Murray, ed., *Images in the Dark: An Encyclopedia of Gay and Lesbian Film and Video* (Philadelphia: TLA, 1994), 428.

32. See, for example, the notice in Jenni Olson, ed., *The Ultimate Guide to Lesbian and Gay Film and Video* (New York: Serpent's Tail, 1996), 199. This notice seems to be one of those Olson took from the "programmers" of the San Francisco International Lesbian and Gay Film Festival.

33. See the unsigned article "James Bidgood Is Anonymous" in the fall 1996 issue of the Webzine *Dent* (members.aol.com/dentmag). The article is the work of Bruce Benderson, who has published a lavishly illustrated account of Bidgood's life and work, including *Pink Narcissus*, in *James Bidgood* (Cologne: Benedikt Taschen, 1999).

34. See Richard Dyer, *Now You See It: Studies on Lesbian and Gay Film* (London: Routledge, 1990), 120–25, 163–65.

35. Thomas Waugh, *Hard to Imagine: Gay Male Eroticism in Photography and Film from Their Beginnings to Stonewall* (New York: Columbia University Press, 1996).

36. Daniel Harris deftly summarizes these motifs as three excuses for men to touch: first, "a maniacal tendency on the part of the actors to engage in unmotivated bouts of wrestling"; second, the " 'appreciation' by an admiring artist"; and third, "a homoerotic form of rescue, as in the many instances of drowning ... or ... heat exhaustion." Daniel Harris, *The Rise and Fall of Gay Culture* (New York: Hyperion, 1997), 112.

37. Unattributed notice in Olson, *The Ultimate Guide*, 199.

38. Some writers on gay film and video still speak as if the documentary were a transparent genre, one in which what is "out there" gets recorded without transmutation. For a recent example of this, see B. Ruby Rich, "Reflections on a Queer Screen," *GLQ: A Journal of Lesbian and Gay Studies* 1 (1993): 82–91. My own view is that a documentary about homosexuality is no less entangled by the paradoxes of gay performance than a theatrical film.

39. I take this as the principal argument of, say, the first three essays in Monique Wittig's *The Straight Mind and Other Essays* (Boston: Beacon , 1992).

40. Dennis Altman, *Homosexual Oppression and Liberation*, rev. ed. (New York: New York University Press, 1993).

41. Mary McIntosh, "The Homosexual Role," *Social Problems* 16 (fall 1968): 182–92, esp. 183–85.

42. See the passages quoted by Dyer, *Now You See It*, 74–75.

Members of the Manson "family" maintain a vigil outside the Los Angeles courthouse during the murder trial. Courtesy of Los Angeles Public Library.

XXX
Love and Kisses from Charlie
Jeffrey Sconce

Few popular demons in American culture have undergone as thorough, endur-ing, and lucrative an exorcism as Charles Manson. Two and a half decades after his conviction and incarceration for the Tate/LaBianca murders he is said to have masterminded, Manson remains a surprisingly public figure. Having already inspired a seemingly endless cycle of paperbacks detailing the sordid life of "the family," and having single-handedly created the now ubiquitous pulp men-ace of the "hippie terror-cult," Manson in the 1990s has continued to generate considerable press—this despite the fact that he has never escaped, can expect absolutely no possibility of parole, and would seemingly have been upstaged by now by the more prolific trio of Bundy, Gacy, and Dahmer. And yet it is Manson who survives, both in a series of correctional facilities in California and in the nation's feverish and apparently insatiable criminal imagination. He remains the psychopath of choice for each new generation of cub reporters and video jour-nalists looking to cut their teeth on an "intense" interview situation. In their time, Geraldo Rivera, Tom Snyder, and even Ronald Reagan Jr. have all gone *mano a mano* with Charlie in lockdown, bringing his disassociative ramblings to a still growing and apparently eternally fascinated audience. With each passing year there appears at least one tabloid story touting Manson's imminent (yet obviously impossible) parole, decrying the supposedly vast recording royalties he receives in jail, or warning of followers still lurking in the California desert, plotting to free him and embark on the killing spree of the century.

For many, the Manson story served as a grisly coda to the failed and now increasingly distant idealism of boomer counterculture in the sixties. In this respect, a generation that watched Jerry Rubin go to Wall Street, Mark Chapman kill John Lennon, Abbie Hoffman take his own life, and Jane Fonda marry Ted Turner must now contend with the equally unnerving bummer that Charles Manson, born November 1934, is over sixty years old. Although Manson himself is not a boomer, of course, he is nevertheless a dominant symbol of that generation's "loss of innocence" for the now burgeoning boomer analysis industry. "Many people I know in Los Angeles believe that the Sixties ended abruptly on August 9, 1969, ended at the exact moment when word of the murders on Cielo Drive traveled like a brushfire through the community," writes Joan Didion in her 1978 memoir of the decade.[1] Debuting the ABC news series *Turning Point* some fifteen years later with an entire episode devoted to "the Manson women," correspondent Diane Sawyer parroted this maxim as the party line on the counterculture's ignominious ending. "There was a sense of possibility then that would survive the Vietnam protests, and the assassinations," said Sawyer, "but it would not survive the day in 1969 when we picked up the newspaper and read about Charles Manson and his followers who brought death."[2]

But there would seem to be something more compelling in Manson's media legacy, something that transcends the tired recirculation of long-standing bromides within mainstream historical and cultural commentary. Born of the sixties, perhaps, Manson has somehow remained meaningful to subsequent generations, and like all true media superstars, he enjoys a celebrity that seems to resonate with a vast cross section of the American public. The Manson persona continues to be important, not only to aging boomers contemplating their harsh fall from Eden, but also to the older God-and-country set who believed Manson to be the inevitable consequence of shaggy hair and electric guitars, as well as a whole new subculture of disaffected youth sporting Manson T-shirts and performing Manson music, all to the horror of elders who do not recognize the knowing irony and rather explicit generational contempt expressed through such gestures.[3] The media may lecture itself every so often about the morality of extending Manson's fame, and as a nation we may occasionally be temporarily distracted by other criminal celebrities, but in the end Manson remains the figure to whom we return collectively again and again as the culture's consummate symbol of evil incarnate. Or as Quentin Tarantino's ambitious mass murderers observe of Manson through the prism of Oliver Stone's *Natural Born Killers*, "It's hard to beat the king."

How has this come to be? Why Manson and not Gacy, or Dahmer, or even

Charlie's military soul mate, Lt. William Calley? How many Americans have
even heard of Dean Allen Corll, a murderer who by the most conservative esti-
mates killed four times as many people as Manson, Tex Watson, and Susan
Atkins combined? Clearly Manson's notoriety is not based on a simple arith-
metic of atrocity, his evil residing somewhere other than in a mere body count.[4]
I would argue that the public longevity of the Manson mythos, like so many
other psychodramas haunting the American mediascape, is fueled by complex
and volatile issues of sex, gender and power—cultural conflicts provoked by
the "sexual revolution" of the sixties that remain unresolved even today. From
the earliest reports of Manson's involvement in the Tate/LaBianca murders,
media attention to "the family" dwelled leeringly on the sexual dimensions of
the group's social organization, leading *Life* magazine, that bastion of American
normality, to dub the entire affair "the strange story of Charles Manson and his
brood of nubile flower children."[5] Exploiting this line of interest, most major
paperback editions covering the case in the years that followed have promised
on their covers that lurid details would be revealed within, ranging from the
secret "sex orgies" of Ed Sanders's *The Family* to the "perversion and passion" in
William Zamora's *Blood Family*. Within this scenario, Manson is not only infamous as a murderer, of course, but also as a psycho-Svengali who was somehow
able to compel middle-class teenage girls to commit unspeakable crimes, be it
the murder of anonymous victims or having sex with a thirty-three-year-old
ex-con. Complementing Manson in this mythos are the Manson women, abused
teen runaways who alternately figure in popular culture as freethinking hippie
sluts or brain-dead hippie slaves.

In this essay I examine how highly sexualized discourses—both prurient and
prudish—surrounding Manson and his "girls" have allowed the events of 1969
to take on the character of a disturbing yet obviously compelling and thus
enduring morality play. Emerging in an era when *Cosmopolitan* and *Playboy*
worked to articulate a new sexual economy beyond the strictly procreative
functions of the American family, Manson's "family" emblematized both the
dread and the desire bound to this cultural transition, making their strange
commune symptomatic of larger sexual contradictions within American society
as a whole. I hope to demonstrate how Manson, in his rather exaggerated roles
as hippie "playboy" and psycho-patriarch, remains a site of cultural fascination
by foregrounding the often repressed ideological connections between male

promiscuity and male domestic control. In this respect, Manson himself is of less interest than Manson as a vehicle of male power, a persona so completely successful at realizing the underlying fantasies and sexual imperatives that structure male American life that he threatens to reveal and thus betray the patriarchal terms of property and power, conquest and control, that provide the foundation of America's sexual, familial, and social order.

Within the Manson mythos, images of Manson's seemingly unfettered and insatiable sexuality are often paired with accounts of brutal social control within the "family" itself. As has been widely reported of the Manson clan, the men of the family ruled over the women, and Manson, in turn, ruled over everyone absolutely. Within this strikingly hierarchical and discriminatory "commune," women were expected to do all the sewing and food preparation while remaining sexually available at all times for the men in the family (and for visitors to the family compound). Despite its seeming sexual liberation, in other words, the Manson family was in fact a model of reactionary gender roles. In this respect, the story of the Manson family, like most accounts of families in America, is ultimately a story of patriarchy. And while Manson remains an unsettling icon of pathological male power "out of control" (precisely by being so "in control"), the Manson women in their dual roles as sluts and slaves express the paradoxes facing women within the confines of American family life, Mansonesque or otherwise. Living in the deviant Manson family, these women were seen as perverse and promiscuous for standing outside the monogamous order of the "normal" family, and yet at the same time they were subject to the most profound humiliation and subordination imaginable as psychotically devoted "daughters" and "wives." If Manson and his family remain notorious, then, it may have less to do with their aberrance in the annals of crime than with our continuing fascination with the roles of domination, devotion, and degradation, which remain extremely relevant in the popular examination of the culture's sexual and social order, structures radically disrupted and yet strangely reaffirmed by the family and its beliefs.

"Love among the Rattlesnakes"

The horse wrangler, tall and ruggedly handsome, placed his hands on the hips of a pretty girl wearing white bell-bottomed trousers and casually lifted her onto a hitching post near the stable; then, voluntarily, almost automatically, she spread her legs and he stood between her, moving slowly from side to side and up and down, stroking her long blonde hair while her arms and fingers caressed his back, not quickly or eagerly but quite passively, indolently, a mood harmonious with his own.[6]

Although the above may seem a rather mundane passage from a nameless romantic novel, it is in fact Gay Talese's lead paragraph in a story about the author's visit to the Spahn ranch, the abandoned movie set where Manson and his followers lived in the months before the murders. Talese knew his audience well. Appearing in *Esquire*, a magazine rivaled only by *Playboy* in its dreamy articulation of male heterosexual fantasy, Talese's opening helped transform a rather dull interview with George Spahn, the eighty-year-old owner of the ranch, into a potentially revealing visit to the legendary sexual wonderland of the Manson compound. Such a strategy was typical of much coverage of the Manson story, which routinely foregrounded the sexual practices of the family (and the victims), sometimes even over the murders themselves.

The *New York Times Magazine*, for example, began its in-depth treatment of the Manson family with the following epigraphs:

> Neither repented they of their murders, nor of their sorceries, nor of their fornication, nor of their thefts.
>
> Revelation 9:21

> Why don't we do it in the road?
>
> The Beatles[7]

Time was particularly salacious in its initial coverage of the story. "His women lolled harem-like around the commune nude or bare-breasted, catering to his every whim," wrote one reporter, who, in case readers lacked the imagination to illustrate this scene in their own mind's eyes, further noted that "one chagrined ranch hand relate[d] discussing business with Manson while one of Manson's girls performed a sex act upon the 'guru.'"[8] During the trial, a reporter for *Newsweek* honed in on Manson's famous sexual vibe by describing a courtroom full of "meticulously lacquered housewives shivering deliciously when Manson fixes them with his compelling stare." The same reporter also felt it significant to note that "a pretty female artist" painting Manson's portrait during the trial was "ejected once from the court room for appearing in a get-up with an exposed tummy."[9]

Such prurience was not limited to the mainstream press. In the months immediately following the arrests, many underground papers championed Manson as a revolutionary hero for having struck terror in the heart of the "Establishment." This did not stop those papers, however, from engaging in Establishment-like feature writing. Amid its own editorial coverage of the murders and trial, for example, the *Los Angeles Free Press* inserted a front-page story headlined "M.D. on Manson's Sex-Life," a report from a psychologist who had lived briefly at the Spahn ranch. In perhaps the most sordid and transparent exploitation of the sexual scandals associated with the family, opportunistic pornographers in 1970 quickly released a low-budget film called *Love in the Commune*, a movie that distinguished itself with the distinctly bucolic perversion of a Manson type "balling a headless chicken."[10]

Even before any arrests were made in connection with the crimes, the events at 10050 Cielo Drive circulated in rumor and reporting as a sexualized scenario. In a classic "blame the victim" response, the American public first seized on the imagined sexual transgressions of the murdered jet-setters. Within days of the Tate murder, and continuing for much of the trial, public gossip traded in bizarre explanations for the murders, each story assuming, as prosecutor Vincent Bugliosi notes, "that somehow the victims had brought the murder on themselves." Bugliosi continues:

> Given Roman Polanski's affinity for the macabre; rumors of Sebring's sexual peculiarities; the presence of both Miss Tate and her former lover at the death scene while her husband was away; the "anything goes" image of the Hollywood jet set; drugs; and the sudden clamp of police leaks, almost any kind of plot could be fashioned, and was. Sharon Tate was called everything from "the queen of the Hollywood orgy scene" to "a dabbler in satanic arts." Polanski himself was not spared. In the same newspaper a reader could find one columnist saying the director was so grief-stricken he could not speak, while a second had him nightclubbing with a bevy of airline stewardesses.[11]

"Live freaky, die freaky" was the popular judgment frequently heard in the wake of the murders, a maxim wholly sexual in its connotations. Fueled by Sanders's book, contemporary interest in the case continues to center on rumors of Satanism, pornography, and even "snuff" films featuring major Hollywood celebrities that supposedly involved the Tate household.

Once arrests were made, however, the stories of Manson's absolute control over his women, sexual and otherwise, quickly emerged as the central fascination in the case. To this day, almost every published account of the family contains some story of Manson's sexual domination, whether it be in seducing new converts, compelling his women to have sex with visitors to the ranch, or in orchestrating elaborate orgies. And as is true in most sensationalistic accounts of sexual excess, the Manson mythos has exploited elements of both revulsion and desire. What provokes outrage in public discourse, after all, can often serve as fuel for fantasy in private thought, and although few would admit it (maybe even to themselves), many men have no doubt been secretly intrigued by Manson's power over women, even as they were outwardly repulsed by it. Such intrigue has certainly fueled the magazine and book industry that seeks to uncover and publish as many anecdotes of Manson's sexual exploits as possible. As Talese's tour of the Spahn ranch demonstrates, this coverage fit particularly well with what was already a primary theme in the articles and advertising of most men's magazines in the early seventies, which promoted fantasies of such sexual control and even promised to reveal the secrets of acquiring such power. Whether Manson himself had ever read *1001 Best Pick-Up Lines for Women*, *Where to Meet Girls*, or any of the other masculine self-help manuals available by mail order, he had clearly mastered their message. Particularly galling (and yet obviously compelling) for critics, not only was Manson able to seduce many different women, he also cultivated and commanded a perpetually renewable harem to service his every desire. "Manson had the greatest scam of all," writes Sanders, almost as if in grudging respect. "He'd tell the girls that if they really loved him they'd go out and bring him back a girl prettier and younger than they were—and he got away with it."[12]

Of course, although many commentators were quick to link the murders to a larger ethos of sexual perversion, few were willing to go so far as to admit that Manson had only mastered an art that many males had been aspiring to understand throughout the sexual revolution of the sixties. As Manson himself said in one of his more lucid moments, "They've been following me around for three years, trying to find something, and wherever I go there's like thirty women. And that really makes them mad. They can't understand what all these women are doing with one guy."[13] Perhaps because Manson was so spectacularly successful as a womanizer, discussions of Manson's "powers" frequently took the form of disavowal. Confronted with a Casanova figure who also happened to be a psychotic cult leader, commentators disguised Manson's obvious success at realizing the *Playboy* fantasies of many of the era's male population by recasting Manson's sexual prowess as psychosis, his magnetism as mania. This disavowal explains why accounts of Manson's sex life concentrate not only on the "immorality" of his sexual excesses, but on attacking Manson's masculinity and heterosexuality. So unsettling, apparently, were the similarities between Manson's seduction of young runaways and the era's more urbane image of the airline pilot seducing young stewardesses that the masculinity of the former had to be discredited in order to preserve the masculinity of the latter.

"One of the mysteries about Charlie is the fact that young women were attracted to this singularly unattractive individual," writes one of the many true-crime authors who has struggled to interpret Manson's legacy in the intervening decades. The implication is that some form of charade beyond the "normal" mechanisms of male heterosexuality must be involved. This same author then focuses her attack by observing, "Other than his brief marriage(s) and his almost as brief activity as a pimp, his primary sexual experience in prison had been homosexual."[14] As this comment suggests, bafflement over Manson's heterosexual charisma has frequently led to attempts to recast him as an impostor of some sort, in this case a homosexual who had somehow learned to "use" heterosexuality as a tool of control over young women. This strategy of heterosexist emasculation has taken a variety of forms. The major newsmagazines, for example, rarely missed an opportunity to comment on Manson's slight physical stature, dubbing him the "diminutive guru," the "pint-sized guru," and the "slight (5 foot 4) defendant."[15] Such attacks no doubt helped ease anxieties that Manson might actually be a "real" man and recast him as a sexual charlatan of some kind.[16] As a stunningly successful example of predatory male heterosexuality, Manson had to be attacked on the terrain of masculinity itself in order to distinguish his "unnatural" and/or "artificial" sexual prowess from that of a normal man.

Perhaps most inventive in this strategy has been Sanders, who, speculating on Manson's fabled sexual stamina (family members claimed Charlie liked to have sex seven times a day), suggests that this "strength" might in fact be a simple case of priapism, a prostate condition that makes it difficult for men to lose an erection.[17] In this way, a common index of masculine pride is rewritten as clinical pathology. Meanwhile, in an essay for *Harper's Magazine* written near the time of

Manson's final sentencing, Frank Conroy wonders whether or not the "rococo architecture of polymorphous perversity" orchestrated by Manson and practiced by the family could possibly compare to the "technicolor prison-cell productions" of Manson's chief sexual outlet: jailhouse masturbation. "The sex games must have become, inevitably, a subdivision of the power games," writes Conroy. "It must have been telling people what to do and having them do it that was the kick, not so much what they actually did." Conroy follows this cogent comment on sex and power with a statement that immediately reaffirms the codes of "true" masculine sexuality underpinning his discussion of Manson. In the ultimate insult one heterosexual male can offer another (beyond allegations of homosexuality), Conroy writes of Manson returning to prison, "I imagine him dying of old age, with his prick in his hand."[18]

Charlie's Angels

Although few critics made explicit connections between the bachelor philosophy promulgated by Hugh Hefner and Manson's oft-quoted creed, "I am the god of fuck,"[19] many commentators did portray Susan Atkins, Leslie Van Houten, Patricia Krenwinkel, and the other "Manson women" as witless vixens whose vacuous personas harbored an explosive potential for violence concealed within a typically *Playboy*-esque mixture of smoldering sexuality and nubile naïveté. And just as popular discourses labored to delegitimate Manson's masculinity, they worked equally hard to construct a certain hyperfemininity around the Manson girls. In a common conceit running from Victorian heroines to Playmates of the month, these women came to signify a volatile passion storming behind an eroticized veil of innocence.

As perverse as it may seem, there is little doubt that the Manson girls provided a site of sexual fantasy, or at least fixation, for the culture at large. As is the fate of many young women in American society, these women's identities were defined almost wholly in terms of their physical appearance, sexual history, and marital status, casting them as objects of both fear and desire. Introducing the world to Susan Atkins, for example, a reporter for *Newsweek* described her first and foremost as "a former acid-dropper and topless dancer," and in his best-selling account of the trial, prosecutor Vincent Bugliosi helped round out his own portrait of Atkins by noting that while in prison, "she did her exercises sans underpants."[20] In perhaps the most strained attempt to exploit an association with the

Manson case, a park ranger for Death Valley National Monument wrote a book based on his intimate knowledge of the desert topography inhabited by Manson and his followers in the days before their arrest. Ranger Murphy recounts this sexual anecdote from the day of the arrest:

> Susan Atkins approached the officers and, pointing to Clem, asked the officers to "unhook him." When George asked the reason he was told, "I want to take him behind the buildings and make love to him one more time." She explained, "He's about the best piece I've ever had, and I may never see him again." The officers knew these were, indeed, unusual women, but her reply flabbergasted them.[21]

During the trial, *Newsweek* reported seemingly extraneous testimony concerning Linda Kasabian's sexual history, noting fastidiously that "she had had sexual intercourse with six different 'family' men on eleven different occasions (four times with Manson)."[22] A hand-drawn illustration for George Bishop's *Witness to Evil*, meanwhile, depicts family member Barbara Hoyt testifying how she "performed 'that oral watchamacallit'" on a visitor to the ranch.[23] Finally, in a more self-conscious examination of this sexualization, the author of a contemporary novella titled *Susan Atkins* wonders in graphic terms "what it would be like to be married to Susan Atkins" and elaborates explicit sexual scenarios around other Manson women such as Kasabian, Van Houten, and Ruth Moorehouse.[24]

Equaling this fascination with the sexuality of the Manson women, however, were infantilizing discourses that portrayed the women as little girls. Thus was Kasabian described at the trial by *Newsweek* as "blue-eyed, dimpled chinned" and as a "pig-tailed woman child."[25] *Time* described her as "girlish, her blonde hair in pig-tails, a small soft figure on the stand."[26] Describing the arrival of Atkins, Krenwinkel and Van Houten at a preliminary hearing, *Rolling Stone* observed, "Three young girls dance down the hallway of the Superior Court Building in Los Angeles, holding hands and singing one of Charlie's songs. They might be on their way to a birthday party in their short, crisp cotton dresses."[27] Reporting from the courtroom, finally, *Newsweek* described the three female defendants as "harpies" who sat "with bird-like heads together, giggling guiltlessly, chattering in strangely childlike voices, smiling innocently and engagingly at the mute, stony jury."[28]

The sexualized woman-child has long been a fixture in patriarchal fantasy, embodying the desired yet contradictory identities of virginal innocence and adult sexuality. The Manson girls were particularly diabolical in this regard, taking shape as the press juxtaposed images of wanton sexual abandon with accounts of girlish middle-class lives abandoned for Charlie. Leslie Van Houten was a prom queen, noted many reporters, while Krenwinkel had sung in the church choir. Such ironic contrasts between debutantes and debauchery helped sensationalize the family and its crimes even more, of course, but they also contributed to the staging of both moral panic and private fantasy in the nation's sexual imagination. It is in this sense of dichotomy and duplicity that the women, Manson, and the family as a whole emblematized the uncertainty surrounding the decade's shifting sexual codes.

Triple XXX

The simultaneous intensity and ambiguity of the Manson family's sexualized kinship structure found dramatic expression during the opening week of the trial. On the first day of testimony, Manson appeared in court with the letter X carved in his forehead. The family, including codefendents Atkins, Van Houten, and Krenwinkel, soon followed suit. Explaining this automutilation, Manson released a statement to the press in which he announced, "I have X-ed myself from your world. . . . I am not of you, from you, nor do I condone your unjust attitude towards things, animals, and people that you do not try to understand."[29] The four defendants bore these marks through the remainder of the trial. Ever the crude semiotician, Manson later converted his X into a swastika.

On a most superficial level, this X can be read in terms of Manson's presumed intentionality. What this gesture lacks in subtlety it more than makes up for as a compelling act of deviance and a calculated image of "Otherness." An X cut into the forehead of any human would command attention, of course, but when Xs were carved into the foreheads of American teenage girls, their impact was immeasurably amplified. Although this objective was most likely not on the family's collective mind, this scarification provided an effective way of disrupting, at least partially, the mass sexual fetishization of these women in the popular press. As opposed to the piercing of ears, here was an act of self-mutilation that was decidedly "antifeminine" in that it did not contribute to the voyeuristic objectification of these women by the media. Those who had bought into such X-rated fantasies surrounding the women were rather rudely confronted by an unambiguous marker of cosmetic disaffection and potential psychosis. Later,

A CBS publicity photo for *Helter Skelter* (1976), the made-for-TV movie about the Manson case, employs collage to create an image of Manson's domination over his "girls." Steve Railsback as Charles Manson; Cathy Paine, Christina Hart, and Nancy Wolfe as the "girls."

when guilty verdicts were finally returned in the case, the female defendants removed themselves even further from the realm of conventional sexual iconography and "sanity" by shaving their heads.

There is a more sinister implication of the X of course, tied to the central issue of gendered power in the family that provides the lingering popular fascination with this case. Quite literally, the Manson X was a mark of the "father," a material sign of Manson's absolute domination over his female followers through a brand signifying power and ownership. In this respect, the X was wholly available for reappropriation within the larger fantasies of masculine power evoked by the case, especially when balanced against the other side of this power equation—the women's apparently spontaneous decision to wear the X as an act of devotion, a pledge of love and commitment to Charlie. Such seemingly blind obedience was already a focus of much public interest in the case, and the wearing of the X only reemphasized the paramount enigma of the Manson saga, a question much more important in the nation's mind than the actual guilt or innocence of the defendants in the murders. Just what was the "real" relationship—sexual, familial, volitional—between Manson and these women?

As objects of terror and titillation, the Manson women shattered the traditional mooring points of gendered society by conflating and confusing such usually distinct social relations as brother and sister, father and daughter, husband and wife. This was perhaps the family's most transgressive act, especially given that Manson seemingly served as the exclusive male partner in each of these relationships. If Manson remains the consummate icon of evil incarnate even today, then, it is in large part because his "family" forced a most public and uncomfortable consideration of the American family's usually occluded drama of oedipalization. As a parable of gender and power, the story of the Manson family presented an example of the intertwined social and sexual mechanisms of oedipalization run alternately amok and astray. Considered in this respect, the recurring obsessions surrounding the case make much more sense. Were the Manson women presexual little girls or adult seductresses? Devoted daughters or eroticized femmes fatales? Was Manson a heterosexual man or some form of asexual or homosexual impostor? Was the "family" actually a family or an ongoing orgy of unrestrained and unchanneled libidinal energy? On the surface, the family's sexual experimentation and apparently communal structure may have evoked both the problems and possibilities of a social organization operating outside the boundaries of the oedipal scenario. But this was more than countered by the absolute power of Manson, whose disturbing public persona reaffirmed the discomforting suspicion that a destructive masculine authority ultimately supported, sanctioned, and censured the era's emerging sexual economy. Sexual liberation, in this case, was the freedom of Manson (and other male family members) to sleep with whomever they chose. Such freedom, of course, was not allotted to the women in the family, replicating the prevailing sexual logic that an airline pilot who sleeps with twenty stewardesses is a playboy, whereas a stewardess who sleeps with twenty pilots is a whore. It was within this authority and omnipotence that Manson ultimately reaffirmed that his family was indeed a family, a social unit that, although it appeared superficially to challenge the sexual order of patriarchy, actually underscored its controlling social order with chilling emphasis, a point perhaps best made by one of the Manson women themselves, who, when asked why she and her friends sat on the steps of the L.A. courthouse sewing a sweater for their incarcerated brother, lover, and patriarch, replied, "We're waiting for our father."

Sexy Sadie

What exactly is the historical legacy of the Manson family twenty-five years later? No longer subject to the immense media scrutiny of the early seventies, Manson and "his" women today nevertheless remain volatile and unstable signifiers, especially as recent attempts to gain parole for the women have intensified. At stake is a historical redefinition of Manson, the women, and the family, often fought around the contentious issue of gendered agency. Were the Manson women helpless victims of Charlie's all-powerful mind games, or were they free-thinking, autonomous criminals completely cognizant of their actions? The latter option would seem to be the opinion of psychologist Clara Livsey, who argues in several places in her book *The Manson Women: A Family Portrait* that female criminals are never taken seriously enough and that their numbers are vastly underestimated.[30] Livsey dismisses accounts of the Manson women as passive victims and argues that they alone should be held accountable for their actions. Even within such a project of recuperation, however, it is doubtful that the Manson women will ever reach the same political status as Valerie Solanas, because as far as crime goes, brutally stabbing jet-setters to death has nowhere near the cultural cachet of artfully plugging Andy Warhol. But this somewhat perverse attempt to reempower these women in the face of Charlie's seeming domination testifies to the continuing importance of these women as symbols and signifiers.

Today, the same boomer analysis industry that sees the Manson case as a signpost for the end of the sixties frequently interprets the story as a warning about the excesses of personal freedom emblematic of the era as a whole. Paradoxically, a story that should serve as a cogent lesson about the excesses of male power implicit in the social structure as a whole becomes instead a parable legitimating a generation's retreat back into the unexamined patriarchal dynamics of "traditional values." Entering this debate over Manson, the women, and their legacy, ABC's documentary series *Turning Point* approached its take on the Manson story through perhaps the most hackneyed, and in this particular case, offensive trope of gender imaginable—the tragic "lost" romance. After probing the consciousness of Krenwinkel and Van Houten with such insightful questions as, "Leslie, were you a *bad* girl?" host Diane Sawyer devotes most of her interview to the women's memories of life with Charlie. Although the women strongly express their repudiation of Manson and their sincere guilt for their parts in the crimes, the overall structure of the documentary cultivates a sense of almost glowing, romantic nostalgia. Incredibly, touted on bumpers throughout the show, the last segment features Sawyer showing the taped interviews of the women to Manson himself in a perverse travesty of *The Love Connection.* "When we come back," promises the announcer, "Charles Manson sees the women who killed for him for the first time in twenty-five years." Back from the commercial, Sawyer introduces her segment with Manson by saying, "It's been twenty-five years since he's seen the women who gave up everything for him." The entire segment then consists of Sawyer setting Charlie up for his video mystery date, working to heighten the audience's anticipation of their strange reunion. Finally, after watching these once teenage murderers now forty-something inmates discussing their former lives in the family, a wistful Manson in full close-up laments of Krenwinkel, "She got old on me." Expressing the general anxiety of boomers everywhere moving into middle-age, perhaps, the showcasing of this comment suggests that, for a nation long fixated on the sexual dimensions of this case, the ultimate crime committed by these women was not murder, but the apparently more horrific betrayal of growing old.

By 1998, however, Manson (and the media) had moved on to fresh meat. British tabloids reported that Manson had become obsessed with the Spice Girls, an all-female pop quintet that Manson reportedly believed to be the Beatles of the new millennium.[31] American video tabloids such as *Hard Copy* immediately picked up the story, reporting that Manson had requested a one-hour audience with the Spice Girls during their upcoming U.S. tour (so that he might "advise" them on their important role in the next century). If authorities would allow the girls to visit Charlie in jail, Manson promised to execute himself afterward with a self-administered lethal injection (his work on earth, apparently, having come to an end). Whether or not this story is true, of course, is of little importance. The tale's frantic circulation on both sides of the Atlantic, however, proves that Manson's peculiar vibe continues to sound in the world's sexual conscious-ness. The story once again activates the full symbolic range of the Manson per-sona. In this latest panic, Charlie could not settle for a mere solo artist. He must have nothing less than the full pop harem of the Spice Girls. But in this respect, perversely, Manson only makes explicit the desires of male Spice Girl fans the world over. Charlie claims he wants to discuss philosophy and the future with the girls, but a knowing public is wise to his "real" goal. Why else would any man want to spend an hour alone with the Spice Girls (and be willing to die after-ward)? Bringing this projection of public fantasy onto the figure of Manson's psyche full circle, management for the Spice Girls announced that in response to the story, the girls would be "beefing up" security on their upcoming U.S. tour. But the question remains: Security from what? A sixty-four-year-old man locked up in California's toughest prison? Or the apparently now timeless sex-ual specter of the Manson mythology?

Notes

1. Joan Didion, *The White Album* (New York: Simon & Schuster, 1979), 47.
2. "The Manson Women: Inside the Murders," *Turning Point*, ABC, March 9, 1994.
3. Most explicit in this regard has been the career of "Marilyn Manson," an Alice Cooper retread who broke into MTV success during the 1990s. Trading on Charles Manson's notoriety, Marilyn Manson's T-shirts featured one of Charlie Manson's most famous quotations: "I am the God of fuck."
4. In large part, Manson's fame hinges on the social position of his more prominent victims—Hollywood starlet Sharon Tate, coffee heiress Abigail Folger, and interna-tional hairstylist Jay Sebring.
5. "On the Trail of Charles Manson," *Life*, December 19, 1969, 2A.
6. Gay Talese, "Charlie Manson's Home on the Range," *Esquire*, March 1970, 101.
7. S. V. Roberts, "Charles Manson: One Man's Family," *New York Times Magazine*, January 4, 1970, 11.
8. "The Demon of Death Valley," *Time*, December 12, 1969, 22.
9. "The Manson Scene," *Newsweek*, January 4, 1971, 20.
10. David Felton and David Dalton, "Year of the Fork, Night of the Hunter," *Rolling Stone*, June 25, 1970, 26.
11. Vincent Bugliosi, *Helter Skelter: The True Story of the Manson Murders* (New York: Bantam, 1974), 78–79.
12. Ed Sanders, *The Family: The Story of Charles Manson's Dune Buggy Attack Battalion* (New York: Dutton, 1971), 71.
13. Quoted in David Felton and David Dalton, "The Most Dangerous Man in the World," *Rolling Stone*, June 25, 1970, 35.

14. Jean F. Blashfield, *Why They Killed* (New York: Popular Library, 1990), 142.

15. "The Family Hour," *Newsweek*, June 29, 1970, 22; "Linda's Punishment," *Newsweek*, August 31, 1970, 29; "Helter Skelter," *Newsweek*, August 10, 1970, 22.

16. Particularly irritated by stories of Manson's diminutive height, supporters of Manson provide the following account of his "true" size on the Web page Access Manson (http://www.atwa.com/index.htm): "This petty and pointless lie has been told by D.A. Bugliosi from the time of the publication of *Helter Skelter* to as recently as his December 8, 1995 appearance on the Discovery Channel's program *Rivals*. Bugliosi spent over nine months in a courtroom in close proximity to Manson, so he must know that this claim is not true. The only reason there can be for him repeatedly saying it is that the height 5′ 2″ is so abnormally short for a white American male that it adds yet another freakishly unique aspect to the Manson caricature. In fact, Manson is at least 5′ 6″. This is born [sic] out by the height indicated on the California Department of Corrections record card reprinted on page 118 of *The Manson File*. It is also born [sic] out by the personal experience of the Webmaster St. Geo, who has observed Manson during over 100 visits at California State Prison-Corcoran. The photo in *Helter Skelter* which purports to show Manson as being 5′ 2″ is clearly incorrect and probably faked. This can be shown by continuing the height scale to Manson's left down to 0′. If Manson was 5′ 2″ tall, as the scale indicates, the scale should reach 0′ where his feet meet the floor. It doesn't. It goes below his feet, out of the photograph, and off the page".

17. Sanders, *The Family*, 65.

18. Frank Conroy, "Manson Wins!" *Harper's Magazine*, November 1970, 58, 59.

19. Sanders, *The Family*, 36.

20. "The Demon of Death Valley," 22; Bugliosi, *Helter Skelter*, 106.

21. Bob Murphy, *Desert Shadows* (Billings, Mont.: Falcon, 1986), 83.

22. "Linda's Punishment," 29.

23. George Bishop, *Witness to Evil* (New York: Dell, 1971), n.p.

24. Kurt Nimmo, *Susan Atkins* (Canton, Mich.: PNG, 1991).

25. "Linda's Punishment," 29.

26. "Of Murders and Messiahs," *Time*, August 10, 1970, 12.

27. Felton and Dalton, "Year of the Fork," 24.

28. "The Manson Scene," 20.

29. Quoted in Bugliosi, *Helter Skelter*, 421.

30. Clara Livsey, *The Manson Women: A Family Portrait* (New York: Richard Marek, 1980).

31. In the mid-1970s, Manson had been linked to the American rock group Heart, a band fronted by sisters Ann and Nancy Wilson. Rumors circulated that their hit song "Magic Man" was actually about Manson, and that profits from the record were being turned over to Manson in jail.

Swinging

Part II: The New Femininity Unveiled

Single

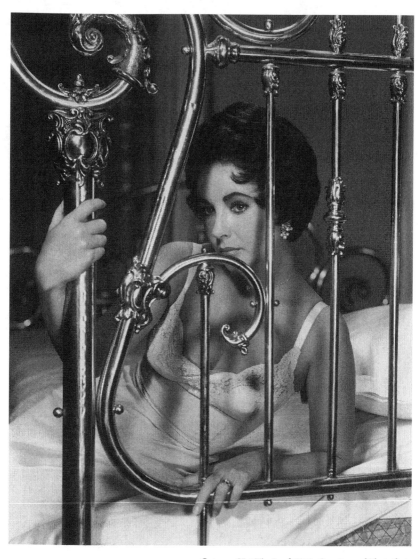

Cat on a Hot Tin Roof, 1958. Courtesy of Photofest.

Elizabeth Taylor

Hollywood's Last Glamour Girl

Susan McLeland

Nationally syndicated advice columnist Ann Landers opens the 1963 *Ann Landers Talks to Teen-agers about Sex* with a description of teenagers' accelerated sexual expectations since her youth in the 1930s. "In our day, 16-year-olds hugged and kissed and called it necking. Today most 16-year-olds go beyond hugging and kissing, and they call it 'making out.'" Landers continues:

> Some metropolitan newspapers printed a full page of pictures of half-nude (and well-known) lovers locked in an embrace on the deck of a yacht. The heroine of this real-life drama is married—but not to him, and she is the mother of three young children. Small wonder our teen-agers get a cockeyed view of morality when such garbage can find a ready market in some of America's "best" newspapers. These are the gods and goddesses their elders have given them to worship.[1]

Although Landers never names the famous lovers, her detailed description leaves no doubt that the target of her wrath is movie star Elizabeth Taylor, and the object of Taylor's affection is her *Cleopatra* costar Richard Burton, who Landers neglects to mention also was married and the father of two young daughters.

The events and the repercussions of the Taylor-Burton affair are best understood in the context of the early 1960s, and especially in terms of Elizabeth Taylor's heavily publicized star persona. The construction and refinement of Elizabeth Taylor's persona in the popular press was a process that began with her promotion as a child star. This process continued through her history of romantic entanglements in the 1950s and culminated with the scandal surrounding her role in the breakup of the Debbie Reynolds–Eddie Fisher marriage, setting the stage for the "role" she would play in the Taylor-Burton affair. Taylor's affair with Burton and its portrayal in the popular press are both dependent upon and in continuity with narrative trajectories originating in the late 1950s and early 1960s. The affair, revealed as part of the promotion of *Cleopatra* (Mankiewicz, 1963), raised additional questions regarding the breakdown in standards of "news judgment." (A decade earlier, the two stars' behavior would have been deemed unspeakable.) This "loosening" of standards, combined with Hollywood's first large-scale encounter with the relatively new phenomenon of paparazzi photography, suggests that not only the couple's behavior but the news *coverage* itself was "scandalous," indicating cultural anxieties about shifting standards of morality and definitions of femininity.

Elizabeth Taylor: Woman with a History

The furor surrounding her affair with Richard Burton did not represent the first time that Taylor had been singled out for aberrant sexuality. She had been vilified less than four years earlier, in September 1958, when her public commiseration with friend Eddie Fisher over the death of her third husband, showman Mike Todd, turned into the equally public breakup of Fisher's "perfect" marriage to Debbie Reynolds. Despite the variety of interpretations available (including a focus on the long-term dissolution of the Fisher-Reynolds marriage, which had been rumored in the gossip columns for more than a year), press reports chose to focus on the two women's roles in the triangle. Reynolds's immediate (and public) decision to fight for her marriage placed the women's representations in stark opposition: Reynolds as the defender of hearth and home, Taylor as home wrecker.

Representations of Reynolds are therefore significant not only for their depiction of what she *is*, but as descriptions of what Taylor *is not*. The discourse surrounding the two women, both separately before the scandal and when they are directly juxtaposed during the scandal, places them at opposite ends of a feminine continuum. Reynolds is portrayed as completely normal, an average American woman plunked down in the middle of Hollywood, whereas Taylor is "abnormal" in almost every sense—overly sexual, extravagant, and desirous in a way that contradicts the ideal for bourgeois American housewives. Yet for fans with a knowledge of Taylor's personal history, the oversimplified "home wrecker" the press depicts during the scandal contradicts their knowledge of another Taylor: the grieving widow who was also the loving young mother of three. Taylor's public persona thus combined a number of seemingly incompatible characteristics: marriage and eroticism, maternity and glamour.

Eroticism versus Marriage

In the 1950s, marriage served to legitimate sexual activity for women and to regulate sexual activity between men and women. As a result, it managed to sanction particular forms and functions for sexuality while it controlled the availability of erotic possibilities—a paradoxical function based in the institution's conflicting meanings for men and women. A variety of scholars have chronicled the centrality of discourses on marriage in containing and repressing women's agency during the post–World War II era. Despite demographic trends that prove that more married women were entering the workplace during the 1950s (to finance the American Dream), women were officially encouraged (or forced) to leave their jobs to marry and raise children. Thus a wife ideally supported her husband's chances for advancement in the burgeoning corporate structure and a consumer economy rooted in suburban sprawl, the streamlined automobile, and the television set.

According to contemporary press reports, Reynolds's experience with marriage appeared to emulate (as closely as was possible in Hollywood) a model in which marriage was posited as the satisfaction of a woman's desires. Virtually since she began dating Fisher in 1953, articles on Reynolds focused on her relationship with the "wholesome" pop star, rather than on her career or her other desires outside the realm of heterosexual romance. A profile of the pair written shortly after their marriage, titled "Young Hollywood at Home," describes their wedded bliss in a "white farmhouse on the shores of the Pacific" that is the very model of stereotypical domesticity. Opening with Debbie's observation that "we face the usual problem of working couples" (despite their extravagant salaries and lifestyles), the article ends with a description of Reynolds and Fisher as "any new-married couple in the neighborhood having old friends in for dinner on Saturday night."[2] The Reynolds-Fisher marriage was rocky almost from the start, complicated by Fisher's waning career, demanding touring schedule, and deepening drug addiction; however, the heavily publicized master narrative of their idealized young love triumphed in the mainstream media over occasional rumors of their increasingly obvious incompatibility.

In contrast, Taylor's three marriages before the scandal can hardly be described as typical or normative. Her first, to hotel heir Nicky Hilton when she was barely eighteen years old, was marked by a spectacular wedding (orchestrated in part by MGM, which provided Taylor's Helen Rose gown and promotional photos of the wedding for a variety of news outlets). The tremendous prenuptial publicity blitz was timed to coincide with the studio's simultaneous release of *Father of the Bride* (Minnelli, 1950). The Taylor-Hilton union, however, disintegrated before the couple returned from their European honeymoon; they never even set up housekeeping in the United States. Taylor moved from her parents' house in Beverly Hills to an apartment in Westwood, which she shared with girlfriend/secretary Peggy Rutledge while she awaited her first divorce.

In 1952, Michael Wilding attempted to introduce Taylor to the joys of domestic life. The pair had two sons, Michael Jr. and Christopher, during their marriage, which lasted until 1956. Although profiles of Taylor as a new mother waxed poetic about her beauty (*Collier's, Ladies' Home Journal, Look,* and *Coronet* referred to her as "the most beautiful girl in the world"), their reveries were marred by discussions of Taylor's failures as a woman—among them, the difficulty with which she adjusted to motherhood, her extravagance, her inadequacy as a housekeeper, and Wilding's dissatisfaction with her growing fame and confidence. Their divergent career paths, in fact, became the official explanation for the dissolution of the marriage.

Taylor's third marriage was to Mike Todd, in 1957. A forty-nine-year-old producer/promoter with a checkered history of huge financial successes and devastating losses, Todd had enjoyed liaisons with a number of Hollywood's most desirable women during his "up" periods. In marrying the much younger Taylor, he elevated her beyond the level of his other dalliances (which included, among others, Gypsy Rose Lee, Evelyn Keyes, and Marlene Dietrich) to the status of the 1950s equivalent of a trophy wife—a role that combined the social and legal protections of marriage with the glamour and eroticism reserved for a different class of women. Taylor and Todd spent much of the fifteen months of their marriage promoting Todd's *Around the World in 80 Days* at a variety of exotic openings, pausing briefly for Taylor to give birth to daughter Liza, then continuing with their jet-setting. No longer garbed in the informal jeans of the "Wildings at home" photographs, Taylor appeared dripping diamonds and wearing low-cut high-fashion gowns designed to emphasize her breasts, waist, and hips, and stared with smoldering sensuality at Todd. Gone was the domesticated, maternal Taylor: in her place, a reenergized erotic charge emerged unencumbered by domestic responsibilities (which, presumably, had been taken over by servants). Images of fabulous wealth and carnal passion combine in Look's "Liz Taylor as Mike Todd Saw Her," which asserts that Todd gave her jewels every Saturday.[3] Todd's unexpected death ended their epic romance and left Taylor alone once again. Her availability would lead to the undoing of what had generally been represented as an ideal union, pitting the passionate Taylor against the domesticated Reynolds in a battle over the institution of marriage itself.

A photo layout from the September 22, 1958, issue of Life magazine typifies how the participants and their roles were interpreted and constructed in the mainstream press during the month that the Fisher-Reynolds marriage disintegrated. Accompanying an article titled "Tale of Debbie, Eddie and the Widow Todd," the photos show Taylor, Reynolds, and Fisher each separately confronting reporters during the week the scandal broke. In the upper left, a slightly-out-of-focus Taylor, her curvaceous figure covered by a conservative suit, but sporting a pair of sparkling brooches, appears to be making a statement to surrounding reporters. The caption begins "INDIGNANT LIZ" and quotes her damning interview with powerful Hollywood gossip columnist Hedda Hopper, in which Taylor retorted, "Mike is dead and I'm alive." To the right of Taylor's picture appears a full-length shot of pigtailed Reynolds, clothed in slacks and rubber thong sandals, diaper pins stuck to her modest blouse, smiling faintly for reporters while she clutches car keys and a diaper bag. Its caption, "WINSOME DEBBIE," depicts a trusting young mother victimized by circumstances beyond her control. "It seems unbelievable to say you can live happily with a man and not know he doesn't love you," she says. In the lower left corner of the page, Life positions a full-length shot of Fisher hugging himself, fists clenched, eyes averted, midway between his house and the omnipresent reporters. This "WOEBEGONE EDDIE" (according to the caption) is the picture of misery, trying to convince reporters that nothing has happened. "Debbie and I are having a misunderstanding. Married people do have arguments and misunderstandings," he rationalizes. The two women's images dominate the page: Reynolds's long shot takes up half, and Taylor's and Fisher's share the other half, yet the medium shot of Taylor (as opposed to Fisher's long shot) makes her appear to be the same size as (or larger than) romantic rival Reynolds.[4]

Press reports such as the one just described constructed Reynolds and Taylor as rivals for Fisher's attention. His causal role in the events was played down, and focus shifted to the two women as the principal actors in the public drama. In this manner, the women were represented in terms of the conflict between the Wife and the Erotic Woman. Under this construction, the Wife, protected by the legal and social institution of marriage, was responsible for maintaining the domestic sphere of home and family, for providing dependable relief from the stresses of a man's hard-fought public role as breadwinner, and for subsuming her own desires in favor of those of her husband and children. The Erotic Woman, whose favors were available without a marital contract, lacked the social approval granted a Wife (who was, if nothing else, proof of a man's "maturity" and economic prowess), but made up for it in her status as a signifier of the man's virility.

From the middle-class woman's point of view, the sexual and social freedom of the Erotic Woman might make her role appear tempting at first; however, her exposure to potential legal and economic catastrophe due to the contemporary lack of social services, the uncertainty of available means of birth control, and the punitive nature of the legal system's approach toward women who were known to be sexually active outside of marriage made this role a virtually unthinkable option for any woman wishing to maintain her status in bourgeois American society. As a result, in popular depictions the Erotic Woman tended to be an outsider—a working-class woman willing to "sleep her way to the top" or a dissolute aristocrat. Without the discipline of a middle-class upbringing, the Erotic Woman lacked the Wife's moral code, and was likely to betray both other women, in her search for an appropriate lover, *and* her latest conquest, if a more attractive target (either economically or physically) came along.

The *Los Angeles Times*'s treatment of the breaking scandal is another example of this type of construction. Its September 11, 1958, coverage of the story (which was syndicated nationwide in major papers such as the *Chicago Tribune* and *St. Louis Post-Dispatch*) included an interview with Taylor and a separate update on the Reynolds-Fisher situation. "I am still in love with my husband," the dependable, devoted wife Reynolds tells reporters. "I am deeply shocked over what has happened ... Eddie is a great guy. Do not blame him for what has happened." Taylor, on the other hand, makes the now infamous statement: "Mike is dead and I'm alive." Taylor continues, "You can't break up a happy marriage. Debbie's and

Eddie's never has been … I'm not taking anything away from Debbie Reynolds because she never really had it."[5]

The photographs that illustrate the articles further emphasize the contrast between the two women: on the front page, pigtailed Reynolds and twenty-three-month-old daughter Carrie smile at reporters from the front seat of the family station wagon; on page 26, Taylor's diamonds and cleavage dominate a photo of Taylor, Fisher, and Reynolds taken at Fisher's Las Vegas opening only three months before. The homely station wagon, on the one hand, signifies Reynolds's maternity; flashy diamonds, on the other, are a potent symbol of Taylor's status as the Erotic Woman. The Wife might have one (modest) stone in the engagement ring her husband had given her. The Erotic Woman, on the other hand, is known for her collection of jewels, acquired through her family's wealth or as payment for her sexual favors. Taylor received them from both sources.

Taylor's excesses in appearance and in other areas are characteristic of the manner in which her persona challenged contemporary representations of feminine sexuality. The contemporary generic description of books on sexual technique as "marriage manuals" suggests how marriage was designed to contain the unruly potentially excessive sexuality of woman.[6] Judson T. Landis and Mary G. Landis, authors of *The Marriage Handbook*, a "scientific" study of marital habits in the United States published in 1953, comment:

> Although [society] no longer controls, and in fact makes it easy for people to break the rules, it still has not changed the penalties for people who do fail to live up to socially approved standards. Public opinion still condemns premarital coitus as a serious form of antisocial behavior *for women;* pregnancy before marriage is still looked upon as a great tragedy and disgrace in the middle and upper-middle class family.[7]

Reynolds compliantly acknowledges the constraints on her sexuality that marriage imposes; Taylor strains against them. Scandal-era articles play on this marriage/eroticism dichotomy in the way they focus on Taylor's checkered marital history. Her overabundance of sexual energy is signaled in the press by the label "Married Three Times"— in a September 10, 1958, *Chicago Tribune* article, for example, the phrase is suspended, in boldface type, between two paragraphs unrelated to Taylor's past.[8] Unlike Fisher's all-American wife Reynolds, who was still a one-man woman in 1958, Taylor had publicly exposed her "failure" at lifetime pairing, the marital ideal during the decade despite a rising divorce rate.

Taylor's hedonism is evident in other appetites as well—food, like sex, satisfies her gluttonous cravings: "My taste buds get in an uproar, and I get a lusty, sensual thing out of eating," she tells *Look*'s Eleanor Harris in 1956.[9] Lacking control over (or refusing to control) her appetites—whether they be for food or for sex—marks Taylor as a particularly dangerous unruly woman, because she upsets the contemporary construction of the feminine as the conservator of the contained domestic body—a body that was constrained as effectively by rigid "foundation" undergarments as by a rigid code of sexual behavior. A woman who desires excessively and ferociously is dangerous, according to Jessica Benjamin, because "the idea suggests power and activity, even as, it would seem, does the image of male desire, the phallus." Because the female is constructed under patriarchy for "the acceptance of passivity," Taylor's active desire is a direct challenge to patriarchal power relations, and a conflation of the binary oppositions that structure sexual difference in the 1950s.[10]

A desiring woman—especially one who desires sexually—is disruptive because she raises "[the] threat of selfishness, passion, and uncontrollability."[11] In *Re-making Love: The Feminization of Sex*, Ehrenreich, Hess, and Jacobs chronicle a variety of prohibitions against women's expressing—much less possessing—sexual desire in 1950s "marriage manuals": "The man was to set the pace, introduce innovations, and decide when foreplay would end and the real business of penetration would begin; the woman had only to respond."[12] Actively, publicly expressing sexual desire as Taylor does violates the gender norms established in the middle-class construction of marriage in favor of the selfish, erotic drives of an "immature" partner.

Taylor's screen roles reinforced her depiction as a primarily erotic, rather than maternal, figure. *Cat on a Hot Tin Roof* (Brooks, 1958) was in national release at the time that the triangle was first publicized. Like Taylor's previous "desiring women" roles (from Velvet Brown on, Taylor's characters unabashedly set and pursued goals of their own), her Maggie the Cat hungers for the wealth of her dying father-in-law, the respectability of marriage, sexual fulfillment—and a child, if that's what it takes to ensure that she secures the first three. To achieve this, she is willing to destroy her husband's best friend, ruin his business partnership, double-cross her back-stabbing in-laws, and spend hours parading nearly naked before her indifferent spouse, begging for his attentions. Each of these actions defies, distorts, or subverts 1950s representations of femininity as the passive receptor and projection of male desire.

Maternity and Glamour

Maternity and glamour represent two more contradictory elements that could not be reconciled in Taylor's persona during the 1950s. The opposition of the two terms is more visible in representations of Taylor than in those of many other female stars whose personas can be said to integrate Hollywood with family life, regardless of the actual condition of their children or careers. This is specifically due to Taylor's association with a particular type of beauty and the corresponding lifestyle that it implied.

Taylor was (and in 1999, still is) the embodiment of the Hollywood glamour girl, a highly stylized model of beauty that emphasizes a balance between the striking and the delicate. Glamour is just one mode of (white) beauty promoted in an effort designed to differentiate stars as products and to capitalize on a variety of women's physical and social types. All Hollywood stars can be said to "put on" glamour for special occasions, particularly for events such as the Academy Awards, which serves as a sort of annual prom night for the movie community; however, some connote glamour on a regular basis, through appearance and/or lifestyle. Glamour is produced through a combination of wealth, exoticism, and eroticism, traits that oppose those associated with middle-class domesticity in the 1950s.

Taylor, for a time, suppressed her glamorous side in favor of a more informal "natural"-style domesticity with Wilding. Her association with Todd returned her to the glamour mode, to which she seemed more visually and temperamentally accustomed, for the remainder of her career. Yet she retained certain associations with the "natural" as well. In contrast with stars such as Joan Crawford, who cultivated their connection to their audience by emphasizing the skill and hard work that made them appear glamorous, Taylor embodied a model of glamour that was seemingly effortless. Taylor's famous "violet eyes" are perhaps emblematic of this form of glamour: a trademark of her originality and intensity, they are not merely blue, as the eyes of less fortunate women might be, they are a "sublime freak of nature." The fact that they are naturally set off by extremely long, thick, and curly dark eyelashes further emphasizes Taylor's status as an extraordinary physical specimen.

Taylor exploited this "natural glamour" in a series of photos taken by her friend Roddy McDowall in the early 1960s. In the photos, Taylor, hair wrapped in a towel, looks as if she has just emerged from a bath. Apparently clean-scrubbed, she still displays the facial features that signify her characteristic beauty: thick, dark eyelashes and eyebrows framing the violet eyes, as well as the "beauty mark" on her cheek that sets off her clear, white skin; delicate, finely chiseled features; full red lips framing her even white teeth. Her slender figure, accentuated by large, full breasts, is partially disguised by the towel wrapped around her body. Taylor's appearance is both flawless and untouched—"naturally glamorous."

But Taylor's glamorous looks are seldom so modestly accessorized: throughout her adult career she is costumed in a variety of low-cut or strapless gowns designed to highlight her beauty and sensuality. Her string of hits in the late 1950s and early 1960s is characterized by the films' reliance on scenes of Taylor in form-fitting lingerie or other revealing costumes: namely, the white slip in *Cat on a Hot Tin Roof*, the slip and sable in *Butterfield 8* (Mann, 1960), and the "invisible" white bathing suit in *Suddenly, Last Summer* (Mankiewicz, 1959). However, the most characteristic signifier of Taylor's status as a glamorous star is her collection of jewels—a collection that had been augmented spectacularly, publicly, and regularly from the days of her third marriage. Jewels signify both the economic power of the man who buys them and the sexual prowess of the woman wearing them. Hard and bright, they provide a visual and tactile contrast to the soft skin of a rounded bosom or a slender neck, reminding the viewer of the sensual pleasures of the body that is adorned with their cold fire.

Photographs and prose in a variety of newspapers and magazines similarly work to draw attention to Taylor's glamorous body and to Taylor as a sexy body. Taylor's mother, Sara Sothern Taylor, writes in a story for the *Ladies' Home Journal* that even as a child, Taylor created a sensation walking down the street; strangers would stop and ask if Elizabeth was in the movies. *Look*'s Eleanor Harris describes Taylor's first appearance at the MGM commissary in "grown up" clothes: she wore "a costume no man who saw her will ever forget: she was wearing a swinging full skirt, a tightly cinched belt and a low-cut white peasant blouse.... Her bosom bounced, she had that look in her eye—and every man at the studio had a new look in his eye, too."[13]

Butterfield 8, 1960. Courtesy of Photofest.

Although Taylor was primarily considered a glamorous figure, she occasionally appeared as a maternal figure in the discourse surrounding her youth and marriages. She had publicly "practiced" mothering in her youth through her collection of pets—among them, a horse, numerous dogs and cats, and a chipmunk named Nibbles who was the subject of a children's book she authored. Nonetheless, Taylor represented an uneasy fit with 1950s notions of maternity, which emphasized self-sacrifice. Taylor's life and career required that she play another role. Taylor's first children, Michael and Christopher Wilding, depended on her not as a caregiver but as a breadwinner, given their parents' extravagant lifestyle and their father's lack of success as a Hollywood leading man.

The nature of Taylor's job as a star demanded a certain level of self-interest; she needed to maintain the face and figure that were her bread and butter, as well as promote the "personal monopoly" on a particular character type that ensured her future employment. Thus Taylor's job officially contradicted the reigning discourse on motherly ideals in the 1950s, as would her later status as a woman of means. By the time Liza Todd was born, Taylor, flush with her third husband's (current) financial success, was able to eschew bourgeois domestic models in favor of the more unconventional arrangements available to the very wealthy. As a result, the Wilding boys and Liza Todd, attended by a full retinue of nannies, tutors, cooks, and servants, accompanied their mother on location and around the world, making their "home" in a variety of hotels, chalets, yachts, and rented estates. Although the children had made occasional appearances in the extra-filmic discourse about Taylor in their infancy, when they served as adorable props for glamour shots of their mother, during the scandal they were curiously absent from representations of Taylor's persona. Taylor had, as well, occasionally played mothers onscreen (in *Giant*, for example) but her most recent role as the patho-logically childless Maggie the Cat could only have contributed to the dominant public perception of Taylor as nonmaternal. Hedda Hopper hints that Taylor's failures as a mother stem from her own mother's deficiencies: "[Elizabeth] never wanted to be an actress. That was her mother's project."[14] This reference to the plague of improper mothering (specifically "momism," or overly ambitious mothering, as it often was described in the 1950s) as the source of children's inadequacies or pathologies offered the only convincing cause-effect chain that might reconcile images of Taylor-as-mother with her role as a glamorous and erotic star. Most other reports chose simply to ignore Taylor's children in favor of her sexuality.

Once the Fisher-Reynolds divorce was announced and confirmed, Taylor, Reynolds, and Fisher moved off of the front pages of America's newspapers and back to the gossip columns. Still, they remained newsworthy, especially in light of certain refinements in their public personas. Fisher was effectively emascu-lated by his passive role in the triangle at the same time that the "immorality" of his behavior led to the cancellation of his television show. Despite a supporting role in Taylor's *Butterfield 8*, he found little success in the entertainment media, although he was able to continue touring and playing Las Vegas throughout the 1960s. Reynolds and Taylor, however, found their careers enhanced by the scandal: its "real-life" casting of the two of them in the mature roles of the "surviving spouse" and the femme fatale provided the intertextual impetus that would allow both women to surpass the ingenue roles they were becoming too old to play. Reynolds's career was virtually revived by the publicity and her portrayal of the long-suffering spouse: after releasing only one film in 1957 and one in 1958, she appeared in four in 1959, two in 1960, two in 1961, and the epic *How the West Was Won* in 1962. She also received a reported one-million-dollar contract for three television appearances.

Denied the best actress Oscar for *Cat,* Taylor went on to be nominated the next year for *Suddenly, Last Summer* and to win for the 1960 *Butterfield 8.* Marriage to Fisher (in 1959) had managed to recuperate her image, and the late 1950s and early 1960s were marked by a series of articles like one that appeared in *McCall's,* "Mr. Edwin J. Fisher: Older & Wiser & Happier," stressing their newfound domestic bliss.[15] By the end of the decade, Taylor would receive the highest salary ever paid to a star for an individual film: one million dollars for *Cleopatra,* which would bring about her next great scandal. Taylor used her "home wrecker" status to boost her career and fundamentally alter her own star image and Hollywood's Erotic Woman stereotype, onscreen and off, during the making of *Cleopatra.*

Her notoriety made Taylor a natural to star in 20th Century-Fox's retelling of the temptress-queen's life story, particularly given Hollywood's tendency to use stars' personal histories to establish their characters' personalities and backstories.[16] Producer Walter Wanger sensed the importance in this link when he agreed to Taylor's demand for one million dollars for the role—an unheard-of sum at the time—and dismissed Fox stockholders' requests that he consider casting an actress already under contract to Fox (among them Marilyn Monroe and Joan Collins) rather than the expensive and scandalous Taylor. Wanger's reply, that he would not and could not make the film without Taylor, suggests that he saw a link between the character of Cleopatra, the queen of a declining dynasty who seduced two of her time's most powerful men and almost brought down their empire, and Taylor, the much-married superstar of a fading Hollywood. The initial flurry of press reports surrounding the production of *Cleopatra* served to dispel any lingering public doubts about Taylor's viability as a star.

When Taylor nearly died during the filming of *Cleopatra* in 1961, those same dangerous desires that were condemned in 1958 were reinterpreted, this time as the symptoms of a strength and a fighting spirit capable of facing and defeating death. She suffered from staphylococcal pneumonia, underwent an emergency tracheotomy, and hovered near death for almost a week. Her daily medical prognosis throughout this period made front-page news around the world. Upon her recovery, Taylor capitalized on the sympathy that her infirmity granted her through a series of interviews and public appearances in which she described in detail her experience of illness, hospitalization, "death," and return to life. *Redbook*'s 1961 profile, "Elizabeth Taylor's Fight for Survival," is emblematic of the success of this narrative construction. In it, Taylor's "excessive" sensuality and tastes are transformed into the appropriate expressions of someone who has been so near to death.[17]

Given the new circumstances, Taylor was once again represented as a maternal figure. She and Fisher were widely photographed with the Wilding boys at Disneyland, for example. While Taylor continued to make movies, Fisher announced his impending "retirement" to manage his wife's career and ensure their domestic bliss. Despite rumors of estrangement between the couple, they sought to cement their union with a child—although physicians had warned Taylor that further pregnancies would jeopardize her life. So, perhaps in an effort to save the Taylor-Fisher marriage, perhaps in tribute to the new life she had been granted, Taylor and Fisher began legal proceedings to adopt a malnourished German infant who required a series of expensive operations. However, Taylor's erotic saga was not to end in connubial felicity: the perpetual act two of her sexual life, her story, continued to sustain her visibility as a star in the public's eye.

Cleopatra and Antony and Eddie

When Taylor recovered and shooting resumed on *Cleopatra* in Rome in late 1961, Richard Burton was called in to replace Stephen Boyd as Mark Antony. With their first scene together as the legendary lovers, Taylor and Burton also "fell in love" and began the passionate affair that would guarantee their newsworthiness (and box-office success) for almost a decade. Taylor was ostensibly "happily married" to Eddie Fisher, the man she had fought so publicly to have; Burton and wife Sybil Williams Burton likewise maintained a facade of domestic harmony. But Taylor, Burton, and the American people were primed for a

Richard Burton and Elizabeth Taylor in *Cleopatra*, 1963.

sexual scandal. MGM hairstylist Sydney Guilaroff alleges in his memoir, how-ever, that 20th Century-Fox publicists had planned for its *Cleopatra* costars to stray—a little bit—for the good of the film:

> The earliest press releases from [Fox publicists Nathan] Weiss and Jack Brodsky, and confidential memos from studio chief Spyros Skouras and other corporate papers, show that Fox had planned for

a mere touch of love between the stars: a couple of kisses, a few nights
out on Rome's Via Veneto and some titillating items for the gossip
columns. Taylor was then supposed to troop dutifully back to her
husband, Eddie Fisher, and Burton to his wife, actress Sybil Williams.
In a pig's eye.[18]

Fox's proposed scenario took into account Burton's (unpublicized) on-
location habit of bedding costars (or, if none were willing, whatever attractive
extras were available), then returning to his wife after the film had wrapped; it
ignored, however, Taylor's feminine insistence on maintaining the 1950s
women's equation of sex with love and marriage. As Taylor later wrote, "Basically,
I'm square.... I have to be really in love in order to sleep with a man and when
I'm really in love I want to be married."[19] Such a statement, however, negates the
legitimacy of her lover's (or Taylor's) previous commitments—in favor of her
current flame. As Fox, Fisher, the Burtons, and the public were soon to learn,
toying with Taylor's sexual energies meant playing with fire. Taylor's renowned
passion, which had been temporarily desexualized by her brush with death, was
reanimated, and with it her ability to wreck even the most flexible and resilient
of marriages.

Public disclosure of the affair, combined with speculation about its effects on
the participants' marriages, occurred in stages throughout early 1962. Fisher's
status as Taylor's husband was immediately jeopardized, and as a cuckolded husband he was subject to public humiliation. The Taylor-Burton affair first surfaced
in gossip (and gossip columns) early in February and made its first televised
appearance February 16, according to Fox publicist Nathan Weiss, who worked in
the studio's New York office. On February 17, Weiss sent publicist Jack Brodsky,
who was on the set in Rome, a frantic cable reading "LAST NIGHTS PERRY COMO HAD
TAKEOFF ON CLEO WITH SLAVE NAMED EDDIE GETTING IN ANTONYS WAY STOP DO THEY
KNOW."[20] By February 18, speculation about the Taylor-Fisher marriage (if not the
Taylor-Burton affair) reigned on the front pages of a number of American newspapers, when Taylor entered the hospital in the wake of a botched suicide attempt
presented as food poisoning. Initial speculation centered on the state of her marriage: wire service reporters were quick to point out that Fisher was out of town
when she succumbed, although there was some confusion over whether he was
in Switzerland or Portugal. Burton's statement to the press, reported in the February 20 *Los Angeles Times*, that he and Taylor were *not* having an affair opened

that rumor for front-page publication.[21] The article disclosing Burton's statement is accompanied in the *Los Angeles Times* with a UPI photo of the grim-faced Fisher eyeing his wife from a distance while she steadfastly avoids his gaze. The juxtaposition of Burton's statement with the tense photograph of Fisher and Taylor provided ample fuel for speculation that the washed-up pop star would soon be discarded in favor of the dashing Shakespearean actor.

Rumors of the rift continued to fly as gossips monitored goings-on in Rome with all the fervor of Cold War Kremlinologists out to decode power relationships in the Soviet Union. Hedda Hopper reported on March 26, "The rumors are flying again. They have Eddie Fisher in New York en route to the coast, and Mrs. Richard Burton back in London. Heigh-ho!" Fisher's hospitalization in New York a few days later was portrayed as a metaphor for the state of the marriage, despite his continuing denials that Taylor had thrown him over for Burton. In a *New York News* syndicated piece run on the front page of the *Los Angeles Times* on March 29, it was reported that "Eddie broke down—'completely,' an intimate said ... after he returned to the United States from Rome where his wife is making a picture co-starring Richard Burton, the English actor with whom she is reported currently in love." Taylor's apparent indifference to reports of Fisher's breakdown were carefully analyzed; on March 30, the *Los Angeles Times* reported that Taylor had phoned Fisher's physician to make sure his situation was not serious, then went back to work (presumably with Burton) on *Cleopatra*.[22]

As these articles and the photos accompanying them would suggest, members of the press were less clearly on the side of preserving marriage above all else in this case than they had been during the Taylor-Fisher-Reynolds triangle —at least as far as the Taylor-Fisher marriage was concerned. Photos would continue to provide proof of shifting alliances in the series of triangles. On March 31, the *Los Angeles Times* printed a front-page photo of Taylor and Burton smiling, arms linked and "on the town" in Rome, over the headline "Liz, Richard Go Night-Clubbing; Eddie Denies Marriage Is on Rocks." The accompanying Associated Press report notes that "Miss Taylor and Burton—both smiling broadly— appeared almost willing to pose [for photographers].... Miss Taylor and Burton have been reported being together frequently off the set but this was one of the few times that they appeared publicly." Fisher, however, continued to contradict the photographic (and other) evidence. The AP article also reported on a press conference Fisher had held the previous day, in which he claimed:

> "The only romance between Elizabeth Taylor and Richard Burton is Marc Antony and Cleopatra, and I might say a mighty good one." During the conference an aide announced "a call from Rome." Fisher took the call in an anteroom, then returned to tell newsmen that Miss Taylor had refused to issue a statement to quiet the divorce reports.
>
> "You know," said Fisher, "you can ask a woman to do something and she doesn't always do it."[23]

Fisher's embarrassment would continue both in print and in photographs. On March 31, Hedda Hopper quoted unnamed Hollywood sources as saying "[Fisher] shouldn't toy with that kind of dynamite if he doesn't have the guts to take it," and "When you leave home and hearth, you can expect the worst." On April 3, when gossip columnist Earl Wilson reported that Taylor and Fisher had (finally) issued a joint statement announcing their impending divorce, the *Los Angeles Times* ran a photo of Fisher rather enthusiastically embracing a grimacing, standoffish Shelley Winters, ironically captioned "PROFESSIONAL ADMIRATION."[24]

But the Fisher-Taylor marriage was not the only one at stake in the wake of the Taylor-Burton affair. And whereas Taylor's public involvement with Burton effectively ended her marriage to Fisher, the double standard that severed sex from love and marriage for men allowed Burton to consider returning to Sybil Williams Burton at some later date. As a result, contradictory reports surfaced. On April 4, the *Los Angeles Times* ran an AP file photo of a smiling Richard and Sybil Burton enjoying dinner together (taken late in February, the caption notes) over the headline "Liz Thinks Burton Will Divorce Wife." Reports on April 4 and 5 speculated on whether Sybil Burton would return to Rome (ostensibly to keep her husband in line). The Associated Press quoted family friend Emlyn Williams on April 4 as saying, "I just cannot imagine that Richard would throw his life away like this. They are exceedingly happy and he adores his daughters.... It's not in his character to be involved in something like this. It's the sort of thing he's always made fun of in other movie stars." On April 5, AP noted that Burton had "cabled his wife Wednesday assuring her of his love despite his public kissing with Elizabeth Taylor." The vitriolic Hedda Hopper had her own take on the relationship; on April 4 she wrote: "Those closest to Richard Burton (they call him Wicked Richard) are taking all bets that he'll never divorce Sybil. 'Where,' asked one, 'would he ever find a wife as tolerant?'"[25]

It is apparent from reports early in April 1962 that reporters were trying to construct a rivalry between Taylor and Sybil Burton similar to the previous rivalry between Taylor and Reynolds. Reports paint Sybil Burton as a blonde, practical homebody who gave up her own acting career to support her husband's. They also note that she has the support of Burton's family (particularly eldest brother Ifor Jenkins) and friends (including Burton's mentor, actor Emlyn Williams, and his wife), and that she shares Burton's Welsh heritage. All of these traits place Sybil Burton in opposition to the raven-haired, four-times-married Hollywood movie star who appeared daily on her husband's arm. Sybil Burton's refusal to engage in a catfight stymied the construction of a triangle. Reporters and photographers who appeared trapped between a perceived demand for "the story" and Sybil Burton's silence were thus obliged to focus on the exotic and continuing romance of the two lovers.

Burton, in fact, benefited greatly from the publicity surrounding the affair. He reunited briefly with Sybil Burton at their villa in Celigny, Switzerland (not far from Taylor's villa in Gstaad), in the summer of 1962. By the end of the year he was back with Taylor, both romantically and professionally, costarring as a pair of battling lovers in *The V.I.P.s* (Asquith, 1963) in London. Burton saw both his marquee value and his salary rise through the union. Despite distinguished performances on stage in London and New York in *Camelot*, among others, and in such Hollywood extravaganzas as *The Robe* (Koster, 1953), *Alexander the Great* (Rossen, 1956), and *The Longest Day* (Annakin, Marton, et al.; 1962), at the time *Cleopatra* went into production Burton had yet to distinguish himself from the pack of handsome British leading men. Laurence Olivier reportedly cabled Burton at the height of the publicity: "Make up your mind, dear heart. Do you want to be a great actor or a household word?" Burton's reply, "Both," indicates that he fully understood the value of his notoriety. The publicity that the affair with Taylor brought him immediately raised his salary (although not to the million dollars per film that she received) and made him a top contender for romantic leading roles both in film and onstage for almost a decade.

The affair recast Taylor in her scarlet woman persona, and no one was going to let her off easily this time. Hedda Hopper, still stinging from accusations that she was responsible for Taylor's bad name in 1958, announced on April 5, "I have not spoken with Elizabeth Taylor since she has been in Rome. This time she's done it all on her own." According to the *New York Times*, the Vatican, in print and over the radio, chastised Taylor for "erotic vagrancy" and issued a thinly veiled demand that she return the German baby she and Fisher had begun adopting (April 5 and 13, 1962); Taylor's life was threatened anonymously (May 21, 1962); and a Georgia legislator sought to revoke Taylor's and Burton's privileges of returning to the United States (May 23, 1962).[26] Continued speculation about how and when Burton would reunite with his wife offered implicit criticism of the long-term attractiveness of romance with one of Hollywood's greatest sex goddesses; Burton's return to Taylor, whether fueled by love or lust or economic pragmatism, vindicated her appeal and helped to establish their stormy relationship as the epic romance of the 1960s.

Taylor's refusal to give up the infant Maria, whose last name had already been changed from Fisher to Taylor (and would, eventually, become Burton), indicates her inability to understand the depth of the accusations against her (she was, after all, planning to marry Burton eventually) and her perception of herself as a fiercely maternal woman. She surrounded herself with her "natural" children throughout the affair (Maria was hospitalized for much of the first few years of her life), perhaps in an effort to ward off criticism that her sexual activities made her an unsuitable mother. Such strategic maneuvering with her children's lives mirrored the character of Cleopatra's efforts to marshal her maternity in a battle against the critical Roman empire and directly contradicted bourgeois constructions of childhood as a privileged and protected period in an individual's life.

Keeping in mind the way that Ingrid Bergman's affair with Roberto Rossellini damaged her box-office appeal in the early 1950s, a nervous Fox rereleased some of Taylor's earlier films to see if the public outcry was weakening *Cleopatra*'s potential box office and then denied that the studio was losing faith in its star.[27] Afraid of audience reprisals against the very expensive film, Fox production chief Peter Levathes told Sydney Guilaroff, "It was so serious that we took a look at the morals clauses in the Burton and Taylor contracts."[28] *Cleopatra* producer Walter Wanger, himself the survivor of a Hollywood scandal, had a more sophisticated view of the situation. Fox publicist Jack Brodsky notes that Wanger argued with Levathes and other Fox executives that comparing the Taylor-Burton affair to Ingrid Bergman's affair with Roberto Rossellini made no sense from the standpoint of star persona or in terms of the film they were making. Brodsky writes, "Ingrid Bergman was a saint to all her fans when Wanger had her in Joan of Arc and when she got in trouble she cracked and destroyed that image. Taylor is the exact opposite, that is her principal attraction, and when she's playing Cleopatra, there should be no trouble."[29]

Fox unabashedly decided to capitalize on what publicity it could receive for its tremendous investment. Fox's marketing strategy for the film challenged head-on critics' complaints about the moral climate on the set. Thus the studio employed popularized Freudian descriptions of the dangers of repression in an openly commercialized form to reinterpret the Taylor-Burton affair as courageous and romantic, and opposition to it as perversely puritanical. Because Taylor's behavior fit the narrative construction of her persona, it was assumed that her actions would ensure "good box office." An outraged public might complain about her offscreen behavior; however, it still bought tickets to see Taylor portray dangerous, desiring women from *Cleopatra* to *Who's Afraid of Virginia Woolf*'s Martha, for which she won her second Academy Award. Although her salary would not long remain Hollywood's highest, she could continue to ask—and receive—at least a million dollars per picture throughout the 1960s.

Representing the Lovers

Which returns us to the opening of this essay, and Ann Landers's desperate diatribe against "the gods and goddesses [the media] have given [teenagers] to worship." For Landers, this publication of the tawdry details of Taylor and Burton's private lust offers evidence of a breakdown of morality in modern culture. It also exposes the fundamental incompatibility of notions of public and private within the star system and the shifting relationships between "gossip" and "news." The first six months of 1962, during which the Taylor-Burton affair would become front-page news and Helen Gurley Brown would publish *Sex and the Single Girl*, marked a turning point in the public representation of sexual mores. Middle-class women were offered the promise of the sort of sexual "freedom" from social, legal, economic, and biological consequences that had been promoted for men since 1953, when the Kinsey report was widely publicized and *Playboy* magazine was first published. Up until this time, the public discourse on women's sexuality in "respectable" news outlets officially contradicted private behavior, hence the rash of "premature" babies born to newlywed celebrities who had obviously been fooling around before their marriages.[30] Taylor's obvious and unpunished affection for Burton, combined with the media's willingness to publish stories and photos of the illicit lovers, backed up Helen Gurley

Brown's assertion that "nice girls do" with impunity far more effectively than another round of anonymous statistics. As a result, the Taylor-Burton affair worked to unbalance publicly the equation of "love," "marriage," and "sexual behavior" for heterosexual women.

At the same time, Taylor's representations also worked to reconcile an opposition between marriage/maternity and glamour/eroticism—a reconciliation that would allow women like Helen Gurley Brown to claim that the glamorous, erotic world of singleness is not (and indeed should not be) confined to women who have yet to find a mate. Taylor embodied Brown's notion of the married woman who acts single—that is, who refuses to "let herself go" by abandoning glamour and sexual desire—and therefore remains a suitable mate for the exciting man she has managed to capture. Co-opting the single style has other advantages for the married woman. If her mate should "let himself go"—by losing the career status and/or sexual drive that made him an attractive partner—then it is, perhaps, his own fault that his still glamorous wife might be admired by someone more appreciative than he has been.

Taylor herself became a poster girl for this "new morality." A number of baby boom–era women credit her for breaking through what they perceived as a repressive and sexist double standard: Susan Douglas notes in *Where the Girls Are: Growing Up Female with the Mass Media* that Taylor's successful sexual exploits were one of her inspirations for ignoring her elders' hypocritical admonitions; in interviews in Gael Green's *Sex and the College Girl* (1964), co-eds cite Taylor's well-publicized conquests as their impetus to challenge the puritanism of the American 1950s.[31] At the same time these young women credited Taylor for releasing them from the double standard, their elders condemned her. As the introduction to this article suggests, Ann Landers holds Taylor responsible for a loosening of moral standards for young American women. Because her public (and well-publicized) behavior defied the conventions of heterosexual monogamous marriage, Elizabeth Taylor the star came to stand for a sexual liberation for women that confounded both second-wave feminists and the private (and rather traditional) Taylor herself, albeit for different reasons. For the second-wave feminist, Taylor remained an avatar of old Hollywood in which a woman's value was determined by her "to-be-looked-at-ness." For Taylor herself, her life was the saga of a traditional feminine woman who continued to seek romantic fulfillment through marriage.

Nonetheless, Taylor's public persona points toward a new conceptualization of women's sexuality that breaks with the binary domestic/erotic model that had structured class and gender relations throughout the immediate postwar era that paves the way for the New Woman of the late 1970s and the 1980s—the woman who wants it all. Thus, despite Taylor's desire to play by the rules of postwar sexual behavior, her actions served to expose the inherent contradictions of marriage and romance. These rules equated feminine sexual desire and practice with the cultural construct of romantic love and with the legal institution of marriage. At the same time, these rules allowed (and even encouraged, according to *Playboy*) men to experiment (hetero)sexually outside cultural and legal constraints—a technical impossibility given that all women hypothetically were either chaste or locked into romantic and/or marital contracts. As a sexually desiring public woman, Taylor made headlines—twice—by compelling famous men to break those contracts and forcing less powerful women to suffer their fallout. That she was rewarded for these transgressions denotes a significant shift in the public representation of feminine sexuality.

Notes

1. Ann Landers, *Ann Landers Talks to Teen-agers about Sex* (New York: Fawcett Crest, 1963), 18, 19.
2. C. M. Wheatland and E. Sharpe, "Young Hollywood at Home," *Ladies' Home Journal*, November 1956, 89.
3. "Liz Taylor as Mike Todd Saw Her," *Look*, July 8, 1958, 59.
4. "Tale of Debbie, Eddie and the Widow Todd," *Life*, September 22, 1958, 39–40.
5. Coverage of the Fisher-Reynolds household was provided in Walter Ames, "Eddie, Debbie Separate," *Los Angeles Times*, September 11, 1958, 1, 26; Taylor's interview appeared in a separate article by Hedda Hopper, "Liz Taylor's Own Story of Eddie's Marital Rift," *Los Angeles Times*, September 11, 1958, 1, 26.
6. See, for example, Barbara Ehrenreich, Elizabeth Hess, and Gloria Jacobs, *Re-making Love: The Feminization of Sex* (Garden City, N.Y.: Anchor, 1986), chap. 2.
7. Judson T. Landis and Mary G. Landis, *The Marriage Handbook* (New York: Prentice Hall, 1953), 131, emphasis added.
8. Seymour Korman, "Eddie Flies Home to Debbie and Has Showdown on Liz," *Chicago Tribune*, September 10, 1958, 1.
9. Eleanor Harris, "The Men in Her Life," *Look*, July 24, 1956, 48.

10. Jessica Benjamin, "A Desire of One's Own: Psychoanalytic Feminism and Intersubjective Space," in *Feminist Studies, Critical Studies*, ed. Teresa de Lauretis (Bloomington: Indiana University Press, 1986), 83.

11. Ibid., 84.

12. Ehrenreich et al., *Re-making Love*, 48.

13. See Sara Sothern Taylor, "Elizabeth, My Daughter," *Ladies' Home Journal*, February 1954, 152; Eleanor Harris "The Elizabeth Taylor Story," *Look*, June 26, 1956, 127.

14. Hopper, "Liz Taylor's Own Story," 1.

15. L. Slater, "Mr. Edwin J. Fisher: Older & Wiser & Happier," *McCall's*, January 1962, 74–75.

16. See, for example, Cathy Klaprat, "The Star as Market Strategy: Bette Davis in Another Light," in *The American Film Industry*, rev. ed., ed. Tino Balio (Madison: University of Wisconsin Press, 1985); Barry King, "Articulating Stardom," in *Stardom*, ed. Christine Gledhill (London: Routledge, 1991).

17. R. J. Levin, "Elizabeth Taylor's Fight for Survival," *Redbook*, May 1961, 76.

18. Sydney Guilaroff, *Crowning Glory: Reflections of Hollywood's Favorite Confidant* (Los Angeles: General, 1996), 217.

19. Elizabeth Taylor, *Elizabeth Takes Off: On Weight Gain, Weight Loss, Self-Image and Self-Esteem* (New York: Putnam, 1987), 36.

20. Jack Brodsky and Nathan Weiss, *The Cleopatra Papers: A Private Correspondence* (New York: Simon & Schuster, 1963), 33.

21. "Elizabeth Taylor Leaves Hospital," *Los Angeles Times*, February 20, 1962, 3.

22. Hedda Hopper, "Romero Will Work in Spain, Honolulu," *Los Angeles Times*, March 26, 1962, sec. IV, p. 11; "Eddie Fisher Reported Suffering Breakdown," *Los Angeles Times*, March 29, 1962, 1; "Eddie Fisher Dodges Quiz on Breakdown," *Los Angeles Times*, March 30, 1962, 1, 11.

23. "Liz, Richard Go Night-Clubbing; Eddie Denies Marriage Is on Rocks," *Los Angeles Times*, March 31, 1962, 1.

24. Hedda Hopper, "20th Signs Koster, Stewart for Comedy," *Los Angeles Times*, March 31, 1962, sec. I, p. 18; Earl Wilson, "Elizabeth and Eddie Say They Will Get Divorce," *Los Angeles Times*, April 3, 1962, 1.

25. Earl Wilson, "Liz Thinks Burton Will Divorce Wife," *Los Angeles Times*, April 4, 1962, 21; "Burton Cables Wife He Still Loves Her; Despite Kisses with Liz," *Los Angeles Times*, April 4, 1962, 1; "Burton Cables His Love to Wife, and Calls Her," *Los Angeles Times*, April 5, 1962, 2; Hedda Hopper, "Cyd Charisse Third Star Cast in Film," *Los Angeles Times*, April 4, 1962, sec. IV, p. 12.

26. Hedda Hopper, "Liz Taylor's Candid Interview Recalled," *Los Angeles Times*, April 5, 1962, sec. II, p. 10; "Vatican Radio Hits Marriage Caprices," *New York Times*, April 5, 1962, 8; "Miss Taylor Is Chided," *New York Times*, April 13, 1962, 27; "Elizabeth Taylor Threatened," *New York Times*, May 21, 1962, 21; "Georgia Legislator Scores Miss Taylor and Burton," *New York Times*, May 23, 1962, 38.

27. Eugene Archer, "Elizabeth Taylor's Public Image Is Subject of Filmmakers' Study," *New York Times*, June 1, 1962, 18; "Fox Says Taylor Reissues Are Not a Popularity Test," *New York Times*, June 2, 1962, 8.
28. Guilaroff, *Crowning Glory*, 218.
29. Brodsky and Weiss, *The Cleopatra Papers*, 65.
30. This epidemic included Rita Hayworth and Aly Kahn as well as Ronald Reagan and Nancy Davis. Stephanie Coontz notes in *The Way We Never Were: American Families and the Nostalgia Trap* (New York: Basic Books, 1992) that this trend reached beyond Hollywood to the rest of the United States in the 1950s, when "young people were not taught [abstinence]—they were simply handed wedding rings" (39).
31. Susan J. Douglas, *Where the Girls Are: Growing Up Female with the Mass Media* (New York: Times Books, 1995); Gael Green, *Sex and the College Girl* (New York: Dial, 1964).

Barbarella, 1968. Courtesy of the Wisconsin Center for Film and Theater Research.

Bringing *Barbarella* Down to Earth
The Astronaut and Feminine Sexuality in the 1960s
Lisa Parks

Hollywood films about the space race, such as *The Right Stuff* and *Apollo 13*, typically depict the women of that era as idly sitting by, nervously glaring at flickering television sets as their husbands hurtle into orbit or cavort on the moon. Such "for all mankind" moments situate the feminine firmly within the armchair of domesticity, suppressing women's efforts to become astronauts themselves during this period. Indeed, during the 1960s thousands of American women would rather have been astronaut heroines racing into space or exploring the moon than housewife witnesses. But despite women's interest in becoming astronauts, their participation in NASA's early space missions was patently forbidden. Dominant public discourses of the period showed a profound mistrust of the physicality of the feminine body and sought to keep women "safe and secure" on American soil rather than to launch them into the dangerous domain of outer space.

Scientists suggested that the extreme unpredictability of the female body, especially during menstruation, made women unfit for astronautic endeavors. Politicians seized upon this research and went so far as to suggest that sending a woman into outer space would pose serious risks to national security. Within this climate of gendered exclusion, the only female astronauts to appear in public during the 1960s were fictional ones. *Barbarella*, a French-Italian science fiction film about the adventures of a female astronaut, appeared in American movie theaters in 1968. The film stars American actress Jane Fonda as a sexy space traveler sent to resolve an intergalactic political crisis. While scientists and politicians positioned feminine sexuality as a threat to the scientific rational and nationalist imperatives of the American space program, *Barbarella* represented

a dangerous alternative: a female astronaut who was sexy, single, and political—
a highly volatile combination.

In this essay I examine *Barbarella*'s representation of the female astronaut in
the context of public debates over the issue of female space flight. I contrast the
official scientific research of NASA and 1960s congressional debates with the
campy and parodic representation of a female astronaut in this 1968 science
fiction film. *Barbarella*'s mise-en-scène and narrative exaggerate the sexuality of
the female astronaut, deflecting attention away from her professional status and
toward the contours of her body. The film's hypersexualization of its protagonist
reflects the impossibility of a "real" female astronaut during the 1960s, for it
demonstrates how feminine sexuality was exploited not only to keep women out
of space, but also to fetishize the only female astronaut in public view. Much like
the discourses surrounding the debates over women's involvement in the U.S.
space program, *Barbarella* offers its viewers a female astronaut who can reach
the public eye only as a fetishized object of sexual display.

But although *Barbarella*'s hyperbolic sexuality might be fodder for a voyeuristic imagination, it also enables the female astronaut to assert power and
control within the narrative. In this science fiction fantasy, sexuality is figured as
a technology of self—a significant, though limited, expression of feminine
agency. In other words, whereas the film constructs the female astronaut as the
object of a fetishistic gaze, Barbarella's body is also a tool of personal pleasure
and political power. I want to consider the film's expression of a bodily feminine
agency that is able to operate within a regime of limited political, professional,
and personal mobility. Read within a context of ongoing struggles over women's
role in the U.S. space program, *Barbarella* is symptomatic of the heavy cultural
constraints placed upon scientific and professional women, but it also suggests
the possibility of a feminine agency based on women's use of their bodies as
technologies of self-realization.

"Astronauttes": Filling the Space Boots of Monkeys and Men

During the early 1960s, about the same time that Jean Claude Forest sketched
the first *Barbarella* comics in France, the American public witnessed a series of
high-profile debates on the issue of female space flight.[1] In 1960, *Look* magazine
reported that more than two thousand women had volunteered to participate in

NASA's space program.[2] By 1962, NASA officials boasted that the organization employed 146 women as aerospace technicians and 77 as mathematicians, but they were unwilling to invite women to participate in flight training programs.[3] In July 1962, after an initial probe led by Victor Anfuso (D-N.Y.), the House Science and Astronautics Committee held a hearing to investigate NASA's exclusion of women from "manned" space missions.

Aviators Jerrie Cobb (1959's Aviation Woman of the Year), Jane Briggs Hart, and Jacqueline Cochran all testified at congressional hearings that were reportedly "woman-packed."[4] Cobb disclosed the names of eleven women who passed the same preliminary physical screening test given to potential male astronauts but were forbidden to become official trainees.[5] She complained with gracious wit, "They [NASA] won't let me take the actual training course, but I see they have a chimpanzee who is being trained to take it."[6] Jane Hart protested, "It's inconceivable to me that the world of outer space should be restricted to men only, like some sort of stag club."[7] The notion that outer space was a domain reserved for monkeys and white men perturbed not only female aviators, but members of the mainstream and African American press as well.

American magazines and newspapers responded to the hearing with editorials supporting the women's position and charging NASA with blatant gender discrimination. A *Saturday Evening Post* editorial noted, "Women in this century have secured the vote. They drive cars, frequent the bars, head corporations and hold important posts in the House and Senate. But one occupation is off limits—no woman is included among our astronauts."[8] In an editorial move that reflected the alliances sometimes forged between African Americans and white women in their struggles for professional mobility, *Ebony* compared the exclusion of women from outer space to the historical exclusion of African Americans from various public spaces. The editorial read, "Male response to female protests against 'for men only' trips to the moon sounded like a replay of white responses to Negro protests against 'for white only' public services and facilities on the planet here below." It continued:

> The twin fears—female invasion into a man's world and Negro domination of large American cities—reflect the insecurity of the male whose only claim to superiority is based on myth.... If he is wise, he will lengthen his launching pad and add two more seats to his space ship, for his "inferiors" are in no mood to again be left behind.[9]

But despite such criticisms, NASA's exclusionary astronaut selection process continued throughout the decade.

Research conducted by the Lovelace Foundation—NASA's medical branch—reinforced the space agency's refusal to allow women into outer space. After conducting a series of experiments on female subjects, Lovelace reported that the temporary weight gain caused by a woman's menstrual cycle and the "tendency to depression, irritability, emotional instability ... [and] diminished ability to concentrate" were enough to keep women on earth.[10] In response to such claims, however, social commentator Slapsie Maxie Rosenbloom asserted that "the male's daily shave was a far greater inconvenience than the female's monthly cycle."[11] Other medical research conducted at the same time, however, suggested that the female body is actually superior to the male in its ability to withstand the physical and psychological effects of starvation, fatigue, and shock.[12] And given that women weigh less, they consume less food and oxygen. Research also suggested that women are "more radiation resistant, less prone to heart attacks, and less troubled by monotony, loneliness, heat, cold, pain and noise."[13]

Although popular press coverage tended to side with Cobbs, Hart, and Cochran, suggesting the viability of female space flight, it also emphasized their roles as wives and mothers. Articles on the hearing identified each of the women's husbands and mentioned that Hart was the mother of eight children. Editors highlighted the feminine attributes of the potential astronauts with headlines and phrases like "Three blondes argued before a House Space Subcommittee," and "Not a brick was hurled, not a single window smashed. The ladies argued politely." Many articles referred to the women as "aviatrixes" or "astronauttes," and most commented on the "spiked heels" Cobbs wore to the hearings. A Johns Hopkins medical professor foresaw the need for female space travelers, claiming, "If man is to colonize the planets, if celestial housekeeping is ever to be instituted, the 'second sex' must have booking on future space flights."[14] But when the members of the "second sex" prepared for NASA training and testified in the halls of Congress, they did not have "celestial housekeeping" in mind.

As the issue of female space flight aroused public controversy in the United States, it also became part of American and Soviet struggles for scientific and technological superiority. Where the United States barred women from space travel, the Soviet Union added women to its ranks of cosmonaut trainees in

1962. In June 1963, Valentina Tereshkova, known to Americans as the "cosmo-miss," boarded *Vostok V* on a mission to test human endurance and physiology under sustained weightlessness.[15] As space historian Walter McDougall explains, "Having no astronautical training, she was presented as proof of the routineness of spacefaring in the USSR—in fact her lack of expertise only proved the super-fluousness of the test pilots on the other flights."[16] Thus, rather than tout Tereshkova's educational background, athletic ability, or bravado, the Soviets signaled their scientific and technological superiority by portraying the first female astronaut as little more than a test subject. Nonetheless, "when Teresh-kova returned to earth ... she became a symbol of emancipated Soviet woman-hood. Kruschchev admonished American bourgeois society for referring to women as the 'weaker sex.'"[17] Tereshkova toured around the world proclaiming the equality of the sexes in the Soviet Union, and, according to McDougall, "Americans bought the Soviet line and berated NASA for 'sexism.'"[18] Cold War competition might thus have had as much influence on press critiques of NASA as did the women's movement. Indeed, the one reason a *New York Times Maga-zine* writer supported female space flight was that "the propaganda value of putting a woman into orbit would be tremendous."[19]

While Valentina Tereshkova's space mission proclaimed Soviet technological progress and Cold War superiority, it also symbolized women's professional mobility and social equality. In 1965, *Science News Letter* reported: "Few activi-ties are today the exclusive domain of the male. Women play football, wrestle, race high speed motor cars, climb mountains ... drive trucks.... Any thoughts by the male of staking out an exclusive domain by leaving Earth for space were dissolved by Cosmonaut Valentina Tereshkova."[20] Indeed, American women seized upon Tereshkova's achievement as they struggled for social equality. In October 1965, when NASA solicited applications for another space exploration mission, it received nearly a thousand applications for ten to twenty positions, and many of them came from women.[21]

Despite the testimony of female aviators, the media's condemnation of NASA, scientific evidence of women's physical fitness, and the success of the Tereshkova mission, NASA still refused to consider women for space flight training pro-grams. NASA officials insisted that women did not "possess extensive education, training and experience in one or more scientific and engineering fields," and such credentials were considered to be crucial prerequisites.[22] George Low,

NASA's director of spacecraft and flight missions, even suggested that integrating women into the program would jeopardize the U.S. lead in the space race: "The present crop of would-be space women do not meet NASA astronaut qualifications, and a special program to train them will slow down the national space program and might prevent the U.S. from getting a man on the moon by 1970."[23] Other NASA representatives concurred with Low, advising that, "in the national interest, women should make a sacrifice by keeping out of space flight at this time."[24] Finally, one official proclaimed that "women astronauts would be a waste in space, a luxury that the United States space effort cannot afford."[25] Thus, although Tereshkova's space flight was heralded as a global success, American women's attempts to become astronauts were perversely transformed into a threat to U.S. national security at the height of the Cold War.

When public debates about female astronauts emerged during the early 1960s, the feminine body was scientifically scrutinized, publicly domesticated, and globally fashioned as an index of national progress. Scientists caricatured the feminine body as prone to sexual and emotional outbursts, claiming that it was simply too unpredictable to launch into orbit. Popular-press articles suggested that women's mobility in the aerospace field would compromise the stability and sanctity of the nuclear family. Soviet political officials used the female astronaut to signal Cold War victories, whereas those in the United States perceived her as a national security risk. Combined, these discourses framed the issue of female space travel in terms of women's sexuality, familial obligations, and national citizenship. Within American culture, then, the ultimate threat would be to rocket an excessively sexy, single, and political female astronaut into outer space. And *Barbarella* did just that.

Barbarella: A Cosmic Comic Comes to Life

Given NASA's opposition to female space travel and American women's challenges to the space agency's gender discrimination, perhaps it is not surprising that the first female astronaut to land on American soil was a character in an imported science fiction film. Jane Fonda, who would later be known as "America's most popular feminist," stars in *Barbarella* as a "cosmos-trotting heroine,"[26] commander of her own spacecraft and a practiced intergalactic diplomat. During the late 1960s many Americans perceived Jane Fonda as yet another screen-bound sex kitten. Her star persona fluctuated from the "pretty girl next door" in American movies such as *Any Wednesday* (1966) and *Barefoot in the Park* (1967) to the "sexy, sultry seductress" in French films such as *Circle of Love* (1964) and *The Game Is Over* (1966). Just before the production of *Barbarella*, Fonda became the subject of two highly publicized sex scandals in the United States. In March 1965, her nude body was splayed across an eight-story-high billboard promoting the premiere of *Circle of Love* at the DeMille Theater in New York. In the ad, Fonda appeared lying on a bed with tousled hair gazing across Broadway toward another billboard, which ironically advertised a film called *The Bible*. A year later, *Playboy* published several candid nude shots of Fonda snapped surreptitiously by a French photographer who had sneaked onto a closed set while the actress was shooting a love scene for *The Game Is Over*.

Both the billboard and the *Playboy* pictures provoked public controversies that filled the pages of newspapers and magazines. In November 1967, just after *Barbarella* began production, the cover of *Newsweek* featured Fonda's bare buns with the headline "Anything Goes: The Permissive Society."[27] Indeed, Fonda became a symbol of permissive sexuality well before she emerged as a popular feminist. Because these nude images entered the public arena without Fonda's permission, they became grounds for retaliatory lawsuits against Reade-Sterling, the distributor of *Circle of Love*, and Hugh Hefner of *Playboy*. Nonetheless, as biographer Thomas Kiernan insists, "it was the billboard more than anything else that established her as America's new sex symbol."[28] When *Barbarella* was released in October 1968, the American public's perception of Fonda as a sex symbol no doubt informed the way film viewers engaged with her role as a female astronaut.

Barbarella originated as a semipornographic comic strip created by Jean Claude Forest in France in 1962. After its successful run in *V Magazine*, the comic was translated into English and published in the avant-garde *Evergreen Review* in the United States. In 1967, Roger Vadim, Terry Southern, and six other writers adapted the comic into a science fiction film script that satirized the repressive bourgeois conventions of Western society. Vadim described the film's lead character as "a kind of sexual *Alice in Wonderland* of the future."[29] The film, starring Fonda (then Vadim's wife) and John Phillip Law, was released in the United States in October 1968. In the aftermath of Fonda's public nudity scandals, Vadim and Fonda reportedly felt that Hollywood "was ripe for a film that would repudiate the Christian sense of sin, celebrate and legitimize the new

Barbarella and the blind angel, Pygar. Courtesy of the Wisconsin Center
for Film and Theater Research.

eroticism and depict a futuristic morality that would make current concern over
present-day morals seem absurd."[30]

Set in the year 40,000 AD, *Barbarella* is the story of a female astronaut sent
on an intergalactic mission by the president of the Republic of Earth to locate a
corrupt scientist named Duran Duran, the inventor of a dangerous weapon
called the positronic ray. On her mission, Barbarella is faced with numerous
spaceship malfunctions and odd encounters with children, machines, men, and
monsters. Riding on the wings of the blind angel Pygar, Barbarella eventually
navigates her way through a kingdom of sadists and prostitutes and thwarts
Duran Duran's efforts to rule the galaxy. Perhaps Barbarella's adventures seem
so fantastically absurd because she is precisely the kind of female astronaut that
NASA officials and American political leaders wanted to keep out of space, for
she embodies all of the characteristics of a frighteningly volatile femininity: she
is sexy, single, and political.

The sexy, single, and political female astronaut challenges traditional gender
norms; she embraces her own bodily pleasures, valuing movement and physical
expression; she evades compulsory heterosexuality and its institutions of mon-
ogamy and marriage; and she advocates political agendas that contradict those

of the Western nation-state. *Barbarella*, however, mitigates this threat by immersing its protagonist in an excessively feminized and campy mise-en-scène. Far from a realist portrayal of female space flight, *Barbarella* is a parodic narrative that ridicules the viability of the female astronaut. Indeed, the only way the film can depict a female astronaut as technologically skilled is by hypersexualizing her work and transforming her body into a fetishized sex object.

Barbarella's adventurous sexuality made it one of several films during the late 1960s to incite moral outrage and cries for censorship in the United States. But despite the film's alleged prurience, critics engaged with *Barbarella* in a variety of ways. Whereas some relished Jane Fonda's "sexy and funny" performance, others characterized the film as "pure sub-adolescent junk," especially when contrasted with Stanley Kubrick's "serious" science fiction film, *2001: A Space Odyssey*, released the same year. One critic complained that *Barbarella* had defiled the recovering science fiction genre: "In the year that Stanley Kubrick and Franklin Schaffner (*Planet of the Apes*) finally elevated the science-fiction movie beyond the abyss of the middle show, Roger Vadim, in a single French-Italian co-production aimed at the American market, has knocked it right back [down] again."[31] A *Los Angeles Times* critic quipped, "You could subtitle the film *2002: A Space Idiocy*."[32] Whereas *2001* was praised for its scientific realism, particularly its portrayals of astronauts in outer space, *Barbarella* lacked such realism altogether, according to critics. As one writer put it, *Barbarella* had "all the gadgetry of science fiction ... but no logic."[33] Given that the film's lead character was a *female* astronaut, it could scarcely be anything but "fantastic," for the specter of a real—not to mention logical—female astronaut was at the time impossible.

Although some measured *Barbarella*'s success against the realism of Kubrick's *2001*, others praised the film's incorporation of the fantastic and read it as a playful satire. Paul Zimmerman in *Newsweek* lauded *Barbarella*'s "universe of yummy decadence" and claimed, "Vadim carries it off with such human style and detachment that *Barbarella* becomes something of an inter-galactic put-on, all satire and supersonic camp."[34] But Stanley Kauffman of the *New Republic* scoffed, "*Barbarella* is only a French sci-fi sex-camp comic strip brought to the screen. I took the sadism about as seriously as the science; they are both just slightly mean jokes on us."[35] Fonda herself described the film as "a kind of tongue-in-cheek satire against bourgeois morality."[36] And Vadim declared, "*Barbarella*, for all its extravagant fantasy, contains a good deal of ruthless satire on the problems of our times."[37]

Indeed, *Barbarella* could be read as an allegory for the international political climate of the 1960s. By positioning a female astronaut as the protagonist of a story about the control of dangerous and catastrophic weapons in outer space, the film's narrative interweaves social anxieties over women's professional mobility with those about the proliferation of nuclear weapons, the escalation of the Cold War, and the colonization of outer space. *Barbarella*'s playful commentary daringly entrusts world peace to a sexy female astronaut who manages to use her own body to resolve intergalactic conflict.

Whereas some critics highlighted *Barbarella*'s lack of scientific realism or its political satire, many feminists and Catholics, among others, were concerned about the film's representations of sex and violence. Feminists asserted that the film sexually objectifies Jane Fonda and turns her into a tortured sex spectacle. *New York Times* critic Renata Adler complained, "All the gadgetry of science fiction ... is turned to all kinds of jokes, which are not jokes, but hard-breathing, sadistic thrashings, mainly at the expense of Barbarella, and of women."[38] Pauline Kael accused Vadim (who had been married to Brigitte Bardot and Catherine Deneuve before Fonda) of "turning each wife into a facsimile of the first and spreading her out for the camera."[39] Vadim even admitted in his memoir that Fonda "didn't enjoy shooting *Barbarella*.... She disliked the central character for her lack of principle, her shameless exploitation of her sexuality, and her irrelevance to contemporary social and political realities." He insisted, however, that "Women's Lib showed through Barbarella's outer space make-up."[40]

Barbarella's release also aroused cries for censorship from the National Catholic Office for Motion Pictures (formerly the Legion of Decency). The NCOMP called *Barbarella* a "sick, heavy-handed fantasy with nudity and graphic representations of sadism," gave the film a "condemned" rating, and forbade devout Catholics to see it. It also criticized the Production Code Administration for having approved the film at all, given that the Code specifically banned the "undue exposure of the human body."[41] *Barbarella* upset conservative moral standards across the country, and it was one of the last films to sneak into American theaters under the proviso "Suggested for Mature Audiences" before the Motion Picture Association of America began rating all American *and* foreign films.

Although the critical reception of *Barbarella* reveals that the film stirred anxieties about the scientific portrayal of outer space, changing international relations, and feminine sexuality, what was strikingly absent was any discussion of the professional female astronaut. This absence was particularly significant given the public controversies that had surfaced earlier in the decade. Moreover, the attention to *Barbarella*'s campy visual style and parodic narrative deflected attention away from the issue of women's professional mobility and instead directed the spectatorial gaze toward Barbarella's excessive sexuality. Indeed, snide attacks on the film's lack of scientific realism constituted a refusal to imagine the feminine body as anything other than sexual, thereby reproducing much the same logic that NASA officials and political leaders had used to exclude American women from the space program a few years earlier. Combined, then, the critical reception of *Barbarella* and the public debates on female space flight reflected profound anxieties, not only about the prospect of sending a woman into outer space, but also about the lack of public control over feminine sexuality more generally.

Barbarella: "The Five-Star, Double-Rated Astronomatrix"

The official title of *Barbarella*'s female astronaut encapsulates her conflicted status. She is, on the one hand, a "five-star" and "double-rated" officer—a skilled state agent, a technical master, an accomplished diplomat. But she is also an "astronomatrix"—a feminized navigator of space, a flying sex spectacle, a roving dominatrix. It is this tension between technological mastery and feminine sexuality that I would like to explore further here, for *Barbarella* offers a female astronaut who could reach public display only by conforming to the visual regime of a masculine fetishistic gaze. The very traits that make Barbarella so threatening within a patriarchal social order—most notably her aggressive, non-reproductive sexuality and her adept use of machinery—are overvalued and transformed from icons of male fear into objects of intense desire. The body of the female astronaut, in other words, is fetishized as both sex object and machine. Nonetheless, embedded within the fetish is the lurking, if sublimated, threat that it contains. The figure of Barbarella, then, is a volatile site, for the fetishistic gaze that seeks to restrain her also imbues her with a sexual power that, under some circumstances, she might turn toward her own ends. Barbarella the sex object, in other words, is also Barbarella the agent, and the technology she most successfully wields is that of her own body. The conditions under which the astronaut uses her body as a technology are far from emancipatory, however, for the film subordinates her desires to those of the state she serves, the narrative whose ends are beyond her control, and the spectator who watches her every move.

Working with director Roger Vadim, production designers Enrico Fea and Mario Garbuglia created colorful and ornate sets, props, and costumes, surrounding the female astronaut with a veritable galaxy of space machinery. Barbarella commands her own customized spacecraft, deploys weapons, and uses gadgets such as a tongue box, a brain wave detector, a mini-missile projector, and a deflagration gun. Designers also technologized the astronaut's nutrition and personal hygiene. Barbarella drinks liquefied food, sleeps in an incubation tank, ingests exaltation-transference pills as a substitute for sexual intercourse, and dons aerodynamic clothing. And while set designers embellished Barbarella with gadgets, scriptwriters created a female astronaut who could speak "scientific" jargon. Pseudoscientific phrases such as "Prepare for acceleration into temporal space," "It must be a galactic phi dialect," and "People's psychocardiograms must be in perfect complement if full rapport is to be achieved" pepper her dialogue. Mise-en-scène and characterization, then, position Barbarella as technologically and scientifically adept.

Although Barbarella appears a competent astronaut, her skills are clearly situated within a gendered power hierarchy. In the opening scene, a nude Barbarella receives orders from the president of the Republic of Earth, a graying paternal figure played by Marcel Marceau, whose face appears on a large video monitor. He greets Barbarella with the word "love," presents the "five-star, double-rated astronomatrix" with her assignment, insists, "We'll have to meet in the flesh someday!" and disappears in a flash. The female astronaut's naked body, while possibly reveling in the physical pleasures of outer space, is also the object of a fetishistic masculine gaze—a gaze that extends from the president in the film's narrative to Vadim behind the camera to the spectator in the film theater. This gaze subordinates Barbarella in the narrative's chain of command: her skills are commandeered for the political ends of the Republic and her body for the eyes of the president.[42]

This gendered hierarchy is perpetuated throughout the narrative as Barbarella's technical skills must be supplemented by those of masculine characters. For instance, when Barbarella's spacecraft, *Alpha 7*, malfunctions, she relies on the expertise of the hypermasculine hairy Catchman or the mad scientist Professor Ping rather than repair it herself, thereby reproducing historical imbalances with respect to the gendered control of transportation technology. Similarly, when in danger Barbarella hesitates to use the weapons at her command, although such weapons are often used against her. Thus Barbarella's technological skill is challenged by the masculine characters within the narrative.

In addition to representing the female astronaut as dependent on the technical authority of men, the film feminizes the technologies that Barbarella does command. The tongue box, for instance, which looks like a designer bracelet, allows Barbarella to decode alien languages when she encounters other beings in outer space. The gadget privileges communication over conflict and enables the female astronaut to mediate alien contact. Weapons such as the mini-missile projector and the deflagration gun, on the other hand, have destructive potential yet are softened by pacifist rhetoric that prescribes their use for "self-conservation" only. In the opening scene, Barbarella identifies herself as a peacenik when she proclaims that unwarranted aggression is a kind of "archaic insecurity," a "neurotic irresponsibility." Further, even if the film itself does not feminize its technological mise-en-scène, many critics have. The sets have been described as "chaos in an interior decorator's salon, or a cosmetics factory," and the spacecraft as "a Revlon lipstick display case."[43]

The astronaut's spacesuit is a technology designed to protect the body from the icy vacuum of space, but rather than wearing bulky space armor like that worn by Yuri Gagarin or Neil Armstrong, Barbarella wears brightly colored, tight-fitting, skimpy outfits that resemble the slinky catsuit made famous by *The Avengers'* Emma Peel. One critic went so far as to describe the film as a "dress designer's field day."[44] Barbarella's space suits focus attention on her body through strategically placed cutouts or peepholes that expose her flesh. Such cutouts carefully direct the gaze through the costume to a skin show and away from the character's professional status. In some scenes, mise-en-scène emulates the peephole framing of Barbarella's space wardrobe. For instance, after she has sex with the Catchman, Barbarella crawls through a transparent, Habitrail-like tube that temporarily "clothes" her body while also spotlighting her nude silhouette.

Barbarella's "softening" or feminizing of the technological is likely one of the reasons critics found the film's scientific realism unconvincing. The film's excessive visual style undermines any potential there might have been for viewers to read into *Barbarella* the prospect of a legitimate female astronaut in command of high-tech space machinery. Barbarella's lipsticklike spaceship, braceletlike dialect decoder, and slinky haute couture space suits launched a flamboyant femininity into outer space, enacting more a masculine fantasy of feminine space travel than a realist adventure. This fantasy underscored the impossibility of an actual female astronaut and reproduced social anxieties about sending a woman into space, but it also temporarily transformed outer space from an exclusively masculine domain into an excessively feminized one. Although the film subordinates the female astronaut to masculine political authority and feminizes her technological skills, *Barbarella* sets up a unique relationship between technology and the feminine body—one that encourages us to consider Barbarella's sexuality itself as a technology. Although Barbarella is certainly the object of masculine sexual desire, she is not passive or immobile. Rather, her body and its movement through space guide and structure the narrative. Further, the narrative's enigma is resolved in part by the sexual agency asserted by the female astronaut. Thus Barbarella's body can be read as a site where the fetishistic masculine gaze and a limited feminine sexual agency collide.

If the object that the female astronaut controls most proficiently and forcefully is her own body, then we might consider it as a "technology of self." Barbarella's relationship to her own body as a technology of power and pleasure coincides well with Michel Foucault's discussion of the "technology of the self," which, he explains, involves an "ethics of self control" when "the relation to self is . . . defined as a concrete relationship enabling one to delight in oneself, as in a thing one both possesses and has before one's eyes." This relationship to the self involves "a different way of constituting oneself as the ethical subject of one's sexual behavior." It is, Foucault argues, a condition in which the relations of oneself to oneself are intensified and valorized.[45] Ethics, in this case, does not refer to an externally imposed social system of values, but rather to a self-directed regime of bodily behavior and style. Foucault's "technology of the self" is significant because it involves a public recognition of the political significance of the body's internal pleasures and desires.

Before moving on, I want to make clear that my analysis of Barbarella's "technology of self" refers explicitly to the fictional female astronaut and not to Jane Fonda herself, for in retrospect, Fonda had major objections not only to the promiscuity of this character but also to the manipulative conditions of the film's production, which were likely intensified in light of the previous exploitation of her body and image. Fonda has been reticent about the film, and she split with Vadim not long after its release. I do not want to erase or ignore Fonda's negative experience with *Barbarella*. Rather, I want to consider how the female astronaut is figured in this film and what kind of agency she is able to assert within a highly constrained matrix of masculine power.

Barbarella is arguably as much about the female astronaut's "technology of self" as it is about her search for Duran Duran. This is established during the film's opening credit sequence: Barbarella floats weightless in midair, slowly and sensually removes her flimsy metallic armor, and releases the film's credits into the frame. Certainly, Fonda is performing a striptease for Vadim, the camera and the spectator here; within the narrative, however, the female astronaut is coming alive, and the first thing she does is revel in the sensations of weightlessness and nudity. Throughout the film, cinematic techniques spotlight Barbarella's plea-sure. After each of her sexual encounters the camera hangs over her grinning face as she squirms in closed-eyed ecstasy, then reveals her nude body in a pile of furs or atop a feathery nest as she hums a tune of postorgasmic delight.

One of the most important scenes with respect to Barbarella's sexual agency occurs when Duran Duran tries to torture her to death by placing her within an

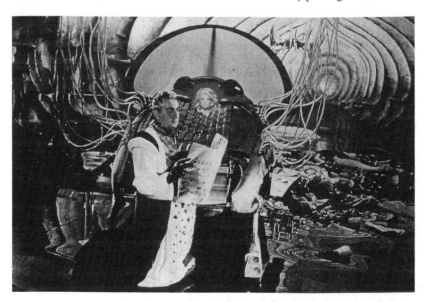

Barbarella, the Orgasmatron, and Duran Duran. Courtesy of the
Wisconsin Center for Film and Theater Research.

Orgasmatron, described by one critic as "part Wurlitzer and part carnivorous plant."[46] With a fierce and languorous orgasm, Barbarella outpleasures and destroys the machine. Her volatile sexual energy prompts an angry and shocked Duran Duran to ask, "What kind of a girl are you? Have you no shame!!?" Here the issue of "sexual ethics" emerges more conventionally, as the condemning and patriarchal Duran Duran morally challenges the sexual power that Barbarella exudes. The kind of sexual ethics Foucault is concerned about, however, is derived internally and is based on the subject's ritualization of her own pleasure. Barbarella's implosive sexuality enables her to combat the forces of evil and prevail for the Republic, but it also allows her to develop a practice of self-stylization.

This female astronaut styles her sexuality as a weapon—as a space technology that enables her to resolve the narrative enigma. When Barbarella's spacecraft fails early in the narrative, she exchanges sex for technical assistance and travel, exploiting her own body to continue her search for Duran Duran. First she ravishes a fur-wearing savage so that he will repair her craft's stabilizers. Then she flirts with the nerdy Professor Ping so that he will examine her broken-down spaceship. Finally, she nests with a blind angel so that he will fly her to Sogo to find Duran Duran. In this final encounter, Barbarella uses sex to restore or "repair" the angel's dormant will to fly. By using her body in such a manner, Barbarella advances the interests of the Republic and at the same time multiplies her own pleasure and rejuvenation.

Despite Barbarella's powerful sexuality, within the narrative she alternates between having control over her body (her autoerotic striptease, sleeping with a furry savage, making love to an angel, and ingesting orgasm pills) and being controlled by nature and/or monsters. Not only is she set back by a major magnetic storm, she is tortured throughout the narrative by a collection of odd creatures. Barbarella's flesh is pecked by the snapping jaws of mechanical dolls and by a cage full of hungry wrens. She is attacked by a clan of Leathermen, placed in the Ultimate Chamber of Death, and tormented in Duran Duran's pleasure organ. In each of these cases, however, Barbarella's body competes directly with the monstrous technologies that try to conquer it. On one occasion, Barbarella's sexuality is so highly charged that it ignites the hand of Captain Dildano during their encounter.

Torture is a strategy deployed within the narrative to keep the sexual and technological prowess of the female astronaut in check. It is a reminder of her

Barbarella and Captain Dildan engage in "exaltation-transference" sex. Courtesy of the
Wisconsin Center for Film and Theater Research.

vulnerability, but this vulnerability is constructed as fleeting or superficial—as
a quick-healing wound on the female body rather than a deep-rooted psychological trauma. In short, Barbarella bleeds one moment and orgasms the next.
Each torture scene in the narrative is, in fact, followed by a sex scene. The film
thus constructs a sadomasochistic sexuality for Barbarella, positioning her as
both sadistic aggressor and docile masochist. Barbarella is subjected to vicious
attacks, but her oscillation between these sexual positions is indicative of the
range of responses she can summon to deal with rapidly shifting political conditions and physical environments.

In addition to being sadomasochistic, Barbarella's sexuality is purely non-
reproductive—mobilized only for pleasure or politics. This state-sanctioned
nonreproductive sexuality is significant because historically the female body has
been co-opted by the state to "build" a national community. Barbarella's sexuality not only dislocated traditional feminine norms, it also dovetailed with
the increased visibility and use of birth control during the 1960s. Indeed, some
of Barbarella's sexual encounters are mediated by the consumption of an
"exaltation-transference pill." By ingesting a pill and touching the palm of a

partner who had a "complementary psychocardiogram," Barbarella could experience sex fully clothed and with no risk of pregnancy. In one scene she identifies the sex pill—clearly a stand-in for the birth control pill—as an important invention because it made "ego support and self-esteem" available to women on Earth.

The technology of the self, then, involves the astronaut's ability, on the one hand, to mobilize sexuality as a weapon in order to compete with external relations of force and, on the other hand, to control the pleasures of the body so that they are ultimately inwardly directed. As Foucault writes, "The individual who has finally succeeded in gaining access to himself is, for himself, an object of pleasure. Not only is one satisfied with what one is and accepting of one's limits, but one 'pleases oneself.'"[47] This tactical use of the body is especially significant when other avenues of power are limited or foreclosed. Because the female astronaut in *Barbarella* is constantly an object of masculine fantasy, any use of her body that ruptures the power of that gaze to control her body is significant. The technology of the self enables us to imagine how this "Alice in Wonderland of the future" might use her body in ways that work against the masculine and state powers that attempt to fix her position, limit her agency, and contain her physicality.

In Barbarella's intergalactic wanderings, her body becomes a battleground between a masculine predatory gaze and a feminine technology of self. The specter of Barbarella's feminine sexuality—her technology of self—was incompatible with NASA's vision of a fully disciplined and nationalized astronaut, and the belief that the female body might experience pleasure (or torture) in space and become unable to perform ultimately kept American women from space travel until 1983. Dominant discourses in the United States during the 1960s showed a profound mistrust of the physicality of the feminine body. Whereas the male astronaut's body was seen as uncompromisingly dedicated to the twin goals of nationalistic expansion and scientific enlightenment, the female body was perceived as too libidinous, too procreative, and thus too unpredictable to send into space.

Barbarella represents a kind of pleasure in the physicality of space exploration that simply could not be voiced by the Lovelace scientists or male astronauts. Astronautics is a bodily act, but NASA and the congressional leaders insisted that the astronaut's body remain purely an expression of state power, not bodily will or desire. NASA officials were unable to imagine a feminine presence in outer space during the 1960s because they understood the female body only in sexual terms. Indeed, patriarchal discourses mark the feminine as undetachable from the body and its erotic, physical potential. As Hilary Radner suggests, "Within the public sphere the female body represents the undisciplined body, and as such is a threat to the public order reproduced by the discourse of discipline and punishment delineated by Foucault."[48] Thus sending a woman into orbit would discursively transform outer space from a place of abstract, disembodied scientific exploration to a physical erogenous zone.

The expressive sexuality of *Barbarella* was precisely why NASA "could not afford the luxury of the female astronaut." Both the fictional female astronaut in *Barbarella* and public debates on female space flight challenged traditional gender norms and provoked anxieties over the place of professional women in the public sphere. When NASA officials banned women from space travel during the 1960s, what they really feared was that a dangerously irreverent and uncontainable feminine body might complicate scientific rational and national imperatives to conquer the unknown domain of outer space. Not only would the female astronaut introduce sexual difference into the spacecraft, she was imagined to be too preoccupied with her own body to observe space "objectively" for science and claim it for the nation.

Barbarella's highly sexualized female astronaut enables us to speculate why women's space flight was impossible in American society during the 1960s. What makes this film such an interesting artifact is its unique means of negotiating state power with feminine sexuality. *Barbarella*, in the context of other media and women's struggles to become astronauts, offers a vision of a feminine heroine who, although controlled by state interests and masculine voyeurism, also manages to use her own body and its sexual potential to assert power. In this sense, Barbarella is not a "free agent," but she does demonstrate how one might use the body as a technology of power within a patriarchal visual regime. *Barbarella* is an important parable, then, because it demonstrates how we might learn to negotiate the internal pleasures of the feminine with the external forces of patriarchy, scientific rationalism, and nationalism.

Jane Fonda's image shifted from that of a public sex symbol in the late 1960s to that of one of America's most popular feminists in the 1970s. One writer called her "the Hollywood feminist with whom most American women could most easily identify."[49] *Barbarella* can be seen as a pivotal, though perhaps difficult, moment in Fonda's public life. The tension within the film—between a con-straining fetishistic gaze and a feminine agency based on bodily pleasure—can in a sense be mapped onto Fonda's own life, for although the media heavily exploited the actress's sexual persona during 1960s, she has always fought hard for control over her body and sexuality. By 1971, Fonda had won an Academy Award for her starring role in *Klute* and had become a political activist who pub-licly denounced the war in Vietnam. In short, Fonda transformed from a public sex kitten to a popular feminist and peace activist in a matter of years. Her recog-nition of the power of her own body and sexuality contributed in large part to this rapid transformation and crystallized with the publication of the *Jane Fonda Workout Book* in 1981—a book that Radner suggests offers "a specifically feminine 'model of self-mastery'" and "provides a narrative that articulates a 'technology' or practice of the self." At the same time, however, this "practice of the self," as Radner points out, is located in a discursive field "in which the strate-gies of domination appear to coexist with tactics of resistance."[50]

In 1976, NASA released a call for shuttle astronauts due to pressure from the White House and the Congress to make the space corps look more like the American population at large. The space agency received more than 6,000 responses, 1,251 of which were from women.[51] A 1978 CBS television news report introduced the first six female astronauts in training and profiled the lives of two.[52] After announcing the astronauts' names, the anchor identified the women as "single" or "married" and then contrasted "single" Dr. Margaret Rhea Seddon performing surgery in a hospital with "married" Shannon Lucid at home in an apron making dinner with her husband and children. Dr. Seddon was reportedly "so confident in her abilities that she joins in the laughter when her men friends joke that her flying duties will include serving coffee, tea, or milk."[53] Although treated lightheartedly, this bifurcation between the single professional woman and the married homemaker reflects an uneasiness over the relation-ships between women's work, sexuality, and domesticity that continue today.

In 1983, more than twenty years after Cobb, Hart, and Cochran testified before Congress, Sally Ride became the first American woman in space. *Barba-rella* came full circle with NASA when officials invited Fonda to attend the launch of Ride's shuttle mission to witness this historical first. This symbolic meeting of the fantastic film star and the first female astronaut encapsulates the range of tactics by which women have moved into outer space. Although seemingly an improbable pair of allies, both Ride's professional achievements and Fonda's film performance compelled patriarchal institutions to grapple with feminine agency. Such intersections, whether they take place on a Florida launchpad or in a campy science fiction film, always carry with them a disruptive potential, for the intervention of feminine agency into science inevitably points up that field's specious mastery and historical occlusion of women. Neither Ride nor Barbarella was content to practice "celestial housekeeping," as one scientist had predicted. Instead, they skillfully used their bodies to produce new knowledges, generate new pleasures, and prove that the exploration of outer space is not just "for all mankind."

Notes

I would like to thank Michael Kackman, Hilary Radner, Moya Luckett, Julie D'Acci, and John Fiske for their comments on earlier drafts of this essay.

1. The phrase that appears as the subtitle of this section is from an article titled "Women Pilots Claim They Are Fit to Be Astronauts," *Milwaukee Journal*, July 18, 1962, 3.
2. "Should a Girl Be First in Space?" *Look*, February 2, 1960, 112–17.
3. "Space Women Expensive," *Science News Letter*, August 4, 1962, 70.
4. "Astronauttes?" *Newsweek*, July 30, 1962, 17.
5. The names of the eleven women are Jan C. Dietrich, Marion Dietrick, Rhea Nurrle Allison, Irene Leverton, Bernice Trimble Steadman, Jean Hixson, Gene Nora Stumbough, Geraldine Sloan, Myrtle Thompson Cagle, Sarah Gorelick, Mary Wallace. See "Women Fight to Join Space Program," *Capital Times*, (Madison, Wis.), July 18, 1962, 2 (in NASA Collection, Box 1, File "Mercury," Wisconsin State Historical Society, Madison).
6. Astronauttes?" 18.
7. "Women Fight to Join Space Program," 2
8. "No Ladies in Orbit," *Saturday Evening Post*, August 25, 1962, 86.
9. "In the Same Boat," *Ebony*, October 1962, 72. Other black publications, such as the *Chicago Daily News*, published editorials condemning NASA's perpetuation of white male dominance in the space flight program as well.
10. "Space May Be a Man's World," *Science News Letter*, March 1965, 24.
11. Quoted in Louis Lasagna, "Why Not Astronauttes Also?" *New York Times Magazine*, October 21, 1962, 55.
12. Ibid., 53.
13. "Women Pilots Claim They Are Fit to Be Astronauts," *Milwaukee Journal*, July 18, 1962, 3.

14. Lasagna, "Why Not Astronauttes Also?" 60, 63.

15. "Women Fight to Join Space Program," 2.

16. Walter McDougall, . . . *The Heavens and the Earth: A Political History of the Space Age* (New York: Basic Books, 1985), 288.

17. Ibid.

18. Ibid.

19. Lasagna, "Why Not Astronauttes Also?" 60, 62.

20. "Space May Be a Man's World," 23.

21. Ibid., 24.

22. "No Ladies in Orbit," 86.

23. Quoted in "Space Women Expensive," 70.

24. Ibid.

25. Ibid.

26. Fonda is described this way in John Simon's review, *Film* 68/69, 150.

27. *Newsweek,* cover, November 13, 1967.

28. Thomas Kiernan, *Jane: An Intimate Biography of Jane Fonda* (New York: G. P. Putnam's Sons, 1973), 180.

29. Quoted in Barbara Seidman, "'The Lady Doth Protest Too Much, Methinks: Jane Fonda, Feminism, and Hollywood,'" in *Women and Film,* ed. Janet Todd (New York: Holmes & Meier, 1988), 193.

30. Kiernan, *Jane,* 206.

31. Dan Bates, "Barbarella," *Film Quarterly* 22 (spring 1969): 58.

32. Quoted in Chris Andersen, *Citizen Jane: The Turbulent Life of Jane Fonda* (New York: Henry Holt, 1990), 160.

33. Renata Adler, "Screen: Science + Sex = 'Barbarella,'" *New York Times,* October 12, 1968, p. 43, col. 1.

34. Paul Zimmerman, "Paradise Found," *Newsweek,* October 21, 1968, 98.

35. Stanley Kauffman, "Three for Fun," *New Republic,* November 9, 1968, 22.

36. Quoted in *Photoplay,* February 1968, 63.

37. Roger Vadim, *Bardot-Deneuve-Fonda* (New York: Simon & Schuster, 1986), 164.

38. Adler, "Screen: Science + Sex = 'Barbarella,'" 1.

39. Pauline Kael, "Film Review," *New Yorker,* November 2, 1968, 182.

40. Vadim, *Bardot-Deneuve-Fonda,* 164.

41. "Four New Movies Condemned by Catholic Office," *The New York Times,* October 4, 1968, p. 34, col. 1. The three other films that received "Condemned" ratings were *Birds in Peru, If He Hollers, Let Him Go,* and *Weekend.*

42. Here I am borrowing from Laura Mulvey's influential essay "Visual Pleasure in Narrative Cinema," in *Issues in Feminist Film Criticism,* ed. Patricia Erens (Bloomington: Indiana University Press, 1990), 28–40, and trying to consider the political mobility of cinematic objectification.

43. Adler, "Screen: Science + Sex = 'Barbarella,'" 1; Renata Adler, "Bolder Sexually—Yet Less Sexy?" *New York Times,* October 13, 1968, sec. II, p. 1, col. 3.

44. James Price, "*Barbarella,*" *Sight and Sound* (Winter 1968–69): 46–47. In 1996 an entire line of haute couture fashion symbolizing the powerful woman of the 1990s was inspired by *Barbarella.*

45. Michel Foucault, *The History of Sexuality,* vol. 3, *The Care of the Self* (New York: Vintage, 1986), 65, 240.

46. Price, "*Barbarella,*" 47.

47. Foucault, *The History of Sexuality,* 66.

48. Hilary Radner, *Shopping Around: Feminine Culture and the Pursuit of Pleasure* (New York: Routledge, 1995), 143.

49. Seidman, "'The Lady Doth Protest Too Much,'" 198. For an excellent discussion of Jane Fonda and the feminine culture of the 1980s, see "Speaking the Body: *Jane Fonda's Workout Book,*" in Radner, *Shopping Around.*

50. Radner, *Shopping Around,* 146, 147.

51. Andrew Chaikin, "Sally Ride," *Working Woman,* November 21, 1996, 42.

52. The first female astronauts in training were Katheryn Sullivan, Judith Resnik, Sally Ride, Anna Fisher, Shannon Lucid, and Margaret Rhea Seddon.

53. "Women Astronauts," *CBC Evening News,* January 13, 1978.

The Avengers, circa 1966. Courtesy of Photofest.

Sensuous Women and Single Girls
Reclaiming the Female Body on 1960s Television
Moya Luckett

During the early 1960s, a number of female writers popularized new forms of feminism. Betty Friedan drew on women's experience to expose their domestic frustrations and thwarted ambitions, and Helen Gurley Brown articulated dissatisfaction with the sexual confinement of marriage. Although Friedan's critiques have retained feminist validity, Brown's more sexually and self-oriented advice has been marginalized, largely because of its seemingly traditional emphasis on beauty, fashion, and seduction. Both women's work nevertheless played an important role in the era's reevaluation and redefinition of women. Whereas Brown forged peculiarly feminine associations among women's bodies, agency, and subjectivity, Friedan offered different interpretations of femininity. For her, Brown's lauded beauty and fashion systems were not a means to power but part of a system that forced women into the home and lured them into false consciousness, entrapping them into a relationship with their bodies to blind them to public life. Both nevertheless agreed that women should have greater access to public space, envisaging a world centered on the expression of female desire. Fulfillment of these demands, however, inevitably required a reconceptualization of the relationship of the female body to space, desire, sexuality, and subjectivity.

By the mid-1960s, Friedan and Brown's work had become highly influential, shaping many forms of women's popular culture. Using her experience in advertising to promote herself, Helen Gurley Brown became the more marketable figure. As a media personality in her own right by 1963, she recorded self-help albums such as 1963's *Lessons in Love;* edited and, in the process, transformed *Cosmopolitan* into *the* single-girl magazine from 1965; and hosted her own syndicated sex-oriented talk show during 1967. The publishing industry swiftly capitalized on her success with a cycle of self-consciously modern sexual fiction for women, largely written by women, that featured young, liberated female heroines clearly influenced by Brown's archetypal single girls. American and British cinema soon followed suit with both adaptations of these novels, such as Jacqueline Susann's *Valley of the Dolls* (20th Century-Fox, 1967), and original material like *Darling* (1965).

By way of contrast, television was slow to adapt, partly because its relatively stronger censorship mechanisms prevented representation of the more sexual heroine and partly because the conventions of prime-time television were so strongly oriented toward male-centered action dramas. Against a backdrop of westerns, military shows, and police/detective dramas, there were a few domestic comedies and even fewer shows centering on female protagonists during the early 1960s; women were cast to the wasteland as wives or decorative foils. Although there were just five female-centered shows in 1960–61, there was a steady, if slow, increase in programs with female protagonists throughout the first half of the decade—from six such shows in 1962 to seven in 1963, ten in 1964, and reaching a decade-high thirteen in 1965. An inconsistent decline began the next year, as women took the lead in ten shows during 1966, seven in 1967, nine in 1968, and ten in 1969. These changes did not necessarily imply that the new feminism lost ground during this period; rather, they mirrored changes in the ratings samples, which had been adjusted during 1965 to take greater account of women and the new teenage baby boomer audience and were then temporarily adjusted back in 1966 to favor the more conventional nuclear family.[1] Seventeen of these shows lasted more than one season—a surprisingly large number given the rash of cancellations that marked television's attempts to engage with the decade's rapid social transformations.[2] Nonetheless, a large number of these programs were set against the conventional feminine backdrop of the family, featuring the mother as pivotal protagonist in domestic dramas (examples include *The Donna Reed Show*, ABC, 1958–66; *Angel*, CBS, 1960–61; and *The Pruitts of Southampton*, ABC, 1966–67). A number of other shows focused on teenage heroines in order to mediate more safely between their domestic settings and public life. With its unprecedented three-year run, *The Patty Duke Show* (ABC, 1963–66) was by far the most successful of these shows, which also included *Peck's Bad Girl* (CBS, 1959–60), *Margie* (ABC, 1961–62), *Fair Exchange* (CBS, 1962–63), *Karen* (NBC, 1964–65), *Tammy* (ABC, 1965–66), and *Gidget* (ABC, 1965–66). With the exception of *Tammy*, all these shows placed their protagonists firmly within the home, although these teenage girls were at least allowed to fantasize about a nondomestic future. Even the working women protagonists of *Hazel* (NBC, 1961–65; CBS, 1965–66), *Grindl* (NBC, 1963–64), and *The Farmer's Daughter* (ABC, 1963–66) were employed as domestic help, revealing how the shows of the first half of this decade were still invested in embedding women within private space. Other female-oriented programs centered on quirky amalgams of work and marriage. For example, *Glynis* (CBS 1963) featured an absent-minded wife helping her amateur detective husband solve crimes; *The Cara Williams Show* (CBS, 1964–65) explored the dilemma of a married couple who had to keep their relationship secret because their employer prohibited staff marriages; *Mona McCluskey* (NBC, 1965–66) examined the comic plight of a Hollywood star married to an air force sergeant who insisted they live on his meager salary; and *Please Don't Eat the Daisies* (NBC, 1965–67) featured a stay-at-home suburban wife who hated housework and divided her time between self-indulgence and writing a newspaper column. Meanwhile, as Lynn Spigel and others have observed, shows such as *Bewitched* (ABC, 1964–72) and *I Dream of Jeannie* (NBC, 1965–70) used fantastic comic displacement to explore the imbalance of power in marriage.[3]

Single women were represented less frequently and even then generally as teenagers or widows. The theme of widowed women combining part-time jobs and domestic duties was repeated several times throughout the decade in shows such as *The Lucy Show* (CBS, 1962–74), *The New Loretta Young Show* (CBS, 1962–63), *The Jean Arthur Show* (CBS, September–December 1966), *Julia* (NBC, 1968–71), and *The Doris Day Show* (CBS, 1968–73). Widows, of course, were easily permitted a certain degree of latitude—they often had to work to supplement small pensions and to keep the family together. As many of these women were also middle-aged, it followed that they did not have the same feminine power as their more glamorous younger counterparts and thus were not so likely to cause havoc in the workplace. In most of these shows, the widow went out to work partly to meet a man so that she could remarry, a gesture that suggested that marriage itself is a family-centered arrangement, devoid of sexuality.

A few shows started to feature single girls working outside the home, mostly from the mid-1960s onward. *My Sister Eileen* (CBS, 1960–61) was an early entry in this genre, focusing on two midwestern sisters working and surviving in New

York. Unfortunately, the show was not particularly progressive: its plain, ambitious, and sensible sister, Ruth, spent much of her time trying to control her flighty, attractive, would-be actress sibling, Eileen. This trend started to gather some momentum in 1964 with the appearance of *Peyton Place* (ABC, 1964–69) and *My Living Doll* (CBS, 1964–65), followed by *Honey West* (ABC, 1965–66), *The Avengers* (ABC, 1966–69), *The Girl from U.N.C.L.E.* (NBC, 1966–67), *The Tammy Grimes Show* (ABC, September 8–September 29, 1966), and *That Girl* (ABC, 1966–71). Unlike the more domestic shows, which were all sitcoms, some of the single-girl shows were dramas (*Peyton Place, Honey West, The Avengers,* and *The Girl From U.N.C.L.E.*).

This latter group featured several seminal shows that started trends and pioneered new ways of representing women on television. *Peyton Place* was American television's first prime-time soap opera; the British spy import *The Avengers* inspired the decade's other female-centered dramas, *Honey West* and *The Girl from U.N.C.L.E.;* and *That Girl* was the decade's longest-running single-girl sitcom and purportedly the first show of its kind to feature a career-girl protagonist, inspiring, among other programs, *The Mary Tyler Moore Show* (CBS, 1970–77). These shows did not merely replace traditional homemaker heroines with swinging singles; rather, they constructed new relationships among the female body, desire, and social space. They accomplished this in a number of ways. *The Avengers* dismantled traditional binaries of sexual difference, producing new models of gender that permitted greater equality. *The Avengers* and *That Girl* focused on active female bodies to show a greater continuity between women and public space. Meanwhile, *Peyton Place* presented both genders struggling for control of the public sphere and suggested that healthy female bodies could exist only outside marriage. These shows' emphasis on the body was quite tactical, for, as Julie D'Acci has argued, viewers " naturally . . . equate women with the body," so it logically becomes a prime site for transformation and reclamation of gender.[4]

One of the much-observed characteristics of the new sixties female icon—whether fictional or real-life heroine—was her ever-mobile, active, and graceful body. In its April 1966 profile of the Oscar-winning new British star Julie Christie, *Life* magazine observed, "The camera catches Julie Christie on the run, which she ever is. . . . she's a 25-year-old British tomboy with a whipcord-and-piano-wire-body. . . . do not confuse her with just any jaunty gamine frugging on the dance floor . . . she burns with a nervous energy that lights up the house."[5] Just two pages before Christie's photo spread, an advertisement for the Chevrolet Corvair features a pantsuit-clad young woman with an Emma Peel-like haircut, holding a briefcase and a Steed-like umbrella. The caption, "The more of a stand-up-and-be-counted individualist you are the more you'll enjoy driving a Corvair," heads four images, the last of which shows the model driving away. The copy is printed at an angle and is filled with short phrases designed to showcase the speed and agility of this sporty car.[6] This association of femininity, speed, public life, youth, and mobility highlights the strategies that would come to define the new modern single girl of the mid- to late 1960s. As this advertisement's implied reference to *The Avengers* suggests, this show would play a prominent role in articulating the media vision of this new feminist-feminine archetype. The insistence on the mobility of this body furthermore emphasizes her departure from the immediately preceding models of feminine beauty that foregrounded the otherworldly, statuesque quality of her appearance, separating her image from all other mundane considerations. The highly passive implications of these representations are evident in a February 1965 *Cosmopolitan* article (preceding Brown's takeover) titled "The Fiber Glass Girls," which features photographs of mannequins based on the day's top models to illustrate the beauty ideal sought by women everywhere.[7]

This image of mobile femininity carried with it inescapable suggestions of feminine subjectivity. Images of female beauty have long been linked to objectivity and passivity. Within phenomenology, corporeal movement has been associated with the ways in which the body experiences the exterior world, producing its subjectivity while creating a relationship between self and other. Nevertheless, phenomenology's truly active body is always gendered male. As philosopher Iris Marion Young observes, studies of women's movements reveal that they depart from phenomenology's ideal of the active subject, typically "fail[ing] to summon the full possibilities of [their] muscular coordination, position, poise, and bearing. Women tend not to put their whole bodies into engagement in a physical task with the same ease and naturalness as men."[8] She suggests that this hesitant motion results from the conditioning that teaches women to view their bodies as separate parts rather than a unified system. Some limbs move while others remain still, effectively existing as objects. This violates Merleau-Ponty's dictum that "for the body to exist as a transcendent presence to the world, it cannot exist as an *object*."[9] This disjointed activity places the woman somewhere between subject and object, limits her agency and the efficacy of her actions, and reveals a doubtful relationship to her physical capacities.

Given academic and broader cultural assumptions about the mobility of the female body and its relationship to subjectivity and public space, it is hardly surprising that *The Avengers* was so influential on both British and American television—indeed, it intrigued American media for years before it even appeared on U.S. television screens.[10] Initial interest centered on its distinctive heroine—Cathy Gale (Honor Blackman), a widowed, educated, glamorous, leather-clad martial arts expert with a Ph.D.—who was almost the equal of her partner, upper-class secret agent John Steed. In March 1965, Liz Smith commented in *Cosmopolitan* that Blackman had created a new feminine archetype, "the humorous, wry, maturely sexy, intelligent woman of action."[11] In still photographs and secondhand plot summaries (she left the show before its U.S. debut), Blackman represented a potent combination of power, activity, and intelligence, characteristics that were articulated through her body.

Her successor, Diana Rigg (Mrs. Emma Peel) added youthful femininity to Blackman's power, intelligence, and physical acumen, prompting Cynthia Grenier to comment in *Cosmopolitan* on Peel's potential as a new role model for the magazine's readers:

> Television is coming on strong in the female take-over.... Great Britain's television series, *The Avengers,* this fall introduced a new heroine, complete with a fashion collection especially designed for her. (The collection is going on sale in retail stores so all female television viewers can live out this fantasy—almost for real.) The program stars Diana Rigg, a lithe twenty-seven year old, as Mrs. Emma Peel, daughter of a millionaire shipping magnate, youthful widow of a famous test pilot and the internationally educated symbol for the jet-age female. Mrs. Peel drives a high-speed Lotus Elan and fights fast, free, and furious with every technique from karate to her own brand of "feinting."[12]

This combination of beauty, intelligence, femininity, and physical power pleased Helen Gurley Brown, who suggested that her readers identify with Peel's performance and take pleasure gazing upon her body. Indeed, Emma Peel's active feminine body helped articulate her agency, while her pleasure in her own

Sexual symmetry and fantasy in *The Avengers*.

appearance helped undermine binary oppositions between subjectivity and objectivity. This was important precisely because it drew on the pleasure of looking at the self that is integral to feminine culture, imbuing it with a new power. Even more than her predecessor, then, Emma Peel was Steed's equal—her femininity forcing changes in the show's construction of sexual difference.

The opening title sequences for *The Avengers* present an alternative vision of the female body. The black-and-white episodes (1965–66) introduce Emma in a series of close-ups featuring her clad first in leather and then in a ruffled dress. After a close shot of Steed looking, the opening alternates among shots of Steed fighting, Steed and the leather-clad Emma fighting, and Emma fighting on her own. The credits conclude with a medium shot of a crouched Emma, ready to spring into action, while Steed's motionless legs are visible in the background. Although the opening consists of a montage of still photographs, the images foreground female motion. Emma's body is introduced with a pan across her arm and a tilt up to her face, and she is seen fighting with arms outstretched and hair flying. Several pictures are blurred, suggesting movement beyond the speed of photographic representation. Her look is also foregrounded, particularly in relation to her desire for her own body, as she admires her own appearance while holding out her collar and gazing at her cleavage. An extreme close-up of Steed's smiling eyes follows as he looks to the right, seemingly at Emma. The next shot features him fighting, an eyeline match implying that he is looking at himself, not Emma. Unobstructed motion, desire, and the gaze at the self are consequently presented as properties distributed across the sexes.

The opening credits for the 1967–68 episodes—Rigg's second and final series and the first to be shown in the United States and shot in color—emphasize similar themes, this time in moving pictures. Steed enters the empty frame and starts to open a bottle. He turns and there is a cut to a shot of a woman pointing a gun at him. A reverse shot reveals that this is Emma (clad in a light yellow jersey catsuit) as she fires the gun at the bottle's cork. In a rapid series of alternating shots, the partners smile and walk toward each other, Emma keeping her gun at hand. Standing by a revealed table, Steed pours two drinks from the bottle Emma has opened, and they share a toast. The next shot shows the table in long shot, with Steed's legs propped up on its left and Emma's on the right. This perfectly symmetrical image indicates that the two genders are balanced, an equilibrium achieved by recasting sexual difference. As the credits identify Steed, we see him in close-up, placing his hat on his head and casting his umbrella over his shoulder. Emma appears from behind an armchair, balancing a gun in her hand as she pushes her hair behind her ear. We then cut to Steed swinging his umbrella and twisting it open to reveal a sword. He practices fencing and then selects a bloom to cut a from a vase of red carnations. Emma catches the flower. The camera arcs with her as she places it in Steed's buttonhole while the two smile and gaze at one another. The final sequence consists of alternating shots of Steed and Emma in combat. Both are initially shown frozen in almost balletic poses. Quick cuts create the illusion of movement until Emma lifts her arms and Steed tosses his umbrella. They come together for the closing shot, facing one another in profile and then turn to the camera. Shot in silhouette, their near identical poses suggest a final symmetry across the sexes. Although Steed's masculinity is not undercut, it is shown to involve a more conventionally feminine concern with appearance and dress. Meanwhile, Emma is shown in motion, in the traditionally more masculine role of the active and potentially dangerous partner, the skilled marksman and fighter with excellent hand-eye coordination.

Both credit sequences redistribute traditional masculine and feminine characteristics across the sexes to produce a new equality while playing with associations among movement, still images, and subjectivity. In the process, they suggest that new forms of femininity can exist only within a changed economy of sexual difference. Emma's motion is particularly important here as it departs from traditions of the motionless, objectified female body.[13] Indeed, throughout *The Avengers* her activity forms an index of her subjectivity. Typically the more mobile partner, she is usually active before the adventure starts, practicing fencing, for example, in "From Venus with Love" (1966), decorating her house in "The Hidden Tiger" (1966), and beating an intruder she finds in Steed's house in "The Thirteenth Hole" (1965). Whereas Steed generally favors tricks to fend off his opponents, Emma uses her body as a weapon. She puts her physical skills to use in adventures, going undercover as a dance instructor ("The Quick-Quick-Slow Death," 1965), a gymnast ("How to Succeed ... at Murder, 1965), a thrill-seeking daredevil ("The Danger Makers," 1965), and a karate expert ("The Cybernauts," 1965).

This dynamic feminine figure is a sharp contrast to the active male body of phenomenology, emphasizing the importance of Emma Peel's active body as a new model of feminine possibility. Her expertise in martial arts underlines her perception of her body as a unified entity, as does her skill in dancing and her excellent hand-eye coordination. Not all women in *The Avengers* are treated in quite the same way, however. For example, in "The Bird Who Knew too Much" (1966), a photographer tells a model to "extend *the* legs"—implying they are not part of her body but rather merely another component in a passive female image. Meanwhile, in "The Girl from Auntie" (1965), Emma is kidnapped and replaced by a young actress, Georgie Price-Jones. The first shots of Georgie objectify her body. As she gets out of a car, the camera frames her from the knees down, following her legs as she walks toward Emma's apartment, balancing clumsily on high heels. The objectifying framing, this figure's ungainly motion, and her curvaceous body highlight that this is not Emma—even before we see the impostor's face. After Steed reveals her true identity, she helps him solve the mystery of Emma's disappearance. But in contrast to Emma, she is a passive, inelegant partner: kindly, well-meaning, disorganized, and badly dressed. Aware of her failings, she tries to improve herself but has limited success. One scene features her reading Emma's books. Once again, her body is introduced in parts.

We see her arm enter the frame from below as she reaches for an apple. Her head then appears as she discards Emma's volume on nuclear physics. Picking up a weighty self-defense text, she reclines on the couch. As she attempts some karate holds, a murderous intruder surreptitiously enters the room. Rejecting an initial movement because it ties her body into knots, she turns to another page and reads, "Should your opponent attack you from behind with a knife or gun, place your right hand over your right shoulder and grasp the attacker's wrist." She rehearses this hold and by chance manages to grab the intruder and throw her to the floor in one fluid movement. Unsure how to follow up, she tries to read and fight at the same time, then gives up and hits her assailant over the head with the book. Her ability to learn this hold at her first attempt nevertheless reveals that women can overcome their culturally induced inability and mobilize their body strength in movement.

Young notes that the context of women's movements is also important, revealing the privileged association between body and space. Disjointed movements are most marked in public places, where women tend to adopt a closed stance to protect themselves from the world. This is a result of women's being conditioned to occupy smaller, more private, spaces and of systems of etiquette that teach them to wait for objects to come into their spatial field rather than to go forward to grasp them. These physical signs suggest their incomplete transcendency while also revealing that women cannot organize space around themselves. Meanwhile, masculine control of public space is evidenced at the level of the male body, whose fluid movements suggest greater continuity between self and other.

The Avengers's representation of an active woman in public space is important, then, because it contributed to the new possibilities advocated within period feminism. As *Cosmopolitan*'s Cynthia Grenier commented, its setting within the public arena of espionage was notable because the spy-genre was "the last male retreat." The world of spies and criminal derring-do ... was sacrosanct male territory. But now this bloody bastion is also crumbling. The girls it seems, are taking over in James Bond land."[14] Besides featuring the agile Emma gracefully moving through highly dangerous public spaces, *The Avengers* also presents a somewhat feminized public sphere (a phenomenon also central to Helen Gurley Brown's project). Traditionally feminine groups, figures, and occupations occupy the show's public space. Villainy is located within marriage bureaus, department stores, dance academies, knitting circles, schools for nannies, and modeling agencies as well as more masculine sites such as science labs, the stockmarket, military camps, and gentlemen's clubs. Rather than simply assigning female villains to feminine spaces and have them dispatched by Emma, there is little systematic sexual segregation. Mostly, both partners are together at the helm, but Emma is the principal investigator in episodes set in scientific laboratories ("A Surfeit of H_2O," 1965; "The Positive-Negative Man," 1967), a dancing school ("The Quick-Quick-Slow Death," 1965), a mechanized house ("The House That Jack Built," 1965), and a comic strip studio ("The Winged Avenger," 1966). Meanwhile, Steed takes the principal role in stories set in a dating agency ("The Murder Market," 1965), the stockmarket ("Dial a Deadly Number," 1965), a knitting circle ("The Girl from Auntie," 1965), and the military ("The Hour That Never Was," 1966).

This fluidity of gender and gendered spaces is perhaps most explicit in "The Girl from Auntie," which features a murderous grandmother who kills with knitting needles. She is a member of a top-ranked knitting circle run by a man. When Steed finally apprehends her, he pulls off her mask, revealing that "she" is a swarthy young man. This involves more trickery (this time with the viewer) as there is clearly a change of actors—the murderous, fighting grandmother was played by an elderly woman. Yet the idea that he was a man all along involves another layer of gender confusion—an expert knitter hit man whose weapon of choice is knitting needles.

The show's emphasis on costuming and appearance also helps feminize public space. Clothing is significant within masquerades, where it helps both partners gain access to enemy spaces and allows them to reorganize those spaces around their presence. Steed's interest in his appearance and his use of specially fortified garments such as steel-rimmed bowler hats indicate that dress is no longer simply a feminine interest. Nevertheless, this still suggests a privileged address to female audiences, implying that some investigations can be solved only through the use of feminine knowledge and indicating the larger, more public significance of the fashion and beauty systems touted by the likes of Helen Gurley Brown.

Nevertheless, this public sphere is not completely equal, featuring few women in positions of power. In the post-black-and-white years of the series, Steed usually initiates the adventures, often through impossible control of the world. In "The Living Dead" (1966), he hails Emma with doctored traffic lights that read, "Mrs. Peel ... We're Needed." In "The Hidden Tiger" (1966), Emma pulls away wallpaper and finds the same words stenciled on the wall underneath. In "The Correct Way to Kill" (1966), these words form the headline on the evening paper Emma buys; in "Never, Never Say Die" (1966), Steed appears on her television screen uttering this sentence; and in "Who's Who???" (1966), he repeats these words as his own image replaces Emma's reflection in her mirror. This development undermines Emma's activity, suggesting that Steed controls public, private, and liminal space and can even appropriate Emma's body.

As part of its project of undermining binary oppositions of sexual difference, then, The Avengers dismantles the rigid dichotomies between subject and object, masculine and feminine, body and subjectivity. This recasts Young's conclusion that gendered differences in movement and perception of space result from "the fact that for feminine existence the body frequently is both subject and object. Feminine bodily existence is frequently not a pure presence for the world because it is referred onto itself as well as onto possibilities in the world."[15] Rather than limiting their mobility and subjectivity, both Emma's and Steed's awareness of their bodies (and the pleasure they take in gazing upon them) increase their agency, help them solve crimes. In "Too Many Christmas Trees" (1965), for instance, Emma and Steed enter a hall of mirrors to fight enemy hypnotists. After Steed is knocked out, Emma monitors the reflections to gauge the positions of their assailants. Although the male villains are confused, she is able to read these images to maintain her bearings. After fending the villains off, she checks her reflection, adjusts her dress, smiles, and reenters the fray. In contrast to more conventional uses of the hall of mirrors, the woman is not lost in narcissistic absorption of her image, leading to her capture and the unmasking of her duplicity.[16] Instead, her look serves to empower her for the continued onslaught, recasting the idea that women's awareness of themselves as image hinders their activity and restricts their conquest of space to position them as neither subject nor object.

Some of the significant discrepancies between the bodies represented in The Avengers and those analyzed by Young result from the show's progressive yet fantastic nature. In contrast, Young's work draws upon more scientific studies of women's movements and the traditions guiding their use of their bodies to conclude that women's liminal subject-object position results from cultural conditioning rather than from any essential physical or psychic traits. Shows such as *The Avengers* and the "new etiquette" inspired by Helen Gurley Brown can therefore be seen as responses to these social conditions. This phenomenological account similarly casts light on the social importance of Brown's body-oriented arguments. If women are conditioned to see their bodies as both subjects (for themselves) and objects (for male others), feminism must prioritize a reclamation of appearance and the body in order to dismantle binary systems of sexual difference. Rather than accomplish this within purely masculine terms, Brown seeks to preserve the same specifically feminine pleasures highlighted in *The Avengers*, breaking down, for example, the equation between the pleasurable look at the female body and its inevitable objectification.

As Hilary Radner notes, Brown's work is therefore quite radical, constituting "a cultural reworking of feminine identity" that simultaneously exists inside and "outside the scene of heterosexuality." Consequently, its pleasures (and its implications for sexual difference and identities) cannot be understood within binary systems of sexual difference where the gaze is always male, the woman always objectified. As Radner points out, beauty systems like Brown's (and the texts they inspire) "move feminine pleasure into another space ... where the masculine gaze is no longer the linchpin in the mechanisms whereby [women] produce identities."[17]

Brown's work, and the popular culture it inspired, thus highlights the female body's role in the construction of subjectivity while simultaneously articulating femininity outside male-defined sexual difference. She prioritized the body of the single girl, partly because her status as self-sufficient, public woman placed her outside the domain of reproduction and partly because she identified with the single girl's economic situation. Within Brown's work, this self-supporting career girl might use beauty rituals to increase her social status, earn herself promotions, and feminize public space. The last of these she accomplishes through her refashioned body, by using a language that masculine culture cannot understand (in part because its significance has been so marginalized).

Brown's refigured female body therefore simultaneously demands changes in women's relationship toward public space. Yet despite her reification of beauty rituals and skills of feminine subterfuge, Brown tactically downgrades women's association with private space. However, as Young notes, women's dislocation from space is also revealed in private spheres, where they are also taught to hold their limbs close to their bodies to occupy the smallest possible area, indicating more fundamental masculine stakes in space itself.

The problems of negotiating women's relationships to this private sphere within new feminist discourses clearly articulated the difficulties inherent in wrenching images of women away from domestic space. Questions of the feminine body's status within private space were nevertheless approached in the popular prime-time soap opera *Peyton Place*, which dealt with feminine secrets, identity struggles, and conflicts over women's place in both public and private life. Based on Grace Metalious's 1956 best-selling novel, the show centers on a group of single women. Constance Mackenzie (Dorothy Malone) is the still-glamorous owner of the town's bookstore, a single woman who masquerades as a widow to hide her daughter's illegitimate birth. Her child, Allison Mackenzie (Mia Farrow), is a blonde, compassionate, intelligent, and ambitious teenage girl who is in love with her friend's estranged husband. The friend, Betty Anderson (Barbara Parkins), purposefully gets pregnant to entrap the town's handsome young heir, Rodney Harrington (Ryan O'Neal), into marriage, loses her baby, and enters into a string of affairs. Although the show's story lines are cleaned up in comparison with the the novel, the program was still cloaked in infamy.[18] *TV Guide*'s Richard Warren Lewis described it as a "continuing saga of temper tantrums, frigid women, adultery, unhappy marriages, illegitimacy, necking and teenage romance."[19]

Prompted by a strong desire to enter public life, Allison spends much of her spare time studying and helping out at the local newspaper. Nonetheless, she is torn between private duty to her single working mother, and the consequent need for her to help with housework, and her more public ambitions. Her fragile appearance underlines these conflicts, suggesting that it might be easier for her to live in her mind and at least disavow gender and physical life. But although her countenance erroneously suggests a need for protection, she nevertheless displays muted but growing awareness that she might gain some power from controlling her image. On her first day at college, she wears a new outfit and takes particular care to look good, revealing that even quiet girls equate increased career success with bodily improvement. Shortly afterward, a scene in the drugstore emphasizes her developing consciousness that she might realize her self through beauty rituals. A young woman's hands are visible in the foreground selecting a lipstick, and as the camera pulls back, we see that they are Allison's hands. The pharmacist reprimands her for choosing too bright a color, and she tells him that is precisely why she likes it. She wants to be noticed, revealing that she is learning the pleasures and power of controlling one's appearance and the looks of others. Meanwhile, the druggist's disapprobation suggests that such orchestrated self-display threatens patriarchal hierarchies. This is reminiscent of Helen Gurley Brown's reworking of feminine beauty rituals, which, as Hilary Radner notes, present

> an arena of reproduction that is primarily narcissistic—in which the woman reproduces, not another, or for another, but herself for herself. It is this self which the "single girl" learns to reproduce on a daily basis under the tutelage of Brown.... Importantly, ... Brown devotes the bulk of the book [1962's *Sex and the Single Girl*] to the problem of embodiment in which the task of the single girl is that of constructing herself as feminine through the disciplined use of makeup, clothing, exercise, and cosmetic surgery."[20]

For Brown, then, the female body makes visible the external effects of its owner's internal desire and agency. But for Allison, its fragility suggests the conflicts between individual will and pleasure and the demands of public and private spheres.

Allison's romantic rival, Betty, is even more conscious of beauty rituals and trusts in their promise of a powerful position in public life. She believes faithfully that her self-created body will allow her to "be someone on my own, as Betty Anderson." When she flees to New York after the failure of her marriage, viewers are presented with a vision of the city as a feminized space, dominated by clothes, filled with single girls, and structured around female looks—in short, the city of Betty's dreams. While Betty is in New York, her desire—and, by extension, that of the viewer—is focused on the female body and the spaces and garments that frame and embellish it. Most of the scenes featuring Betty and her new friend, Sharon, include shots of the girls looking at their bodies, their reflections or each other. In all the scenes with Sharon, the camera focuses on the details of her lifestyle—her exercises, her wardrobe, her apartment decor, and her movements across the screen. This is combined with an emphasis on Betty's gaze as she is seen repeatedly staring at Sharon, smiling at her own reflection, or admiring her own body as she seductively dances. But the fabricated nature of these essentially private spaces highlights the duplicity of this vision, stylistically departing from the documentary-style shots of the cityscape that open these scenes and hold a recognizable stamp of "truth" about the city that these interiors do not possess.

The pleasure and power that these women gain from gazing at the female body is perhaps best demonstrated in a scene where Betty visits Sharon at the designer store where her friend works as a model. A clerk leads her to Sharon, who is trying on "a heavenly sheath." Betty is almost hypnotized by the commodities within the store and, more markedly, by the image of Sharon modeling furs. As a gesture of friendship, Sharon lets Betty wear a fur stole. As she moves to the center of the room, the camera tracks in to reframe the two women in medium shot beside the mirror. The bond between them is expressed in terms of a shared love of clothes and in the way they both move in front of the mirror, exchanging reflections with one another. While Sharon looks on, Betty apes the seductive style of a model, smiling at her reflection. The monumental nature of this moment—Betty's appropriation of her own glamorized image, her transformation into the self of her dreams—is underscored with a zoom in to a medium close-up as romantic music swells.

At first Betty flourishes in New York, until she discovers that these seemingly self-generated feminine pleasures have their cost. In order to live like this, a woman has to sell herself to a man. Although she loves her married sugar daddy, Phil, Sharon has to self-medicate with pills and alcohol to withstand the torment of their affair, and she is slowly destroying her body. Although the pleasures of looking at oneself might not be subject to the control of a male gaze, *Peyton Place* reminds us that the consumer goods required to produce this look can be purchased only with men's money.

This male economic power reveals how foundational elements of public life resist feminization. Betty discovers that there are few jobs for the crowds of women at employment agencies, most of them poorly paid. As Sharon notes, the seventy-five-dollar weekly wage paid to most secretaries and working women restricts them to "salads at the automat ... and nights with good books." Such poverty prevents women from carving out identities for themselves in public life. These scenes reveal that once the single female enters the public sphere, her body becomes subject to the disciplinary forces of patriarchal culture and cannot always be so easily used for her own ends—regardless of Helen Gurley Brown's advice.[21]

Peyton Place thus shows how the male-dominated economy seizes women's bodies back as objects, even as women struggle to establish themselves as corporeal subjects. Betty is punished for trying to short-circuit this system, for taking pleasure in her newly adorned body without providing service for any man. On her first date as a consort, she is sexually attacked, prompting her to return to Peyton Place.

In this important respect, *Peyton Place* mediates between the extremes of Brown's and Friedan's work. Friedan demanded increased career opportunities for women, conceiving a feminized public space built around increased social and economic power for women. As she noted: "My answers may disturb the women and the experts alike, for they imply *social change*. But there would be no sense in my writing this book at all if I did not believe that women can affect society, as well as be affected by it; that, in the end, a woman, as a man, has the power to choose and make her own heaven or hell."[22] In contrast, Brown's glamorous single girl suggested a glamorous image of women, toying with work, preening, and flirting, an image of power that could be recuperated to suggest the affluence of working women. This allowed the media to repress the gendered segregation of the economy and the discrepancies in men's and women's wages. These issues concerned Friedan, as she was aware that women also needed to control the economic spheres within which their bodies circulated. It was easier for the media to recuperate the potentially dangerous single girl as a sign of the nation's economic success. Rather than heralding the end of marriage, the lowly spinster's self-fulfillment was used to articulate the benefits capitalist culture held for all social groups.

As this suggests, *The Avengers* and *Peyton Place* gained some of their popularity with women because they did not reduce the single girl to a metaphor for national affluence. Throughout its Emma Peel episodes, *The Avengers* represents a social context that is both fantastic and in turmoil, but its disturbances relate to a reassessment of nation and history as well as sexuality. Within its narrative world, gender stability results from social changes and is always equated with the single man or woman, whereas marriage is envisioned as pathological. Although *Peyton Place* glamorizes the body of the single girl, it also shows her glamour and sense of self as compromised because contemporary public and private life is itself torn between images of past and future. Within this system, women have incomplete mobility, and both genders suffer from the impossibility of realizing their dreams.

Perhaps the closest approximation of the "safe" single-girl ideal comes in the successful sitcom *That Girl*, in which the heroine, Ann Marie, strives for success as an actress but finds merely a continuing series of temporary jobs. Although many of these are disappointing, even humiliating, she soldiers on with minimal loss of glamour or enthusiasm. Although she relishes her independence, it is also compromised and rendered safe as her parents and, most significantly, her fiancé, Don, are always close by, ready to protect her. Meanwhile, the different generic conventions of comedy mandate an always happy ending, a reassuring return to stasis, and suggest a certain levity.

Feminist debates in the 1960s thus shifted the conventions of social and corporeal arguments of subjectivity, the body, and agency by inserting gender. This was a significant move, for, as feminist theoreticians Elizabeth Grosz and Teresa de Lauretis remind us, most theories of the body and subjectivity purport to be gender-neutral. Grosz comments:

> It is significant that none of the male theories discussed here [those of Freud, Lacan, Merleau-Ponty, Nietzsche, Derrida, and Deleuze and Guattari] is very enlightened about or illuminating on the question of sexual specificity. None seems prepared to admit that his researches, if they make sense of the body, do so with reference to the male body. None seems aware that the specificities of the female body remain unexplained.[23]

As she points out, theories of masculinity and femininity based on these models have limited use for the study of the female body, precisely because "the 'masculinity' of the male body cannot be the same as the 'masculinity' of the female body, because the kind of body inscribed makes a difference to the meanings and functioning of gender that emerges."[24] Brown's articulation of femininity as productive self-creation clearly fits in with this model as it refers specifically to woman. Correspondingly, *Peyton Place* centers its conflicts over this idea of a gendered body, highlighting how corporeal difference is very much at stake in the regulation and ordering of private and public spheres. Friedan's model is perhaps less specific, as Friedan deals more with an exchange of power between genders and relies on a more fixed and opposed model of essential biological difference.

Although both authors responded to an array of female frustrations with private, domestic, and public life, neither of their models fully resolved the issues that women dealt with on a daily basis. This was ironically productive, however, for the gap between and within their positions stimulated debate about female sexuality. During the mid-1960s, there was not only greater and more public exploration of the relationships among women's minds, bodies, physical capabilities, and mental acumen, but it was performed with more passion and in more detail than ever before. This in itself shifted the terrain of debate about sexual difference. As Teresa de Lauretis has observed, analyses of gender (both social and theoretical) tend to be performed within a binary axis of sexual difference, one that defines the feminine against a male norm.

> With its emphasis on the sexual, "sexual difference" is in the first and last instance a difference of women from men, female from male; and even the more abstract notion of "sexual differences" resulting not from biology or socialization but from signification and discursive effects (the emphasis here being less on the sexual than on differences as *différance*), ends up being in the last instance a difference (of woman) from man—or better, the very instance of difference in man. To continue to pose the question of gender in either of these terms once the critique of patriarchy has been fully outlined, keeps feminist thinking bound to the terms of Western patriarchy itself.[25]

Clearly, Friedan's and Brown's status as popular rather than academic writers helped here, for it freed them from responsible intellectual paradigms while making their work accessible to the millions. Their work is significant, however, because it helped recast popular analyses of sexual difference so that *woman* was no longer a fixed term, inevitably opposed to the male. Instead, interpretations and representations of the feminine were cast against one another, temporarily displacing the male element. In January 1966, for instance, *Look* published a special issue on "the American woman" to analyze the massive volume of writings on "the woman question." The fact that these questions publicly remained unresolved suggested that femininity might more profitably be seen as a set of identities in flux. In practice, however, such questions were only being raised in order to find the answer, to fix some position for women in public and private life.

Certainly, there was little continuity even across archetypal models of the new feminist woman. Television shows such as *The Avengers* and *Peyton Place*, which are synonymous now and were then with the new swinging single-girl ideal, represent sexuality, femininity, and public and private space in ways that cannot be easily reconciled. Although national difference clearly plays a role in these programs' definitions of sexuality, it does not account for those definitions, as revealed by the shows' popularity on American screens. All these texts highlight the pleasure of the woman's look at her own body, a structure that is replicated in the female viewer's look at the woman on screen. This look itself recalls the address of women's magazines, indicating that gazing upon the female body is a foundational aspect of female sexuality. Despite Helen Gurley Brown's progressive recuperation of this look, and the beauty rituals upon which it is based, it seems to have limited use for changing the social inequities shown in *Peyton Place* and discussed by Friedan. Given women's expertise in reading the female body, however, the possibilities raised by multiple representations of active female bodies cannot be so easily dismissed. Even if these shows cannot solve very real social inequities, they might help undermine the gendered binaries on which those inequities are based, exposing their roles in constructing those separate gendered spheres that help immobilize feminine bodies and compromise women's subjectivity.

Notes

1. "Upheaval in the Networks," *Business Week,* November 13, 1965, 46–47.
2. The seventeen were *The Donna Reed Show* (1958–66), *National Velvet* (1960–62), *Hazel* (1961–66), *The Lucy Show* (1962–74), *The Nurses* (1962–65), *The Patty Duke Show* (1963–66), *The Farmer's Daughter* (1963–66), *Peyton Place* (1964–69), *Bewitched* (1964–72), *I Dream of Jeannie* (1965–70), *Please Don't Eat the Daisies* (1965–67), *The Avengers* (1966–69 in the United States, 1960–69 in the United Kingdom), *That Girl* (1966–71), *The Flying Nun* (1967–70), *Julia* (1968–71), *The Doris Day Show* (1968–73), and *The Ghost and Mrs. Muir* (1968–70). All data on TV shows' networks and dates are from Tim Brooks and Earle Marsh, *The Complete Directory to Prime Time Network TV Shows: 1946–Present,* 5th ed. (New York: Ballantine, 1992).
3. Lynn Spigel, "From Domestic Space to Outer Space: The 1960s Fantastic Family Sit-Com," in *Close Encounters: Film, Feminism, and Science Fiction,* ed. Constance Penley, Elisabeth Lyon, Lynn Spigel, and Janet Bergstrom (Minneapolis: University of Minnesota Press, 1991), 205–36; Susan J. Douglas, *Where the Girls Are: Growing Up Female with the Mass Media* (New York: Times Books, 1995) 106–120.
4. Julie D'Acci, *Defining Women: Television and the Case of Cagney and Lacey* (Chapel Hill: University of North Carolina Press, 1994), 43.

5. "Julie Christie: Style and Verve of an Antigodess," *Life*, April 29, 1966, 61.

6. Chevrolet advertisement, *Life*, April 29, 1966, 59.

7. "The Fiber Glass Girls," *Cosmopolitan*, February 1965, 30–31.

8. Iris Marion Young, *Throwing Like a Girl and Other Essays in Feminist Philosophy and Social Theory* (Bloomington: Indiana University Press, 1990), 145.

9. Ibid., 150.

10. Two years before its U.S. debut, for example, *TV Guide* printed a feature article on *The Avengers*. Robert Musel, "Violence Can Be Fun," *TV Guide*, May 9, 1964, 12–14.

11. Liz Smith, "Honor Blackman: Queen of the Kinks," *Cosmopolitan*, March 1965, 26.

12. Cynthia Grenier, "Secret Agent Girls," *Cosmopolitan*, April 1966, 56–57.

13. See Young, *Throwing Like a Girl*, 148.

14. Grenier, "Secret Agent Girls," 55.

15. Young, *Throwing Like a Girl*, 150.

16. See, for example, the conclusion of *The Lady from Shanghai* (Orson Welles, Columbia, 1948).

17. Hilary Radner, *Shopping Around: Feminine Culture and the Pursuit of Pleasure* (New York: Routledge, 1995), xi, xiii.

18. Producer Paul Monash cast his daughter Stephanie as one of the Cross daughters in the show's pilot, suggesting that he wanted to maintain these characters in some form. Although the network and the sponsors eagerly approved the pilot, controversy soon arose. Because the network had invested an unprecedented amount of time and money in developing the show, it wanted to ensure its success; to this end, Irna Phillips, "the queen of soap opera," was hired as a consultant. Phillips immediately disagreed with Monash as to the show's direction and announced that the pilot should be scrapped. "'When I saw it—the sensational story of Selena Cross and her father—I told ABC it ought to be shelved.... I did not think that this was the kind of thing to give an American public—a father seducing his stepdaughter.'" Quoted in Richard Warren Lewis, "The Battle of *Peyton Place*, Part I," *TV Guide* January 16, 1965, 8. Edgar J. Sherick, head of ABC, agreed, leading to an all-out battle among Phillips, ABC, and Monash. Because the novel pivoted around public expressions of illicit female sexuality (illegitimacy, premarital sex, adultery, rape, incest, abortion), producers did not know how to start the serial and had further problems trying to decide what the initial recurring problem should be. The female-oriented story of Betty's miscarriage won out over the network's more male-oriented suggestion of murder. (ABC also wanted Betty to become pregnant again as quickly as possible, revealing the network's highly conventional approach to female sexuality.) See Richard Warren Lewis, "The Battle of *Peyton Place*, Part I," 6–9; and "The Battle of *Peyton Place*, Part II," *TV Guide*, January 23, 1965, 24–27.

19. Lewis, "The Battle of *Peyton Place*, Part I," 6.

20. Radner, *Shopping Around*, xi–xii.

21. See Radner's discussion of this process in ibid., 142–45.

22. Betty Friedan, *The Feminine Mystique* (New York: Dell, 1963), 10.

23. Elizabeth Grosz, *Volatile Bodies: Towards a Corporeal Feminism* (Bloomington: Indiana University Press, 1994), xiii.

24. Ibid., 58.

25. Teresa de Lauretis, *Technologies of Gender: Essays on Theory, Film, and Fiction* (Bloomington: Indiana University Press, 1987), 1.

Courtesy of Photofest.

The "Coloscopic" Film and the "Beaver" Film
Scientific and Pornographic Scenes of Female Sexual Responsiveness

Eithne Johnson

When William Masters and Virginia Johnson published *Human Sexual Response* in 1966, they sought to explain why they, as scientists, felt it necessary to study sex. Thus they introduced their book to the reader with an extended prefatory quote from the venerable gynecologist Robert Latou Dickinson:

> Our vigorous protests against the sensual detail of pornographic pseudo-science lose force unless we [doctors] ourselves issue succinct statistics and physiologic summaries of what we find to be average and believe to be normal, and unless we offer in place of the prolix mush of much sex literature the few pages necessary for a standard of instruction covering sex education.[1]

In *Human Sexual Response*, Masters and Johnson provided the public with documentation of their laboratory sex research, which involved extensive experiments proving that sexual "responsiveness" is indeed an average and normal expression of human anatomy and physiology. Through the publication of this volume, in which they instructed an eager public in new norms for sexual behavior, Masters and Johnson, who began laboratory sex research in the 1950s, became known in the 1960s for their observational-experimental apparatus and the scientific imagery that it enabled. Since the nineteenth century, photography and film have been instrumental in experimentation. Indeed, developments in photography and film have enabled experiments in the study of the human body, particularly its anatomy and physiology. According to Lisa Cartwright, the early popular cinema, in particular the "genre of the facial expression film," owed a "debt to experimental physiology and its surveillant gaze." Pointing to the cultural significance of this debt, she writes, "The fascination with the physiological and technological spectacles of 'life' was a transversal phenomenon, cutting across popular, public, and professional cultures."[2] I suggest that this fascination continued during the period marked by the "space age" and the "sexual revolution," especially as various technological spectacles brought sex "on/scene" in relation to the "naked ape."[3] Masters and Johnson kept the films that documented their research from the public, depriving their audience of the "images" their prose described. Nevertheless, their work received much attention. That the sex researchers filmed their volunteer test subjects' genitals was especially significant, because the explicit depiction of genitalia was taboo in the popular cinema. On April 29, 1966, a week after *Human Sexual Response* was published, *Time* commented:

> It was the book's extraordinarily detailed account of the female's arousal and progression to orgasm ... that attracted the most immediate attention. The descriptions are based upon observations and color movies made of 10,000 orgasms, achieved by 382 women and 312 men, under laboratory conditions, sometimes in coitus, sometimes by masturbatory techniques.[4]

That the so-called beaver film emerged in theaters shortly after *Human Sexual Response* was published suggests a popular response to the much remarked upon absence of anatomically explicit films in the popular market.[5] Although it would be difficult to prove that any individual filmmakers were inspired specifically by *Human Sexual Response*, the popular press provocatively referred to the sexology laboratory as a scene of sex film production. *Newsweek*, for example, referred to the researchers' coloscopic device as a "plastic penis with a light and camera mounted to its base."[6]

When the "beaver" film emerged on public movie screens in 1967, it was perceived as threatening to the existing sexploitation film business.[7] According to popular porn film histories, the 16mm "beaver" film marked a shift from sexploitation to hard-core pornography, precipitated by new sexual norms and liberal legal rulings that were exploited by entrepreneurial filmmakers.[8] In a 1967 report to the California State Legislature, Thomas Lynch and Charles O'Brien stated that in some California cities, arcades included viewing machines that could run a "continuous reel" of four hundred feet of film, for a total running time of twelve minutes. They described such reels as follows: "The films usually feature a single female. They range from strip-tease to extended close-ups of undulating shaven genitals simulating sexual intercourse."[9] In their book *Sinema*, Kenneth Turan and Stephen Zito maintain that "sometime around 1967, an unknown and very enterprising San Francisco exhibitor began to screen a type of film that was then doing good business in the mail order houses and in some of the more daring peep-show arcades, where they were 'looped' together in continuous shows."[10] As James Fulton reported for *Adam Film Quarterly* in 1969, "You have to live in a fairly large city and drive up one of those well-traveled boulevards to really believe it. Beaver Splits, says one marquee. San Francisco Beaver, says another."[11] In his analysis of porn films and the theaters that played them near Times Square in 1971, Joseph Slade noted that "the original Avon was the first in New York to screen 'beaver' films, i.e., those showing pubic hair, five or six years ago."[12] In contrast to the viewing machines, which could run the arcade patron fifty to sixty cents for the full twelve-minute reel, the "beaver" film offered five films edited—still referred to as "looped"—together for an hour's screening time, which, according to Fulton, cost five dollars admission in 1969.[13]

Obviously, such films were intended for men's entertainment. For this reason alone, feminist critics might condemn the films on the basis that they "objectify" women and their genitals for men's visual pleasure. However, it is important to consider the "beaver" film within the broader context of the "democratization" of sex across the century. As Lawrence Birken suggests, the issue of women's "sexual subjectification" deserves as much attention as the issue of "objectification."[14] Given the public attention to the sexology laboratory as a scene of sex film production, I suggest that the "beaver" film's transition to public exhibition symptomatically represents, on the one hand, a popular negotiation of the sexologists' claim that the female body is sexually "responsive" and, on the other hand, a resistance to the nonpictorial physiological imagery privileged by scientific sexologists.[15] Rendering "responsiveness" as a technical and automatous performance, Masters and Johnson depended on a variety of imaging techniques, such as radiography, electrocardiography, and film, including the "coloscope," "an instrument for the visual examination of the vagina and cervix" that they modified to film the female genitals.[16] In contrast to what Cartwright would identify as the "modernist logic of abstraction and analysis" produced through such experimental research, the "beaver" film's "participatory realism" can be traced to other popular forms, including the striptease act, the stag film, and amateur filmmaking, which, according to Patricia Zimmermann, had established aesthetics and practices by 1962.[17] Although both the "coloscopic" film and the "beaver" film were motivated by a fascination with the female body and especially the female genitals, the "beaver" film imaged female sexual agency as a seemingly spontaneous response to an intimate male observer, rather than a mechanical response to a scientific observer.[18]

The Coloscopic Film and "Modernist" Sexual Imagery

Female orgasmic experience can be visually identified as well as recorded by acceptable physiologic techniques. The primary requirement in objective identification of female orgasm is the knowledge that it is a "total-body" response with marked variation in reactive intensity and timing sequence.[19]

Laboratory observation and experimentation can be traced back to previous sex researchers. According to Janice Irvine, "Working in the early decades of this century, [Robert Latou] Dickinson not only observed sexual response during intercourse and masturbation, but constructed a phallus-shaped glass tube through which he observed the physiological responses of orgasm inside the vagina." Masters and Johnson were well aware of Dickinson's work, as their book's preface indicates. As Irvine notes: "Despite their reputation as pioneers, most of Masters and Johnson's research was not innovative.... In many ways the impact of Masters and Johnson was largely symbolic."[20] In fact, they created their own language and imagery through the experimental research process.[21] Synthesizing research from various disciplines, including comparative biological and evolutionary theories, Masters and Johnson's laboratory experiments were less about what Michel Foucault has characterized as the confession of secrets from a docile body than about the construction of "responsiveness" as a set of signs taken to represent the hard-core of orgasmic performance.[22] Supplying what they called "physiologic summaries" as well as what Cartwright defines as "graphic" and "nonpictorial" imagery, Masters and Johnson positioned their work as "modernist" science rather than "pornographic pseudoscience." Directing the reader's attention to an anatomo-physiological mise-en-scène ordinarily understood as inaccessible to the naked eye, they divided *Human Sexual Response* into female and male sections, with chapters detailing the researchers' meticulous examination of the genital and extragenital areas. *Human Sexual Response* included the following "graphic" and "nonpictorial" illustrations, in keeping with the "modernist logic of abstraction and analysis": cross-sectional diagrams of the genitals with dotted lines to indicate the trajectory of motion for erection, contraction, retraction, and so on; radiographic plates showing the content medium's effect on the cervical cap; and microscopic images of the secretory Bartholin's gland.

But, as the press enthusiastically indicated, film technology had been instrumental in their analysis of the genitals in extreme close-up. On January 7, 1966, *Time* anticipated the publication of *Human Sexual Response*, drawing attention to the sexology laboratory as a scene of sex film production under the subheading "Bed & Camera": "In 1954 [Masters] persuaded the university to set up special laboratories containing a bed, electrocardiographs, electroencephalographs, biochemical equipment, flood lights and color-movie cameras."[23] In their book, Masters and Johnson referred to the visual aspects of such research; for example, "The degree of individual clitoral-body retraction has been estimated with the aid of direct coloscopic observation." Referring to their "coloscope," Masters and Johnson explained, "The artificial coital equipment was created by radiophysicists. The penises are plastic and were developed with the same optics as plate glass. Cold-light illumination allows observation and recording without distortion"[24] Cartwright explains how this belief in the technology's capacity to see better than the eye emerged: "Physiology—the discipline for which the film motion study was a crucial technique—regarded the body in terms of its living functions and processes, and its practitioners devised methods and techniques to facilitate a temporal, dynamic vision of the body in motion."[25]

According to Masters and Johnson, their films have been destroyed; but, fortunately, examples of "coloscopic" filmmaking can be found that help explain their work as well as its influence on other scientific sex researchers. In 1973 at the Institute of Medical Physiology, Dr. Gorm Wagner made a film that was given the appropriately scientific title *Physiological Responses of the Sexually Stimulated Female in the Laboratory*.[26] According to the film's guide, "The physiological responses shown in the film are based on those mainly described by Masters and Johnson (1966)." Hence the film was designed to illustrate the scientific signs of "responsiveness" for the female body across the four-phase "human sexual response cycle." Echoing the legacy of physiological image making described by Cartwright, the guide ends with the following assertion: "A dynamic medium has been used to document dynamic responses in the human female."[27] Other examples of "coloscopic" film include a sequence that appears in the A&E *Biography* production on Masters and Johnson and a sequence in zoologist Desmond Morris's television series on the "human animal." Such excursions into the vaginal canal are nonpictorial, illuminating that interior, ordinarily invisible space and the apparent anatomo-physiological phenomena of color changes, lubrication, and contractiveness. As the popular press repeatedly noted, the sex researchers explored the vagina with an "artificial" penis-camera.[28]

Justifying their laboratory investment in female test subjects—privileged by a three-to-one ratio—Masters and Johnson stated, "Direct observation of hundreds of women using mechanical and manual masturbatory techniques through repetitive orgasmic experiences has emphasized the fundamental questions, 'How?' and 'How much?'"[29] By attaching recording devices to the surface of the body and/or inserting them into orifices, Masters and Johnson produced sexual "responsiveness" in degrees of "intensity" and "duration." According to Jonathan Crary, nineteenth-century experiments in perception resulted in observation techniques that enabled the quantification of sensation in response to external stimuli; a century later, Masters and Johnson's experiments were particularly concerned with such measurements.[30] The guide for the Danish "coloscopic" film provides the following example: "Surface electrodes on the thorax makes EKG-recording possible during the experiments."[31] To establish correlations between physiological response and intensity of sensation, Masters and Johnson relied mostly on such artifactual evidence for "objective" verification, occasionally supplemented by "subjective" report. For example, "artificial coition" with the penis-camera "provides opportunity for observation and recording of intravaginal physiologic response to sexual stimuli." Another example involved measuring uterine contractions during orgasm; thus, they found, "inevitably, the degree of excursion of recorded corpus contractive response [illustrated by the accompanying readout] parallels the study subject's subjective and the observer's objective evaluations of the physical and emotional intensity of the orgasmic experience."[32] In other words, the greater the peak on the recording device, the greater the orgasm.

Negotiating the "productivist" and "consumerist" tendencies within sexual science, Masters and Johnson sought to optimize female sexual pleasure for heterosexual coupling, but their emphasis on masturbation as the index of maximum orgasmic intensity also decoupled the vagina and the organic penis.[33] Based on their experiments, Masters and Johnson elaborated a hierarchy of orgasmic intensity outcomes for women: first, in rank order, "self-regulated or automanipulative techniques"; second, "partner manipulation, again with established or self-regulated methods"; and last, "coition."[34] Apparently, automanipulation by self or by penis-camera—which was designed such that the "penile-thrust" was controlled by the test subject—was most effective for the women "volunteers," although that may be because such orgasmic performances best accommodated laboratory cinematography. The production environment, with its intense illumination, provided Masters and Johnson with a spectacular show: on women's bodies they observed skin flushes, breast enlargement, and genital colorations, which they identified as the "sex skin." Considering this "excitement phase" effect, *Time* noted, "the labia minora ... turn bright pink, a process that Dr. Masters compares biologically with changes in the female monkey's exposed 'sex skin.'"[35] Indeed, Masters and Johnson understood their project as a scientific effort to come to grips with the "nature" of human primate sexuality and to rectify "cultural fallacies" about sex among humans. Situating their laboratory experimentation within the "natural" data from animal-primate research, Masters and Johnson maintained, "Observations of higher animal patterns of foreplay first sensitized investigators to the clinical importance of effective autostimulative techniques by emphasizing the obvious response that such effective foreplay can develop in the human of the species."[36] Building a "natural" argument for foreplay, they not only argued for effective female sexual stimulation prior to intercourse, but also redefined all female orgasms as clitoral rather than vaginal. Moreover, based on Mary Jane Sherfey's appropriation of their work for her evolutionary model of female sexual "insatiability," Masters and Johnson concluded that the female body was naturally superior for orgasmic performance. With the "sexual revolution" and the "space age" as cultural backdrops, Masters and Johnson's "modernist" sexual science suggested a voluntary female cyborg, penetrated by the penis-camera and launched on the artifactual "reflex arc" of the technologically monitored orgasm.[37] Significantly, only the female test subject was reliably found capable of "status orgasmus," defined as "rapidly recurrent orgasmic experiences."[38]

The "Beaver" Film and "Participatory Realism"

The first beaver movies—whose main attraction was the visible pubic region of the women (and later men) who posed for them—were nothing more than short loops, several loops making up a show, in which, for once, the stripper followed the request of the boys in the front row and actually took it all off.[39]

Histories of science have shown that public responses to laboratory and clinical research demonstrate both fascination and fear of experimentation involving human test subjects. As Masters and Johnson's research was publicized, the possible consequences were debated, often returning to the issue of filming sex. Some commentators extolled the technical superiority of the researchers' instrumentation, praising this contribution to scientific knowledge. As Buckley described it in the *New York Times Magazine*, the laboratory was "dazzlingly ultramodern."[40] Critics were concerned that sex had been made too technical and too automatous through the new scientific sexology, with its observational-experimental apparatus. Before *Human Sexual Response* was even in the bookstores, psychiatrist Leslie Farber sarcastically described the experience of volunteering: "Going to work in a somewhat businesslike manner while being measured and photographed, would have to provide its own peculiar excitement. (Thank you, Miss Brown, see you same time next week. Stop at the cashier's for your fee)."[41] Referring to Farber's criticism, *Newsweek* noted that he "protested the coldly clinical way in which Masters in the laboratory separated physical sex from its total human element."[42] In a 1970 report, *Newsweek* returned to the scientific scene of sex film production, summarizing the initial criticism: "Masters had built a rather bizarre device: a plastic dildo connected to a camera, which could photograph the interior of the vagina. Partly because of this apparatus, the authors were accused of dehumanizing sex, and concentrating on technique at the expense of romance and morality."[43] By frequently referring to the coloscope as a "penis-camera" or "dildo-camera," the popular press drew attention to the invasive and literally inhuman form of penetration used to investigate the genitals of the female test subjects. Although Masters and Johnson's research claimed to liberate a normal and average human sexuality from society's traditions and taboos, it raised anxieties about the impact of the results on social relations. On the one hand, technological devices—the penis-camera and the vibrator—could be seen to realize the body's "natural" orgasmic potential, especially for the female body. On the other hand, technological manipulation could be understood as crossing the line to cyborgian sexuality.[44] If female sexual physiology were indeed insatiable—whether due to evolution or experimentation—perhaps only a vibrator or artificial penis could reliably satisfy, rendering the organic penis obsolete.

That so much film pornography emerged in the late 1960s must be understood in relation to Masters and Johnson's "modernist" attempt to isolate the signs that would demonstrate female sexual "responsiveness" and their scientific contention that the female body has the same "natural" capacity for orgasmic performativity as the male body. In *Hard Core*, Linda Williams defines the illegal "beaver" film as "a second stage in the formation of the new genre"—the hardcore feature. Rather than follow the evolutionary model of the popular porn film histories, she argues that film pornography "emerges more from" *scientia sexualis* than *ars erotica*.[45] Referring to Gertrude Koch's assertion that film pornography tends to a "clinical-documentary" style, Williams elaborates on the genre's epistemological link to *scientia sexualis:*

> We might call this ... feature the principle of *maximum visibility*. In the hard core proper, this principle has operated in different ways at different stages of the genre's history: to privilege close-ups of body parts over other shots; to overlight easily obscured genitals; to select sexual positions that show the most of bodies and organs; and, later, to create generic conventions, such as the variety of sexual "numbers" or the externally ejaculating penis—so important to the 1970s feature-length manifestations of the genre.[46]

The fact that some women's genitals were shaved for some "beaver" films—as in the marquees that proclaimed "Ruthless Shaved Beaver"—points to the practical exercise of this "principle."[47] Similarly, it is possible that the sexology laboratory's volunteers also had to be shaved in preparation for filming "clitoral retraction" or the "sex skin."[48] However, "modernist" scientific films were designed to be nonpictorial in order to foreclose on subjective visual pleasure. Referring to the "physiological" spectacles of the early facial expression film, Cartwright suggests that "close-ups and foregrounded bodily movement likely would have repelled their audiences."[49] Similarly, Masters and Johnson's book provided extraordinarily detailed observations, such as the following: "Microscopic tumescence of the clitoral glans always develops with sexual tension, regardless of whether this vasocongestive process continues into a clinically observable (macroscopic) tumescent reaction."[50] Given the many signs of "responsiveness" generated through *Human Sexual Response*, with its provocative allusions to the "coloscopic" film, the "beaver" film might have aspired, in the new legal term of "socially redeeming value," to reveal even more than it did. That it did not—nor has film pornography generally—suggests popular resistance to the "'distanced,' analytic viewing" assumed by the scientific observer.[51]

Much as laboratory sexology was organized to observe sexual anatomy and physiology, the "beaver" film was formally organized to observe physical performance and to display female genitals. Produced to attract and to entertain men, the "beaver" film integrated vulva display into the organic body imagery privileged in both the naturalistic aesthetic of amateur film and the full-body exhibitionism of the striptease act. Indeed, the "beaver" film aimed to "position the spectator as an active participant rather than a passive spectator," in keeping with what Zimmermann identifies as the amateur film aesthetics of this period.[52] In *I Know It When I See It*, Michael Leach quotes Justice Potter Stewart's description of the "beaver" film:

> Instead of a woman in tights doing jumping jacks [as in the early silent film, *Her Morning Exercise*], in a beaver, a nude woman lies on a bed and does leg raises, spreading them as they get high. Though these were a sensation for a few months, once viewers learned what a variety of vaginas [vulvas] looked like they were either sated, satisfied, saddened, or all three.[53]

This description points to the range of acceptable responses that such imagery might evoke in viewers—noting the affective position of the viewer, who may not coldly assess the scene but who is, rather, forced (in terms of the conventions of the genre) to develop a relationship with the spectacle, which either attracts or repels. Reflecting on the viewer's experience of such films, Slade suggested: "The man in the audience does not control the pacing of the action or the explicitness of the images, as he does when he reads; he may see more than he wants to see. When a girl on screen spreads her legs so wide that her ovaries are visible, her sheer presence forestalls consideration of her other attributes."[54] The viewer may even lose "sensation." After raving about the moments when "the whole screen is full of forbidden flesh," Fulton remarked, "Surprisingly enough, you find yourself getting bored even though, when you glance up at the screen, the *Thing* is still there in all of its glory." According to Fulton, sensational pleasure depended more on the "presence of an actress, a girl capable of generating the kind of gutsy excitement that a man is willing to pay five dollars for."[55]

Known by its generic name, the "beaver" film invited viewers to expect a genital exhibit, much as the press called attention to the sexology laboratory's focus on the genitals when *Human Sexual Response* was published. On the marquee, the "beaver" film presented itself as a new cinematic "attraction."[56] Regarding the early cinema's exhibitionistic strategies, Gunning writes, "Founded on the moment of revelation, the cinema of attractions frequently redoubles its effect of appearance by framing the attraction with a variety of gestures of display." For example, he describes how early exhibitors generated suspense about what would be screened by talking it up before running the projector; this cultivated delay, or "disjunction," could even shock audiences. Furthermore, Gunning argues that "such disjunction could also be used to an erotic effect, as the scopophilia implied by this mode becomes thematized. Edison's *What Happened on Twenty Third Street, New York City* provides a complex example."[57] Because the "attraction" effect of that film may be lost on contemporary viewers, Gunning explains that the location was well-known for attracting male onlookers who were hoping to see women's skirts lifted by the winds. In 1967, the "beaver" film's generic name served as a way of framing its "attraction" and intensifying audience anticipation. Moreover, the street vernacular distinguished it as a "homemade" film in comparison to the technically sophisticated practice of scientific filmmaking.[58]

According to Williams, the "beaver" form began by "showing women stripping to display their naked pubis" and progressed to displaying the "split beaver," then the "'action beaver,' with 'action' restricted to the woman herself or another woman fondling the genital area and sometimes simulating cunnilingus."[59] By comparing the stag film with the classical Hollywood cinema, Williams argues that "the stag film oscillates between the impossible direct relation between a spectator and the exhibitionist object he watches in close-up and the ideal voyeurism of a spectator who observes a sexual event in which a surrogate male acts for him." Thus, she explains, "two shots typify this oscillation": the "'split beaver' (genitals visible, legs ajar)" and the "meat shot, which shows more of the 'genital event' than ever before seen by a mass audience (but which is still not the full narrative event that we will encounter in hard-core features)."[60] Although it is useful to compare the "beaver" film to the early cinema, the stag film, and the classical Hollywood cinema, it is important to consider other historically relevant filmmaking practices. The fact that the "entrepreneurs" who made "beaver" films could be prosecuted for obscenity may account for the "beaver" form—its initial preference for women rather than men (due to the penis) and its undisciplined "homemade" aesthetic.[61] However, fear of prosecution cannot explain why the "beaver" film was popularly considered an innovation over the stag film. Although the "beaver" film certainly included genital display and eventually showed genital action, its style did not fit so neatly into the "primitive" stag aesthetic because it aimed for a more naturalistic positioning of the viewer in relation to the performer that can be traced to amateur filmmaking. Regarding the significance of "naturalism" to amateur filmmaking, Zimmermann explains: "Naturalism was prized as a purer form of uninterrupted observation.... Naturalness represented a pure, uninterrupted, value-free form of observation that could better evoke an emotional response."[62]

Unlike stag filmmaking, with its "oscillation" between the primitive exhibitionism of the genital "show" and the classical voyeurism of the genital "event," "beaver" filmmaking aspired to the sensation of intimacy, spontaneity, and participation in the scene through the naturalistic "eye" of the amateur filmmaker. According to John Morthland, who described the variety of pornographic films that emerged in the late sixties:

> In terms solely of fantasy-fulfillment, the cheap loops, with their one-to-one shooting ratio, flash frames, audible director's cues, shadows, visible light stands and all, are every bit as good as the more "professional" productions. Nothing is asked of these films except that they make that connection between the viewer and the heaving, throbbing mass of flesh on the screen.[63]

As Leach referred to the "sensation" generated by the "beaver" film, Morthland alluded to the amateur film's claim to a more authentic "connection" between the viewer and the onscreen action. In their celebratory history of the genre, Al Di Lauro and Gerald Rabkin maintain that "the stag film or dirty movie was, and is, the *cinema vérité* of the forbidden, an invaluable record of the images openly unacknowledged feelings about sex assume."[64] By implicitly drawing on cinema verité's claim to naturalism, Di Lauro and Rabkin uncritically reiterate what

Zimmermann explains is the "alternative, although certainly nascent, view of amateurism as a liberated zone."[65]

Though Di Lauro and Rabkin inaccurately conflate all stags with a historically specific film practice, their comment points to film pornography's link to amateur filmmaking. Although comparison between the "beaver" film and amateur film would require much more close analysis, which is difficult because most amateur productions are home movies that are unavailable for academic research, Zimmermann's research provides a way for thinking about this possible link. In *Reel Families*, Zimmermann traces the discourses that shaped U.S. amateur filmmaking and its orientation to domestic life. Emphasizing "human values and sensibilities, energy, and spontaneity," the amateur film discourse directed filmmakers to focus on family and friends with a "commitment to subjective responses in both artist and viewer."[66] Amateur film discourse was also influenced by empiricism and modernist scientific claims to objectivity, as in the "time-motion study." Hence the discourse could accommodate both pictorialism's "beauty" aesthetic and science's "social production of the body as a natural, unified, and composed unit."[67]

According to Zimmermann, World War II brought about a change in amateur filmmaking based on the "participatory realism" that resulted from field use of cameras. As a result, what had been considered mistakes and inconsistencies in professional cinematography could be regarded as a more naturalistic aesthetic; in Hollywood productions, shaky camera work suddenly seemed to create "a more intimate and a more sensory spectator experience," which, Zimmermann maintains, "induced audience participation in represented experience."[68] By the early 1960s, influenced by the "moving camera" style of documentary productions, amateur filmmaking privileged "unscripted 'real life'" as captured by the mobile camera-eye: "The camera metaphorically and visually metamorphosized into a spontaneous participant, gradually shedding its obtrusive, objective technological demeanor through a disguise of human characteristics."[69] Such a "provocative aesthetic," incorporating the camera as a "body appendage," also marks the "beaver" film. Due to its undisciplined, "homemade" aesthetic, the "beaver" camera could either be stationary, relying on the zoom for spatial variation, or handheld, moving around the performer's body. Intimacy and spontaneity in the "beaver" film stemmed from its "hybrid" documentarylike approach to performance that bordered on the "presentational" (acknowledging the camera) and the "representational" (acting as if the camera were not there).[70] For example, the performer might respond self-consciously to offscreen direction and/or commentary. This "live" spontaneity resembled both the home-movie production process, which ideally includes responsive family members, and the striptease act, which ideally includes a responsive audience.

The implied proximity of the "beaver" camera to the observer's body as a sensing-seeing, participatory "eye" was very different from the distanced, analytic observation imposed between the sexologists' penis-camera and their own bodies, which did not even have to be in the same room as their mechanical device. Whereas the "coloscopic" film constructed a stable point of view to go with its scientific mise-en-scène, the "beaver" film offered a less predictable point of view on its apparently spontaneous, seemingly unscripted scene of sexual display. In this way, it alluded to the striptease act, in which the stripper's movements and gestures ideally work to attract the viewer's eye. According to Williams, the stag film "retains many of the theatrical elements of the striptease —without, however, the striptease's most basic element: the coincidence of stripper and audience in the same theatrical space and time." Following an argument by David James, Williams claims that erotic entertainments develop a "highly ritualized, theatrical quality" as "compensatory substitution for sexual relations themselves."[71] Unfortunately, this argument presumes that participating in sexual relations is inherently more "natural," less "theatrical," and therefore more psychologically gratifying than experiencing erotic entertainments. One could just as easily argue that the sex laboratory has a "highly ritualized, theatrical quality" without concluding that its inscriptive practice is "compensatory substitution" for sex itself. Whether or not a "compensatory substitution" theory explains the "beaver" film style, it is important to consider how the "beaver" film appropriated the striptease act to the naturalistic style of amateur filmmaking as it was practiced in the 1960s. As popular histories of film pornography suggest, both the strip show and the "beaver" film could be available in the same parts of a city, possibly in the same buildings.[72]

As in the theatrical striptease, the "beaver" performer makes a spectacle of her body through basic movements—bending over, going to a bed or couch, kneeling, and so on. The performer's legs may open and close rhythmically, as if "flashing" the genitals at the viewer.[73] Additionally, props, such as clothing or pillows or drapery, can be used to attract viewer attention and provoke interest in the scene. In a brief memoir, Jane Smith describes the directions she received during her first "beaver" film, which was staged "to represent what a man might see as he watched a girl get ready for bed, supposing she'd left the shade up and the lights on in her apartment":

> Okay, now stand up. . . . You dropped something on the floor, bend down and get it. Reach up to your right for something on the shelf. Now take off your panties . . . slowly. Walk toward the camera, you're going to pull down the shade—no, you changed your mind. Go back to the couch. Kneel on the couch . . . spread your heels. Lie on your back . . . Okay, now turn on your front. Look at the camera. Open your mouth. Lick your lips.[74]

Even though the director elaborates a rudimentary scene for acting as if unaware of being seen, he also urges Smith to look into and flirt with the camera. A teasing suspense results from her movement toward the camera, as if to close off the view; at the same time, her act of looking at the camera acknowledges the viewer's participation in this scene, implying an intimacy that the "coloscopic" film negates and the striptease act ideally solicits. Moreover, like the home movie, the "beaver" film implies intimacy between the camera-eye and the performer, whose "name" sometimes appears on a clapper or chalkboard at the head of a loop. As genital display is integral to the form, so is the performer's face. She may even flirt or wink at the camera. Smiles may become grimaces, and giggles may become guffaws.

Such exhibitionism bears comparison with Kelly Dennis's analysis of the hard-core "beaver" magazine: "The magazine problematizes voyeurism *by acknowledging the viewer's look.*" Regarding the value of the face for amateur photos in *Hustler*, Dennis states: "The latter rule, that faces be visible, is scrupulously honored: so much so that, in conjunction with the distance of the nonprofessional photograph and the mundane, 'homey' details of the model's surroundings, the 'Beaver Hunt' photographs appear to be portraits rather than spectacularized porn."[75] The "beaver" film made no claim to the personal authenticity of amateur "beaver" photography; however, in comparison to the nonpictorial style of "modernist" scientific imaging, the "beaver" film offered a more organic, naturalistic style of body display. Its action typically took place in an ersatz domestic space, such as a motel bedroom. This points to the secrecy of the work as much as to its banality. As in the home movie and the amateur photograph, the "beaver" performer's expressive agency was not necessarily controlled by the production scene. Basic movements, and their effects on clothing, concealed parts of the body inadvertently. For example, in the "Laurie" loops, her baby-doll nightie slips at points, covering areas that she is trying to reveal.[76] The camera operator could also lose sight of the performer as she moved around.

More like undressing than burlesqueing, the verité removal of relatively ordinary clothing marked the "beaver" performance as more "naturalistic." To evoke the sensory "connection" for male viewers with the "heaving, throbbing mass of flesh on the screen," "beaver" performers were typically in motion; they fidgeted, shifted, rotated, gyrated. In the solo beaver film, sensory arousal was conveyed through the performer's licking her lips; sucking on her fingers; kissing her limbs; rubbing up against fabric, furniture, or stuffed toys; and touching her breasts and genitals. Without the goal of orgasm, such gestures emphasized sensory foreplay, which Masters and Johnson had argued was crucial to the female's progression to orgasm. Of course, the "beaver" film's failure to show performance to orgasm might also be attributed to a sexist reaction to deny female sexual pleasure and/or to assuage male performance anxiety given the purported inadequacy of the penis to effect orgasm in women during intercourse.[77] The anatomical shots ranged from medium to extreme close-ups, sometimes with a zoom. The solo "beaver" performer might even end her act by moving her body to signal readiness for sex, or, as the sexologists put it, for "mounting": gyrating her hips and presenting her vulva.[78] In this way, their performances should be understood as "naturalistic" for the period, quoting the signs of sexual "responsiveness" that primatology and sexology had already documented for the "naked ape." Thus the "beaver" film produced an exhibitionistic, amateurish scene that might be considered a parody (in terms of its emphasis on excessive, undisciplined motion) of the sexology laboratory's scientific scene of an "involuntary" (engineered and standardized) orgasmic performativity.

"Thank You, Miss Brown, See You Same Time Next Week"

In a 1967 feature titled "Anything Goes," *Newsweek* worried that a "permissive society" "cannot agree on standards of conduct, language and manners, on what can be seen and heard."[79] Surveying art, film, fashion, and literature, this "special report" concluded that the "new generation" had demanded more nudity and sexual explicitness in everything. As a representative of this generation, mini-skirt designer Mary Quant exclaimed: "Am I the only woman who has ever wanted to go to bed with a man in the afternoon? Any law-abiding female, it used to be thought, waits until dark. Well, there are lots of girls who don't want to wait. Mini-clothes are symbolic of them."[80] Significantly, Quant, Norman Mailer, and others argued that because nudity and sex are natural, sexually explicit representations can be frankly naturalistic rather than prurient. Though Masters and Johnson took a dim view of pornography, their work was also organized around naked bodies engaged in sex acts. Both pornography and sex research were invested in gendered bodies: whereas "big breasts" or shaved vulvas were prized in pornographic films, "responsive" genitals were required for "coloscopic" films. In a *Life* profile, Masters commented: "What people do when they read about our work is confuse the segmental kind of photography we do with the stag movie kind of thing."[81] By focusing on "graphic" and nonpictorial data, as gathered through the coloscope, among other imaging techniques, Masters and Johnson aspired to investigate the "nature" of sex itself. Like laboratory sexology, the "beaver" film privileged the female body. However, instead of objectively verifying arousal at the microanatomic level with a penis-camera, the "beaver" film elaborated a more subjective, "participatory" camera-eye approach to the performer. Whereas the insensate camera-penis could literally penetrate the female body, the camera-eye could wander lustfully across the body's surface. Instead of representing "nature" itself, as claimed by scientific realism, the "beaver" film promised to show natural bodies, as if spontaneously captured in a moment of sexual intimacy. In its inconsistent way, "beaver" filmmaking also reflexively called attention to the process of filming a "live" performance, which was clearly an important aspect of the sex laboratory and much remarked on in the popular press.

Both laboratory sexology and the "beaver" film asserted that women could have sex at any time. According to Masters and Johnson's criteria, their study volunteers had to satisfy the scientific demand for normal humans whose natural sexual behaviors could be observed and recorded in the laboratory. To the researchers' surprise, they did not lack for test subjects. As *Life* science editor Albert Rosenfeld explained, "Potential subjects were not only willing but eager to cooperate"; once in the laboratory, "these perfectly normal people were able to perform in an apparently free and natural manner."[82] Though their test subjects may have performed freely, they did not do it for free. Like the "beaver" perform-ers (at least reportedly), the laboratory's "volunteers" were paid for their partici-pation.[83] Putting a price on performance may have influenced the outcome, although Masters and Johnson could counter that the involuntary nature of sex-ual responsiveness could not be consciously controlled. In fact, Masters and Johnson pointed to an unexpected benefit—the release of "sexual tension"—that accrued from participation for single women in particular.[84] As discussed in the popular press, the female "volunteers" could experience any number of methods to achieve this release of tension, including "artificial coition" with the penis-camera.

In comparison to the "ultramodern" laboratory, which some critics found chillingly inhuman, the "beaver" film favored a homey location, simulating sex-ual intimacy through the home-movie aesthetic. Certainly, "beaver" actresses probably had little or no control over the productions, so their agency was cir-cumscribed by the social context of performing in illicit films that would circu-late among men. But their film performances must be understood in relation to the contemporary shift in social mores through which women were perceived—and, as Quant's remark quoted above suggests, perceived themselves—as "natu-rally" sexually responsive.[85] Moreover, as it elaborated various scenarios—solo, lesbian, heterosexual coupling, and group sex—the "beaver" film also marked a refusal of both the "familialism" that dominated amateur film discourse and the heterosexuality that dominated sexual science.[86] Exploiting amateur film's claim to a "liberated zone," the "beaver" film projected an anti-home movie, naturalistically evoking a spontaneous sexual "responsiveness," freed from the marriage contract.[87] The fictive "Miss Brown" (perhaps Farber was alluding to Helen Gurley Brown) and the "beaver" performer signify two competing, "con-sumerist" representations of the "single girl." Unlike the laboratory volunteer, who strategically traded genital exposure for mechanical sex once a week, the lively Lauries, Lynnes, and anonymous others appeared to be freely uninhibited and ready for sex at any time. Paradoxically, then, the "beaver" film offered a new scene of pleasure for a female sexual subject, one in which she could perform freely in an "amateur" setting liberated from both the demands of reproduction and the supervision of a scientific gaze.

Notes

My thanks to Mike Vraney and Lisa Petrucci of Something Weird Video for making copies of "beaver" tapes available and to dissertation cochairs Thomas Schatz and Henry Jenkins for reading the larger draft on which this essay is based. I would also like to thank Hilary Radner for her suggestions on how to edit that draft into this chapter. As always, my thanks to Eric Schaefer for being there and for sharing research materials from his new study of sexploitation film.

1. Quoted in William Masters and Virginia Johnson, *Human Sexual Response* (Boston: Little, Brown, 1966), v. According to Walter Kendrick, medical texts on prostitution and sex hygiene manuals were once included in definitions of pornography. See Walter Kendrick, *The Secret Museum: Pornography in Modern Culture* (New York: Viking, 1987).

2. Lisa Cartwright, *Screening the Body: Tracing Medicine's Visual Culture* (Minneapolis: University of Minnesota Press, 1995), 13.

3. As I argue in my dissertation, sex research in the 1960s situated a sexually responsive "naked ape" within the broader scope of evolutionary sciences by synthesizing ideas from primatology, ethology, gynecology, and anthropology. That the human animal became a naked subject for laboratory sex research points to Donna Haraway's observation that "apes could be 'humanized'; humans could also be 'naturalized.'" See Donna J. Haraway, *Primate Visions: Gender, Race, and Nature in the World of Modern Science* (New York: Routledge, 1989), 140. The term *on/scene* comes from Linda Williams. See her "Pornographies On/Scene" in *Sex Exposed: Sexuality and the Pornography Debate*, ed. Lynne Segal and Mary McIntosh (London: Virago, 1992) 233–65. The term *naked ape* comes from the zoologist Desmond Morris, whose book of that title popularized ideas about primatology in the late sixties. Desmond Morris, *The Naked Ape* (New York: McGraw-Hill, 1967).

4. "Problems of Sex," *Time*, April 29, 1966, 51 (physiology sec.).

5. In preparing to write this essay, I watched approximately thirty-eight "beaver" films that had been transferred to videotape. Two films appeared twice; one performer appeared in two different films. I focus here on solo acts, because the form began that way. See the Bucky Beaver line from Something Weird Video, Seattle, Washington.

6. "Sex under Scrutiny," *Newsweek*, April 25, 1966, 80 (medicine sec.).

7. Sexploitation filmmakers referred to the entrepreneurs who made the "beaver" films as the "heat artists," because it was feared that their racier films would attract the attention of law enforcement. See Eric Schaefer, "The Inside Story of Storefront Theaters," in *Something Weird Blue Book* (Seattle, Wash.: Something Weird, 1997), 2–6.

8. See Kenneth Turan and Stephen F. Zito, *Sinema: American Pornographic Films and*

the People Who Make Them (New York: Praeger, 1974); Michael Leach, *I Know It When I See It: Pornography, Violence, and Public Sensitivity* (Philadelphia: Westminster, 1975); Al Di Lauro and Gerald Rabkin, *Dirty Movies: An Illustrated History of the Stag Film 1915–1970* (New York: Chelsea House, 1976). I refer to such books as popular film histories because they are written in a journalistic style for broader appeal than academic film histories.

9. Thomas C. Lynch and Charles A. O'Brien, "Obscenity: The Law and the Nature of the Business" (a report to the California Legislature, filed in Box 33 of the archives of the 1970 Commission on Obscenity and Pornography, LBJ Library, University of Texas, Austin), 88. My thanks to Eric Schaefer for sharing this information based on his archival research.

10. Turan and Zito, *Sinema*, 77.

11. James Fulton, "Dirty Movies Are Dirtier Than Ever," *Adam Film Quarterly*, February 8, 1969, 75.

12. Joseph Slade, "Pornographic Theaters Off Times Square," *Transaction*, November–December 1971, 37.

13. Lynch and O'Brien "Obscenity," indicated 1967 prices for the viewing machines; Fulton, "Dirty Movies," 75.

14. Birken suggests that sexology is implicated in this "democratization"; he also asks, "If cultural conservatives see the sexualization of women and children as contributing to their objectification, can we not also see this sexualization as a form of subjectification?" Lawrence Birken, *Consuming Desire: Sexual Science and the Emergence of the Culture of Abundance, 1871–1914* (Ithaca, N.Y.: Cornell University Press, 1988), 133, 149.

15. Cartwright discusses the "graphic method" of image production in the science of physiology and links it to the elaboration of "scientific cinema's nonpictorial mode of representation." *Screening the Body*, 12.

16. Masters and Johnson, *Human Sexual Response*, 338.

17. Cartwright, *Screening the Body*, xvi; Patricia Zimmermann, *Reel Families: A Social History of Amateur Film* (Bloomington: Indiana University Press, 1995).

18. I use *female*—rather than *feminine* or *woman*—because in their research Masters and Johnson isolated the genitals as essentially sexed, even as they sought to democratize relations between the sexes on the basis of their "modernist" notion of the genderless "human sexual response cycle."

19. Masters and Johnson, *Human Sexual Response*, 128.

20. Janice Irvine, *Disorders of Desire: Sex and Gender in Modern American Sexology* (Philadelphia: Temple University Press, 1990), 78.

21. As Masters explained to Tom Buckley, they carefully rewrote their manuscript "to make the language as technical and noninflammatory" as they could. Tom Buckley, "All They Talk about Is Sex, Sex, Sex," *New York Times Magazine*, April 20, 1969, 98.

My point is not to dismiss their research as faulty or inaccurate as to the "real" of sex; instead, I am interested in their contributions to imaging sex.

22. Michel Foucault, *The History of Sexuality*, vol. 1, *An Introduction*, trans. Robert Hurley (New York: Vintage, 1980[1978, 1976]).

23. "The Nature of Sexual Response," *Time*, January 7, 1966, 65 (physiology sec.).

24. Masters and Johnson, *Human Sexual Response*, 51, 21.

25. Cartwright, *Screening the Body*, 11.

26. This film is available from Multi-Focus, Inc., San Francisco, California.

27. Guide for the film *Physiological Responses of the Sexually Stimulated Female in the Laboratory* (San Francisco: Multi-Focus, Inc., n.d.), 1, 5.

28. Although the plastic penis-camera and vibrator were prosthetic devices employed for research purposes, Masters and Johnson were also sensitive to implanted prostheses, such as the "artificial" vaginas that had been surgically constructed for their test subjects who had been born without organic vaginas. In this way, they also stretched the boundaries of the "natural," even as they attempted to document the "nature" of sex.

29. Masters and Johnson, *Human Sexual Response*, 63.

30. Jonathan Crary, *Techniques of the Observer: On Vision and Modernity in the Nineteenth Century* (Cambridge: MIT Press, 1990), 145–46.

31. Guide, *Physiological Responses*, 2.

32. Masters and Johnson, *Human Sexual Response*, 21, 116.

33. Birken explains that sexology negotiates "productivist" ideas (revolving around procreation and the perpetuation of the species and the family) and "consumerist" ideas (revolving around sexual pleasure and individual experience). See *Consuming Desire*.

34. Masters and Johnson, *Human Sexual Response*, 133.

35. "The Nature of Sexual Response," 65.

36. Masters and Johnson, *Human Sexual Response*, 63.

37. This sentence echoes Haraway's descriptions of the launching of HAM, the first primate-cyborg, into space: "He rode an arc that traced the birth path of modern science—the parabola, the conic section." *Primate Visions*, 138.

38. Masters and Johnson, *Human Sexual Response*, 131.

39. Turan and Zito, *Sinema*, 77.

40. Buckley, "All They Talk about Is Sex," 98.

41. Leslie Farber, "I'm Sorry Dear," *Commentary*, November 1964, 50.

42. "Secrets of Sex," *Newsweek*, April 26, 1965, 51 (medicine sec.).

43. "Repairing the Conjugal Bed," *Newsweek*, May 25, 1970, 51.

44. Pointing to the possible consequences of the scientific reengineering of human sexual relations, Roger Vadim's *Barbarella* (1968) projected a futuristic fantasy in which coition is considered "dangerous to maximum efficiency." In one scene the

eponymous heroine (Jane Fonda) is trapped inside the "Excessive Machine," which is a musical masturbatory device the antagonist plays in order to pleasure her to death. Barbarella survives, but the machine breaks down, striking a blow against cyborgian sex. Mixing up sexual experimentation and space exploration, *Barbarella* can be understood, at least in part, as a popular reaction to scientific test subjects. Its opening striptease and its celebration of "spontaneous" heterosexual intercourse suggests cultural resistance to sexology's dispassionate observation and its preference for a cyborgian performativity designed to deny arousal and participatory identification in the observer. Danny Peary, *Cult Movies 2* (New York: Dell, 1983), 8–11.

45. Linda Williams, *Hard Core: Power, Pleasure, and the "Frenzy of the Visible"* (Berkeley: University of California Press, 1989), 96, 36.
46. Ibid., 48.
47. Fulton, "Dirty Movies," 75.
48. Masters and Johnson did not share such preproduction preparations with the public; given that Masters was a gynecologist, it is likely that he would have been familiar with such presurgical preparations as shaving the pubic area.
49. Cartwright, *Screening the Body*, 14.
50. Masters and Johnson, *Human Sexual Response*, 49.
51. Cartwright, *Screening the Body*.
53. Leach, *I Know It When I See It*, 40–41.
54. Slade, "Pornographic Theaters Off Times Square," 40.
55. Fulton, "Dirty Movies," 75.
56. Tom Gunning has made the argument for looking at early films in terms of a "cinema of attractions." At a lecture he gave at the Massachusetts Institute of Technology in Spring 1998, he hypothesized that the "terrain of modernity" is etched by discourses of "wonder"—also "astonishment," "shock," and "amazement"—that mark "threshold" experiences organized around a "new" technology or its "reenchantment." Listening to his lecture, it occurred to me that sex films—whether scientific or popular—that emerged in the mid-1960s to early 1970s were elaborated as modern "attractions," promising technological and physiological spectacles.
57. Tom Gunning, "'Now You See It, Now You Don't': The Temporality of the Cinema of Attractions," *Velvet Light Trap* 32 (fall 1993): 6, 8.
58. Kelly Dennis notes that the word *beaver* was slang for a "man's beard in the mid-nineteenth century" and that "'beard' has a longer history as a reference to the female genitals." Kelly Dennis, "'Leave It to Beaver': The Object of Pornography," *Strategies* 6 (1991): 161 n. 34.
59. Williams, *Hard Core*, 96–97.
60. Ibid., 80.
61. Such films were made in color or in black and white; some were silent and some included sound.

62. Zimmermann, *Reel Families*, 132.

63. John Morthland, "Porno Films: An In-Depth Report," *Take One*, March–April 1973, 11–17.

64. Di Lauro and Rabkin, *Dirty Movies*, 26.

65. Zimmermann, *Reel Families*, 132.

66. Ibid., 37, 42.

67. Ibid., 41.

68. Ibid., 111.

69. Ibid., 125. In the 1920s, Soviet filmmaker Dziga Vertov coined the term *kino-eye*. This enthusiasm for a kind of camera-eye was shared by documentary filmmakers who had elaborated the direct cinema and cinema verité practices in the 1960s. But, as Zimmermann notes, amateur film discourse in the United States has tended to avoid thinking of the camera reflexively as a means for "instigating analysis of abstract principles in spectators." Ibid., 89.

70. Thomas Waugh makes this distinction in "'Acting to Play Oneself': Notes on Performance in Documentary," in *Making Visible the Invisible: An Anthology of Original Essays on Film Acting*, ed. Carole Zucker (Metuchen, N.J: Scarecrow, 1990).

71. Williams, *Hard Core*, 76, 77. As Williams explains this theory, "Each historically successive form of representation of sexual acts using living, moving bodies must compensate its viewers for the formal limits of the medium" (77).

72. See Schaefer, "The Inside Story of Storefront Theaters." For a local analysis of urban-space adult entertainment, see Eric Schaefer and Eithne Johnson, "Quarantined! A Case Study of Boston's Combat Zone," in *Hop on Pop*, ed. Henry Jenkins, Tara McPherson, and Jane Shattuc (Durham, N.C.: Duke University Press, forthcoming).

73. Former stripper Margaret Dragu offers this definition of "flashing": "It means stretching your g-string to offer the audience a glimpse of pubic hair. This is a tease in g-string off areas, but it is all you get in g-string on areas." Margaret Dragu and A. S. A. Harrison, *Revelations: Essays on Striptease and Sexuality* (London, Ont.: Nightwood Editions, 1988), 161.

74. Jane Smith, "Making Movies," in *Sex Work: Writings by Women in the Sex Industry*, ed. Frederique Delacoste and Priscilla Alexander (Pittsburgh, Penn.: Cleis, 1987), 137.

75. Dennis, "'Leave It to Beaver,'" 145, 146–47.

76. See *Bucky #55*, Something Weird Video, Seattle, Washington.

77. Dragu and Harrison offer the following theory for the popularity of sexually exhibitionistic shows: "Watching strippers does not provide men with opportunities to have sex. In fact, watching strippers is an abdication of the pursuit of sex. *Revelations*, 130–31. Considered this way, it is possible to acknowledge the pleasurable experience of a viewer who can watch (an activity that requires further analysis), but cannot touch. Of course, showing a naked woman performing orgasm naturalistically

might have been too great a risk for these entrepreneurs, given that this was the first hard-core film form to venture across the border to public screenings.

78. Strippers may also end their acts with simulated humping motions.

79. "Anything Goes: Taboos in Twilight," *Newsweek,* November 13, 1967, 74.

80. Quoted in ibid., 76.

81. Quoted in "Two Sex Researchers on the Firing Line," *Life,* June 24, 1966, 51.

82. Albert Rosenfeld, "A Laboratory Study of Sexual Behavior" (book review), *Life,* April 22, 1966, 12. It should be noted that the volunteers were selected from the educated, urban classes. Although African Americans volunteered, Masters and Johnson noted that their sample had "been weighted toward the Caucasian rather than the Negro race." *Human Sexual Response,* 15.

83. Recalling her initiation into the "beaver" film business, Jane Smith writes: "My friend Ruby told me about the movies. 'They're always looking for new chicks,' she said. 'You get twenty-five dollars, and they pay you right on the spot.' Twenty-five dollars was a lot of money in 1967. Hamburger was three pounds for a dollar; a loaf of bread was a quarter. Minimum wage was a dollar and forty cents an hour." "Making Movies," 136.

84. Masters and Johnson, *Human Sexual Response,* 305.

85. Eric Schaefer makes a similar point regarding the burlesque film, which also catered to men: "Even if gender norms were continually recuperated, burlesque films, with their unique history and mode of production, had the capacity to expose the instability of those [gender] norms and deny their hegemony." Eric Schaefer, "The Obscene Seen: Spectacle and Transgression in Postwar Burlesque Films," *Cinema Journal* 36 (winter 1997): 63.

86. Zimmermann (*Reel Families*) discusses the ways in which the amateur film discourse has emphasized the family at the expense of other social formations. Pointing to what Birken (*Consuming Desire*) would identify as the discipline's "productivist" tendencies, Irvine argues that "sexology has responded to cultural fears about the survival of heterosexuality and the institution of marriage by claiming to improve heterosexual and marital relationships through better sex." *Disorders of Desire,* 11.

87. Zimmermann, *Reel Families,* 132.

Illustration by Jacqueline Tomes from *Freckled and Fourteen*, by Viola Rowe, 1965.

Rusty Fems Out
Straightening Hair, Sexuality, and Gender in *Freckled and Fourteen*
Erica Rand

Dancing was fun. And better exercise than most indoor sports. The only thing was that she didn't see what was wrong with girls dancing together. Or even boys with boys. It was unreasonable the way everyone wanted to pair off opposite sexes just to dance. She and Jeri danced together often, and Jeri always let her do the leading.[1]

That's what eighth-grader Rusty is thinking a third of the way through *Freckled and Fourteen*, Viola Rowe's 1965 novel written for girls aged eleven to thirteen. Here's my fantasy rewrite of the next chapter:

Rusty was still feeling angry, frustrated, and confused when the doorbell rang the next day. She opened it to find her favorite relative, Aunt Erica. Rusty's friend Jeri always raved about Aunt Erica's beautiful red nail polish, but Rusty especially loved the way Erica always showed up on holidays with women who dressed just like Rusty wanted to dress—in pants and vests instead of those frilly dresses that Rusty's mom was always trying to get Rusty to wear. Maybe Aunt Erica would understand.

"Rusty," Aunt Erica said, after Rusty blurted out everything she'd been thinking, "your feelings are perfectly natural. It sounds to me like you're growing into one of the most wonderful kinds of women in the world, a butch lesbian. I know that it can be hard dealing with people, even in your family, who want you to act more feminine or date boys. Maybe sometimes you think you're the only one with these feelings. But you're not. There are lots of girls just like you, and special girls like Jeri who will let you lead them around the dance floor—and even make you feel like you're really the one in charge."

Rusty didn't quite understand why Aunt Erica smiled to herself at that last comment about being in charge, but she found herself smiling back. She smiled even more when Aunt Erica explained to her that there were lots of different kinds of wonderful girls, including butch girls who liked boys, butch girls who liked to date girls, and even girls, like Aunt Erica, who weren't butch at all and liked to date girls, too. She said that Rusty could always count on her to value Rusty's own life choices, whatever they turned out to be, and to stand by her if she faced prejudice from family, friends, and society. For the first time in ages, Rusty saw that even if she might have some hard times coming, she also had a lot to look forward to. "I guess," she thought, "I can be butch, or a dyke, or both—or even neither if I'm different later—and there will always be people who love me."

As I discuss later, my fantasy rewrite, in which Rusty's lesbian aunt comes to the rescue with love, hope, and more information about sex/gender intersections and variations than many adults have today, deviates wildly from *Freckled and Fourteen*. Rusty learns there that straightening out her gender, desires, and "kinky" hair is the key to acquiring love of all kinds. A young reader who shared Rusty's dance preferences in the 1960s would have had to turn elsewhere for cultural products that affirmed or understood her. Where might she have gone?

In *Barbie's Queer Accessories*, I argue that the world of Barbie offered one source of lesbian representation in the 1960s, if only at the level of subtext.[2] I note that although Mattel presented Barbie as heterosexual, especially after Ken appeared in 1961 so that Barbie could get a life, certain Barbie products might well have pleased consumers with an eye to a dyke reading, such as the 1963 Barbie Travel Pals carrying case that portrays a moment of girlfriend intimacy in which Midge cups Barbie's face while Barbie seems almost to be fondling Midge's breast. These products occur among others that suggest for Barbie an identity as a sexually liberated girl of the 1960s. (In the Barbie novels, for instance, Ken waits at home while Barbie dates a boy in every port, including some who seem to stretch the boundaries of the permissible; in *Barbie's Hawaiian Holiday* [1963], written when Barbie in plastic was a white girl with a white boyfriend, Barbie even dates outside the race.)

But did girls of the 1960s notice then the lesbian subtexts I discerned in the 1990s? I interviewed some lesbian adults who remembered using Barbie to act out lesbian fantasies in the 1960s or remembered their negative attitudes toward Barbie—"I preferred trucks"—as a marker of protobutch identity. Yet these consumers described reacting not to perceived lesbian subtexts, but to Barbie's high visibility as a feminine, sexual character. This is not to argue that no 1960s girls found a lesbian fantasy catalyst in the Travel Pals. It is simply to say that I did not find adults who recalled being those girls, and to point to what I consider a central rule about content analysis, a staple of cultural studies: meanings that critics discern to reside "in" a product do not necessarily correspond to the meanings extracted by consumers.

This stated, however, I undertake here precisely the limited venture of content analysis with a study of *Freckled and Fourteen*. It's a book that meant a lot to me in the 1960s, and I returned to it when an invitation to contribute an essay on lesbian representation to this volume made me realize something that I had never quite noticed when I was working on Barbie: there was a big disjunction between my 1990s reading of 1960s products and my 1990s memory of my own 1960s cultural consumption. The 1960s, in the ad language of the time, were my Wonder Years, ages one through (almost) twelve. So I was a girl in the sixties, and, in many ways, of the sixties, with a child's collection of experiences, values, and accessories that were associated with adult movements for political and sexual liberation. I baby-sat for a commune, saw *Hair*, studied "Jews and civil rights" in Sunday school, and stayed out of school to protest the firing of the school superintendent who had overseen mandatory integration of my district. I had beads, flower power decals, a poster declaring "War is not healthy for children and other living things," and guitar teachers who kept "splitting for California."

What I don't seem to have acquired while situated among all those people and products outfitting me for liberation was knowledge about lesbians. In fact, I don't remember any cultural products depicting lesbians, overtly or subtextually, or how I learned anything about them. By 1974, when a crisis broke out after a girl I knew announced that she was bisexual, I certainly knew what that meant; a year later, at the latest, I was thinking that the term *lesbian* might apply to me. But I have no idea where I learned about women, real or fictional, to whom the term might apply. I also don't remember looking for lesbians, which perhaps contributed to why I didn't find them, along with the dictates of hit-or-miss library perusal. There were a few books I might have hit upon; a friend my age, for instance, remembers reading a children's novel about two girls in boarding school who were separated after being caught kissing.[3] But missing such books might be described as overdetermined (and perhaps happy) accident; certainly then, as now, little existed in terms of lesbian images in children's culture.

I do remember, however, the cultural products for children from which I learned about the heterosexual world of teen romance that I was, presumably, to enter: those "teen" novels directed toward younger-than-teen readers. In fifth grade, I checked out seven a week, reading one a day, no doubt as a substitute for interaction with live children, until I had exhausted the library's supply. These books had two reigning plot features. One, which could be described as pro-girl, demonstrated that it was okay to be smart (instead of popular). The other was anti-sex. The protagonist, for instance, learned to resist inappropriate behavior at make-out parties—when some naively longed-for access to the cool crowd materialized in an overture, usually suspect, from a popular student. Or she learned that the quiet, brainy Norwegian exchange student was a better object of desire than the horny captain of the football team.

Freckled and Fourteen concerns the transition to that high school world where smart girls date quiet boys who don't pressure them for sex. I decided to write about this book because it stood out in my memory as a book that I owned, kept, and read more than once, although I remembered virtually nothing of the plot. It's about a tomboy nicknamed Rusty who deals with being adopted, learns to thin and straighten her hair, gets her wayward older brother Alan back on track, comes to enjoy being a girl, resolves to get her grades up to college-scholarship level in anticipation of family financial strain, and starts a romance with a smart, quiet boy named Sammy, who, unlike Alan, puts working before flirting.

In this essay, I examine the book's complex and sometimes convoluted narrative of sexual awakening, gender rigidity, family feeling, and subterranean ethic notions. I would also like to address something else here: what this book meant to girls who read it when I did, what lessons they learned or rejected, what "knowledge" they took from it, what pleasures and/or pains it generated. But I can't really unearth this now. Even if I could locate people with vivid memories of *Freckled and Fourteen*, what would I have found? Memories are notoriously unreliable, hardly transparent accounts of what occurred in either the material world or the imagination. As I have discussed in relation to Barbie, memories are transformed by time, filtered through adult understandings of how the past shapes the present, and expressed through both conventions of storytelling and the relationship between writer and informer. So I do not expect to conjure 1960s girl consumers through a 1990s adult reading. I offer later, however, some conjectures about what this book may have offered, for better and for worse, in light of other accounts about the role of cultural consumption in the lives of girls who, in terms of sexuality, gender, or both, were coming out queer.

If girls' reactions to *Freckled and Fourteen* must remain largely inaccessible thirty years later, some evidence exists of adult response. I got my own copy from the Arrow Book Club (after bypassing it for several months because I was too embarrassed to ask for a book on the troublesome matters of feeling ugly and growing up). Arrow, the branch of the Scholastic Book Clubs for grades four through six still in operation today, distributes order forms through teachers, who then collect orders and money in class and distribute the books when they arrive. The book's appearance as an SBC selection indicates that SBC's corporate reviewers liked it, considered it suitable to represent the image they project of being purveyors of educational and wholesome reading material, and expected it to meet with the approval of the teachers and parents upon whom their sales depended. I was unable to obtain information from SBC about the book's sales record, the years in which it was offered, or the blurb copy used on order forms.[4] But its duration as an SBC selection—I know of one girl who got it a few years before I did—suggests that the blurb copy, at least, was acceptable to gatekeepers, and that it sold enough to remain on the list.

Adult reviews are mixed. In "The Best Books of the Season for Children," Ethna Sheehan praises it for "excellent values expressed through an appealing story," although, she adds, "the writing is undistinguished."[5] *Grade Teacher's* reviewer, clearly struggling to cram summary and evaluation into forty words or less, manages a seemingly positive comment that "the book doesn't let [Rusty] find answers to her problems too easily."[6] *Kirkus Reviews* notes, "A little bit too much of Rusty's girlish emoting, but otherwise a sturdy and solid book of its type."[7] Least enthusiastic is the *Library Journal's* reviewer, who calls it "an average, at times dull junior novel for younger teenage girls."[8]

What these reviewers share, despite mixed opinions of the book's quality, is an apparent lack of desire to criticize the novel's portrayal of Rusty's transition to girlish heterosexuality. Sheehan again is the most enthusiastic about how Rusty "becomes interested in her appearance and in a boy, and makes advances toward true femininity and appreciation of being a girl." The other three merely register this feature in the plot summary: "In addition to adjusting to becoming a girl instead of a tomboy"; "*Freckled and Fourteen* ... but before that it was tomboyish and thirteen. This is a year of changes and adjustments for Rusty Eastman; "Already suffering from the pangs of becoming a young lady, tomboyish 14-year-old Rosalind."[9] Although I don't want to read too much into such brief comments, it seems safe to suggest that the reviewers were not outraged by this feature of the plot. Their language suggests "growing pains"—that purportedly natural, if difficult, part of growing up. That one author refers to Rusty's "girlish emoting" and another uses Rusty's hated given name, Rosalind, implies also that they, like Sheehan, see Rusty's femininity as her "true" self.

This is just what the novel wants the reader to see, although many convolutions of plot and character development suggest coercion rather than organic development. The novel begins when Rusty, walking home from school with her best friend Jeri, sees signs that Jeri has become interested in boys. Rusty takes Jeri's gushy, "Oh, Rusty, he's the dreamiest" (20), uttered about Rusty's own brother Alan, as a betrayal—"It was all too evident that her friend was no longer faithful to their ideals" (21)—and as evidence that adults had been right to warn them away from their exclusivity:

> Many a time since the first week of their first year in junior high they had marveled at their good fortune in finding each other among all the boy-crazy girls and girl-chasing boys and all the other chirps and mopes and just plain ughs. They had spurned the friendship of other girls, even though some people—parents, for instance—had tried to warn them. So now what they'd been warned against was coming to pass. Their undying friendship was about to die. (23–24)

Besides introducing grief that sounds suspiciously like romantic longing, set in the context of adult warnings that recall those coded admonitions to nuns against "special friendships," the first chapters also present other sources of despair for Rusty: her freckles and, more distressing, her red "kinky" hair. Interestingly, the trajectory of the hair plot runs in direct opposition to the sex/gender plot. In the latter, Rusty must change what others don't accept. In the former, Rusty learns to accept what others like already, although she will make changes here, too, that please everyone involved. The two plots work in tandem, however, within the overall theme of learning to embrace what biology gives you.

This theme is underscored in two incidents during the walk home from school that emphasize Rusty's perception of her hair as a curse of nature. In the first, two boys harass Rusty and Jeri: "[They were] making loud noises that might have been meant to resemble 'the wild and terrible cry of Tarzan.' Or, Rusty thought, the boys were probably stupid enough to think the sounds coming from their lips were Indian love calls." One yells, "Hey Rusty, where did you get that red hair? Out of a bottle?" Rusty reacts angrily:

> For one black moment she was stunned. Then she was filled with
> wrath. Not because a boy had dared to tease her about the color of
> her hair. She was used to that. Hadn't it been carroty red all her life?
> What shook her was being accused of getting it from a bottle. As if
> she would choose to have this kinky carroty mop! As if she wouldn't
> prefer nice straight dark hair like her brothers'. (15–16)

Rusty would also prefer blond hair, which we learn soon after when her disappointment with Jeri's reaction to the boys is described, in a passage that
screams "crush," in terms of a "suspicious impatience" that interrupts Rusty's
ordinary attentiveness to her friend's charms: "She scarcely noticed Jeri's smooth
blond hair, which she usually envied; or the light blue of Jeri's eyes and the pale-
ness of her lashes and brows, or even the fact that not a single freckle marred
Jeri's fair skin" (17).

The second incident has Rusty comparing herself to her brother's crush
object, Dawn Borden, whose eyes looked "more blue than the sky" and who had
"the kind of inconspicuous brown hair that Rusty especially envied" (22),
although Dawn claims to prefer Rusty's: "You have the prettiest hair, Rusty, and
your wave looks so natural. Don't tell me that you not only have natural red hair
but a natural curl? I mean a real permanent wave, and not the kind that grows
out?" (24–25). Rusty, furious, interprets these comments as a sign of Dawn's
phoniness, and rails to her brother later about how much she hates having "red
kinky hair" unlike everyone else in the family, adding in rage, "I'm probably
adopted" (27).

These episodes introduce one of the most incoherent yet persistent features
of *Freckled and Fourteen:* while Rusty's hair and freckles most obviously star in a
drama of family identity, they figure also in an interconnected drama of racial
identity. It's a drama written between the lines and, I suspect, unintentionally.
Unlike the carefully planted subtext, which I discuss later, that explains away
Rusty's butchness as a cultural product of imperfect parenting, this one appears
only in telling adjectives and juxtapositions. Rusty repeatedly describes her hair
as "kinky" and different from the hair of all the other (white) people she knows,
despite their variety of hair coloring. Freckles, which might be seen otherwise as
tokens of fair skin, are dark marks that, it seems, color the whole; it is Jeri's skin
that is "fair."

Not that Rusty or her author ever identifies anyone in the novel as "white."

Like many white people in white-dominated societies, Rowe presents white as the default category that does not need to be named; there are people and "Indians," not white people and Indians. Yet the novel also reveals that, as recent scholars on whiteness have noted, "white" is not thereby a given; white identity, white privilege, and the understanding of whiteness as generic, normative, and ideal must continually be constructed and maintained.[10] In *Freckled and Fourteen* the work of constructing whiteness is largely evidenced by the telling absence of reasonable comparisons that might actually throw Rusty's racial origin into question. "Indians," who are stereotyped as having straight hair, appear twice, first in the incident described above—as people whom Rusty's peers can but imagine and ill impersonate—and later when Rusty, upon learning that she is, in fact, adopted, fantasizes about who her biological parents might have been. After "foreign acrobats" fleeing a feud or vendetta and "royalty" fleeing from Communists, she considers "American Indians," ultimately deciding that her hair makes this heritage implausible: "Before she'd figured out why they would leave their papoose behind she realized that no American Indian was likely to have hair the color of hers" (60).

Rusty's racial musings end there, despite her inability to find her visual kin among the other white people she sees around her, who all have straight, smooth hair in shades of blond and brown. Her kinky hair doesn't make her wonder, as well it might, if she's African American, for instance, or Jewish (an identity often viewed in racial terms).[11] Nor do red hair and freckles induce her to consider ethnic identities, such as Irish, that would identify white as variable or non-monolithic.[12] Of course, not all redheads are Irish nor are all Irish people redheads. Nor does kinky hair characterize all people, or only people, who are of African descent and/or Jewish. "Race" is a cultural construct precisely because the idea of biologically distinct peoples is a fiction. My point is not that Rusty *has* Jewish, Black, or Irish "blood," but that her failure to consider any of these possibilities is striking in a novel about a girl who considers her hair a clue to her origins—and whose frame of reference includes habits of ethnic stereotyping, as her comment about "Indian love calls" indicates. Ultimately, Rusty seems to be white and unethnic because her author won't let her consider otherwise.

But only her hairdresser knows for sure. When Rusty, on her path to girlish femininity, eventually does get her hair done, the hairdresser provides the final confirmation that Rusty is a white girl by dismissing Rusty's amateur assessment of her hair as "kinky." After the hairdresser enthuses over Rusty's "naturally curly" hair, Rusty replies, "But it's kinky!" The hairdresser says, "Not really. Just a tight wave. If it's set with big rollers ... it will fall into beautiful big waves. You'll see. After it's thinned a little. And shampooed" (155). Ironically, in this scene that implicitly affirms racist standards of beauty (kinky hair is undesirable), Rusty is rescued from the appearance of kinkiness through a strategy for approaching white standards that was sometimes used by just those African American and Jewish girls who might be considered her kin if the text didn't banish them: she has her hair straightened.[13] Rusty remains perilously close to the kinky-haired even in her departure from them.

This tenuous hold on a distinctly unkinky identity illustrates the extent to which constructing whiteness requires continuing cultural and textual work—work for which Rusty's hair provides a fitting symbol. As the text emphasizes, getting "beautiful big waves" requires much transformative labor. After being thinned and set on rollers, Rusty's hair is "brushed and combed and pushed and coaxed and pinned and sprayed" (155) to create a look that will need extensive home maintenance and repeated renewals at the beauty parlor. It requires great expenditure of resources that are elsewhere denoted to be in insufficient supply: after spending her money on her hairdo, money that Rusty is otherwise conserving to help her parents send her to college, Rusty must wait for her next allowance to purchase the rollers she now needs. It also, one would think, requires some psychological labor, given that the opinion all around that Rusty now looks much better can hardly jibe easily with previous affirmations from the same people that she was beautiful beforehand.

If Rusty's racial identity is the matter that dares not speak its existence as an issue, the opposite is true of Rusty's gender identity, although the related question of her sexual identity is engaged as obliquely as race through the adult cautions, dreamy descriptions, and high emotions mentioned earlier that hint at Rusty's romantic feelings for Jeri. Just as Rusty never asks, "Am I white?" she never asks, "Am I heterosexual?" and the text tries to present Rusty's transition as one, not from lesbian to heterosexual, but from presexual to sexual; boys are just the natural object of Rusty's newly awakening sexual interest.

Rusty's gender identity, however, is a subject of explicit concern, and the one around which most plot points revolve, often quite unfelicitously. Even Sheehan, the enthusiastic reviewer, seems not exactly to buy the connection Rowe tries to establish between Rusty's discovery of her adoption and her reconciliation with her femaleness; "Somehow" she writes, "the shock helps Rusty to grow up."[14] Sheehan's skepticism is understandable. The plot makes sense only if the reader sees Rusty's transformation not, as Sheehan does, in terms of the ascent of nature ("true femininity"), but in terms of psychological coercion—an explanation that lies close to the surface despite Rowe's best efforts to indicate otherwise.

Rowe clearly intended to weave into Rusty's adoption woes an explanation for why she'd been, contrary to nature, a tomboy. When Rusty's parents finally talk to her about her adoption, they apologize for not telling her long before she found the papers and then for another crime of parental negligence:

> Mr. E. chuckled a bit. "With the others all boys, we've always figured we were especially lucky that we got you to round out the family."
>
> Mrs. E. said, "But I'm afraid we let the boys make too much of a tomboy out of you. We're going to try to do something about that. From now on things will be different."
>
> "Right," Mr. E. agreed. "We like our boys. But we want our girl, too."(104)

This scene explains Rusty's tomboyishness as a development against nature imposed from outside: Rusty's brothers turned her into a tomboy. And, for the moment, this conversation seems to suffice. It concludes with tears and hugs all around and Rusty returning to thinking of the Eastmans as her parents, rather than Mr. and Mrs. E.

But Rusty soon hypothesizes more insidious implications of the Eastmans' plan to help Rusty be a girl: her parents must not have liked the tomboyish girl she'd been and still was. Actually, Rusty had begun to see feminine behavior as a condition and catalyst for maternal love earlier, soon after discovering her adoption. When her mother hands her a bag from the Sweet Sixteen Shop containing her first bra—in a scene highlighting the "perfectly natural" ascent of puberty that is supposed to root Rusty's transformation in nature—she concludes that her mother wants her to be like those boy-crazy "chirps," and must not love her as she is: "For a little while [before seeing what the bag contained] she'd thought Mrs. E. actually cared about her" (64). Later, when Rusty goes to Jeri's house to confide her adoption news, Jeri's bedspreads and curtains, cross-stitched by Jeri's mother, no longer strike Rusty primarily as "too frilly and girlish" but as tokens of maternal love (93) in a bedroom implicitly contrasted to Rusty's own, which had been decorated, at her own insistence, in brown plaid (31).

After the adoption news is out in the open, Rusty determines to win the love of her adopted parents, especially her mother, by acting more like the girl they desire, even though the effort makes her feel like "a stranger even to herself" (109). Fearing that she could not camouflage her disappointment at sacrificing formerly beloved boyish outdoor activities, she forgoes the family vacation and arranges to stay behind doing more female-coded activities: cooking and cleaning for her uncle, whose housekeeper's family emergency has left him stranded. This uncle, a lawyer named Lawrence who is charmingly nicknamed Uncle Law, is the relative-confidante whom I rewrote into Aunt Erica to give Rusty a better ally. I'm not sure I changed the ally's sexual orientation; Uncle Law's bachelor status and distaste for sports hint (given the novel's association between gender normativity and heterosexuality) that he and Aunt Erica may have something queer in common. He functions quite differently than his replacement, however, guiding Rusty gently toward accepting her parents, which means, in Rusty's mind, becoming the "girl" they want.

As the novel progresses, Rusty confirms her suspicion that girl things are indeed the key to bonding with her mother. When Rusty asks her mother for permission to visit the hairdresser, she's "touched by how pleased her mother looked" and "guessed it was natural for mothers to want their daughters to look nice. Even adopted daughters" (154). She marvels at how her mother knows without asking that she has been hoping with her hairdo to get the attention of Sammy, Rusty's crush interest. (That Sammy displaces Jeri from this role is suggested by the fact that he is Jeri's cousin and by mirror illustrations at the beginning and end: in the first full-page illustration, Rusty and Jeri walk home from school together; in the last, it is Rusty and Sammy.) Rusty responds happily when Mom says just the right things and offers to help her learn the art of hairnet use at bedtime: "It was nice to have someone to talk to about girl things. There were some things boys just weren't hip to at all" (164–65). By the end of the book, Rusty can tap into her own special knowledge of girl things—knowledge that seems to come from within rather than without. "A girl can tell," she informs her brother when she advises him about his own romantic woes (210).

The description of Rusty's newfound female intuition serves to blunt the impression of psychological violence. Rusty's femininity, it seems, has not been coerced into being; instead, she has "come out" as the girl she has always been deep inside. Rowe also gives Rusty a future boyfriend who appreciates some of her less girlish qualities. The novel ends as Sammy tells Rusty about a summer job for both of them, working as "junior helpers" in a recreation department sports program for young children; Rusty is valued as an athletic girl. Yet another, more sinister message comes through with the coming to fruition of Rusty's prediction that she can join her family by femming out. Rusty's new gender expression, portrayed, like Rusty's hair, as acceptance of nature, comes just as much from hard work and the conscious imposition of cultural standards. Although the text tries to suggest that Rusty needs the guidance of the (Uncle) Law only until natural female feeling emerges—after which mom takes over as the confidante—both the evidence of labor and the size of the stakes suggest that rules have become not superfluous but internalized. And the impetus to internalize is clear. Femming out gets Rusty closeness with her mother, a future boyfriend, reconciliation with her brother, and new friends. Love, in short, is the reward; femininity is its precondition.

Reading this novel as an adult, I find some pleasure in the way that the narratives of return to the natural undo themselves in contradictions, implausible plots, and counternarratives of cultural violence that cannot help but show themselves. I'm not saying here that Rowe fails to suppress a true nature that Rusty had before the advent of culture. The roles of culture and biology in the formation of gender and sexual identity remain undetermined. Besides, regardless of biological factors, culture clearly affects how people express the gender and sexuality they understand to be theirs; if ballet had been one of her brothers' favorite approved-for-boys activities, Rusty's closet would probably have harbored toe shoes instead of "her favorite baseball and bat" (31). The issue, for me, concerns what feels authentic, right, and desired;[15] my point is that the novel doesn't quite manage to make its own accounts of nature convincing.

I also feel some sympathy for the author, whose biographical sketch hints that the novel's convolutions are, perhaps, the mark of her own painful "inning." It validates her, in way that suggests protesting too much, not merely as heterosexual but as the producer of heterosexual girls besides—she has a husband, son, and "married daughter." It attributes to her mixed gender, at least if we decode her bio by the rules of her novel, which uses sports expertise to signal masculine tendencies: "Like Rusty ...," she says, "I am interested in most sports, but the typewriter gets priority." In this light, the newspaper column she wrote at the age of seventeen, "The Feminine Viewpoint," may well betoken a "viewpoint" as difficultly acquired as it is labeled naturally "feminine." One source of Rowe's acculturation is implied by her current position as a Sunday school teacher for children Rusty's age. (This also explains why Rusty periodically gets help at church—learning, for instance, that if God is "everyone's Father . . . maybe it didn't matter so much if she never did find out who her natural parents were" [128]—and why Rusty's new feminine garb is a modest brown.)

But my pleasure in close reading and sympathy for Rowe fade fast when I imagine the huge damage done to butch girls, both dykelets and straightlets, by texts and Sunday school teachers like these, purveyors of messages that femming out will get you harmony with nature and the love of family, God, friends, and dates. I know too many butch women and FTMs who struggled as children against such cultural coercion—before, during, and ever since the 1960s—facing rejection, harassment, and imposed self-doubt along with the pain, oppression, and injustice that result. Thinking of them, I rage against this text that contributes insidiously to the enforcement of gender normativity for girls. Thinking of girls of all genders who wanted to dance with their girlfriends, and girls with kinky hair who lived with ethnic notions that silky smooth was better, I want to time travel back to Viola Rowe's Sunday school class, and snatch her out of there before she inflicts more damage.

Yet I don't presume to hypothesize exactly what any such girls—each, of course, different—drew from this text, or to conclude that it was all negative. Many autobiographical accounts of childhood reading and other forms of cultural consumption testify to pleasures and strength drawn from cultural products that offered no apparent place, or no positive place, for the consumers to find themselves. Cherríe Moraga and Deborah Bright have written about butch sexual fantasies wrested from heterosexual narratives. Moraga, in an essay about fem/butch desire coauthored with fem dyke Amber Hollibaugh, engages cultural narratives on a general level, discussing her early erotic identification with male figures in "capture" fantasies and the pleasures it gained and cost her.[16] Bright writes more specifically about her fondness, and that of friends who were also protolesbians in the early 1960s, for strong film actresses who challenged conventional feminine stereotypes:

> These transgressions of the norms of femininity were often "punished" or regulated by the monogamous, heterosexual logic of the film narrative, but that didn't matter much. For reception is driven by desire and what many young, middle-class, proto-dykes saw in

these films in the early 1960s were concrete (if attenuated) suggestions of erotic possibilities that they could not name and that their
own experience did not provide.[17]

Bright's account of desire evading the dictates of plot and message is echoed in
numerous accounts by dykes who found something for themselves in pulp fiction from the 1940s through the 1960s that purported to depict lesbians when
these were the only lesbians in cultural products that they could find, even if they
also bought, at least temporarily, the novels' negative stereotypes about lesbians
being depraved, doomed, and abnormal.[18]

Dorothy Allison, writing of selective reading at a younger age, describes what
she got from two beloved books that she read at eleven and twelve, Morton
Thompson's *Not as a Stranger* and Mary Renault's *Fire from Heaven:*

> Both were romances about the seemingly predestined triumph of
> young boys with large ambitions. What I loved about these books
> was that mix of the real and the marvelous, the tragic and the hope-
> ful. The mean and bitter parts of life were there in full measure, but
> they did not stop the heroic dream of meaning and purpose, the
> sense that even the most difficult beginning could be part of a larger
> story. At the time I ignored the fact that they were about boys and
> that I was a scared little girl. I pretended it didn't matter, that life for
> a girl could be just as hopeful and deliberately plotted. I ignored the
> way both novels made the women characters important only in their
> relationships to the men who were the real focus.[19]

Allison also drew from *Not as a Stranger,* which, she states, "change[d] the way I
thought about fiction, about the way I thought about myself and the poverty
into which I had been born," a sense of "the power and complications of sexual
desire," made believable in relation to, but not exact translation of, what she saw
around her.[20]

Allison comments, too, that from previous reading ("everything and anything that came within [her] reach" starting at the age of five, including biogra-
phies, histories, science fiction, her mother's adventure novels, and her father's
porn, but no children's books), she took context rather than content, along with
some hope. Despite skepticism and certainty that fiction was about "imaginary
beings," she also read with a "passionate, romantic conviction that fiction was, at
times, about a better world than the one that I knew."[21] Joanna Kadi offers a

related account of rewards, plot driven or otherwise, found in texts that hardly offered validation of self:

> Books shone brightly on the desolate landscape of my childhood, in ways both profound and basic. They provided me with fantasy, escape, a reality in stark contrast to the one around me. I especially loved reading about children with happy home lives and positive experiences with a friendly, bustling outside world. But equally profoundly, books, and the children who inhabited their pages, betrayed me by ignoring my world. Where was I? Where were workers? Arabs? Rarely to be found. And if found, never a good word. Stupid janitors who couldn't think, idiotic truck drivers who couldn't write, dirty Arabs who couldn't be trusted. And still I read, still I coveted shelves full of books, still no one could offer a better present than a book. Still I carried a deeply buried and mostly jumbled desire to carve my own niche in this world.[22]

Kadi and the other adult lesbians I have quoted above all remember childhood engagement with cultural products that ignored or demeaned facets of the identity that they understood then or would come to claim: gender, class, sexuality, race, ethnicity. Each ignored, adapted, overlooked, read against or in spite of seen messages. This does not mean that they failed to be influenced by messages that might well be termed harmful or, I presume, that they don't have their own fantasy rewrites or retrospective wishes for cultural products that dispensed less toxin-saturated pleasures. They have all written eloquently about the destructive messages encoded in products for children and adults, past and present. By citing countertextual readings, I don't mean to diminish what they were countering.

Yet it is crucial, I think, to see in their writings the evidence of interpretive as opposed to passive readers. Too often cultural critics, professional and otherwise, presume that consumers take in the messages that the critics deem them to emit, condescendingly ascribing to consumers (excluding, of course, the critic her- or himself) a passive, absorptive mode of consumption. This is especially the critical habit when the consumers in question are children. I found doing research on Barbie, for instance, that people often told me with great assurance what girls "learned" from Barbie, dismissing possibilities for deviation even (or especially) when they remembered their own childhood stances toward Barbie as far more creative or idiosyncratic.

I want to avoid making this same mistake with *Freckled and Fourteen* and the corollary mistake of presuming catastrophic effect—girls ruined forever by this one text. My friend Nancy Bullett clearly wasn't. She's more hip to lesbian/gay/ bisexual/trans issues than any other straight person I know. Like me, she vividly remembered having the book, which belonged to her freckled older sister, at home. She could picture the cover and the Scholastic Book Club's logo on the spine. All she remembered of the effect, however, was that after she read it, she wanted to have freckles and red hair, too.[23] After I told her about the anti-butch plot, she was horrified and angry, commenting later that she really wished that she'd had other models then, or the tools to decode destructive messages in cultural products like this one. As an advocate for queer youth, she has good reason to be angry, especially because, although *Freckled and Fourteen* may circulate little now, anti-queer youth culture is hardly a thing of the past. Despite Ellen's coming out and the advent of women's professional basketball—which doesn't, of course, get the cultural affirmation accorded to women's figure skating and gymnastics—kids who don't conform to dominant sexuality and/or gender norms still get brutalized and still have insufficient cultural support. Nonetheless, it is also important to see Nancy as a *Freckled and Fourteen* "survivor," who ignored or put behind her its dubious messages, just as the women I have cited above worked against the grain of the cultural products that worked against them.

Is that what I did with *Freckled and Fourteen*? Rereading the book in preparation for writing this essay, I found that a few parts seemed vaguely familiar, but nothing came back to me about why I kept returning to it. I can hypothesize, however, one reward that Rowe might have offered me, as a fem kid who figure skated and hula hooped, in the process of femming out Rusty. I do remember clearly what I hated about *Little Women*, which, for some reason that now eludes me, I read at least ten times in elementary school. I hated the fact that Jo, the independent one, the writer, had a male nickname. Here was the part of culture that denied my identity and aspirations: the habit of coding strong, smart females with masculine names and attributes. This habit seemed to be everywhere, and, at the time—long before I knew anything about why cross-gender identification might suit some girls more than an increase in approved ways to enjoy being a girl—I railed against girls who, like Jo, took male nicknames. This seemed to me complicitous with antifeminism: How could women get rights if female achievements always got male labels? Perhaps, then, I saw in Rusty—who, it is hinted, may return to her given name, Rosalind—a girl with a mix of attributes that didn't have the overarching label "tomboy." After all, Rusty, like me, was good at math—which we learn in one of those subtle anti-dyke moments when she trades her career aspiration from gym teacher to math teacher—and she didn't lose her smarts at the hairdresser.

Who knows? Maybe, to the contrary, Rusty was the first butch girl I had a crush on. In 1997, I was shocked and delighted to discover in Rusty's early dancing pleasures a children's version of the fem/butch dance scene that yields me much adult pleasure. Was this what brought me back to the book? As Bright and others suggest, when cultural products give form to desires and identities in scarce representational supply, the articulation of them at all may be more compelling than narrative attempts to dismiss them. Today, I'm as thrilled to discover that the novel to which I returned was a dyke novel as I am saddened to see the advent of Sammy in Jeri's place. Was I thrilled or saddened back then?

I don't know. What I do know is that, whether any, all, or none of these hypotheses about my own consumption are true, *Freckled and Fourteen* accurately betokens dominant social messages of that time, with rigid gender and sexual codes that offered insufficient space for butch girls who wanted freedom to cross, fem girls who wanted the freedom to figure skate and be good at math, or girls of all genders who wanted to dance with each other. Significantly, what comes through as well, at least in my adult reading, is the cultural work required to naturalize gender and sexual norms, which never really manage to stand as natural here, along with the extent to which construction of ethnicity is integral to the construction of gender/sex norms. "Freckled" and "fourteen" are not separate issues. Rusty's new hairdo is simultaneously a white-out and fem-out. She needed one to have the other; "white" is an unspoken yet crucial ingredient of the feminine ideal promoted by the novel. She needed both to straighten out. What she really needed, however, was in short supply in 1965 and remains so today: better allies, better Laws, better narratives, and better books than the one she stars in. Survival stories testify to how much we can get around and, occasionally, to keen pleasures attending cross-reading. But it just shouldn't always be so hard to find what you need.

Notes

My thanks to Tracey Guillerault for her research assistance with this essay; to my siblings, nieces, and nephews, who give me the pleasures of being an aunt; and to all the butch, fem, and trans people who have added so much to my life, my knowledge, and, in some cases, my dance card.

1. Viola Rowe, *Freckled and Fourteen* (New York: William Morrow, 1965), 79. Page numbers for further quotes from this work appear in parentheses in the text.

2. Erica Rand, *Barbie's Queer Accessories* (Durham, N.C.: Duke University Press, 1995).

3. This book was *Prelude,* by Madeleine L'Engle (New York: Vanguard, 1968[1945]), which was "adapted for young people," as the copyright page puts it, from the first part of her novel *The Small Rain,* the latter written circa 1945 and republished in 1984 (New York: Farrar, Straus, & Giroux) with a new introduction by the author that tries to explain away, indirectly, why she was so preoccupied with lesbian temptations when she wrote the text. The synopsis on the jacket flap of the children's adaptation—which might well have had many readers looking for other books by the famous author of *A Wrinkle in Time*—has the same indirection. It explains that we follow the protagonist Katherine at boarding school "through all the torment, loneliness, and adorations and passions of a fifteen-year-old girl." Reading it, I wish L'Engle would have been even more obscure about her subject, so that its homophobic content would have been easier to miss. My thanks to Avi Chomsky for remembering this book and tracking it down.

4. I did get, however, the current teacher's pack of order forms (*Scholastic/Arrow Book Club News,* April 1997, grades 4-5-6), which indicates the dubious promotional copy that sometimes emerges when educational products meet the sales pitch. For instance, the ad copy for *We Are Witnesses: Five Diaries of Teenagers Who Died in the Holocaust,* by Jacob Boas, in the "Teacher's Book Guide"—an enclosed color poster marked "Photocopy to send home and/or post in your classroom!"—sounds a bit too much like it is trying to sell a scary thriller movie that will not, however, be too scary, but "unfortunate": "Unfortunately, they were sentenced to death under Hitler's mad rule." (The students' order form adapts this sentence to "Unfortunately, there is no happy ending.")

5. Ethna Sheehan, "The Best Books of the Season for Children," *America,* November 20, 1965, 645.

6. A. Izard, review of *Freckled and Fourteen, Grade Teacher* 83 (November 1965): 109.

7. Kirkus Service, review of *Freckled and Fourteen, Kirkus Reviews,* July 1965, 631.

8. Elizabeth M. Guiney, "Review of *Freckled and Fourteen* by Viola Rowe," *Library Journal* 90 (November 1965): 5100.

9. Sheehan, "The Best Books," 645; Izard, review, 109; Kirkus Service, review, 631; Guiney, "Review," 5100.

10. For a survey of literature on the construction of whiteness, see Charles Gallagher, "White Reconstruction in the University," *Socialist Review* 24, nos.1–2 (1995): 167–71. As Gallagher demonstrates in his study of white college students dealing with what they considered the apparent ascent to power of people of color in the era of "multiculturalism," the frequent assertion by scholars of whiteness that white people do not view their whiteness as a marked category is not universally applicable. His argument may apply to Rusty; like the students studied by Gallagher who were struggling with economic changes such as decreasing job prospects, Rusty has a reason, her adoption, not to take for granted her race or its privileges. However, the novel's nonarticulation of this matter also situates it within a signifying context in which whiteness is the norm that does not need to be named.

11. For the development of the idea that Jews are a race of biologically distinct people, often considered dark (although, simultaneously, Jews of color are frequently rendered invisible), and the interconnections between racism and anti-Semitism, see Paul Kivel, *Uprooting Racism: How White People Can Work for Racial Justice* (Philadelphia: New Society, 1996), 147–54.

12. Interestingly, the racial identity of Irish people has often been called into question. For an account of mid-nineteenth-century arguments that Irish people were fundamentally Black and possibly of African origin, see David R. Roediger, "Irish-American Workers and White Racial Formation in the Antebellum United States," in *The Wages of Whiteness: Race and the Making of the American Working Class* (London: Verso, 1991); and for a history of anti-Irish racism in Ireland, see Liz Curtis, *Nothing but the Same Old Story: The Roots of Anti-Irish Racism* (Belfast: Sasta, 1996[1984]).

13. On the history of straightening Black hair, see Beryl Wright, "Back Talk: Recoding the Body," in *Lorna Simpson: For the Sake of the Viewer* (exhibition catalog, Museum of Contemporary Art, Chicago) (New York: Universe, 1992), 19–22; Kobena Mercer, "Black Hair/Style Politics," in *Out There: Marginalization and Contemporary Culture*, ed. Russell Ferguson, Martha Gever, Trinh T. Minh-ha, and Cornell West (New York: New Museum of Contemporary Art/Cambridge: MIT Press, 1990), 247–64. As Mercer points out, hair functions as a crucial "ethnic signifier" because, unlike other physical features, it can be altered relatively easily (250). He also suggests that the distinction between natural and straightened hair, given much political significance in the 1960s and later in relation to Black identity, does not really hold up as a distinction between nature and culture because "natural" styles are also importantly products of cultural understandings and, often, transformative activity (253). From this angle, Rusty's hairdo must be seen not as a move from nature to culture, but as a move from one culturally invested style to another. As Mercer's essay also indicates, the contradictory notion that Rusty can bring out her natural beauty at the hairdresser's is hardly an idea limited to Rowe alone.

14. Sheehan, "The Best Books," 645.

15. I use the expression "feels authentic" for two reasons. On the one hand, I gesture, somewhat approvingly, toward postmodern skepticism about whether one might speak meaningfully of a true, authentic identity that exists before or apart from cultural adaptation, or of identity as a unitary essence unmarked by contradiction and fragmentation. On the other, and more important, I want to acknowledge the extent to which gender and sexual identity are often experienced as natural or innate, however simple or complex, unitary or fragmentary they are experienced to be. To me, this should bear more weight than theoretical analyses about where identity comes from. What matters is the right to claim the identity that feels authentic, not whether "authenticity" is an appropriate label.

16. Amber Hollibaugh and Cherríe Moraga, "What We're Rolling around in Bed With: Sexual Silences in Feminism," in *Powers of Desire: The Politics of Sexuality*, ed. Ann Snitow, Christine Stansell, and Sharon Thompson (New York: Monthly Review Press, 1983), 396–97.

17. Deborah Bright, "Dream Girls," in *Stolen Glances: Lesbians Take Photographs*, ed. Tessa Boffin and Jean Fraser (London: Pandora, 1991), 152.

18. On the stereotypes, pleasures, and circulation of pulp fiction purportedly about lesbians, see Jan Zita Grover, "Dykes in Context: Some Problems in Minority Representation," in *The Contest of Meaning: Critical Histories of Photography*, ed. Richard Bolton (Cambridge: MIT Press, 1989), 170–73. Grover, who came out as a young adult right around when *Freckled and Fourteen* appeared, also discusses her own struggle to find lesbian representation then and reaction to what she did find (163–66). See also Nina Levitt, "Conspiracy of Silence," in *Stolen Glances: Lesbians Take Photographs*, ed. Tessa Boffin and Jean Fraser, 61–66, for a photographic "inversion" of some lesbian pulp fiction covers.

19. Dorothy Allison, "Not as a Stranger," in *Skin: Talking about Sex, Class and Literature* (Ithaca, N.Y.: Firebrand, 1994), 79.

20. Ibid., 78, 80.

21. Ibid., 77–78.

22. Joanna Kadi, "Writing as Resistance, Writing as Love," in *Thinking Class: Sketches from a Cultural Worker* (Boston: South End, 1996), 9.

23. Conversations with Nancy Bullett, February and April 1997. Christine Quinn offers another testimony that the book accomplished, or was thought by adults to accomplish, one of its explicit goals of making hair and freckles like Rusty's look more desirable. She remembers being given the book in 1987, when she was a child being teased about her own Rusty-like hair and freckles. Conversation, April 1997.

Select Bibliography

This bibliography presents a select list of titles on the 1960s for further reading and research on sexuality and representation in this period. For titles referenced in the essays and introduction, please see the note sections at the ends of the individual contributions. This bibliography was prepared by Allan D. Campbell and Moya Luckett; we would like to thank Allan for his assistance.

Adelman, Clifford. *Generations: A Collage on Youth Cult.* New York: Praeger, 1972.

Altman, Dennis. *Homosexual: Oppression and Liberation.* Rev. ed. with an introduction by Jeffrey Weeks. New York: New York University Press, 1993.

_____. *The Homosexualization of America.* New York: St. Martin's, 1982.

Andersen, Chris. *Citizen Jane: The Turbulent Life of Jane Fonda.* New York: Henry Holt, 1990.

Anthony, Earl. *Spitting in the Wind: The True Story behind the Violent Legacy of the Black Panther Party.* Malibu, Calif.: Roundtable, 1990.

Armstrong, David. *A Trumpet to Arms: Alternative Media in America.* Boston: South End, 1991.

Bad Object-Choices (ed.). *How Do I Look? Queer Film and Video.* Seattle, Wash.: Bay, 1991.

Baer, Jean L. *The Single Girl Goes to Town: A Knowing Guide to Men, Maneuvers, Jobs, and Just Living for Big City Women.* New York: Macmillan, 1968.

Battcock, Gregory (ed.). *The New American Cinema.* New York: Dutton, 1967.

Bell, Arthur. *Dancing the Gay Lib Blues.* New York: Simon & Schuster, 1971.

Bennett, Tony, and Janet Woollacott. *Bond and Beyond: The Political Career of a Popular Hero.* New York: Metheun, 1987.

Bernstein, Matthew, and Gaylyn Studlar (eds.). *Visions of the East: Orientalism in Film.* New Brunswick, N.J.: Rutgers University Press, 1997.

Bishop, George. *Witness to Evil.* New York: Dell, 1971.

Biskind, Peter. *Easy Riders, Raging Bulls: How the Sex-Drugs-and-Rock 'n' Roll Generation Saved Hollywood.* New York: Simon & Schuster, 1998.

Bodroghkozy, Aniko. "Groove Tube and Reel Revolution: The Youth Rebellions of the 1960s and Popular Culture." Ph.D. dissertation, University of Wisconsin-Madison, 1994.

Breedlove, William, and Jerrye. *Swap Clubs: A Study in Contemporary Sexual Mores*. Los Angeles: Shelbourne, 1964.

Bronski, Michael. *Culture Clash: The Making of Gay Sensibility*. Boston: South End, 1984.

Brown, Helen Gurley. *Having It All*. New York: Pocket Books, 1982.

_____. *Sex and the Office*. New York: Random House, 1964.

_____. *Sex and the Single Girl*. New York: Bernard Geis, 1962.

Bugliosi, Vincent. *Helter Skelter: The True Story of the Manson Murders*. New York: Bantam, 1974.

Carson, Clayborne. *In Struggle: SNCC and the Black Awakening of the 1960s*. Cambridge: Harvard University Press, 1981.

Case, John, and Rosemary C. R. Taylor (eds.). *Co-ops, Communes and Collectives: Experiments in Social Change in the 1960s and 1970s*. New York: Pantheon, 1979.

Cleaver, Eldridge. *Soul on Ice*. New York: Dell, 1968.

Cohen, Mitchell, and Dennis Hale (eds.). *The New Student Left: An Anthology*. Boston: Beacon, c. 1966.

Coontz, Stephanie. *The Way We Never Were: American Families and the Nostalgia Trap*. New York: Basic Books, 1992.

Davis, Angela. *An Autobiography*. New York: Random House, 1974.

de Beauvoir, Simone. *The Second Sex*. New York: Knopf, 1953.

D'Emilio, John. *Sexual Politics, Sexual Communities: The Making of a Homosexual Minority in the United States, 1940–1970*. Chicago: University of Chicago Press, 1983.

D'Emilio, John, and Estelle Freeman. *Intimate Matters: A History of Sexuality in America*. New York: Harper & Row, 1988.

Denning, Michael. *Cover Stories: Narrative and Ideology in the British Spy Thriller*. London: Routledge, 1987.

Didion, Joan. *Slouching Towards Bethlehem*. New York: Farrar, Straus & Giroux, 1968.

_____. *The White Album*. New York: Simon & Schuster, 1979.

Dobrow, Larry. *When Advertising Tried Harder: The Sixties, the Golden Age of American Advertising*. New York: Friendly Press, 1984.

Douglas, Susan J. *Where the Girls Are: Growing Up Female with the Mass Media*. New York: Times Books, 1995.

Doyle, Jennifer, Jonathan Flatley, and José Esteban Muñoz (eds.). *Pop Out: Queer Warhol*. Durham, N.C.: Duke University Press, 1996.

Dyer, Richard. *The Matter of Images: Essays on Representation*. London: Routledge, 1993.

_____. *Now You See It: Studies on Lesbian and Gay Film*. London: Routledge, 1990.

Echols, Alice. *Daring to Be Bad: Radical Feminism in America, 1967–1975*. Minneapolis: University of Minnesota Press, 1989.

Ehrenreich, Barbara. *The Hearts of Men: American Dreams and the Flight from Commitment.* Garden City, N.Y.: Anchor, 1984.

Ehrenreich, Barbara, Elizabeth Hess, and Gloria Jacobs. *Re-making Love: the Feminization of Sex.* Garden City, N.Y.: Anchor, 1986.

Ephron, Nora. *Wallflower at the Orgy.* New York: Bantam, 1970.

Faderman, Lillian. *Odd Girls and Twilight Lovers: A History of Lesbian Life in Twentieth-Century America.* New York: Columbia University Press, 1991.

Falkof, Lucille. *Helen Gurley Brown: The Queen of* Cosmopolitan. Ada, Okla.: Garrett Educational Corp., 1992.

Fanon, Franz. *The Wretched of the Earth.* New York: Grove, 1963.

Farber, David. *The Age of Great Dreams: America in the 1960s.* New York: Hill & Wang, 1994.

_____. *Chicago '68.* Chicago: University of Chicago Press, 1988.

Farber, Stephen. *The Movie Rating Game.* Washington, D.C.: Public Affairs Press, 1972.

Feigelson, Naomi. *The Underground Revolution: Hippies, Yippies and Others.* New York: Funk & Wagnalls, 1970.

Firestone, Shulamith. *The Dialectic of Sex: The Case for Feminist Revolution.* New York: Morrow, 1970.

Foucault, Michel. *Ethics: Subjectivity and Truth,* ed. Paul Rabinow, trans. Robert Hurley et al. New York: New Press, 1997.

_____. *The History of Sexuality,* vol. 1, *An Introduction,* trans. Robert Hurley. New York: Vintage, 1978.

_____. *The History of Sexuality,* vol. 3, *The Care of the Self.* New York: Vintage, 1986.

Fraser, Ronald (ed.). *1968: A Student Generation in Revolt.* New York: Pantheon, 1988.

Friedan, Betty. *The Feminine Mystique.* New York: Dell, 1963.

Friedan, Betty, and Howard Horne. *Art into Pop.* New York: Methuen, 1987.

Gilbert, Harriet, and Christine Roches. *A Woman's History of Sex.* London: Pandora, 1987.

Gitlin, Todd. *The Sixties: Years of Hope, Days of Rage.* New York: Bantam, 1987.

_____. *The Whole World Is Watching: Mass Media in the Making and Unmaking of the New Left.* Berkeley: University of California Press, 1980.

Grant, Linda. *Sexing the Millennium: Women and the Sexual Revolution.* New York: Grove, 1994.

Green, Gael. *Sex and the College Girl.* New York: Dial, 1964.

Green, Jonathan. *It: Sex since the Sixties.* London: Secker & Warburg, 1993.

Greer, Germaine. *The Female Eunuch.* New York: McGraw-Hill, 1971.

Greer, Rebecca E. *Why Isn't a Nice Girl Like You Married? Or, How to Get the Most Out of Life While You're Single.* New York: Macmillan, c. 1969.

Hall, Stuart, and Tony Jefferson (eds.). *Resistance through Rituals: Youth Subcultures in Post-War Britain.* London: Hutchinson, 1976.

Harding, Sandra G., and Jean F. O'Barr (eds.). *Sex and Scientific Inquiry*. Chicago: University of Chicago Press, 1987.

Harris, Daniel. *The Rise and Fall of Gay Culture*. New York: Hyperion, 1997.

Harris, Norman. *Connecting Times: The Sixties in Afro-American Fiction*. Jackson, Miss.: Jackson University Press, 1988.

Haskell, Molly. *From Reverence to Rape: The Treatment of Women in the Movies*. New York: Holt, Rinehart & Winston, 1974.

Hayes, Harold T. P. *Smiling through the Apocalypse: Esquire's History of the Sixties*. New York: McCall, 1969.

Heath, Stephen. *The Sexual Fix*. New York: Schocken, 1984.

Heidenry, John. *What Wild Ecstasy: The Rise and Fall of the Sexual Revolution*. New York: Simon & Schuster, 1997.

Hillis, Marjorie. *Live Alone and Like It*. New York: Sun, 1936.

Hocquenghem, Guy. *Homosexual Desire*. Rev. ed., with a preface by Jeffrey Weeks. Durham, N.C.: Duke University Press, 1993. French original published Paris: Editions Universitaires, 1972.

Hoffman, Abbie. *Revolution for the Hell of It!* New York: Dial, 1968.

Irvine, Janice. *Disorders of Desire: Sex and Gender in Modern American Sexology*. Philadelphia: Temple University Press, 1990.

"J." *The Way to Become a Sensuous Woman*. New York: Dell, 1969.

Jackson, George. *Soledad Brother: The Prison Letters of George Jackson*. New York: Coward-McCann, 1970.

James, David E. *Allegories of Cinema: American Film in the Sixties*. Princeton, N.J.: Princeton University Press, 1989.

Jay, Karla, and Allen Young (eds.). *Out of the Closets: Voices of Gay Liberation*. Rev. ed. London: GMP, 1992.

Jeffords, Susan. *The Remasculinization of America : Gender and the Vietnam War*. Bloomington: Indiana University Press, 1989.

Jezer, Marty. *Abbie Hoffman, American Rebel*. New Brunswick, N.J.: Rutgers University Press, 1992.

Kaiser, Charles. *1968 in America: Music, Politics, Chaos, Counterculture, and the Shaping of a Generation*. New York: Weidenfeld & Nicolson, 1988.

Katz, Jonathan Ned (ed.). *Gay American History*. New York: Thomas Y. Crowell, 1976.

———. *The Invention of Heterosexuality*. New York: Dutton, 1995.

Katzman, Allan (ed.). *Our Time: An Anthology of Interviews from* The East Village Other. New York: Dial, 1972.

Keith, Michael C. *Voices in the Purple Haze: Underground Radio and the Sixties*. Westport, Conn.: Praeger, 1997.

Kendrick, Walter. *The Secret Museum: Pornography in Modern Culture*. New York: Viking, 1987.

Kennedy, Elizabeth Lapovsky, and Madeline D. Davis. *Boots of Leather, Slippers of Gold: The History of a Lesbian Community.* New York: Routledge, 1993.

Kesey, Ken. *One Flew over the Cuckoo's Nest.* New York: New American Library, 1962.

Kiernan, Thomas. *Jane: An Intimate Biography of Jane Fonda.* New York: G. P. Putnam's Sons, 1973.

Kinsey, Alfred C., Wardell Baxter Pomeroy, and Clyde E. Martin. *Sexual Behavior in the Human Male.* Philadelphia: W. B. Saunders, 1948.

Kinsey, Alfred C., Wardell Baxter Pomeroy, Clyde E. Martin, and P. Gebhard, *Sexual Behavior in the Human Female.* Philadelphia: W. B. Saunders, 1953.

Klein, Michael (ed.). *The Vietnam Era: Media and Popular Culture in the U.S. and Vietnam.* London: Pluto, 1989.

Kopkind, Andrew, and James Ridgeway. *Decade of Crisis: America in the Sixties.* New York: World, 1972.

Krassner, Paul. *How a Satirical Editor Became a Yippie Conspirator in Ten Easy Years.* New York: Putnam, 1971.

Leary, Timothy. *The Politics of Ecstasy.* New York: Putnam, 1968.

Lessing, Doris May. *The Golden Notebook.* New York: Simon & Schuster, 1962.

Linden-Ward, Blanche, and Carol Hurd Green. *American Women in the 1960s: Changing the Future.* New York: Twayne, 1993.

Livsey, Clara. *The Manson Women: A Family Portrait.* New York: Richard Marek, 1980.

Lobethal, Joel. *Radical Rags: Fashions of the Sixties.* New York: Abbeville, 1990.

Lorde, Audre. *Zami: A New Spelling of My Name.* Trumansburg, N.Y.: Crossing, 1983.

Lyons, Paul. *New Left, New Right, and the Legacy of the Sixties.* Philadelphia: Temple University Press, 1996.

Marcus, Greil, and Michael Goodwin. *Double Feature: Movies and Politics.* New York: Outerbridge & Lazard, 1972.

Masters, William, and Virginia Johnson. *Human Sexual Response.* Boston: Little, Brown, 1966.

McDougall, Walter. ... *The Heavens and the Earth: A Political History of the Space Age.* New York: Basic Books, 1985.

McLuhan, Marshall, and Quentin Fiore. *The Medium Is the Massage: An Inventory of Effects.* New York: Bantam, 1967.

Mekas, Jonas. *Movie Journal: The Rise of a New American Cinema, 1951–1971.* New York: Collier, 1972.

Mercer, Kobena. *Welcome to the Jungle: New Positions in Black Cultural Studies.* New York: Routledge, 1994.

Miller, Jim. *"Democracy's in the Streets": From Port Huron to the Siege of Chicago.* New York: Simon & Schuster, 1987.

Miller, Neil. *Out of the Past: Gay and Lesbian History from 1869 to the Present.* New York: Vintage, 1995.

Miller, Toby. *The Avengers*. London: B.F.I. Publishing, 1997.

Morgan, Robin (ed.). *Sisterhood Is Powerful*. New York: Random House, 1970.

Morris, Desmond. *Intimate Behavior*. New York: Bantam, 1972.

Mousa, Suleiman. *T. E. Lawrence: An Arab View,*. trans. Albert Butros. London: Oxford University Press, 1966.

Nagel, Julian (ed.). *Student Power*. London: Merlin, 1969.

Newton, Huey. *To Die for the People*. New York: Random House, 1972.

Nimmo, Kurt. *Susan Atkins*. Canton, Mich.: PNG, 1991.

Obst, Lynda Rosen (ed.). *The Sixties: The Decade Remembered Now by the People Who Lived It Then*. New York: Random House/Rolling Stone Press, 1977.

Olson, Jenni (ed.) *The Ultimate Guide to Lesbian and Gay Film and Video*. New York: Serpent's Tail, 1996.

Omi, Michael, and Howard Winant. *Racial Formations in the United States: From the 1960s to the 1990s,* 2d ed. New York: Routledge, 1994.

Packard, Vance. *The Sexual Wilderness: The Contemporary Upheaval in Male-Female Relationships*. New York: David McKay, 1968.

Peck, Abe. *Uncovering the Sixties: The Life and Times of the Underground Press*. New York: Citadel, 1991.

Rabinovitz, Lauren. *Points of Resistance: Women, Power and Politics in the New York Avant-Garde Cinema, 1943–1971*. Urbana: University of Illinois Press, 1991.

Rechy, John. *City of Night*. New York: Grove, 1963.

Reich, Charles A. *The Greening of America: How the Youth Revolution Is Trying to Make America Livable*. New York: Random House, 1970.

Reich, Wilhelm. *The Mass Psychology of Fascism*. New York: Farrar, Straus & Giroux, 1970.

Reid, Mark A. *Redefining Black Film*. Berkeley: University of California Press, 1993.

Robinson, Frank M., and Nat Lehrman (eds.). *Sex American Style*. Chicago: Playboy Press, c.1971.

Robinson, Paul. *The Freudian Left: Wilhelm Reich, Geza Roheim, Herbert Marcuse*. Ithaca, N.Y.: Cornell University Press, 1990.

Roget, Marie, and Hector Roget. *Swingers Guide for the Single Girl: Key to the New Morality*. Los Angeles: Holloway House, c. 1966.

Ross, Andrew. *No Respect: Intellectuals and Popular Culture*. New York: Routledge, 1989.

Rout, Kathleen. *Eldridge Cleaver*. Boston: Twayne, 1991.

Rubin, Jerry. *Do It! Scenarios of the Revolution*. New York: Ballantine, 1970.

Russo, Vito. *The Celluloid Closet: Homosexuality in the Movies,* 2d ed. New York: Harper & Row, 1987.

Said, Edward. *Orientalism*. New York: Vintage, 1979.

Sanders, Ed. *The Family: The Story of Charles Manson's Dune Buggy Attack Battalion*. New York: Dutton, 1971.

Sayres, Sohnya, Anders Stephanson, Stanley Aronowitz, and Fredric Jameson (eds.). *The 60s without Apology*. Minneapolis: University of Minnesota Press, 1984.

Segal, Lynne. *Straight Sex: The Politics of Pleasure*. London: Virago, 1994.

Segal, Lynne, and Mary McIntosh (eds.). *Sex Exposed: Sexuality and the Pornography Debate*. New Brunswick, N.J.: Rutgers University Press, 1992.

Sitney, P. Adams (ed.). *The Film Culture Reader*. New York: Praeger, 1970.

Sontag, Susan. *Against Interpretation*. New York: Farrar, Straus & Giroux, 1966.

Spigel, Lynn, and Michael Curtin (eds.). *The Revolution Wasn't Televised: Sixties Television and Social Conflict*. New York: Routledge, 1997.

Spock, Benjamin. *Decent and Indecent Behavior: Our Personal and Political Behavior*. New York: McCall, 1970.

Stanton, Domna C. (ed.). *Discourses of Sexuality: From Aristotle to AIDS*. Ann Arbor: University of Michigan Press, 1992.

Stoler, Ann Laura. *Race and the Education of Desire: Foucault's History of Sexuality and Colonial Order of Things*. Durham, N.C.: Duke University Press, 1995.

Streitmatter, Rodger. *Unspeakable: The Rise of the Gay and Lesbian Press*. Boston: Faber & Faber, 1995.

Suárez, Juan A. *Bike Boys, Drag Queens, and Superstars: Avant-Garde, Mass Culture, and Gay Identities in the 1960s Underground Cinema*. Bloomington: Indiana University Press, 1996.

Tanner, Leslie B. (ed.). *Voices from Women's Liberation*. New York: New American Library, 1971.

Teal, Donn. *The Gay Militants*. Rev. ed. New York: St. Martin's, 1994.

Thompson, Hunter S. *Hell's Angels: A Strange and Terrible Saga*. New York: Random House, 1966.

Turan, Kenneth, and Stephen F. Zito. *Sinema: American Pornographic Films and the People Who Make Them*. New York: Praeger, 1974.

Tyler, Parker. *A Pictorial History of Sex in Films*. Secaucus, N.J.: Citadel, 1974.

_____. *Screening the Sexes: Homosexuality in the Movies*. Rev. ed. New York: Da Capo, 1993.

_____. *Sex Psyche Etcetera in the Film*. New York: Horizon, 1969.

_____. *Underground Film: A Critical History*. New York: Grove, 1969.

Ullman, Sharon. *Sex Seen: The Emergence of Modern Sexuality in America*. Berkeley: University of California Press, 1997.

Umansky, Lauri. *Motherhood Reconceived: Feminism and the Legacies of the Sixties*. New York: New York University Press, 1996.

Vadim, Roger. *Bardot-Deneuve-Fonda*. New York: Simon & Schuster, 1986.

Wallace, Michele. *Black Macho and the Myth of Superwoman*. New York: Verso, 1990.

Warhol, Andy, and Pat Hackett. *POPism: The Warhol Sixties*. New York: Harper & Row, 1980.

Waugh, Thomas. *Hard to Imagine: Gay Male Eroticism in Photography and Film from Their Beginnings to Stonewall.* New York: Columbia University Press, 1996.

Weiss, Andrea. *Vampires and Violets: Lesbians in Film.* New York: Penguin, 1993.

Weiss, Andrea, and Greta Schiller. *Before Stonewall: The Making of a Gay and Lesbian Community.* Tallahassee, Fla.: Naiad, 1988.

Westhues, Kenneth. *Society's Shadows: Studies in the Sociology of Countercultures.* Toronto: McGraw-Hill Ryerson, 1972.

Williams, Linda. *Hard Core: Power, Pleasure, and the "Frenzy of the Visible."* Berkeley: University of California Press, 1989.

Willis, Ellen. *No More Nice Girls: Countercultural Essays.* Hanover, Conn.: Wesleyan University Press, 1992.

Wittig, Monique. *The Straight Mind and Other Essays.* Boston: Beacon, 1992.

Wolf, Daniel, and Edwin Fancher (eds.). *The* Village Voice *Reader: A Mixed Bag from the Greenwich Village Newspaper.* Garden City, N.Y.: Doubleday, 1962.

Wolfe, Tom. *The Electric Kool-Aid Acid Test.* New York: Farrar, Straus & Giroux, 1968.

Contributors

Abdullah Habib AlMaaini is an Omani writer. He has published three Arabic collections of poetry and fiction as well as numerous translations and essays on literature and film. His contribution to *The Space between Our Footsteps: Poems and Painting from the Middle East* is the most recent of his works published in English. He cofounded the Committee for the Establishment of the Cinema in the Gulf Cooperation Council Countries in 1994 and the Omani Film Association in 1996. He is currently a graduate student in film studies at the University of Texas-Austin.

Eithne Johnson teaches media studies and popular culture in the Department of Sociology at Wellesley College. She is a Ph.D. candidate in the Radio-Television-Film Department at the University of Texas-Austin. Her essay in this volume is drawn from her dissertation, "Sex Scenes and Naked Apes."

Mark D. Jordan is Asa Griggs Candler Professor of Religion at Emory University. Among his books are *Ordering Wisdom: The Hierarchy of Philosophical Discourse in Aquinas* and *The Invention of Sodomy in Christian Theology*. A sequel to *Invention*, titled *The Silence of Sodom: Homosexuality in Modern Catholicism*, is forthcoming.

Moya Luckett is assistant professor in the English department at the University of Pittsburgh. She is finishing a manuscript titled *Cities and Spectators: A Historical Analysis of Movie Going in Chicago, 1905–1917*. She has published articles on feminine culture, most recently in *The Revolution Wasn't Televised*.

Susan McLeland is a lecturer in the Radio-Television-Film department at the University of Texas-Austin and at Austin Community College. A former editor of the *Velvet Light Trap* (1993–94), she recently completed her dissertation on star scandals in poststudio Hollywood.

Leerom Medovoi is assistant professor of English at Portland State University. He holds a Ph.D. from Stanford University in the Program of Modern Thought and Literature; his dissertation is on Cold War ideology and masculine rebellion in the consumer youth culture of the 1950s. His work has been published in such journals as *Cultural Critique* and *Socialist Review*. He has chapters in two forthcoming volumes, *Back to the Raft: Race and Masculinity* and *American Culture in the 1950s*, and a book based on his dissertation is also in press.

Lisa Parks is assistant professor in the Film Studies department at the University of California at Santa Barbara. She completed her doctorate in the Media and Cultural Studies Program at the University of Wisconsin-Madison. She has published articles on gender, film, and television in *Critical Matrix*, *Feminist Collections*, and the *Velvet Light Trap*, and is currently writing a book titled *Cultures in Orbit: Satellite Technologies and Visual Media*.

Hilary Radner is associate professor in the Department of Film, Television, and Theater at the University of Notre Dame. She is the author of *Shopping Around: Feminine Culture and the Pursuit of Pleasure* and coeditor of *Film Theory Goes to the Movies* and *Constructing the New Consumer Society*. She has published essays on feminine culture most recently in *Cultural Values* and *Contemporary Hollywood Cinema*.

Erica Rand teaches in the Art department at Bates College. Her writings include *Barbie's Queer Accessories* and essays in *Genders*, *Eighteenth-Century Studies*, *Art Journal*, *Journal of Homosexuality*, and *Radical Teacher*. Among other activist projects, she works with the Maine Rural Network and Outright/Lewiston-Auburn, an organization for lesbian, gay, bisexual, and transgender young people.

Jeffrey Sconce teaches film and television studies at the University of Southern California. His work has appeared in the edited collections *Film Theory Goes to the Movies* and *The Revolution Wasn't Televised*, as well as in the journals *Screen*, *Wide Angle*, *Science as Culture*, and the *International Journal of Cultural Studies*. His book on myths of presence in electronic media is forthcoming.

Janet Staiger is professor of cultural and critical studies in the Department of Radio-Television-Film at the University of Texas-Austin. She is the author of *Interpreting Films: Studies in the Historical Reception of American Cinema* and *Bad Women: Regulating Sexuality in Early American Cinema* (Minnesota, 1995) and coauthor, with David Bordwell and Kristin Thompson, of *The Classical Hollywood Cinema: Film Style and Mode of Production to 1960*. She is also editor of *The Studio System*. Her work has been widely anthologized.

Justin Wyatt is the author of *High Concept: Movies and Marketing Hollywood* and *Poison*. A former market research analyst in the film industry, he is associate professor of media arts at the University of Arizona. His work has appeared in such journals as *Wide Angle*, *Film Quarterly*, *Sight and Sound*, *Cinema Journal*, and the *Journal of Film and Video*. His book on marketing independent cinema is forthcoming. He holds a Ph.D. in film and television studies from the University of California, Los Angeles. At the University of Minnesota Press, he is editor for the book series Commerce and Mass Culture.

Index